# Too Funny for Words

*A Contrarian History
of American Screen Comedy
from Silent Slapstick to Screwball*

DAVID KALAT

McFarland & Company, Inc., Publishers
*Jefferson, North Carolina*

LIBRARY OF CONGRESS CATALOGUING-IN-PUBLICATION DATA

Names: Kalat, David, 1970– author.
Title: Too funny for words : a contrarian history of American
screen comedy from silent slapstick to screwball / David Kalat.
Description: Jefferson, North Carolina : McFarland & Company, Inc.,
Publishers, 2019 | Includes bibliographical references and index.
Identifiers: LCCN 2019010732 | ISBN 9781476678566
(paperback. : acid free paper) ∞
Subjects: LCSH: Comedy films—United States—History and criticism. |
Silent films—United States—History and criticism. |
Screwball comedy films—United States—History and criticism.
Classification: LCC PN1995.9.C55 K36 2019 | DDC 791.43/617—dc23
LC record available at https://lccn.loc.gov/2019010732

BRITISH LIBRARY CATALOGUING DATA ARE AVAILABLE

ISBN (print) 978-1-4766-7856-6
ISBN (ebook) 978-1-4766-3652-8

Front cover images: *top* Carole Lombard and Fredric March nurse their injuries
as Walter Connolly looks on in *Nothing Sacred*, 1937; *left* Cary Grant, Rosalind Russell
and Ralph Bellamy do the institution of the press no favors in *His Girl Friday*, 1940;
Buster Keaton and costar Virginia Fox are spooked by *The Haunted House*, 1921
(all images author collection)

Printed in the United States of America

*McFarland & Company, Inc., Publishers
Box 611, Jefferson, North Carolina 28640
www.mcfarlandpub.com*

Too Funny for Words

ALSO BY DAVID KALAT

*A Critical History and Filmography
of Toho's Godzilla Series,* 2d ed.
(McFarland 2010; paperback 2017)

*The Strange Case of Dr. Mabuse: A Study
of the Twelve Films and Five Novels*
(McFarland 2001; paperback 2005)

For Sam and Sheila.
Buster Keaton never unleashed half the havoc you did
whenever you said, "Smokey bit me."

# Acknowledgments

This book didn't write itself. It was dragged, painfully, into existence thanks to an enormous number of people.

I want to thank Jeff Stafford and Turner Classic Movies for giving me a forum to start to explore these ideas in public. The time I spent working alongside the likes of Susan Doll, Greg Ferrara, Pablo Kjolseth, Kimberly Lindbergs, Richard Harland Smith, R. Emmet Sweeney, and Nathaniel Thompson was humbling and eye opening. I am also deeply grateful to the online community of readers who visited the TCM website to post their reactions and commentary—since most of them posted under online handles and pseudonyms it's hard to credit them properly here, but I hope you know who you are.

I am also indebted to the community of slapstick aficionados who have variously hosted theatrical revivals and film festivals, rescued old comedies for release on home video, and engaged in deeply-researched scholarship and historical documentation. This community includes Joe Adamson, Brian Anthony, Robert Arkus, Serge Bromberg, Phil Carluzzo, Rusty Casselton, Ralph Celentano, Rob Farr, Paul Gierucki, Ken Gordon, Tommie Hicks, Cole Johnson, Tim Lanza, Bruce Lawton, Steve Massa, Ben Model, Wayne Powers, Ben Redwine, Richard Roberts, Ulrich Ruedel, Steve Rydzewski, Salvatore Salonia, Maurice Saylor, Chris Seguin, Bill Shaffer, David Shepard, Andrew Earle Simpson, Yair Solan, Tom Stathes, Dave Stevenson, Rob Stone, DJ Turner, Brent Walker, Ed Watz, and Bret Wood.

My parents, Jim and Ann, first introduced me to this world by taking me to a pizza restaurant in Durham, North Carolina, that projected old movies onto the wall to keep customers happy while they waited. It was there that I first encountered Buster Keaton, and my life was changed forever. They happily bought me books (like Walter Kerr's *Silent Clowns*) and later gave me a treasure trove of Buster Keaton videos as a Christmas gift.

My children, Ann and Max, have carried this passion forward as if it were a family heirloom. It was a tremendous joy to attend Slapsticon with them, year after year, even as they were surrounded by old men griping about how today's generation won't watch old movies.

Last but not least, I owe more thanks to my wife Julie than I can ever quite say. In real life I am the inept bumbling fool that Buster Keaton made a career out of pretending to be. I injure myself, destroy what I'm supposed to protect, and mismanage the most basic of tasks. For more than 25 years she has patiently put up with my antics, perhaps in the hope that I'll outgrow this phase. She is my best friend, my surest coach, and the person I most admire.

# Table of Contents

# Introduction: The History
# of the History of Silent Comedy

We begin our story at the end. The end of what, you ask? The end of silent comedy. It is March of 1949, 20 years after sound came to Hollywood and laid waste to the traditions of silent slapstick. It is St. Patrick's Day, and the California Country Club is playing host to an event called the Mack Sennett Alumni and Remember When Association.

The aging wrecks of once sprightly comedians have convened, decked out in ill-fitting finery that went out of fashion back in the days of Prohibition. They are here to reminisce, to drink, to throw pies at each other. Mack Sennett, one of the true pioneers responsible for creating Hollywood as we know it, has seen to it his friends don't waste their efforts on something so ephemeral as mere fun. He's brought cameras—to record their shenanigans for posterity. This is how he built his empire—by letting funny people do what came naturally and let the cameras roll.

This is not the first time these old coots have gotten together to "remember when." Just the year before, the same cast of grizzled characters fêted Sennett at the Masquers Club. Just 10 years before, they were recreating their shtick on camera for a serious movie, Irving Cummings' *Hollywood Cavalcade*. The gags are the same—the gags have always been the same, since Woodrow Wilson was elected president. Only the bodies have changed—the Keystone Kops have grown fat and gray, the once vampy Bathing Beauties now saggy and wrinkled.

Old age comes to us all—it is meaningless to make much out of it. It is just the accumulation of days on a calendar. But Sennett and his geriatric chums are more than just old. They are old-fashioned.

Once the unrivaled Kings of Comedy, these men and women are now relics of a form and a style long since relinquished to the dusty upper shelves of the attic. Resentful, the crusty-fusties of the Remember When Association drew the battle lines: *We knew what was funny, we knew what was sexy, we knew how to make good pictures. You upstart youths don't know a damn thing. Get a haircut!*

To prove his point, Sennett assembled clips of his classic silent comedies into a compilation film, *Down Memory Lane*, distributed by Eagle Lion in the late summer of 1949. A few years later, Sennett went to the Cannes Film Festival for a retrospective of his classic shorts. He schemed ideas for a biopic about his storied life. In short, he clung tenaciously to his achievements and zealously defended them against the changing times.

Nothing came of his biopic idea, but no matter. *Hollywood Cavalcade* was for all practical purposes a biography of Sennett—wildly unreliable and inaccurate, sure, but likely no more inaccurate or unreliable than the one Sennett would have made about himself. The man turned himself into a legend, and even he started to believe the hype.

*Hollywood Cavalcade* was a symptom of a larger phenomenon. Throughout the first few decades of the sound era, Hollywood struggled to come to grips with its silent past. Or, put another way, the increasingly corporate movie-making industry struggled to spin its messy, anarchic past into a PR-friendly packaged narrative.

In September 1949, the same year as Mack Sennett's self-congratulatory Remember When bash and recycled *Down Memory Lane* clip-job, critic James Agee published in *Life Magazine* the first substantial critical and historical overview of silent comedy. It was a landmark essay, the foundational stone upon which all subsequent critical and historical study of slapstick comedy would be built. It begins with Agee asserting that old-school silent comedy achieved better and more satisfying laughs than anything since, and that the reason talkie comedy could not compete was the basic flaw of talking in a comedy. In short, silent comedy was by definition "Comedy's Greatest Era," the title of his essay.

Mary Pickford once said, "It would have been more logical if silent pictures had grown out of the talkie instead of the other way 'round." It is a much quoted and deeply beloved remark among silent film aficionados—almost a mission statement. Kevin Brownlow quoted it at the end of *The Parade's Gone By* as a summing-up sentiment, and Walter Kerr used it to open his book *The Silent Clowns*. There is certainly some sharp theoretical insight there—most art forms do follow a backwards progression from high fidelity into increasing abstraction and reductionism. Go to any art museum and take a look—the photorealistic images of people and landscapes are the older paintings, and the crazy scribble scrabble are the recent ones. By the same logic, should not the abstracted reductionism of Black and White silent movies have been a modernist improvement upon full-color talkies?

Mack Sennett's notion of a Remember When Association became the default approach to celebrating silent comedy. Eventually Sennett and his friends went the way of all flesh, but their followers continued the rite in their stead, dressing up in the fashions of the twenties and nostalgically longing for an innocent age gone.

Personally, I find this whole thing curious. At practically every significant retrospective of silent comedy I have attended or arranged, there are some if not several guests who make a point of dressing in 1920s fashions. Screenings of other silent films—like *Metropolis*, or *Dr. Mabuse*—don't provoke the same reaction.

Consider three successive screenings at the National Gallery of Art in the early 2000s. The first was for Fritz Lang's *Dr. Mabuse the Gambler*. I had been asked to introduce the show, which due to its massive length was shown on two separate afternoons. On the first day, I got into a lively conversation with the crowd about terrorism, James Bond, and *24*. I took my seat and watched as the first two and a half hours of *Mabuse* unspooled. The next day I returned to introduce the second half, and found the same faces eagerly staring at me from the crowd. These were no casual lazy-day movie-goers, but a serious crowd ready to engage with a then 80-year-old movie as a current and living work of popular culture. A few years later I was back in the exact same auditorium for a retrospective of shorts by Georges Méliès. This time the crowd included a number of school groups from the Washington, D.C., public schools, who watched in rapt attention and fascination at crude special effects and magic tricks created half a world away, generations before they were born. My third silent film experience at the National Gallery was a Charlie Chaplin double feature, and it was for this show and this show alone that certain members of the crowd felt compelled to raid their grandparents' closets. Please understand—I am not poking fun.

**Buster Keaton contemplates a world of classic films in *Sherlock Jr.***

I have to count myself among their number: when I was 18, I went to a revival of *The General* in a restored theater in Detroit, wearing my own homemade Buster Keaton outfit.

What's especially odd about this nostalgic thrall is that almost without exception, the people caught in its grip are too young to have had any genuine nostalgia. People who actually lived in the 1920s are few and far between these days. Our nostalgia, however palpable it feels, is artificial.

So where does it come from?

One answer to that question has been staring us in the face all along: there it is in *Down Memory Lane*, there it is in "Comedy's Greatest Era." It's baked into the plot of *Hollywood Cavalcade*, it's in the titles of Robert Youngson's compilation films *When Comedy Was King* and *The Golden Age of Comedy*. The history of the history of silent comedy has been a nostalgia industry since day one. By treating the advent of sound as a dividing line between Then and Now, any celebration of "Then" turned into a pining for something lost. Over time, that nostalgia became a self-feeding phenomenon.

The great slapstick comedians represent inconvenient facts. The story reads better if the great silent clowns not only did their best work on just one side of the silent/talkie divide, but did *all* of their work there. Like an adolescent who comes across her pacifier and blankie in a closet and marvels at how these items ever meant so much, Hollywood found the stubborn presence of its silent clowns to be an uncomfortable reminder of its own infancy. As Hollywood collectively looked back on its history before sound, it struggled to draw a distinction between Then and Now that would keep all the embarrassing pacifiers and blankies on the other side. As a result, any discussion of silent comedy would overemphasize the primitive aspects of physical comedy. *Hollywood Cavalcade*'s version of the Mack Sennett story says that slapstick comedy came about as a consequence of a bumbling fool (played in the film by Buster Keaton) being unable to execute a dramatic scene correctly. The implication is obvious: real skill and specialized talent might be needed to survive in today's Hollywood, but *back then* any jackass could be a slapstick clown. Why, you could do that stuff by accident.

That the great filmmakers and comedians of the recent past were heroic figures with unusual skillsets and whose artistry and entrepreneurship reflected the best of American principles, well, that was a notion at odds with the orthodoxy that the film industry had progressed to maturity. As such it was a viewpoint that was infrequently and poorly articulated. The men and women who were themselves a part of that history did themselves no favors by insisting that the silent era was a superior one—because such an argument only validated the idea that the arrival of sound marked the crossing of a Rubicon, and that you had to choose sides, silent vs. sound.

It is also a losing proposition. If you want to make the case that what distinguishes silent comedy as fundamentally superior is that it is silent, you have to contend with the inescapable fact that silent film is a dead form, obsolete and abandoned. Like insisting that Aztec culture is fundamentally superior to every civilization that followed, it is a self-defeating stance to take. Nevertheless, this is precisely where most fans and champions of silent comedy set up base camp.

The other problem is that taking sides in a dispute between silent and talkie comedy implies a distinction that fuzzes into ambiguity the closer you look. If you want to say that *The Jazz Singer* killed off silent filmmaking, that is not an outrageous position to take, but it is nonetheless a position that tends to fall apart under scrutiny.

For one thing, even setting aside the gimmickry of *The Artist* or Mel Brooks' *Silent Movie*, there remain an array of films whose makers digested the aesthetics of silent comedy and managed to make sound films in that tradition: Jacques Tati's *Playtime*, Pierre Etaix's *Yo-Yo*, Pixar's *Wall-E*. Arguably, much of the realm of animated cartoons from the 1930s through the 1960s recapitulated silent comedy aesthetics in a raucous, noisy new style. Filmmakers like Blake Edwards or Jackie Chan have self-consciously paid homage to the silent comedies that inspired them, and they did so in modernist talkie films.

Chaplin, Keaton, Lloyd, and Langdon all continued to make movies without breaking their stride. It may be the popular consensus that their talkie era work was so diminished as to be incomparable to their silent greats, but that's a matter of opinion, not an objective fact.

Even if we were to agree that the talkie era work by Chaplin, Keaton, Lloyd and Langdon was of such diminished quality that it couldn't be connected to their silent work, that still leaves Laurel and Hardy, Our Gang, and Charley Chase as silent era comedians who made the transition to talkies without missing a single step or changing their aesthetics at all. (Speaking of Hal Roach, I'd argue that Harry Langdon's work at Roach in talkie shorts was a perfect translation of his experimental anti-comedy, and that he too made the transition without changing his style.)

What of the Three Stooges? Nothing about their act was dependent on sound—they could have been silent stars, if they just started making movies earlier. They represent the survival of physical slapstick well into the 1950s!

What of directors like Leo McCarey, Frank Capra and Ernst Lubitsch, who got their start in silent comedy but are best known for talkie comedies?

The fact of it is, the very existence of silent comedy is an almost inexplicable anomaly. It is not as if the traditions of comedy had been leading towards this. George Bernard Shaw did not go to bed at night wishing he could jettison all the dang words from his plays. Quite the contrary, at the moment that the movies came into being, nearly every form of comedy you could encounter in any media was centered around words.

The only meaningful tradition of "silent" comedy that predates the birth of the movies was the history of clowning. There is a line of thought that seeks to define the silent comedies of the 1910s and 1920s as a modern reinterpretation of clowning traditions. There is a respectable argument to made on this count, but you won't find it from me.

My resistance to that line of thinking is simple: whatever common ground you may find between silent "clowns" and their non-movie antecedents are mostly coincidental. A rhinoceros looks like a triceratops not because they share any close relatives but because they independently evolved to live in similar environments.

If silent comedy cinema was truly just a new medium by which to explore existing traditions of clowning, then you'd expect the great silent clowns to actually *be* clowns, to have come from a clowning background. You'd expect the filmmakers to be turning to the history of clowning for inspirations for their films. Basically, you'd expect exactly the opposite of what the history of slapstick actually was.

Silent cinema poached its comedians from vaudeville more than any other source—that is, from a tradition of live comedy that was heavily dependent on puns, dialect comedy, songs, and other forms of wordplay. The very word "slapstick" refers to the mechanism to produce a sound effect to accompany on-stage comic violence that punters in the back row could hear.

There were the occasional silent comedians who came from

Poster for the Three Stooges.

unambiguous clowning backgrounds (Poodles Hanneford, I'm looking at you), but the field was absolutely dominated by comedians who came from vaudeville, not the circus. Charlie Chaplin, Buster Keaton, and Harry Langdon were stage stars before they filmed a single frame, and their stage acts were not silent. Charley Chase started out with a primarily musical act built around his singing. Billy Bevan came from Australia's music hall traditions. The prominent comedy stars who didn't come from vaudeville or music halls just came straight to the movies (see Harold Lloyd, for example), they didn't start as clowns.

During these early stage careers, the men and women who would become the great silent comedians weren't trying to excise dialogue from their acts. They happily incorporated dialog comedy and other sounds into their physical comedy acts naturally—and only jettisoned the words when the technology forced them to. When the first silent comedy features were made, the filmmakers drew from source material from the legitimate stage and from literature—from essentially "talkie" sources.

Placed before the silent cameras, however, these comedians had to improvise and adapt. Whatever performing skills they may have honed on the vaudeville stage had to be warped to suit the limitations of silent cinema. The major comedians of the era (Chaplin, Keaton, Lloyd, Langdon, Arbuckle, Chase) just happened to do this better than anyone else. They had competitors and peers, and some of those competitors and peers tried alternate approaches to adapting to the silent screen. Some are better remembered than others today. Put another way: many different kinds of artists tried different kinds of screen comedy in the silent era, and some of these were more successful than others—they are the ones that have been remembered and celebrated. But we shouldn't assume by that result that their style of physical slapstick was somehow predetermined.

The Marx Brothers, W.C. Fields, and Will Rogers all made silent comedies—but their particular approach to comedy did not adapt to the silent form very well. Their silent films are poorly remembered if at all, and they found their fame later when they could deploy words to their advantage, as had generations of comedians before them.

If the defining feature of silent comedy is silence, then we are only talking about a 20-year cycle firmly bounded at both ends by technological developments. But if we acknowledge that the key figures of silent comedy emerged from non-silent comic traditions, and that their silent work was in many ways an accident of history, we not only have the privilege of conflating silent and talkie comedies into a single history, we are also better situated to recognize just how astonishing their silent accomplishments really were.

Basically, there were a set of comedy aesthetics associated with silent films that were prevalent and popular in the 1910s and '20s but a different set of comedy aesthetics associated with talkie films were prevalent and popular in the 1930s and '40s. That's a lot of qualifying weasel words, but it's an easier stance to defend—and phrasing it this way shifts the emphasis away from the technological shift and onto an aesthetic shift.

The technology was never the central story here anyway, and putting it at the center was a mistake.

Just imagine, as a thought exercise, that sound technology had been part and parcel of the movies since Day One—that when Fred Ott sneezed, we heard "*A-choo!*," that when the workers filed out of the Lumière factory we could hear them grumbling about their lousy jobs. This isn't so much of a stretch, really—there are experimental films with prerecorded sound from this early period. The technology was not ready for primetime but there's a plausible alternate history where sound-on-film emerged in the late 1800s.

In fact, there is an extant film from 1900 that is in color, with a prerecorded synchronized soundtrack. Choke on that, *Jazz Singer*! Experiments with sound recording predate experiments with motion pictures—indeed the inventors behind the movies had always intended to include sound as part of the technology. The technology existed at the dawn of cinema, but it was tricky, awkward, and expensive—and the support from audiences and filmmakers just wasn't enough to overcome those logistical and financial hurdles.

For argument's sake, let's imagine that history took that different path, and sound was part of motion picture technology right from the very beginning. Would this have changed things so very much? I doubt it—the early history of cinema is dominated by forceful personalities, great visionaries whose pioneering work helped establish what the movies were and what they meant to audiences.

Film technology didn't come to us with an instruction manual. The "language of film" had to be discovered by trial and error. It took people like G.A. Smith, Edwin S. Porter, Thomas Ince, D.W. Griffith, Georges Méliès, Louis Feuillade, and so on to experiment—and it took the filmgoing audience to provide feedback on what they liked, what worked, and what didn't. If those early filmmakers had been given sound as part of their movie toolbox, they'd still have had to work through that whole messy process of trial and error to find their way to the film language we know today—and their audience would have had to react to each step, just as they did in the history we know.

The people were the artists they were because of their peculiar idiosyncrasies and personal quirks. Had they been given an extra tool to play with, they wouldn't have suddenly been different people or had different sensibilities. The trajectory of American slapstick followed the course that it did because Mack Sennett was an anarchist rebel who liked to ridicule authority and convention. He had an eye for talent, and attracted ex-vaudeville comedians and their English music hall compatriots—such as Charlie Chaplin. Audiences responded overwhelmingly in favor of this, and turned Chaplin into a star—and inspired legions of copycats to follow his example.

Movies represent an enormous and complex feedback loop. On one end are the content providers: the visionary artists, and the businessmen and investors who support them. At the other end are the recipients: audiences and critics. The cycle depends on both ends—if audiences and critics respond poorly to something, then the content providers will have a powerful incentive to stop making it. If the audiences and critics respond positively, then there will likely be more.

The addition of sound at the outset of the evolution of film might have changed the movies the early pioneers made, but wouldn't have changed any of the personalities involved.

You could argue, however, that the vaudeville comedians taking to the screen around 1910–1915 might have done more dialogue-based comedy, instead of the physical slapstick, had they had the ability.

Perhaps.

But doesn't it strike you as odd that silent comedy as an artform took root so powerfully in the United States, more so than anywhere else in the world? Other countries (like France, Germany, and Russia) made terrific silent dramas, and science fiction films, Gothic horror, adventure yarns, detective thrillers, high-minded art films ... but America cornered the market on comedy.

There's more: America also cornered the market on comedy *with foreign comedians*. The talent existed abroad, but came to Hollywood to flourish. Chaplin didn't become a star in his native England. That was never even on the table.

What was different here? Well, among other things, America at the dawn of the 20th century was a place dominated by polyglot immigrant enclaves in fast-growing urban centers. To appeal to mass audiences in America meant trying to appeal to an exceedingly wide array of folks, of all races and social classes and educational backgrounds. In turn, this meant that movies that appealed to Americans were likely to be highly exportable, and better equipped to translate across national lines. The environment encouraged visually-based comedy, physical slapstick and thrills, because this had the broadest possible appeal. A man getting clonked in the face with a brick is funny no matter what language he speaks.

This simple fact put a heavy thumb on the scale in favor of the development of a primarily visual, language-independent form of comedy in the earliest days of cinema—and this thumb would have been on that scale whether or not sound technology existed at the time.

I'm not saying that the very same movies would have been made, or the same comedians would have risen to the top—but in our imaginary alternate universe where sound caught on in 1900, I believe the form of silent-style physical slapstick comedy would still have arisen in the early decades of the 20th century.

Now, I want to turn that thought experiment on its head: what if sound never caught on? If *The Jazz Singer* never sang Mammy, then would silent comedy have thrived into the '30s and '40s?

In the years since Charlie Chaplin first rose to stardom, movie-going audiences around the world had experienced the First World War, in which traditional notions of national pride and military honor were cruelly thrust up against efficient modern technology. Ten million died, but worse yet were the survivors—maimed, disfigured things that returned home with shellshock to communities that had no place for them. Then came the Russian Revolution, further proof that the old way of doings things was permanently over. The world began to slide into a global Depression…. That Depression didn't hit the United States until after *The Jazz Singer* opened, but Europe had been feeling it since the end of the war. If we want to be specific about America, we should take note of women's suffrage, Prohibition, and the anarchist terrorism of the 1920s. Simply put, those golden years of silent slapstick were also years in which piece by piece the world lost its innocence. It seems unreasonable to expect that the audience that lived through these things would want the same things from their entertainment as the people who did not.

In other words, audience tastes were moving away from silent slapstick even before the advent of sound. The aesthetic shift happened to coincide with—and was benefited by—sound technology, but it wasn't dependent on it. This is, in fact, the story charted by this book—the inevitable transformation of silent slapstick into talkie screwball.

And we can see this aesthetic shift in action, well before *The Jazz Singer*, if we take a look at Harry Langdon's *Three's a Crowd*.

In 1927 Harry Langdon was riding high, arguably the highest of all the great comedians at that moment in time. Three films in a row had been huge hits: *Tramp, Tramp, Tramp,*

*The Strong Man*, and *Long Pants*. And for his next feature, Langdon made a bleak black comedy called *Three's a Crowd*. It's a harrowing tragedy with scarcely any laughs. Set aside the questionable wisdom behind making this thing (it's a defiant work of iconoclastic film-making by an artist who wasn't listening to any advisers), it marked the turning point as his career began to slide into oblivion. *Three's a Crowd* has been tagged with the infamy of being the film that tanked Harry Langdon's career. While this myth is easily debunked, the fact that *Three's a Crowd* is a disorienting and deliberately off-putting experiment has always singled it out for criticism. It isn't hard to imagine that something like this would destroy one's career.

That being said, *all* of Langdon's films are weird creations, and he shot into pop super-stardom in 1926 and 1927 on the basis of stuff that was really quite strange, so *Three's a Crowd*'s quirks should be measured against that benchmark, by which it doesn't come off nearly as bizarre as if you compare it to, say, anything made by anybody else.

According to Frank Capra, the problem with *Three's a Crowd* was rooted in Langdon's misconceived direction of the film—an error that existed because, well, because Langdon went and made it without Capra. Capra had been with Langdon since 1925 and had been a key creative collaborator on Langdon's most acclaimed works. Fundamental personality clashes drove them apart and Langdon fired Capra; *Three's a Crowd* was the first feature he made without any Capra involvement of any kind.

Capra needed to insulate his ego from the humiliation of being fired, and so told the story that he was the source of all Langdon's success—and by extension, Langdon's fall from popularity was attributable to Capra's absence. Mind you, Capra told this story after Langdon had passed away, after Capra himself had become a Hollywood fixture, and during a period where access to Langdon's films was virtually impossible—Capra's version of the story had no one to dispute it.

*Three's a Crowd* does not appear to have been treated as a flop in its day. Critical reception appears to have been positive, and its box office performance not too far off the mark. The perception of it as a failure developed later, in hindsight, in large part due to Frank Capra's sour grapes retconning.

To the extent that *Three's a Crowd* did fall short of commercial expectations can be explained by a variety of factors—1927 saw something of a Langdon glut. When he quit Mack Sennett's studio to strike out into features at Warner Brothers/First National, Sennett still had a handful of unreleased Langdon films waiting in the queue. Looking to capitalize on someone else's investment, Sennett sat on them until Langdon's First National features started to come out, then released them. And these were now pretty stale items—made in 1925 by a less experienced comedian, juxtaposed with his latest and most daring works. This may well have tested audience patience to the limits.

But here's the thing: focusing on these minutiae is causing us to miss the big picture. As long as the argument stays focused on "was *Three's a Crowd* a flop because Capra was fired" or "were audiences tired of Langdon's man-baby character," we are ignoring the fact that across the board, and all at the same time, the great silent comedians hit rocky shores together.

In the case of Harry Langdon, we have an intensely personal and daringly experimental work—*Three's a Crowd*—underperform at the box office, and in response Langdon retreats to familiar material and makes *The Chaser*, a more pedestrian and conventional comedy.

His career was in a tailspin, and he went from comedy superstar to being largely marginalized to being a has-been. (Let me be clear: I think Langdon's late period sound era work is wonderful, but we're talking here about commercial success measured on the ground, in the day.)

The same thing happened to Harold Lloyd—his personal, perfectionist project was *The Kid Brother*, the recipient of more gag-writing and cinematic effort than anything he'd made before it. Yet it grossed a mere $2.4 million, less than his previous *For Heaven's Sake*. Lloyd was so disappointed by this he allowed the film to fall into complete obscurity for the next 30 years, unscreened and unrevived (although it is today hailed as a masterpiece). Having been bitten on his personal project, he followed it up with *Speedy*—which got an Oscar nomination and rave press, but grossed even less than *Kid Brother*. In strictly commercial terms, Lloyd was on a slide. Harold Lloyd never again made a silent film, and never again made a movie widely accepted as a classic.

Now consider Buster Keaton. When historians talk of sound killing the silent comedian, Buster is Exhibit A. One day, he's making *The General*, the next he's a washed-up alcoholic has-been slumming with Jimmy Durante. But how much of this is to blame on sound? Buster's unhappy marriage had a lot to do with his drinking, and his misguided manager Joe Schenck was responsible for selling Keaton's contract to MGM, the entirely wrong studio for him. If Keaton had ended up, say, at Paramount—or had never married Natalie Talmadge—or both—we'd be having a very different conversation. That's not a sign that sound was fundamentally inhospitable to him—just that he had a run of very bad luck.

Also, drawing that line in the sand between Keaton's "good" films and his "bad" ones is trickier than it sounds. Yeah, you don't have to take much convincing to put *The General* on the "good" side and *What, No Beer?* on the "bad" side ... but where exactly is that line?

*The General* cost Buster $750,000 to make. Adjusting for the changing value of the dollar, that's just under $11 million in today's money. It was an expensive undertaking—and a huge investment not just of money but of Buster's effort. The painstaking attention to period detail, the hundreds of extras, the crashing of the train into the valley—Buster held nothing back. And what feedback did he get for all this? The *New York Times* panned it. *Variety* panned it. *Life* panned it. Critical consensus was that Raymond Griffith's Civil War comedy *Hands Up!* was the superior film.

As for audiences ... well, it gets tricky. Keaton biographer Tom Dardis published some box office figures that have been disputed and debunked, but they stuck around long enough to infect a lot of what is written about Keaton's films, so putting a fine point on what his various films earned is always subject to some controversy. Although the details are fuzzy, it's safe to say the box office returns weren't what Buster was hoping for. He shored up, and played it safe by making his next film, *College*, in the same mold as Harold Lloyd's successful *The Freshman*. This is not the action of a man who felt vindicated in his creative experiment.

And what of Charlie Chaplin? Following the success of *The Gold Rush*, he embarked on *The Circus*. David Robinson described this as "a production dogged by persistent misfortune. The most surprising aspect of the film is not that it is as good as it is, but that it was ever completed at all." Chaplin suffered a nervous breakdown, quit for eight months, and then never even mentioned the film at all in his autobiography. Like Lloyd and *The Kid Brother*, he let it quietly vanish and didn't revive it for many years.

*The Circus* was, like *The General*, an uneconomical production marked by excessive spending, which set the bar very high for it to be considered a profitable success. Despite strong reviews it performed disappointingly; although it won an Oscar (beating out *Speedy*) it failed to surpass the box office returns of *The Gold Rush*.

Chaplin retreated even more than his peers, and didn't make another film until 1931. Have you spotted the pattern?

All four of the top comedy stars of silent slapstick—Chaplin, Keaton, Langdon and Lloyd—made expensive, experimental, personal films in 1927. All four of these movies were received in ways that disappointed and demoralized their makers. All four of the filmmakers responded by pulling back, making less ambitious follow-ups in 1928 (or in Chaplin's case, not even making a film at all).[1]

In other words, the audience reaction to these films was consistent. Slapstick comedy from the very best practitioners operating at the height of their powers, making the films for which they would be best remembered and for which they expected to be the proudest, was dismissed. You simply cannot come to the end of 1927 and believe that the future of silent slapstick comedy looks promising or bright.

Audiences had spoken with their pocketbooks and the world of American screen comedy was going to have to respond by recalibrating what it offered in the way of movie comedy—an aesthetic shift was signaled, before *The Jazz Singer* was even a gleam in Warner Brothers' collective eyes.

If we had access to a time machine and used it to kidnap Al Jolson and avert the release of *The Jazz Singer*, it wouldn't change history. Audiences were moving away from Keaton, Lloyd, Chaplin, and Langdon already—even though these comedians were still making terrific movies. The quality of their films had not diminished—not one bit.

It's not that the movies got worse, it's not that sound was competing, it's not that the aesthetics had (yet) changed. The reason audiences were turning away in 1927 was, as discussed above, the cultural climate was changing. The world was a different place. The 1927 world needed different jokes and different kinds of jokes than the 1914 world.

And there was a new breed of comedian who had come along to tell those new jokes.

In the span of time between Buster Keaton's first talkie, *Free and Easy* in 1930, and Charlie Chaplin's last silent, *Modern Times* in 1936, the following took place: W.C. Fields made *It's a Gift* and *Man on a Flying Trapeze*; the Marx Brothers finished all of their Paramount films including *Duck Soup* and still had time to move to MGM and make *Night at the Opera*; Ernst Lubitsch transitioned to sound and made all four of his naughty operettas and then: *Trouble in Paradise*, *Design for Living*, and *The Merry Widow*; Frank Capra made *It Happened One Night* and inaugurated the screwball era; the first *Thin Man* movie arrived; Fred Astaire and Ginger Rogers started making musicals; and *Theodora* went *Wild*; Mae West began her career and made such gems as *She Done Him Wrong* and *Belle of the Nineties*; and Leo McCarey made *Ruggles of Red Gap*. In other words, silent slapstick looked tired and atavistic compared to this fecund new world of sound comedy. Is it really any surprise that silent comedy gave way? It really doesn't matter how bad or how good the scripts MGM gave to Buster Keaton in the 1930s—a new kind of comedy had blossomed and it suited the needs of the contemporary audience.

Conventional wisdom will tell you that the arrival of talkies killed off silent film, espe-

cially silent comedy. This book is my ramshackle, poorly organized, often incoherent coun-
terargument. This book tells a story about Joan Crawford and Harry Langdon, Charley
Chase and Cary Grant, Ernst Lubitsch and Mack Sennett—it's going to build a bridge from
F. W. Murnau's *Sunrise* to Howard Hawks' *His Girl Friday*. It sounds like a sprawling mess,
and I'm sure it will be, but bear with me.

# Hey, Down in Front!

Let's say you just saw *The Gold Rush*, or *City Lights*, and are overwhelmed with the genius of Charlie Chaplin. You want to see more of this genius, you want to chase it back into the past to see from whence it came. If you sit down to watch his short comedies from 1917, the ones he made at Mutual, you will be delighted. They are at least the comic and cinematographic equal to his later features. Here in the Mutual comedies is a fully formed comic personality, full of humanity and tolerance, whose films are innovative works of cinema, trenchant social critiques, and transcendent physical comedy all in one.

If you skip back just one year, however, to the shorts he made at Essanay in 1916, suddenly that perfection is tarnished. Here we find rough edges and primitivity. These things are funny enough and quite well made for their time, but the Essanay shorts appear to be rough drafts for the Chaplin to come.

Skip back just another year or two more, though, and you will land somewhere altogether else. These are the shorts that Charlie Chaplin made at Keystone Studios following his arrival in Hollywood in 1914. Frankly, it is hard to see these as rough drafts. It isn't just that Chaplin's Keystone shorts are cruder than the phrase "rough draft" would imply—it's more that they seem to have wholly different comic ambitions altogether.

Keystone producer Mack Sennett's style of comedy was built on riffing on a specific kind of melodrama that was common then but extinct today. It is extraordinarily difficult for modern audiences to connect with these films because we lack the basic cultural assumptions that underlie the humor. Sometimes, though, lightning struck and the result was a film that could connect with audiences both then and now with equal power. Which brings us to *Kid Auto Races at Venice*.

*Kid Auto Races at Venice* is an important film in Chaplin's canon—this is the first film in which he appears in the costume he would soon make famous. Despite that historical significance, *Kid Auto Races* rarely gets much respect. Historians and Chaplin-o-philes will make their dutiful pilgrimage to check it off their lists, but few will admit to genuinely enjoying it. Which is to my mind a shame, since this movie is one of the few of Chaplin's Keystone films that actually *works* today.

To really understand this crucial turning point in Chaplin's life, we need to jump back in time even further, to a time when Charlie Chaplin and his half-brother Syd were ragamuffins in London. They were so poor they had to trade who got to eat on which day. Nobody knew for sure who Syd's father was, and while the identity of Charlie's papa was known, fat lot of good it did since the man himself was gone. Mama Chaplin was succumbing to a family history of mental illness. Charlie and Syd were in and out of orphanages and institutions. If Charlie's future films ended up ruminating on social injustice and the arbitrary cruelties of life, we should not be surprised.

Syd and Charlie had a way out of this daily nightmare: they went into show business. They each joined Fred Karno's troupe of music hall entertainers. In America they called this stuff "vaudeville." Same difference really. You should have something like *Saturday*

*Night Live* in your mind at this point—an ensemble troupe of performers offering a live show with comedy sketches and music. Charlie was but one of a number of talented performers who took the Karno stage—and if he "popped" out of that background, think of that as akin to someone like Eddie Murphy suddenly outstripping his co-stars on *SNL* (I'm sorry—was that reference too old? How about Tina Fey? Kate McKinnon?).

The main show Karno did involved a sketch called "Mumming Birds." It went through a number of name changes and cast changes over the years, but we don't need to worry over the details—the point is, it was a show-within-a-show in which a vaudeville (sorry, music hall) performance is heckled and interrupted by an unruly audience, in particular one conspicuous drunk. Various comedians played that drunk—Billy Reeves, Billie Ritchie, Charlie Chaplin. Chaplin did not originate the role, but he perfected it, and became a megastar. On the basis of this performance he got himself headhunted by Hollywood, and a job offer at Keystone.

Try to imagine Charlie's mindset at this point. One day he's literally a starving artist, facing down a family implosion, and the next he's a much-sought-after entertainer. His ability to make people laugh is a gift that can transform his life—but while *we* know how this story ends, Charlie has no way of knowing where this is leading, or when his luck will run out.

Charlie's earliest days at Keystone were legendarily awful. He had difficulty ingratiating himself with the established comedians on the lot (who may have worried about his prima donna way of stealing the limelight), and he fought with his director Henry Lehrman. Unfamiliar with the mechanics of film production, he missed his cues, was stiff in front of the camera, lost. According to Denis Gifford's biography of Chaplin, the first film Lehrman shot with Charlie went so badly, the thing was junked (Gifford does not reveal the title of this aborted project).

Chaplin was humiliated. Moreover, he was scared. Mack Sennett, the impresario behind Keystone, was now making noises about canceling the contract with the unreliable Englishman and sending him back to London. So Charlie reached deep into himself to try again—and the next film they shot was *Making a Living*.

If you want to set down the book now and go watch *Making a Living*, knock yourself out. I don't recommend it, but I'm not the boss of you. After having seen it, if you can recall any of it meaningfully, then you're a better person than me. I've seen it dozens of times in different versions, I even *own* a couple of prints, and I barely recall a single frame. It's as forgettable and disposable as they come. Sennett laid Chaplin off for a week, and returned to considering firing him.

Then, on January 10, 1914, in the city of Venice, California there was a race. I grew up calling these things "box cars," but they called them "kid autos." Either way, we're talking about gravity-operated miniature cars driven by children. Lehrman and Chaplin trundled off to improvise a film there.

This sort of thing was standard practice at Keystone. Many of the films were properly scripted and worked out in advance, more or less, but the grueling pace of production was so demanding that it simply wasn't an option to do this for every picture. Some were just made up on the spot, if there happened to be a convenient location or event that could be used to prompt the act of creation.

Chaplin fans and scholars generally dismiss *Kid Auto Races at Venice* as not evidencing enough in the way of forethought or creative imagination to warrant much attention. It's got just one joke, repeated and stretched out for 10 minutes. There's no deep social critique, no elaborate miming, no interplay with other characters—none of the details that critics go looking for when they dig through these early seminal works. Legend has it Charlie improvised this in 45 minutes—it hardly took much longer to make the movie as it takes to watch it. To the extent it gets much notice in the critical press it is for Charlie's appearance. This was the first time that audiences saw Charlie in his "Little Tramp" costume, and that has historical significance no matter how you cut it. By the way, the phrase "Little Tramp" has been completely taken over by Chaplin's legacy such that if you're talking about a Tramp, you're talking about a funny little guy with a Hitler moustache and a bowler hat. But for audiences at the time, this iconic image was meant to carry its own connotations. A "tramp" was what we might today call a homeless drunk. So, in the interest of making you think about Chaplin's character in the proper context, that's what I'll call him here.

Poster for *Kid Auto Races at Venice* (Library of Congress Prints and Photographs Division, LC-USZC4–4714).

There are as many different legends about how Chaplin came up with his Homeless Drunk costume as there are historians to tell them. No two are the same, and they tend to contradict each other quite dramatically. I don't trust legends. But if you ignore them, one thing jumps out—this character was in general appearance, behavior, and comic constitution the same as the one Charlie played on the Karno stage. It makes sense, doesn't it? Chaplin comes to Keystone, has trouble slotting into the expectations the company has for him, his job is on the line—so what would you do? Rely on the tried and true—go back to the character that made you a star in the first place.

Here's where it gets interesting—the character of the Drunk that Chaplin played in "Mumming Birds" was a disruptive element who derailed a performance by professional entertainers. The character of the Drunk that Chaplin plays in *Kid Auto Races* is a disruptive element who derails a documentary film by professional filmmakers.

The genius of *Kid Auto Races at Venice* is that like any contemporary fake documentary it pretends to be a straight documentary recording of the race. Nothing in the film aside from Chaplin's intrusion is played for laughs—this is a newsreel record of a real event at which some stray homeless drunk wandered into the frame, obscuring the action. When the camera crew waved him off, he noticed the camera—and became fixated on the idea of getting himself into the movie. "*Hey, ma!*" Over and over again, in every shot, here comes

Charlie. He doesn't do anything especially funny once he's there—the joke is how he continually insinuates himself into the frame, unwanted. He becomes the self-appointed star of a hijacked movie.

He's smitten. He won't take his eyes off the camera. He flirts with it. It's been said that certain charming movie stars knew how to "make love" to the camera. This fellow rapes it. Sorry for the rude language, but there it is—he's forced himself on this movie. The camera pans away, burly men shove him away, the crew switches the camera off and relocates altogether ... and he returns, always, center of the frame.

Bear in mind: Charlie had been hired by Keystone to be a part of a comic ensemble that included such established stars as Mabel Normand, Roscoe Arbuckle, and Ford Sterling. There was no intention to turn him into a standalone star (or at least, if that was Charlie's desire, it wasn't shared by his employers). But that's what he would do—the real-life Charlie Chaplin hijacked his movies as thoroughly and selfishly as his character here invades this one little movie.

It is worth noting that "Mumming Birds" worked a clever meta-textual trick: it was a music hall show about a music hall show being disrupted. Take away the disruptions, and you'd still have an intact show. Translating that into cinematic terms was tough. *Kid Auto Races at Venice* maintains the meta-textual element, but it was the only instance in the entire history of silent comedy that it was done like this. The idea of interrupted performances became a reliable workhorse for slapstick comedians. Charlie Chaplin and Buster Keaton, Laurel and Hardy and Harry Langdon, Charley Chase and Snub Pollard ... you'd be hard pressed to find a notable comedian of the period who didn't make a movie about some kind of show being turned on its head. But once and only once was this disrupted show presented as if it had actually happened.

Oh, but wait. It did happen.

There was an actual race, remember? Those were actually professional filmmakers recording that race. Some weird-looking guy who appeared to be drunk did disrupt the filming of the race. These events happened as we see them—it's just that the filmmakers were cognizant of the eventual entertainment value of what they were doing.

It is the same joke structure of *Borat*, of a reality-age culture that seeks the thrills of commingling fiction with fact. Never mind that its fictional nature is obvious, the joy is in the pretense. The makers of satirical news programs like *Brass Eye* and *The Day Today* reveled in conning genuine politicians and publicity-hungry celebrities onto what they believed to be a real news show, only to be punk'd. *The Office* and *Modern Family* are but two of the increasingly common trope of the faux-documentary sitcom. *Kid Auto Races at Venice* is a reality-age silent comedy, minted nearly one hundred years ahead of its time.

# Mack Daddy, Daddy Mack

Mack Sennett was a miserly skinflint whose extraordinary ability to identify and nurture talent made his studio *the* jumping-off point for more superstars than anywhere else. The litany of film greats who started here, even if they went on to achieve greatness elsewhere, is astonishing—not to mention all the has-beens and already-ares who cycled through his orbit as well.

But Mack Sennett's films remain difficult territory for film fans. Call him the King of Comedy if you wish, but a great many of his productions fall flat to today's audiences, or require a patience or mindset that only the most dedicated fan can muster. Seeing as I am one of those patient, dedicated fans, I offer up here a tribute to—and primer on—the man who invented American slapstick.

One of the reasons Sennett's earliest comedies feel foreign to modern audiences is that we have grown accustomed to looking for something that wasn't there yet. The kind of silent comedy that developed in Sennett's wake was oriented around "hero" comedians—the likes of Charlie Chaplin, Harold Lloyd, or Buster Keaton, whose personality served as the organizing principle of the films around them. Sennett's comedies played by a different set of rules, and often acted as parodies of a particular style of melodrama as popularized by Biograph Studios.

To understand Sennett's slapstick, you have to start with D.W. Griffith's dramas. Mack Sennett, born Michael Sinnott, signed up with Biograph in late 1907 as an actor. They paid him $5 a day, and he was glad of it—the boy wanted more than anything to be a serious actor, and here he was now a regular player at the world's premiere movie studio. He arrived at around the same time as D.W. Griffith, who quickly ascended to the spot of "Director-General."

During the years 1908–1913, Griffith directed some 450 films—most of them one-reelers, all of them silent. A fair number were identified as "farces," but the exact figure is hard to pin down. Not all farces were self-identified as such, which leaves it up to interpretation: what is a farce? I might find something funny you don't, and vice-versa. So, let's put down an estimate of 150 or so Biograph comedies. The number I have in front of me is actually 152, but that seems weirdly specific for a figure I've just said is a fudge, so I'm rounding down to an even 150.

The biggest hit of these farces—and indeed the biggest Biograph hit of any genre—was *The Curtain Pole*, in which Mack Sennett was cast as a clumsy idiot whose havoc knows no bounds. It's built around just one joke—if you hold a long pole horizontally, it will whallop people in the head—but if you do the same joke over and over for 10 minutes, it becomes something superlative. This may not be the *first* slapstick movie, but it is just about as fully formed and perfect an example as you will find that early in the history of movies.

Griffith knew enough to keep making *Curtain Pole*–ish farces, since audiences paid good money to see them, but he didn't much enjoy making them himself. Griffith thought such

**Mack Sennett wields the titular Curtain Pole in the 1909 Biograph film of the same name.**

tawdry nonsense was beneath a serious artist, and his talents were better suited to directing domestic melodramas and adaptations of classic literature. He figured since Mack seemed to have a feel for this kind of thing, he could delegate the comedies to him altogether.

Meanwhile, Sennett couldn't quite figure out what Griffith was even talking about. *Serious art? Are you kidding me?* Griffith's films ran a scant 10 minutes and made no allowance for the actors to ever even speak. You can "adapt" all the classic literature you want, but the absurd limitations of the form (at that time) were destined to undermine you. At least, that's how Sennett saw it. He thought Griffith's melodramas were already so pretentious as to border on the ridiculous—it wouldn't take much to push them over the edge.

Sennett's farces, first at Biograph and then later at his own studio Keystone, differed little from the Griffith template. He used the same situations, the same character types. But he would exaggerate everyone into some ludicrous extreme. (This is one of the reasons why I find it hard to tally how many farces Sennett made at Griffith—the difference between a serious one that veers into unintentional self-parody and one that aims for parody but soft-pedals it is awfully slim.)

It's not that Sennett was unsuited to making Griffith-style art: *The Lonely Villa*, hailed as the first full-blown example of Griffith's "cross-cutting" was scripted by Mack Sennett. But Sennett and Griffith were operating on wholly different levels. On long walks together, Griffith would elaborate on his theories of how cinema should evolve, how he could use cinematic devices like editing to elide the less important bits so as to fit longer stories into the available running time, how he could use other devices like close-ups to emphasize the good bits. In these same walks, Sennett merely kept harping on how funny police could be if they were bumbling morons.

Exactly where the idea for the Keystone Kops came from is unclear. Too many alternate theories and competing anecdotes have been told. Many of these anecdotes are terrific (I especially like the one in which Sennett was stuck outfitting his police characters with ill-fitting costumes because Griffith had taken all the good ones already, and the result prompted the Chicago police department to issue a formal complaint. Sennett was delighted, and decided to stick with the misfit uniforms). But the fact is funny cops predate Sennett, both in film and vaudeville, so worrying too much about origins is a fool's game.

The Keystone template as it now emerged was this: a mischief-maker causes some havoc, and the Kops descend on him to restore order. The mischief-maker could be any force of selfish wickedness—a Ford Sterling, for example. But the reason these old Ford Sterling shorts seem so odd to us today is we're accustomed to looking for something that wasn't there yet—we've become inclined by the later development of slapstick comedies to expect our identification and sympathy to align with the star. But there's no reason to root for Ford Sterling—he's a bastard. The point isn't to root for him, but to revel in the catharsis of absolute social disorder. Authority is defied, social norms violated—this is rebellion, packaged as entertainment. This is rock and roll, circa 1914.

The appeal of slapstick comedy was for its era comparable to the safe rebellion of rock and roll. It was a way of rebelling against a system that you actually still had to live and function within. Few rockers ever really dropped out—fewer still their fans—which is why they now seem so odd in their '60s and '70s as establishment figures. They sold the illusion of rebellion.

Sennett gave audiences a space to gather in mixed groups, mingling classes and races and genders, and laugh in communion at the foolishness of authority figures, at the absurdity of social graces, at the overwhelming silliness of life.

That, and he hired some amazing comedians.

Chaplin, obviously. And once, just for kicks, Sennett put himself on camera alongside his new star. *The Fatal Mallet*, which Sennett also directed, finds Charlie stealing away Mack's girlfriend Mabel Normand. You watch this thing today for the historical curiosity of seeing Mack and Charlie side by side, pummeling each other. But there's a weird undercurrent here, a troubling subtext: Mabel Normand was Mack Sennett's great unconsummated love in real life, Charlie Chaplin was indeed a disruptive intruder whose presence was realigning Mack's relative power and influence over others. Maybe things would have turned out

**Mack Sennett, King of Comedy.**

differently if, during their contentious contract negotiations, they'd just taken out some big-ass hammers and had at each other.

But Chaplin was just the biggest name among big names—Sennett also had Harold Lloyd, long before he put on his famous glasses, before he even played "Lonesome Luke." A highlight of Lloyd's intersection with Sennett was *Courthouse Crooks*, because it features Lloyd doing what he would always do—running. This is quite possibly the earliest and most seminal appearance of anything resembling the Harold Lloyd we would come to know later.

By the 1920s, Sennett's preternatural ability to spot talent had too often come into conflict with his unwillingness to pay people what they were worth. He'd lost Lloyd, who went on to become *one of* the greatest box office draws of the age. He'd lost Chaplin, who went on to become *the* greatest box office draw of the age. He'd lost Roscoe Arbuckle and Charley Chase—and the list goes on.

So when he saw the bidding war going on for the truly bizarre vaudeville star Harry Langdon, Sennett made sure he won that war and gave the nutty little man space to do his thing. Chaplin hadn't just quit over money—he'd chafed against the restrictions on his creative freedom. Langdon would have no such cause to complain. (Langdon will feature later in this book, as an example of the apotheosis of silent slapstick before its transformation into screwball. We'll cycle back to him in time.)

One major comedian that Sennett didn't employ was Buster Keaton, but they worked together nonetheless. During Buster's time at Educational Pictures in the early 1930s, after Sennett's various studios had imploded and vanished, Mack was hired to direct Buster in the two-reeler *The Timid Young Man*. It starts off with a virtual remake of Harry Langdon's *The Hansom Cabman*, with Buster now cast as the man waking up from an epic bender trying to shake both a hangover and a gold-digging vamp insisting he'd promised to marry her. Buster flees to the woods, where he joins forces with a pretty hitch-hiker to embark on remakes of scenes from several of Keaton's silent classics (*The Balloonatic, The Battling Butler*), before winding the whole thing up with standard-issue Keystone-style violence. It's an odd but amiable blend of the two men's differing comic aesthetics.

So, that's Mack in a nutshell. Not a bad legacy for a failed actor.

# Irony and the Fat Man

There are two historical events that have colored Roscoe Arbuckle's reputation and legacy, generally for the worse.

In the 1920s, Arbuckle was the center of a scandal that had lasting consequences for his own career and for Hollywood at large. Any attempt to take stock of Roscoe Arbuckle must at some point grapple with that traumatic event, at the very least to explain why he went from an international movie star one day to a blacklisted pariah the next, why he worked under the pseudonym "William B. Goodrich" and eventually returned to movies only in reduced circumstances.

However, while grappling with the scandal would be a prerequisite to a thorough understanding of Arbuckle's career, doing so merely serves to keep that tragic event entwined with his story. He was a wronged party in the proceedings, which had nothing to do with truth or justice. By continuing to talk about the scandal, its damaging effect on his reputation is perpetuated.

Because here is something that is really, really uncomfortable for fans of silent comedy to hear: people don't know who Roscoe Arbuckle is anymore. There was a time, way back when, when the scandal still dogged Arbuckle's reputation and continued to haunt his name. Back then, you could carve the world into two kinds of people, and you could distinguish between them by saying the name "Fatty Arbuckle." One camp immediately thought of a dead flapper and a ruinous trial, while the other (smaller) camp was knowledgeable enough to know that Arbuckle was acquitted, the judge apologized to him from the bench, and that he started rebuilding his screen career as a beloved comic when he happened to die young.

Time passed, and now if you mention the name "Fatty Arbuckle" you get a different set of reactions. You still have the inner retinue of informed film buffs who know the full story and resent how the scandal has overshadowed Arbuckle's memory—but here's the thing: the other group simply goes, "Who?"

The general public has completely forgotten Arbuckle. (And you want to really feel the sting: it's my experience that the average American has forgotten Harold Lloyd, too. Outside of specialist audiences, ordinary people have *maybe* heard of Buster Keaton and Charlie Chaplin, and that's it. End of story. Forget all those "Who's the Fourth Genius?" debates—now there aren't even Three Geniuses anymore.)

Arbuckle's *fans* haven't changed, but the context around them did. Once upon a time, they were his defenders, fighting against the way history had sullied his reputation. But now *they* are the ones who sully his reputation, by keeping the memory of the scandal alive.

If we Arbuckle fans simply stopped talking about the thing, it would be quickly completely forgotten.

There is no longer any reason to argue over whether he should be called "Fatty Arbuckle" or "Roscoe Arbuckle." His fans take umbrage at "Fatty," since we know he hated being called that ("I've got a name you know" he used to respond). But nowadays nobody other than us is talking about him at all. All we have to do, as a community of film aficionados, is just keep calling him "Roscoe Arbuckle." The rest of the world, having never heard of him, will have no reason to object, and we can quietly change his name back on his behalf without any fuss. The same thing applies to the scandal—most people have no idea that ever happened. So as long as we don't talk about it, we can let it be buried and move on with honoring Arbuckle's memory the way it should be—as a comedy genius.

As discussed in the previous chapter, producer Mack Sennett got his start under D.W. Griffith, helping the great man make melodramatic pot-boilers for the Biograph Company. A typical Griffithian melodrama would have a damsel in distress, a villain, a hero.... Sennett made farce comedies that used the exact same template but pushed everything to extremes. The characters in a Sennett short were grotesque exaggerations, outsized caricatures who raced through the familiar story beats like a bull in a china shop. The humor came from the mismatch between the outsize absurdity of the characters with the expectations set by the apparent genre.

Consider the issue of Arbuckle's weight. Right from the start, Arbuckle's size was emphasized. He was called "Fatty" throughout his run at Sennett, and to Arbuckle's dismay that insulting nickname followed him even when he left the studio. Audiences knew what to expect from a fat comedian—jokes about his weight, of course. You know the kind: he sits down in a chair and it disintegrates beneath him; he sits on a park bench and turns it into a seesaw, flinging whoever was on the other side of the bench into the air; a gargantuan belly that doesn't fit through doorways; an endless appetite...

These however are *not* the jokes you find with Fatty Arbuckle. Instead, in film after film, he is presented as agile and effortlessly strong. If anything, he seems improbably dainty and balletic. The cruel name is there to set up a fat joke that then never comes.

Similarly, Arbuckle's silent comedies often cast him as a sexually desirable ladies' man—or put him in drag, whereupon he is taken by the other characters as a convincing woman, despite the total lack of femininity. There are obvious jokes to be had by putting Fatty Arbuckle in a frilly dress, but his films decline to make those jokes—and instead establish an ironic distance from the usual comedy fare. His comedy starts to take on characteristics of meta-comedy, comedy about comedy.

Arbuckle's comedy is always aware of the audience—not in the sense of Oliver Hardy looking straight down the camera lens at the viewer, or Groucho Marx breaking the Fourth Wall to talk directly to the crowd, but rather in the sense of choreographing everything with the implicit understanding that someone is watching.

Roscoe Arbuckle was a comedy genius whose groundbreaking work fundamentally defined large swaths of what silent slapstick was all about, but he is most commonly remembered today through his connection to Buster Keaton. From 1917 to 1919, Arbuckle's movie career would be tied up with Keaton's. And then, of course, Keaton went off to make his run of unfailingly superb solo shorts in 1920, while Arbuckle would be arrested a year later and his screen career was driven off a cliff. Here is where we cycle around to that *second* hiccup in Arbuckle's legacy that I mentioned at the top of this chapter—Arbuckle's career seemingly came to an end right as Keaton's begins, so there's a natural tendency to view their collaborations as being more significant in terms of Keaton's role, since he was the rising, as opposed to waning, star. Add to that the fact that Keaton has many, many more fans than Arbuckle does—so there are many people whose only exposure to Arbuckle is

**Is Roscoe Arbuckle holding Buster Keaton down in this picture, or pulling him up? You decide (courtesy Paul E. Gierucki).**

through, and in relation to, Keaton. Between those two aspects, it becomes habit to read Arbuckle's films in connection with Keaton first and foremost.

Consider *Backstage*, a 1919 two-reeler co-starring Keaton and Arbuckle, and one of their last collaborations before Keaton went solo. Many books on Keaton observe the similarity between this film and later Keaton works—such as the fact that it features an early version of the falling wall gag Keaton famously used in *Steamboat Bill, Jr.* wherein he survives by standing miraculously where the window hole happens to be. Or that the opening scene in which one reality is torn apart and revealed to be a stage set being dismantled was also reused in *Steamboat Bill, Jr.* Or that the overall tone and structure of the short prefigures Keaton's *Playhouse*. According to this brand of conventional wisdom, these similarities are evidence that Keaton was the primary creative influence at work in *Backstage* and the reason for that similarity.

The problem with this line of thinking is that it proceeds from a familiarity with Keaton's films and a relative unfamiliarity with Arbuckle's; where overlap is found between the aesthetics of Arbuckle/Keaton collaborations and later Keaton films the assumption is simply, "well that must mean Buster was the common denominator." It seems churlish to me that critics routinely deny Arbuckle the credit for any great comedy ideas that surface in the films he made with Keaton.

There's a signature Arbuckle gag that appeared several times in his filmography—1913's *Mother's Boy*, 1915's *Fatty's Plucky Pup*, and in 1917's *The Rough House*. The bit involves Arbuckle discovering that his bed is on fire. What will he do?

If this were any other slapstick clown star, you'd probably find him running around frantically, jumping up and down, waving his arms in an expression of panic. He might rush to get a garden hose, and spray himself in the face with it. Then he'd spray the hose all through the house, destroying furniture and furnishings as thoroughly as if he'd let the fire run its course.

This is not what Arbuckle does. Instead he moves deliberately, carefully, to get a single cup of water, walk it carefully to the adjacent bedroom to splash its contents on the burning bed. Then he traipses patiently back to the sink to retrieve another. He pauses to take a refreshing drink from the third.

It's a good gag, and worth repeating (and, it should be noted, appears to have originated with Max Linder around 1910). But part of what charges it with such comic energy is the context: Roscoe Arbuckle was one of the first stars to emerge out of the chaotic comedy of Mack Sennett's Keystone studio. Sennett's ethos was centered on mayhem and havoc. Sennett style slapstick was about "going big." Small complications would lead to massive overreactions and violence. And in this world of excess, Arbuckle made his name by subverting the formula. His contemporaries would tear the world asunder for a joke—Arbuckle, faced with something as genuinely calamitous and demanding of immediate attention as a raging indoor fire, took his time to daintily fill a demi-tasse of water, one splash at a time. No hurry. Nothing worth expending any real energy on.

And in that simple gag we find the essence of Arbucklian comedy distilled. In a world dominated by slapstick, Arbuckle created his laughs out of comic irony. He was postmodern before anyone else had even gotten around to being modern.

In a gag he repeated at least as often as the burning bed routine, Arbuckle is about to change clothes when he turns to the camera, gets the attention of the cameraman, and directs him to pan up so as not to expose Roscoe's nudity.

Keaton repeated the joke in his first solo short *One Week*. It's hard not to see that as a direct lift from Arbuckle—but the connection is rarely commented on.

To fully grasp the relative contributions of Keaton and Arbuckle in their collaborations, it helps to spend some time with some of the films Arbuckle directed for other comedians. For example, Arbuckle directed an oddity called *Curses!* starring Arbuckle's nephew Al St. John in a silly parody of cliffhanger-style serials. It's the kind of gag-a-minute parody that *Airplane!* does for disaster movies.

Then there's *The Movies* with Lloyd Hamilton. Although his career was cut short by alcoholism, during his heyday Lloyd Hamilton was a talented and funny slapstick clown with a persona not unlike that of Roscoe Arbuckle. They worked together in the 1920s when Arbuckle was forced into working as a pseudonymous director in the aftermath of his scandal, trial, and subsequent exoneration. Together, Arbuckle and Hamilton collaborated on three short comedies, of which only this one is known to survive. Hamilton makes a great Arbuckle stand-in *The Movies*, a film ripe with absurdity and self-referentialism. The story involves a young hayseed (Hamilton) who is warned by his country folk family to stay away from the moving pictures—but no sooner does he arrive in the big city than he is recruited by talent scouts to join the picture business. The reason they want this inexperienced rube? Because he's a dead ringer for—wait for it—Lloyd Hamilton, who wants his lookalike to handle his more dangerous stunts for him!

In the same vein is *My Stars*, in which Virginia Vance plays a movie-struck gal, who can't stop swooning over her movie mags and the pictures of her favorite stars. Hoping to get her attention back, Johnny Arthur takes to lavishly appointed impersonations of the various stars—but he can't quite keep up with her fickle fixations. Finally, he hits on a well-timed Harold Lloyd impersonation, just in time to sweep her off her feet and into a Harold-Lloyd-esque stunt-addled chase climax.

Taken together, these are a disparate mix of films made over a spread of many years for a variety of corporate entities involving many different kinds of comedians and performance styles. Yet there is a common thread—theatrical and/or cinematic self-referentialism, and a preference for absurd sight gags over raw slapstick. And since these are the dominant characteristics of something like *Backstage*, it starts to be more plausible that these are the comic characteristics of Arbuckle's vision. Perhaps they recur in Keaton's later work not because they were unique to him, but because Arbuckle was his friend and mentor and he was profoundly influenced by him?

# First Things First, but Not Necessarily in That Order

Marie Dressler's 1914 comedy feature *Tillie's Punctured Romance* is a hugely important work in film history—just about any film reference will tell you so. Here's what Wikipedia has to say: "*Tillie's Punctured Romance* is notable for being the first feature-length comedy in all of cinema." Wow. I mean, right? Just wow.

Except … it's hard to give credit to *Tillie's Punctured Romance* for being the "first feature-length comedy in all of cinema" when there was another feature-length comedy released four months earlier, on August 10, 1914. And you want to know the best bit? This earlier film, arguably the true first comedy feature in film history, is a gender-bending treat that suits today's mood much better than the fusty old melodramatic complications of *Tillie's Punctured Romance*.

The film in question is *A Florida Enchantment* by Sidney Drew. It is fabulous by many measures, but let us uncover its fabulousness in stages:

The story begins when Lillian Travers (Edith Story) makes a surprise visit to her boyfriend Dr. Cassadene (Sidney Drew). The surprise is on her when she catches him in what sure seems like a comprising position with a wealthy widow. He makes the requisite apologies, they make up, but it all goes pear shaped again when he blows their next rendezvous, once again caught with the same widow. She gives him a third chance—and as she comes out of her house to meet him, there he is, entangled in the clutches of three fawning women. If this were any other movie, you'd expect Lillian to blow her top and walk out on him, continuing the cycle of sit-commy complications that you've come to expect by this point.

This is where things veer sharply off course.

Lillian comes into the scrum of clingy ladies and gives Cassadene the cold shoulder. Instead, she plants a big wet one on the respective lips of the pretty young things. What Cassadene doesn't yet realize is that there is no point in his apologizing. She just isn't that into him anymore. His sweetie has taken a weird drug that changes people's sex. She's started growing facial hair, and developed an interest in women.

She fakes the disappearance of "Lillian" and adopts a new identity as "Lawrence Talbot." Yep, werewolf fans, she beat ole' Lon Chaney, Jr., to that name, and helped establish its pedigree as the name for a person with metamorphic abilities.

Eventually, the farcical complications of Lillian/Lawrence's transformation implicate Cassadene, and he takes the same drug—and instantly becomes a mincing, preening stereotype. For those of you who don't know of him, Sidney Drew was a master of awkward comedies of social manners. Given his fussy mannerisms, it's a short hop to feminizing him all the way.

To be clear—these are very broad stereotypes. But what's striking is that the stereotypes are not played hurtfully—they are simply used as an efficient visual shorthand to get the admittedly offbeat idea expressed quickly, without words, in a film with a tight running time.

Role reversal comedies are a genre unto themselves, and this early example of the form plays by much the same rules as *Tootsie* or the like. But to find this kind of gender-bending comedy in 1914 is startling. The sexual stereotypes are clumsy, but you could condense this film down and restage it as a *Saturday Night Live* sketch today.

*A Florida Enchantment* was based on a book by Archibald Clavering Gunter. With a name like that, you know it's gotta be old. The book was written in 1892 (if you'd like, you can find the text online for free), and by the time Sidney Drew got to it, it had already been adapted into a play.

Sidney Drew was an established stage performer from a prominent theatrical family—he's the uncle of John, Lionel, and Ethel Barrymore. In 1911, much to the snickering of his Barrymore clan, he joined the flickers and started making short comedies. By 1913, he was one of the leading lights of the Vitagraph company, where he specialized in domestic farces. Thanks to his fame and talent, he was in a position to exert some professional control over his work, and *A Florida Enchantment* finds him not only starring, but producing and directing as well.

Let's linger on that—as I've mentioned before, there is a line of thought among some film historians that would have you believe that this kind of auterist comedy was the sole province of Charlie Chaplin, Buster Keaton, and Harold Lloyd—indeed, that their status as the "Three Geniuses" derives from their unique role as the sole Hollywood clowns who made their own films. Yet here we find a largely forgotten name, Sidney Drew, exercising that kind of personal artistic vision as well.

His auteurship continued—and by 1918 he'd started his own production company (the VBK company) to make comedies for Metro.

*A Florida Enchantment* was released about a month after Sidney Drew got married to one of his co-stars, Lucille McVey (using the stage name Jane Morrow). She plays "Bessie" in the film. She fairly instantly graduated to bigger things—marrying Drew and becoming "Mrs. Sidney Drew" in his continuing cycle of short comedies. This is significant because the "Mrs. Sidney Drew" role had been a component of Drew's act all along, dating back to his days on the stage. The original Mrs. Drew, Gladys Rankin, was also a screenwriter (more gender-progressivism from the Drew clan!) and an integral part of Drew's life, both at work and at home. Her death at the end of 1913 was a horrible, tragic loss for Sidney.

Her passing was a cruel blow, and the speed with which he remarried should not distract us. He set out to make *A Florida Enchantment* while he was grieving—and its story, about a couple who decide to soothe their heartache by remaking themselves as new people, carries added poignancy with this knowledge.

As for whether this counts as the "first feature-length comedy in all of film," we can debate that if you want. Because to be fair, some of the historians who venerate *Tillie's Punctured Romance* as some kind of significant landmark are circumspect about how they phrase it, inserting qualifying words to gerrymander *Tillie* away from anything that might challenge it—Mack Sennett had that film before cameras in April 1914, and was finished as of July 1914, before *Enchantment* was finished.

It may be the first feature comedy, but who knows. I just happened to see *A Florida*

**Edith Storey (left) shows Jane Morrow a good time in the ground-breaking gender-bending comedy *A Florida Enchantment*.**

*Enchantment* at a film convention more or less by accident, without knowing anything about it beforehand, and so I have to admit that there may yet be other worthy discoveries still buried. No point sticking my neck out to make claims I can't back up.

The primary reason anyone still watches *Tillie's Punctured Romance* is its alleged status as the first American feature comedy. Actually sitting through it is a bit of a chore. *Tillie* has an excellent cast, but they don't get to do anything all that funny. Perhaps in 1914, its style and content connected more viscerally with audiences, but very few people today find *Tillie* especially entertaining.

Which means the best part of this anecdote is, the fact that Sidney Drew got there first isn't even the best part of his accomplishment. Being first is a fairly drab kind of triumph, the sort of thing that appeals to a *Guinness Book of World Records* mentality. Drew's film does something much cooler: it's still funny today.

Indeed, there is some evidence the film works even better with today's audiences than with 1914 ones. *Variety* hated it so much in 1914, its reviewer wrote that the film should never have been released at all. And the fact that it is virtually unknown today, compared to *Tillie*, suggests that it wasn't a huge popular success in its day. But no matter—it works perfectly today, and with one exception needs no apologies.

That one exception though is for the blackface. (Deep sigh.) What can I tell you? It's set in and was filmed in Florida, and the characters have black servants. White actors were cast in these roles, and made up to look black. The racial stereotypes aren't any worse than usual for the era, but just putting someone in blackface has so much negative baggage already, the damage is done.

That being said, though, this is a film about the slipperiness of identity. Men become women and vice versa—why not swap races while you're at it? And this brings us to one fleeting moment of near-redemption:

Lillian has forcibly administered the sex-change drug to her maid, and the man-maid immediately makes a pass at the other maid. And in this sequence there is a brief moment where the man-maid (played by Ethel Lloyd) starts to powder his/her face aggressively ... and we have the possibility of having a white actress playing a black man pretending to be a white woman. There is no payoff, but there are times I fantasize about that scene continuing, Ethel layering fake whiteface on top her blackface, and playing a woman as a man as a woman...

# Slapstick While Black

Times change.

A 21st-century audience simply cannot watch something like *A Florida Enchantment* the same way the audience of 1914 did. Our modern perspective is forged by living and functioning in a world with a different set of notions about race relations and gender roles. Dealing with this issue, however, is one of the thorniest aspects of trying to cultivate interest in old-timey comedies.

Despite these festering wounds, I love silent comedy, and I do not wish to watch it slide into cultural irrelevancy. The only way to keep these films and these comedians even mar-ginally, passingly, culturally relevant is to keep bringing new audiences to them—and the sadly plentiful racist gags that recur throughout these films are a significant barrier to that.

But not all racist gags are created equal. Consider what ought to be the third rail of American comedy—blackface. Touch it at your peril. It was a blackface gag in *A Florida Enchantment* which brought us to this topic, but for a moment let's step outside the world of silent slapstick to watch how blackface was handled in the 1976 Richard Pryor/Gene Wilder buddy picture *Silver Streak*.

Director Arthur Hiller had been reluctant to work with Pryor—the comic's reputation had preceded him, and Hiller was worried he'd be difficult. And, just once, he was.

The scene in question occurs when Pryor's character is trying to help get Wilder's character safely past the various federal agents who are out in force looking for him. He takes a can of shoe polish, a gaudy jacket, and a radio and tries to disguise this red-haired Jew as a black man. Gene Wilder rubs shoe polish on his face and leaps into the broadest, most cartoonish racial caricature he can summon. That's a given. What happens next deter-mines the context of this gag, and how the joke is pitched.

As written, the script called for a white man to enter the bathroom while Wilder was blacking himself up and accept the ruse, believing him to be black. That's where Pryor drew a line. Although Pryor didn't articulate what bothered him about the staging, it's easy enough to figure out: in this version, the joke centers on the implication that this absurd racist stereotype is close enough to the truth about black people that it's convincing. It gives audiences a place to laugh *at* black people.

Pryor instead suggested an alternate staging—why not have a black man come in instead, the shoeshine man for example, and immediately see through the incom-petent disguise. *"You must be in a lot of trouble,"* he could say, and shake his head in disappointment at the world. Then, when Wilder later manages to fool the cops with this blackface act, the joke isn't directed at black people, it's directed at Wilder's character and the foolish white people who can't see past the fake skin color.

Pryor had to basically go on strike to force Hiller to shoot it his way—but he was right. Pryor's version not only rehabilitated the ethical stance of the joke, he just plain made it funnier. It was one of the bigger laughs of the movie—a signature moment. A small tweak, but one that shifted the focus of the joke in a crucial way—and it's to Pryor's credit that he saw how to rescue the scene with such a subtle change.

In addition to his blackface routines in *The Jazz Singer* (1927), Al Jolson made an entire film about blackface minstrelsy with 1930's *Mammy*.

With that example as a guide, let's return to the realm of silent slapstick to examine how certain jokes are pitched, and how those nuances change the hurt.

Let's start with the simplest, and least horrendous, of the jokes on offer—one I'll call "The Black Reveal." A good example can be found in Buster Keaton's *Seven Chances*. Buster has to get married in a few hours or forfeit an inheritance—so he's desperately proposing to every woman he sees. The proposals and rejections get faster and faster as he goes. As he walks down the street, there's a woman ahead of him in a fur coat and fancy hat. He speeds up to meet her—and stops abruptly upon seeing that she's black. No proposal is made—it is to be taken for granted that she's not an option.

Of course, thanks to miscegenation laws, it was literally and legally true in many places that she was not a prospective bride, but I'm wrestling here with reconciling what these movies meant to their audiences at the time of their manufacture with how we watch them today.

As a silent comedy, this is a form in which nearly all of the jokes must be expressed in purely visual terms. Not only that, but since comedy depends so much on pacing, the joke not only has to land entirely visually, but it also makes a huge difference how long it takes the viewer to process what they're seeing. If the punchline depends on rapidly revealing to the audience that once again Buster's hit a matrimonial dead end, then having the "wrong woman" be a different skin color is a convenient visual shorthand that gets the joke across quickly.

We can see that in the numerous variations of this joke throughout the same film, what matters is the quick reveal, not the racial component. Earlier in the film Buster spotted a woman on the far side of the room. As he sat next to her, she lowered her newspaper to reveal—a baby on her lap! Moments thereafter he finds what he believes to be a possible bride—but once she's removed her hat and coat she turns out to be a child, not a grown woman at all. (I should also mention that just before his encounter with the black woman, he tries to propose to a woman on a bench until he realizes she's reading a Hebrew newspaper.)

There are different ways to handle this "joke" that show different degrees of tolerance and sensitivity. In *His Marriage Wow*, Harry Langdon performs his variation on the same gag. Harry leaves his wedding in a typically Langdonian state of disorientation and gets into the wrong taxi, next to a black bride. Instead of the scene being about *his* reaction to *her*, however, it's about *her* reaction to *him*. She immediately starts screaming at this unwelcome intruder and hammering her fists on him until he leaps from the moving vehicle into the arms of his actual bride. Not unlike Richard Pryor's fixes to *Silver Streak*, this was a way to deliver largely the same visual gag but pivoted so as not to be about laughing at the minority character but laughing with them.

Nevertheless, the essence of the Black Reveal is the concept that on sight, based solely on skin color, one can make conclusions about a person's place in society, their capabilities, their worth as a person. It may be a visual shorthand, but that visual shorthand is the very basis of racial prejudice.

Of all the Black Reveals I've seen, one stands apart from the others and deserves a separate mention of its own. It occurs in the Charley Chase short *Isn't Life Terrible*, in which Charley sets out on an epically disastrous family vacation. Early on, he accidentally takes the hand of a different girl instead of his daughter's hand, and only later realizes he's taken the wrong child along and left his own daughter behind alone. And, perhaps because the skin color difference helps telegraph the joke best in the accelerated pace of this two-reel silent short, sure enough the wrong kid on his arm is black. In any other film of the era, that would be the punchline—a quick "a ha!" reaction as he sees the girl is black, some quick panicked double takes, and then move on. But Charley Chase has set up the premise so that there's no way to swap the kids back again, so after that first "*a-ha!*" gag, the black girl stays in the film as his ersatz daughter. Suddenly the joke has changed—instead of being about the reaction to her skin color, it becomes an extended sight gag. More to the point, the sight gag isn't at her expense, or to do with any racial stereotypes—it's just indulging in the visual incongruity, back in the days of racial separation, to see a white family with a black child. She continues to be treated as their child, though, as if skin color is just a mask...[1]

Which brings us to Racial Joke #2: "Swapping Colors." This can refer either to white characters getting blacked up or black characters getting whiteface on.

Once again I'll lead with a Keaton example, this time from *College*. Buster's character has to disguise himself in blackface to get hired as a waiter. When the girl he loves and his romantic rival come in to eat, he only escapes the humiliation of being recognized as their waiter because he looks black (sort of). In other words, once again here's a situation that's using the racial angle as a visual shorthand—in a modern comedy, you could have a similar premise but have the comedian use other means to hide their identity (a fake accent, for example, or other sort of disguise).

Also notable, Keaton's shuck-and-jive routine is contrasted directly with the actual black waiters and waitresses around him who seem perfectly competent at their jobs. Keaton, meanwhile, catastrophically misunderstands the in/out system of the kitchen doors, can't take or deliver orders correctly, and seems generally unsuited to any aspect of the job. As with Pryor's redo of the blackface gag in *Silver Streak*, this blackface sequence ends up doing nothing but making fun of Keaton's character, not the African Americans he's trying to pass as.

One comedian who used blackface (and whiteface) extensively was Larry Semon. I'm not sure I've ever seen a film of his that didn't at some point have a white character get a bucket of paint dunked on his head, or a black character get coated in white flour. Or both.

I've never quite known what to make of Semon's seeming obsession with this kind of joke. I definitely get the feeling he thought there was nothing funnier than seeing a person who appeared to have changed skin color. But exactly what made that funny is up for debate. Is it because changing races is so transgressive, that just to think of the taboo is hilarious?

Racial Joke #3 is "The Scaredy Black." The idea here is linked, on some level, with the role played by supporting comedians of all races to help their top-billed stars land the jokes. The slapstick shenanigans of silent comedians needed someone to react to them, to help the jokes go bigger. Comic performers like Edgar Kennedy or Jimmy Finlayson basically built their careers on making funny reactions to the havoc unleashed by the likes of Laurel and Hardy. So, it's not necessarily a bad thing that there were so many black performers like Spencer Bell, Curtis McHenry, and "G. Howe Black" whose paychecks came from making funny double takes...

Except, all these black supporting players were there to act scared. Edgar Kennedy got to simmer like a pot set to boil over, Homer Simpson's "D'oh!" is the direct descendant of Jimmy Finlayson's annoyed grunt. There were an array of ways to react to slapstick, unless you were black, in which case abject terror was all that was on offer. And since it traded on long-standing stereotypes of black Americans as superstitious and ignorant, no matter how brilliantly Bell and his colleagues sold their scaredy acts, they reinforced an oppressive system.

Fans of slapstick comedies have a reflexive defense that seeks to minimize the hurt inherent in these images. "You have to watch these films through your 1920 glasses." For example, in his book *The Funny Parts*, film historian Anthony Balducci makes the claim that back then "everyone was fair game as long as a stereotype served the plot or made people laugh."

The problem with that defense, however, is it speaks from a position of unacknowledged privilege. No matter how stupidly a white comedian behaved, it wouldn't incline audiences to think of white men as inherently stupid. There are simply too many disparate pop cultural representations of white men (rich, poor, dumb, smart, heroic, villainous, decent, cowardly, etc., etc.) that no particular representation holds any special power.

But minorities—be they racial, religious, sexual, what have you—get such infrequent representations, how they are portrayed in those limited roles takes on disproportionate weight. And when those portrayals conform to existing prejudices, it only serves to reinforce those attitudes, in an endless feedback loop.

The way the media depict minorities is fundamentally part of this—the images of black men in the media have a direct influence on the life expectancy of a black man caught up in any interaction with a cop. To argue that everyone is equal game for stereotypes is to suggest that stereotypes have an equal effect on all people, which is demonstrably untrue.

There is another problem with the reflexive defense of "Slapstick comedians were equally opportunity offenders. Everybody got theirs." That's sometimes true, but not always, and the devil is in the details.

By way of illustration, consider Charlie Chaplin's *The Immigrant* (by the way, one of my very favorite films of all time. If my house ever catches fire, I'm running back in to save my print).

*The Immigrant* came out in June 1917. Now, just four months earlier, Congress passed the Immigration Act of 1917. At the time, the country was gripped by the same asinine xenophobia and nativism as it is today, and there were politicians then who whipped up anti-immigrant scapegoating for their own benefit.

President Wilson vetoed the thing, but the groundswell of anti-immigrant hysteria was enough to override the veto and get the Immigration Act of 1917 into law. The Act declared most of Asia as a "Barred Zone," forbidding immigration from the entire region. It enumerated the types of "undesirables" who would be barred from any country: "homosexuals," "idiots," "feeble-minded persons," "criminals," "epileptics," "insane persons," alcoholics, "professional beggars," "mentally or physically defective persons," polygamists, and anarchists. And it imposed a literacy test to exclude the uneducated.

Notice how many of those "undesirable" character types describe Chaplin himself, or his screen persona? This did not go unnoticed. The biggest movie star in the world knew firsthand what it meant to be unwanted and adrift, to be hungry and destitute, to be distrusted. He knew alcoholism and madness first hand. He made a living playing criminals and beggars. And so, he made a movie.

It happened backwards. He'd been working on a film about slapstick shenanigans in a restaurant. As he improvised on camera, he hit upon the idea that it would be funny if his character had never been in a restaurant before, and this opened up whole new avenues of jokes. As the thing developed, though, he realized it was funny without making a whole hell of a lot of sense. He needed some context. He needed a first act.

And so, working backwards to justify a situation in which a grown man has his first encounter with a restaurant, he decided his first act would be about watching this guy immigrate to the United States.

But here's the sheer brilliance of the set-up: Chaplin gets a lot of sharp jokes in about the very things the xenophobes were anxious about. The film shows a boat full of poor people, who don't speak English, who eat weird smelling food, and bring various diseases and criminal activities with them. If you've got a chip on your shoulder about immigrants, this film has jokes that come from your perspective. Only, they don't quite land the way they seem to be aimed.

Instead of appearing like a mass of dangerous unassimilable others, the immigrants in the film are portrayed as sympathetic people. For all the differences that are depicted, they are fundamentally like us. Audiences had been watching Chaplin cavort through two-reel shorts for three years by this point, and there's little in *The Immigrant* they hadn't seen in one form or another before. These people aren't so different after all, the film seems to whisper.

Charlie Chaplin was the world's most highly paid entertainer. The entire film industry has been reshaping itself around him. Put his name on a film and it will turn a profit, simple as that. He's so marketable, films that have exactly nothing to do with him are using looka-likes to try to buffalo audiences and cash in on his appeal. In other words, he has power. He can do literally anything and the audience will follow—so he plays an immigrant. He plays an immigrant who can't read and has no money, one who is clearly willing to at least consider theft and murder even if he doesn't go through with it.

Under the law that was just passed, this guy would be barred from entry. The most popular performer in the world uses his bully pulpit to show that, if you're going to draw up lines of us versus them, he is choosing the "them" side. Chaplin is siding with the outsiders, the excluded, the unwanted. This isn't casual or coincidental, this is the politics of the personal.

He doesn't have to do this—he's already in. He's safely integrated, he's rich and powerful and comfortable. If he wanted to, he could poke merciless fun at those smelly foreigners and their funny accents and we'd all laugh with him, at the powerless and the downtrodden. But this is an artist who has always chosen the path of mercy, and inclusion.

Meanwhile, Chaplin's chief copycat, Billy West, dropped a needless little nugget of racist comedy into his 1917 short *The Hobo*. West plays the caretaker of a train station, and nestled in the middle of an otherwise quite well-made and amusing short film, he meets a "black" couple who have come to collect their children. The adults are white actors in crude blackface, and the wife of the couple is an enormous man in drag. The children are a gaggle of about a dozen kids, who have evidently been stored in a locked storage bin with a handful of air holes. After releasing the kids from the locker, Billy West gives them a huge watermelon to eat while sitting on the train tracks.

I know, hilarious, right?

There's no tolerance there. It's just pointing and laughing at the other. It's just mean spirited, and the very essence of the joke presupposes a division between the people being pointed at and laughed at, and the people doing the laughing.

Back in 2008 I somehow managed to attend three separate theatrical screenings of the exceedingly obscure silent comedy *Uncle Tom's Gal* starring Edna Marian. There's a cruel irony in the fact that the film gods saw fit to preserve this horrifyingly ugly monstrosity for posterity while films like Laurel and Hardy 's *Hats Off* vanished off the earth. I know it's wrong for a film geek like me to ever wish for a film to be destroyed, but all I'm saying is, if a film had to be destroyed, I'd rather live in a world that still had *Hats Off* but had lost this.

Some background: the book *Uncle Tom's Cabin* was in its day intended as an anti-slavery tool, and by depicting the terrible reality of slavery in the South helped encourage abolitionists. Problematically, the novel's depiction of the slaves was also tainted by stereotypes that later became so vilified that the book became more notorious for its racist content than its anti-racist agenda—in other words, the book *Uncle Tom's Cabin* became a victim of the very cultural shift we're talking about here, left behind by a society that moved on.

In the short comedy *Uncle Tom's Gal,* a movie company is making a film of *Uncle Tom's Cabin,* and for no reason at all has decided to shoot on Edna's farm. She's an avid movie buff given to daydreaming of being a star, and she insinuates herself into the production. Early in the picture, Edna sidles up the camera with Hollywood glitter in her eyes. Already, the film is starting to offend on several levels: first is the way the horrifying caricature of slavery itself (with such lines as "Now you charcoal babies belong to me" and the image of the plantation owner brutally whipping his slave) is just jarring to find in a comedy. This was the problem with the book *Uncle Tom's Cabin*—the text itself hits wrong notes and raw nerves. Problem #2 is that the "filmmakers" have cast white actors in blackface. And problem #3, is the way movie-struck Edna reacts to all this racial cruelty with giggly, giddy glee.

What's she smiling about? It sure looks like she's getting off on watching a black man being whipped. That can't be right, can it? Surely she's just excited by the prospect of being so near a film crew … but that's not what it looks like.

Soon, Edna fully insinuates herself into the movie and is cast as the leading lady … in some of the grimmest, meanest blackface you'll ever find.

At each of the screenings, the hosts screening it gave some variation of the apology "This movie was made in the 1920s, things were very different back then and this will be very un–PC comedy. So, put on your 1925 glasses to enjoy this."

I get what they were trying to say—that films like this are artifacts of a different world that operated under different values and we cannot fairly expect things from the past to fit with the way we think about things now. Or, to cast out another hypothetical for use as an analogy—what if a future society decides that images of men dressing up as women constitutes a horrifying gender-based hate crime. Suddenly, old episodes of *Monty Python's Flying Circus* and *The Kids in the Hall* would be tainted with negative cultural associations that they do not now have. Most of the time *The Kids in the Hall* handled gender issues with great sensitivity and nuance, not only better than other comedies of the 1990s but better than most dramas. If a future society were to re-interpret those images with negative connotations, it would fundamentally distort what the original was meant to convey.

Fair enough, but you cannot say that *Uncle Tom's Gal* wasn't offensive in 1925, that people weren't hurt or humiliated by the dehumanizing imagery. What you can say is that the people who found it offensive or who were humiliated by it were not in a position to voice their discomfort openly. A mainstream audience of whites were permitted to laugh at this, to vicariously mock blacks, and never have it questioned. Yes, in today's PC culture that joke crosses a line that hadn't been drawn in 1925—but saying the line hadn't been drawn openly isn't the same thing as saying there was no line.

It's more comforting, certainly, to tell ourselves that these old comedies were harmless. But ignoring someone's hurt doesn't erase your guilt. Nelson from *The Simpsons* once described "a victimless crime" as "punching someone in the dark." Mean-spirited jokes that poked fun at ethnic minorities, at gays, at women, at foreigners—these jokes had victims. And in the pre–PC days, those victims were effectively silenced, which gave the illusion of no victims. But notice how the people who usually say, "It's all in good fun" are the ones making the joke, not the ones receiving it.

When I go to classic film festivals, or revival screenings, or other gatherings of film geeks, what I see is a crowd of predominantly white, middle-aged men. People who look like me. Showing a film like *Uncle Tom's Gal* doesn't do much to open that tent to people who don't look like me. And when people who do look like me debate how offensive this stuff is, we do so at a remove—we can never really know how hurtful a stereotype is, if it isn't our stereotype.

I'm no censor. That Billy West scene I described above—the one with the family eating watermelon? I'm the guy who restored that film and published it on DVD under my own label. Real censors don't usually go out of their way to show you the thing they want to suppress. Even though I find that joke deeply offensive, I didn't cut out the scene (although I could have and few would ever have known the difference). Instead, I made a point to buttress that short with what I considered counterexamples—I packed in some Ernest "Sunshine Sammy" Morrison shorts.

When he was less than eight years old, he was sharing the screen with Harold Lloyd—arguably, upstaging Lloyd. He went on to be the primary supporting costar to Snub Pollard, and then producer Hal Roach gave him a fulltime contract. It was the first long-term movie contract given to a black actor in Hollywood. Roach started hiring other children to surround Morrison in his own starring series—and this is how Our Gang began.

Eventually, Morrison got too "old" and Our Gang continued on without him—so when the Little Rascals did their version of *Uncle Tom*, called *Uncle Tom's Uncle* in 1926, it was up to Joe Cobb to put on the blackface and be whipped by Mikey Daniels. Because that's what you want from comedy, right?

When I watch Morrison, what I see is a sharp-minded kid who adheres to no stereotype. But that's just me—not everyone saw him the same way. As the Civil Rights era dawned, Morrison was shoved aside—along with so many other black comedians of his era, who were perceived by a new generation as having been Uncle Toms themselves.

Such as Mantan Moreland—a brilliant comedian whose presence enlivens many an otherwise trashy B-movie. Moreland almost always upstaged his costars—we'll encounter him again later in this book, stealing the attention away from Lucille Ball. Comedians of that caliber are few and far between.

The curious thing about Moreland is he had two discrete personas. One was more in the mold of the dumb black servant, a role he played—and ennobled—in films like *King of the Zombies* (you should absolutely watch this movie, but only because of him; if he weren't in it, it would be justly forgotten). But that was in movies aimed at whites. At the same time he also performed live and in low-budget films aimed exclusively at black audiences, with a different shtick. Left to be himself, Moreland's comedy was sped up to a crazy degree. He and whatever comedian he'd be with at the moment would banter back and forth so quickly they trampled all over each other's lines, running out ahead of the dialogue and racing off into oblivion. It was a singular act, depending on a razor-sharp comic timing that would exhaust almost anyone.

Moe Howard loved Moreland's double-talk act. When Shemp died, and the hunt was on for a new third Stooge, and under pressure to push the Three Stooges away from violent slapstick and into dialog comedy, Moe proposed Moreland. The execs at Columbia rolled their eyes and patiently explained to Moe that under no circumstances were the Three Stooges to be integrated.[2] Joe Besser got the gig instead (in the parallel universe where Mantan Moreland joined Moe and Larry after all, the Stooges kept making shorts long after the Moe-Larry-Joe combo fizzled out).

Moreland later complained that the worst thing to happen to him professionally was the Civil Rights era, as he was shoved into obscurity by a generation that felt instinctively embarrassed by him.

So, here I am, 21st-century white guy, looking back at Morrison and Moreland as examples of black comedians whose acts don't strike me as racially problematic, and whose memories I wish to rehabilitate in the face of this overly sensitive backlash that suppressed them … but who am I to say that Mantan Moreland wasn't offensive? If it was blacks in the 1960s who said he was an embarrassment, what gives me any authority to disagree? Even if I could draw a line between "these comedians were offensive Uncle Toms selling out their race" and "these comedians subverted the system," the result would be to lend support to the notion that some comedians from the past deserve to have had their careers destroyed, their films suppressed, and their names forgotten.

But these kind of arguments fly above the level at which most people engage with movies—and certainly the level at which kids engage with movies. The problem with letting the unreconstructed sexual and racial attitudes of the past out today without some kind of filter, is that they propagate their worldview into younger viewers. I know that makes me sound like I'm more worried about today's kids being corrupted by watching too many old movies than by watching the anything-goes stuff of contemporary TV, which must make me sound insane, but since I spend so much time trying to cultivate new viewers for old movies, it's an issue that weighs on my mind.

Black faces appear rarely in silent comedy. When they do, they are the butt of mean-spirited jokes more often than not. At *best*, and this is pretty rare, they are neutral figures in the background. This is unfortunate, and because it's in the past we can't change it. Acknowledging it is better than trying to pretend it wasn't hurtful.

# @RealCharlieChaplin

It's mid-summer 1928. A California district court of appeal is considering a case involving alleged fraud. On one side stands Charles Millikan, the lawyer representing Charlie

Chaplin. On the other are Ben Goldman and J.J. Lieberman, representing Mexican actor Charles Amador, AKA "Charlie Aplin."

Amador's lawyers are putting forth the argument that, yeah, no question about it, Amador was ripping off Charlie Chaplin's appearance and persona. But, they contend, that's OK, because Chaplin himself had ripped it off first—and therefore he had no viable claim of ownership.

I won't leave you in suspense: Amador lost this argument. He lost the original trial, he lost this appeal—and when he tried to get the Supreme Court to listen to him, they shrugged him off. The ruling in *Chaplin v. Amador* established that, as far as the Court was concerned, Chaplin was the creator of his comic identity and therefore had intellectual property at stake. But...

Charlie Chaplin did his best work amidst a swarm of parasites—copycats and imper-sonators who profited from his comic gifts. His resentment of them knew no limits. He excoriated them in the press, he sued them in the courts, and when he died he bequeathed his enduring hatred of them to the succeeding generations of film buffs and scholars who would chronicle his art. But this self-imposed prejudice does us no good service. There's a different story waiting to be told, if we can for a moment consider Chaplin's mimics on their own terms.

Chaplin himself was inconsistent in his treatment of copycats, and his response evolved over time. There were several categories of legitimate copies, which Chaplin himself tended to overlook if not forgive, and even the illegitimate ones had a positive role in developing Chaplin's artistry.

The first thing we have to wrap our heads around is that Charlie Chaplin's rise to suc-cess was meteoric in every possible sense. As a teenager in England he was shuffled between orphanages and institutions, living in slums and starving. Less auspicious roots can scarcely be conceived. Yet even in his earliest roles on the stage, minor supporting parts in minor plays, he garnered critical attention and favorable reviews. When he joined Fred Karno's troupe in 1908, he was just one comedian amongst an ensemble of equals, yet once again distinguished himself from the pack in the eyes of critics and audiences. (Karno's U.S. tour folded after Charlie left—no one was even interested in booking the rest of the show without him.) This emerging fame got him a movie gig with Mack Sennett, where once again he was employed as one funnyman among multitudes—Mabel Normand, Roscoe Arbuckle, Ford Sterling, etc. And yet once again he earned a disproportionate share of the lauds. In just months he had become not only Mack Sennett's MVP, but one of the biggest movie stars in the world.

It is against this backdrop of astonishing success that his competitors must be judged. Everyone's doing the same thing, but here's a guy who does it so much better—naturally they try to follow his lead. In any other field of human endeavor this is the approved approach. If someone is winning, you observe what they're doing to win and appropriate their techniques into your own. In business it's "benchmarking," not plagiarism.

The first time audiences saw Chaplin in a movie was on February 2, 1914, in a short titled *Making a Living*. The Little Tramp character didn't surface until the following week, *Kid Auto Races at Venice*. Just eight months later (roughly coincident with Chaplin's 28th Keystone short), the first faux-Chaplin film arrived: *Love and Surgery*, starring Billie Ritchie.

Ritchie looks like Chaplin, but his performance isn't very Chaplinesque. Ritchie plays an identically costumed tramp, and copies some of Chaplin's mannerisms (like that wad-dling walk), but emphasizes the violent slapstick and aggression that Chaplin was already starting to weed out of his own performance. Ritchie isn't merely a Chaplin mimic—he's specifically a mimic of Keystone-era Chaplin. Except Ritchie insisted that in fact he was not a Chaplin imitator, Chaplin was an imitator of *his*.

To evaluate this claim, let's turn back the clock to the turn of the century in London where Fred Karno inaugurated the latest installment of his "birds" sketches—*Jail Birds, Early Birds, Mumming Birds*... (no *Angry Birds*, though).

It was a self-referential show-within-a-show in which some of the Karno company played the goofy vaudevillians performing on stage while the others played rowdy audience members heckling the show or otherwise getting into mischief. The lead heckler, called "The Inebriate" or "The Tipsy Swell," was first played by a comedian named Billy Reeves. Reeves then passed the role to Billie Ritchie, who then was replaced by Charlie Chaplin.

It was Ritchie's contention that much of Chaplin's screen persona and costume were in fact his innovation from the Karno days, and Chaplin took over these from him. That famous waddling walk that I said Ritchie copied from Chaplin? Well, evidently Chaplin himself copied it from Karno's Fred Kitchen.

Remember these details from a few chapters back: Chaplin's first film at Keystone was such a misbegotten disaster it was abandoned and destroyed, Charlie was benched for weeks, and Sennett considered firing him. Ritchie's claim is that it was in this troubled debut that Chaplin feared he'd blown his Hollywood chances. He was discouraged and full of self-doubt. Ritchie, being Chaplin's friend, told his buddy to rely on what had worked at Karno, and gave him Ritchie's own Tramp costume. Ritchie added that while he bears his friend no ill will for his success, he also did not feel constrained from continuing to play that role himself as well.

Now, it is not a hard thing to poke holes in Ritchie's story. Many of Chaplin's most dis-tinctive mannerisms predate his time at Karno and were part of his actor's DNA all along (there are pre–Karno press clippings to establish this). Let's also note that the Tipsy Swell role was originally Billy Reeves.'

In interviews and his autobiography, Chaplin claims to have devised the costume him-self—and while his story sounds like a self-serving myth, a better-researched and more detailed account by Denis Gifford also credits Charlie with the costume.

The thing is, a fair number of Chaplin-o-philes stop there, assuming that once they've established Ritchie's story as an exaggeration or worse, they've resolved the issue. But there's another issue, wrapped up inside the question of who invented the costume, which nobody addresses.

Ritchie had not only worked alongside Chaplin at Karno, but both men worked at Keystone together, too. When Chaplin first started in films, he was directed by others, like Henry Lehrman. Lehrman was the director of that first abortive misfire of Charlie's, he directed the first released film in which Chaplin appears, and he directed the first film in which the Little Tramp appears—and by that point their working relationship was pro-foundly soured.

Lehrman quit. He had been one of the principal architects of the Keystone studio, its comedy brand, its corporate identity. But he was sick of Chaplin and his growing influence, and left to start his own studio, L-KO where he could do things his way. And he hired Billie

Ritchie to come with him. L-KO was basically created to be a factory for fake Chaplins, and he encouraged Ritchie to push the imitation.

And this is where our story gets complicated—because Lehrman had been involved in developing Chaplin's screen persona. As the director of several of Chaplin's earliest films, not to mention his role as a guiding creative force at the studio independent of his specific screen credits, Lehrman undoubtedly influenced Chaplin. Just as Ritchie, having played Chaplin's role in *Mumming Birds* before him, had some influence as well. These guys overstated their case, but they were an undeniable part of Charlie's early development, and that gave them some legitimacy to adapt the role on their own terms.

If you disagree with my logic, bear in mind that it is the same logic that Chaplin himself used in laying artistic claim to ideas and material that he had a tangential connection to.

At Essanay, he would make a film version of the *Mumming Birds* sketch, entitled *A Night in the Show*, without paying royalties to Karno. He continued to feel entitled to use that sketch, which he did not write or originate. In the early sound era, his brother Syd Chaplin was planning a talkie feature version to costar him and Charlie.

Also at Essanay, Chaplin remade his Keystone short *The Rounders* as *A Night Out*, casting Ben Turpin in the role played by Roscoe Arbuckle in the Keystone version. He remade the Keystone short *The New Janitor* several times, as *The Bank* and *The Floorwalker*. And if you think he was entitled to remake those films because he'd made the originals, that doesn't quite explain how he could remake *The Knockout* as *The Champion*, when *The Knockout* had in fact been written and directed by Charles Avery and Chaplin merely played a small role in it. For that matter, he took a key gag from Roscoe Arbuckle's *Fatty and the Broadway Stars* and put it in his unfinished short *How to Make Movies* as if it was his. Perhaps most conspicuously, Chaplin's legendary bread roll dance from *The Gold Rush* (a routine indelibly associated with the Little Tramp) had been filmed nearly a decade earlier by Arbuckle in *The Rough House*.

In a bigger sense, by contemporary standards of intellectual property rights, Chaplin should never have had the right to take his Little Tramp character with him when he left Keystone, because that role and its distinctive costume were developed at Sennett's studio using Sennett's time, money, and resources, for use in films by Sennett (unless you agree with Ritchie and conclude that the Tramp predated Sennett altogether).

The point I'm trying to make is not that Chaplin was a plagiarist, but that in the era in which he lived and worked, the rules of authorial ownership of creative products was very loosey-goosey, and that lassitude worked to his benefit. Chaplin took these iffy claims and made of them great art we now love. I'm glad he did, we all are the better for it—but the same logic also bestows a certain legitimacy upon the copycat antics of Billie Ritchie working for Henry Lehrman.

Apparently Chaplin understood that. Even when he sent his lawyers storming after his other impersonators, he never sued Ritchie. After Ritchie's untimely death Chaplin employed the guy's widow to make sure she was taken care of.

So we can establish one category of Chaplin mimics as semi-legitimate—the kind of thing analogous to the arguments over Pink Floyd, when you had competing band lineups each laying claim to the band name and music catalog.

To continue our music analogy, another category of Chaplin mimics that he seemed OK with would be tribute bands—performers who adopted his likeness in situations where he did not perform. Tribute bands perform all the time for small-scale venues like local bars, and the real acts rarely get riled up because it doesn't really qualify as competition.

Dan Kamin noted that Mabel Normand could be counted as the first Chaplin mimic, imitating Charlie in *Mabel's Married Life*. And he's in that movie with her! *Motion Picture Magazine* in July 1915 published a piece by Charles McGuirk that insisted that imitating Chaplin was the way fans showed their appreciation for their hero—and that to the extent other comedians imitated him, that was the highest possible form of screen comedy!

In early 1915, Stan Laurel played a Chaplin-alike in a stage show called *The Keystone Trio*, with his co-stars aping Chester Conklin and Mabel Normand. They toured the vaudeville circuits and survived on the strength of Stan's mimicry of his former Karno costar. At almost the exact same time, Bert Wheeler, later of the Wheeler and Woolsey comedy duo, played a Chaplin clone on stage that won critical raves—and the real Chaplin even signed to Wheeler a photo of Wheeler in his Tramp costume, inscribed "to my worthy imitator." Chaplin also seemed more touched than threatened by circus clown Charlie Rivel's impersonation, an act which Rivel kept doing for over a decade. In 1927, the Royal Albert Hall hosted a competition for Chaplin mimics, in which Chaplin himself secretly participated.[1]

In 1917, cartoon pioneers Otto Messmer and Anton Sullivan launched a series of unauthorized animated shorts starring a caricature of Charlie the Tramp. According to Messmer and Sullivan, their animators worked from a series of photos of Charlie which the comedian gave them expressly for that purpose (at least Messmer and Sullivan said that's what happened).

There is one last category of Chaplin imitator that escaped his wrath—the fellow travelers. And to keep with the music analogy we can compare them to the kinds of musicians whose style is dictated by the successful performers of the day. When the Beatles hit it big, you had a slew of British Invasion acts with a similar sound. In the wake of the Clash and the Sex Pistols, countless small punk acts modeled their sound on the chart-topping punk pioneers.

Nineteen fifteen saw Harry Watson as the tramp Musty Suffer, not a Chaplin clone per se but again a figure drawn from the same raw ingredients (more on him next chapter). Also in 1915, Harold Lloyd started his solo career in a character devised to mirror Chaplin's—unlike the other mimics, he did not copy the costume, but inverted it. Around the same time, Charlie's own brother Syd brought his Gussle character to Sennett—and like Harold Lloyd it wasn't a direct clone but a character whose appearance and mannerisms were derived from Charlie's.

The tipping point for the Chaplin imitators, and the moment when Chaplin's response to them profoundly changed, was 1916, his time at Essanay. And it had to do with money.

Some numbers: The first acting contract Chaplin had ever had, at the age of 17, was the equivalent of roughly about $15 or $16 a week. When Karno signed Charlie to a one-year commitment in 1908, he paid him the equivalent, more or less, of $25 a week. Keystone started him at $150 a week. Essanay wooed him away with a staggering $1250 a week.

In 10 years, Charlie's pay had rocketed from $15 to $1250 a week, increasing almost tenfold in just one year. And, on top of this, Essanay offered him a $10,000 signing bonus!

Or did they? George Spoor, the S part of S&A (get it? S&A=Essanay), balked at the contract. He said he didn't owe that kind of bonus to anyone, and he hadn't even heard of this Charlie Chaplin guy, and how in the hell could he be worth 15 times what the company was paying anybody else?

From today's perspective we can see Chaplin was a genius, waiting for the chance to shine, but Spoor in 1915 had no way to know that. Essanay would only pay such sums if they thought it would rebound to them as profit—and Spoor's hesitance suggests he was unsure of Chaplin's ability to make them that kind of profit.

Flash-forward a year. Chaplin's contract at Essanay was nearing its end, and he negotiated a better one at Mutual. In March of 1916—14 months after starting work for Essanay— he signed a deal with Mutual for a mind-reeling $670,000 for one year—that's more than 10 times what Essanay was paying. And there was a $150,000 signing bonus.

In two years, Chaplin had jumped his earnings by over a hundredfold. He became the highest paid entertainer in the world. Some reports say his Mutual contract represented then the highest salary ever paid to anyone in the world in any field.

Look at the same facts though from George Spoor's perspective: he dug deep into his pockets to pay Chaplin the big bucks when such a thing represented a genuine act of faith. He believed in Charlie when it was a gamble, when it was hard to do. Just when that gamble was starting to pay off, Chaplin was going to take away the stardom that Essanay created and give it to a competitor.

Let's add this to the mix: I suggested that it was of questionable ethics for Chaplin to take the Tramp character with him from Keystone to Essanay, but really all he took from Keystone was the costume. It was at Essanay that the Tramp as we know him evolved—the personality, the social critique, the tragic dimensions, the sense of grand cinematic aesthetics—all of that was created at, by, with, and for Essanay. When Chaplin decamped for Mutual, he was absconding with Essanay's intellectual property.

It was every bit the messy divorce—and like a spurred and angry ex-lover, Spoor became enraged and jealous.

Because, there's one last detail I haven't mentioned. When Chaplin left Essanay for Mutual, he still contractually owed Essanay four shorts.

Obviously with Chaplin gone, their ability to get those remaining shorts was FUBAR, as they say. The last thing Chaplin had finished before departing for Mutual was his two-reel *Burlesque on Carmen*. Looking to get some of theirs back, Spoor withheld *Carmen* from distribution in order to turn it into a mini-feature, with which he could get more profits than from a two-reeler.

Spoor tasked the project to Leo White, one of Chaplin's stock company, who shot additional material with Ben Turpin, another of Chaplin's regular costars. The expanded version of *Carmen* came out in April of 1916, just in time to compete head-to-head against Chaplin's first short at Mutual.

This was when Charlie starting suing. Chaplin argued that he had a contractual stipulation that no film could go out with his name without his approval, and that this bastardized version of *Carmen* would harm his reputation because negative critical response would be directed at him, and people wouldn't make the distinction that he hadn't made it.

Essanay responded: (a) Chaplin invalidated his contract when he walked out early, so they aren't held by its terms; (b) the film clearly identifies Chaplin as the star, not the filmmaker; (c) the reviewers and audiences like the longer version, so there's no harm to his reputation on that count; (d) oh, and since we paid for *Carmen* in the first place, we own it and can do anything we want to with it.

The court agreed, and eventually got around to ordering Chaplin to pay *them* damages.

But as damages go, Chaplin felt that just letting the altered version of *Carmen* slide was the worst thing that could happen to him. Because at the moment that the court agreed that Spoor was permitted to make Chaplin films without his approval, the flood gates opened. Emboldened by the verdict, Essanay took the scraps of footage Chaplin had left behind for *Life*, and outtakes of other projects, had Leo White shoot some new footage, and assembled the result as another film, *Triple Trouble*.

At the time, it was not standard practice to officially copyright motion pictures. Doing so cost money, and with short films pouring out of movie companies like water from a spigot for an intended theatrical life that was measured in days, it didn't seem worth it. While Chaplin had been at Essanay, some pirates had taken to copying his films. Jules Potash and Isadore Peskov had gotten a hold of a print of *The Champion* and overprinted its footage onto footage of Annette Kellerman's undersea fantasy flick *Daughter of the Gods*, to make a seeming new pastiche about Chaplin interacting with mermaids. This they called *Charlie Chaplin in a Son of the Gods*. They did the same thing a short while later to create another overprinted patchwork they called *Charlie in a Harem*.

Meanwhile, a film called *Miss Minerva Courtney in her Impersonation of Charlie Chaplin* was a remake of *The Champion* starring the actress in full Tramp makeup and costume playing Charlie's role.

Chaplin didn't own *The Champion*, and Essanay didn't seem to care. These ripoffs vexed Chaplin, but he had little recourse. His attempt to sue Essanay over *Carmen* misfired. Charlie was now actively competing against himself.

In 1917, he unleashed a wave of lawsuits against his copycats—suing Potash and Peskov's New Apollo Feature Film Company, suing the makers of *The Fall of the Rummy-Nuffs* which also recycled actual Chaplin footage to make an unauthorized new film, and other companies who tried to pass off their work as actual Chaplin films

And then there was Billy West. Russian-born Billy West played a Chaplin mimic on the vaudeville stage in an act he called The Real Charlie Chaplin. That should have been a provocation, but remember Chaplin tended to overlook his stage imitators. West did something that virtually none of his competitors in the Chaplin mimicry business did—he observed his subject so closely as to capture all of the minute details of his performance. West didn't just copy the costume—he cloned his body language, his physical grace, his nuances.

A Chicago-based film start-up hired West to bring his act in front of the cameras, and managed to film a single short,

**Bobby Dunn, allegedly the "first Keystone Kop," also worked as a Chaplin mimic.**

which was subsequently purchased by a tiny outfit called Unicorn. Unicorn lasted for about three films before West's contract was bought up by the newly formed King-Bee organization, in the summer of 1917.

Seeking to avoid a head-on confrontation with Chaplin's lawyers, King-Bee never rechristened Billy West in a name meant to sound Chaplinesque, they merely copied everything else. They hired top-notch comedy directors like Arvid Gillstrom and Charley Chase to direct. They hired Leo White to bring his intimate knowledge of Chaplin's style to the team, they hired Oliver Hardy as the heavy.

West nailed Chaplin's mannerisms perfectly—which was an accomplishment too easily underrated. If copying Chaplin this closely was so easy, more of the mimics would have done it. Instead, most of them settled for copying the costume. Secondly, West's films are genuinely well made. And lastly, he copied Chaplin's settings, plots, and themes. He copied Chaplin's tragic notions, his social satire. He was Chaplin margarine.

Twenty-four films into the 26-film contract, West retired from his Chaplin clone role. He moved on, trying out a new (failed) comic creation, and eventually establishing himself as a producer of other comedians' films. His former producers sued him, much as Essanay countersued Chaplin for the same reasons, and replaced him with Harry Mann—an actor hired to play Billy West playing Chaplin (wrap your heads around that one).

Mann was no Chaplin, though—he wasn't even a satisfactory West mimic. So the producers found a new guy—Mexican actor Charles Amador.

And here's where we came in: Amador, billed as Charlie Aplin, made his debut in the film *The Race Track* in 1920. It was the first of a proposed series of 12 shorts, but using the name "Charlie Aplin" had the very effect that canny Billy West had successfully avoided. They got themselves sued.

For the film that effectively ended the faux-Chaplin business, *The Race Track* is a historical anomaly. We have the title, we have the effect—but no film. It was never publicly shown, so we have little documentation about what it contained. It is a "lost film" as far as the terminology goes—but that word doesn't capture the fate of this thing. When Amador lost his suit, the court ruled the film must be destroyed. Yeah, this is a "lost" film, just like an ash tray is full of "lost" cigarettes.

But we know these things about it: F.M. Sanford and G.B. Sanford, the producers, had made just this one pilot for the proposed 12-film series, and then headed off to New York to screen it for some state's rights distribution chains.[2] They had sent out announcements publicizing their new hire "Charlie Aplin," "in this famous character." And this was what Chaplin and his attorneys objected to—the idea that the mimics wouldn't just fool the public, but fool the film business. If anyone was going to be selling "Charlie ***plin in this famous character" films, he wanted to be the one making the sale.

At this point, the Sanfords and Amador made a startling and potentially game-changing declaration: "We have no desire to use the name Charles Aplin or Charlie Aplin or any other name similar in spelling or pronunciation or appearance to the plaintiff's name," they told the judge. They were prepared to sign an affidavit to that effect. Suddenly a huge proportion of Chaplin's case had just been taken off the table. But, the defendants continued, although we're more than happy to give up on any confusingly similar name, we stand firm on all other aspects.

The nature of the case had changed. It was now no longer about whether the fraud consisted of the misleading promotion—but about whether Chaplin could establish that he had intellectual property rights in the vagueries of clothing and performance.

Amador's lawyers started to lay out the story that I described above: the first appearance of the Tramp costume and characterization on stage, in the form of Billy Reeves and Ritchie, the role of Lehrman in developing the character, the aspects borrowed from other comedians. Their assertion was simply that the burden of proof was on Chaplin to prove he had originated the role and therefore had the standing with which to police who else got to play it. The judge was indeed worried by all this, and even the appellate court (which upheld Chaplin's win) agreed that the evidence was conflicting as to whether Chaplin had created the character. But, the trial court and appellate court agreed, there was sufficient evidence that Chaplin originated that character *in movies*. So, while he may not have been the sole author of the role, he was the first one to do it in a movie, and the courts decided to draw a tight line around that narrow sphere.

Thus, Chaplin had won a legal ruling that said he had the right to control that character in movies. It was the end of the Chaplin copycat business—or, rather, it would have been, if there was still such a thing.

Chaplin's final legal victory came in September 27, 1928, when the United States Supreme Court refused to hear Amador's appeal. By that point, the copycats had long ago piffled out all on their own.

What ultimately killed the mimics wasn't the strong arm of the law, but Chaplin's own artistry. As we saw with Ritchie, putting other folks in the same clothes is easy, but doesn't necessarily rise to a full-blown imitation. Chaplin was a moving target—constantly adding to and improving on his creation.

Chaplin softened his portrayal, moving away from violent slapstick; the mimics softened theirs. Chaplin started imbuing his films with social commentary; the mimics tried to follow suit. Chaplin made grander films with more cinematic flourish; the mimics improved their aesthetics. And then, in 1921, Chaplin made *The Kid*, a feature film of (maudlin) emotional intensity. The mimics gave up. There are two-reel Chaplin-alikes that are as good as some of the Keystone and Essanay shorts, but no Chaplin copycat ever came close to copying the achievement of *The Kid*. Chaplin simply out-competed the competition.

Which leaves us with an interesting question: would Chaplin have evolved so far, so fast, if not forced to compete against himself? Without the influence of the copycats, pressuring him to constantly top himself, would Chaplin have matured to his fullest? In other words—do we owe the mimics a debt of thanks?

# Cruel and Unusual

The first film in the "Mishaps of Musty Suffer" series, *Cruel and Unusual*, appeared in theaters on March 1, 1916. For the next two years, Musty Suffer's mishaps unspooled over a raucous cycle of unruly two-reel shorts, full of surreal imagery and violent slapstick. Largely forgotten today, but available to the curious in an outstanding set of DVDs, the

Musty Suffer films are remarkable both for what they are and also for what they are not. They are artifacts of what happens when talented and inventive people go significantly out of their way to take the road not traveled. And to understand just why these singular oddities deserve special attention beyond their immediate joys, we need to focus on the significance of that date—these would make sense if they'd been a few years before, or a few years after. But 1916? That's just nuts.

Last chapter focused on the extraordinarily long shadow cast by Charlie Chaplin, and just one manifestation of the immense influence he had on other comedians and filmmakers. The story of Musty Suffer is the mirror image of that—instead of an influential artist whose genius is acknowledged, this is the tale of a forgotten weirdo who never meaningfully influenced anyone else.

But this is in itself a puzzle of sorts.

We start with Harry Watson, Jr., the titular "Musty Suffer" himself, a turn-of-the-century vaudeville comedian from a theatrical family. Like many vaudevillians of his day he was drawn to the allure of the new world of movies, and joined with early cinema pioneer George Kleine to make some feature comedies in early 1915.

We haven't gotten very far into our story before hitting another anomalous date—recall from a couple of chapters ago that it isn't hard to find a source that claims that the very first feature comedy in American movie history was the Charlie Chaplin film *Tillie's Punctured Romance* released in December 1914. Even if you accept my claim that *A Florida Enchantment* deserves to be considered the first feature-length American screen comedy, finding Harry Watson making *feature* comedies in February 1915 marks him as a precocious talent, significantly ahead of the curve.

After a few fitful starts, Watson and Kleine made two key tweaks to their approach: (1) Watson started playing a disheveled tramp, and (2) they stopped making features and switched to one-reel shorts. These two tweaks were not simultaneous. In March 1916 Watson started releasing two-reel shorts under the name "Musty Suffer," but it was a half year earlier when he committed to the tramp character.

So what we have here is a weird, anomalous backwards regression. *Other* comedians started in shorts and tried to graduate up to features; *other* comedians started off playing Chaplin-alike tramps and then developed their own distinctive screen characters. But Harry Watson, Jr., is doing this in reverse, and in his own context seemingly unconcerned with the tide of pop culture around him.

I used the word "surreal" to describe the comic style at work here. That's another date anomaly: Surrealism emerged as an artistic movement after the Musty Suffer series started. And I also used the word "cartoon," another anachronism. The cartoons of 1916 had not yet taken on the rambunctious slapstick they would once Warner Brother's Termite Terrace started cranking out Looney Tunes. The one cultural touchstone that seems to inhabit the same world as Musty Suffer are the *Dreams of a Rarebit Fiend* newspaper cartoons by Winsor McKay.

Chaplin had risen to fame and gotten his first movie gig from having played a belligerent drunk on stage; he went through a couple of iterations of his homeless drunk characterization before hitting on a combination of costuming, makeup, and mannerisms that resonated around the world. But his fame meant that the iconography he had created to signal "homeless drunk" simply came to signal "Charlie Chaplin," and to today's audiences does not fully carry the same signifying power. Let's face it, it's hard to think of a "tramp" without thinking of Charlie Chaplin.

Harry Watson's homeless drunk seems to owe nothing whatsoever to Chaplin's. Chaplin used a combination of misfitting clothing, bowler hat, and chocolate bar mustache—all of which were easily replicated by imitators. Watson enhances his already craggly features with exaggerated makeup and a suit of rags, and ends up with a look that was all his own. Where Chaplin was a sympathetic figure, an intelligent and deeply affecting soul trapped by circumstance at the bottom rung of society's ladder, Musty Suffer is almost a cipher— a slapstick cog in a surreal machine. He is there to be the brunt of violent physical humor, a human cartoon.

But to be drawing these distinctions at all is to be reminded of the incongruity of that date: March 1916 is the month that Charlie Chaplin's contract at Essanay came to an end.

In case you skimmed or skipped the last chapter, here's a quick refresher: Chaplin started appearing in movies at Keystone Studios in early 1914, and within months had catapulted to being a beloved movie star burning brighter than the rest of the Keystone stable. Chaplin jumped ship for better terms (more money, more control) at Essanay in early 1915. That relationship was somewhat rocky—Chaplin fulfilled his end of the bargain by making extraordinarily popular and profitable films for the company, but he was an increasingly temperamental employee. In March 1916, Essanay released the last of Chaplin's official productions for them, a two-reel short called *Police*. But after he moved on to his next home,

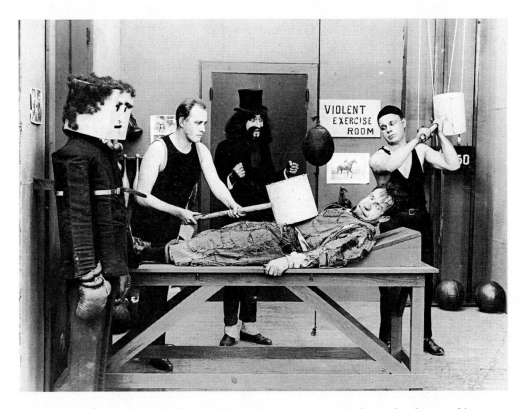

**The misadventures of Musty Suffer get off to a ridiculous start in 1916's *Cruel and Unusual* (courtesy Undercrank Productions/Library of Congress).**

and started making films at Mutual Films, Essanay continued to turn out Chaplin films by recutting and reconfiguring footage he'd left behind.

Chaplin had walked out while he still contractually owed Essanay another four films. The studio felt they were legally entitled to get as close to those four films as they could, by any means necessary. Chaplin sued, claiming the claptrap they were boggling together in his absence and sending out with his name on it would hurt his reputation—but he lost that suit and was ordered to pay Essanay damages. The ruling emboldened Essanay to keep making phony-Chaplin films, and helped embolden the burgeoning industry of Chaplin mimics (who didn't have the same legal justification, but went for it anyway). From mid 1916 through 1917, Chaplin was in an ongoing competition against other comedians who tried to cash in on his name and image by making faux-Chaplin films.

In other words, during the *exact* period that Charlie Chaplin was in an existential struggle with mimics, the Musty Suffer films unfolded as a film series about the slapstick misfortunes of a tramp, with essentially zero connotations in common with Chaplin's work.

If you were to tell me that the films of Musty Suffer were not actually of this Earth but were artifacts that fell into the world from a fracture in the space-time continuum from some other parallel dimension, I'd go, "Yeah, that explains it."

# Life, Police and Trouble

This is the story of three movies. One of these movies was never made. The second was made, but has at times been alleged to be a wrongheaded bastardization of its creator's true intentions. The third film is most decidedly a wrongheaded bastardization, but was deceptively promoted as being the real deal. This is the story of *Life*, *Police*, and *Triple Trouble*.

The crux of this story is our collective fascination with trying to restore a creator's true intentions. It's always a selling point to say that some particular edition of a movie restores the original director's cut, or finally presents the director's original vision. But this is a deeply problematic quest.

For many decades, the story of Chaplin's year at Essanay was told in shorthand, so as to focus more critical time and attention on his later, more popular works. In broad strokes, then, the general understanding went that towards the end of his contract at Essanay Studios, Chaplin started developing plans to make an ambitious feature film to be called *Life*. But the studio was having none of that—their star comedian was already horribly in arrears in turning in his contractually obligated series of short films. Theaters were waiting impatiently for more Chaplin two-reelers—there was no way the studio could justify abandoning those paying customers to wait indefinitely while Chaplin developed his feature.

And so, the story goes, Chaplin transitioned some of the *Life* material into a two-reeler called *Police*, and then quit.

But he'd quit before fulfilling his contract—the studio was still owed some more shorts. And so they took to helping themselves—taking more unused material from *Life* and shooting some new scenes to pad it out to length, and sending that out to theaters as *Triple Trouble*.

Many years later the home video age made it possible for a wider number of film enthusiasts to pore over films in detail. People could now carefully compare *Police* with *Triple Trouble* in greater depth, and it was here that the nuttiness began.

*Police* consists of three major comic sequences. In the first, Charlie is released from prison and immediately set upon by ravenous "reformers" seeking to rob him while pretending to help him. In the second sequence, he attempts to find a bed for the night at a "flophouse" but can't get in without any money—and the reformers took his last dollar. In the third sequence, he meets up with a former cellmate, and the two go to burgle a house together. The occupant of the house is Edna Purviance, who gives the thieves dinner and only asks that they not disturb her sickly mother upstairs. The other crook is unwilling to agree to those terms, though. Charlie is agog, having experienced his first encounter with basic human kindness, and decides to side with Edna over his cellmate. Cue the slapstick finale.

There are many who think of *Police* as Chaplin's best film at Essanay (Walter Kerr being one of them). It is an accomplished and mature comedy with many textures. Go watch it.

Now, here's where it gets messy: there are two previously unseen Chaplin sequences in *Triple Trouble* (the rest is nonsensical padding or reused footage). One of these sequences takes place in a flophouse…

No, I said that wrong. It takes place in *the* flophouse. It is inarguably the same set as the one used in *Police*, and the supporting cast in the scene are largely the same. The most logical explanation is that these two scenes—the flophouse scenes in *Police* and in *Triple Trouble*— were shot at pretty much the same time. This is consistent with the conventional wisdom— that this material was originally developed for use in *Life*, and just ended up being cut into two different films.

But remember I said there were *two* new Chaplin sequences in *Triple Trouble*. In one of these, Charlie is a janitor at a richy-rich's house, where Edna Purviance is a housemaid. Is this part of the same movie?

Filmmaker Don McGlyn convinced himself that it was, and undertook an extensive documentary project in 1992 to present his argument to the world, along with a "reconstruction" of what he believed the intended film was meant to be. His was the most elaborate and intense articulation of this idea, but he wasn't the first to float the idea that *Police* was butchered on its original release. Ted Moss' Chaplin biography from 1975 makes the same claim.

To give that argument its due, let's agree that *Police* was released after Chaplin had departed Essanay. We can also stipulate that

**Back cover of 1916's *The Charlie Chaplin Book* promoting Chaplin's Essanay films.**

Essanay certainly did release butchered and reworked versions of Chaplin films once he'd left (such as *Triple Trouble* and *Burlesque on Carmen*) so they don't get the benefit of the doubt. Furthermore, the copyright filings for *Police* include a narrative description of the film in which the flophouse scene described is the one seen in *Triple Trouble*.

Taking this as factual background, and recognizing the obvious visual clues that the two flophouse scenes must have been shot at the same time, McGlyn concluded that both scenes, and the stuff with Charlie and Edna as servants, all belonged to the same movie. And so he put them all "back together again" and premiered it within his 1992 documentary *The Chaplin Puzzle*.

In the ensuing decades since then, the McGlyn recut of *Police* has been rejected as the authentic version. *The Chaplin Puzzle* is all but unavailable, except as a fuzzy off-air recording someone posted to YouTube.

The problem is, as persuasive as the argument might have been to McGlyn on paper, once all the scenes got shoved into one movie, it became a bloated unfunny mess. The pieces just didn't fit together—instead of illustrating Chaplin's genius, McGlyn's three-reel version of *Police* is an illogical jumble.

So what was going on? If these scenes don't fit together, what did Chaplin have in mind?

Well, far be it from me to try to impute the motivations behind decisions made when my grandparents were small children. But there's another documentary that helps shed light on all this: Kevin Brownlow and David Gill's *Unknown Chaplin* from 1983. That film presented Chaplin's reams upon reams of outtakes from various films, demonstrating his working method. Basically, once he had a general premise for a scene, he'd set up the camera and start improvising on film. Over and over, again and again. Good ideas would be embellished, bad ones discarded. Little by little, he honed something out of nothing. But along the way, not only did he use up massive amounts of time and filmstock, but he abandoned perfectly good jokes as well.

The mistake comes in assuming that just because both flophouse scenes were shot on the same set, they were both for the same movie. That idea presupposed Chaplin had any intention of ever using both, rather than just discarding footage and moving on. Eventually, *Police* took shape in such a way that the longer version of the flophouse scene didn't suit, and it was discarded in favor of the scene that was used.

Chaplin never complained that the released version of *Police* didn't reflect his intentions. Meanwhile he did object very publicly to both *Carmen* and *Triple Trouble*. It's reasonable to conclude that *Police* is exactly as Chaplin wanted it—and any footage he shot along the way and tossed was just that—outtakes. As Chaplin fans we are fortunate that Essanay made those outtakes available in the form of *Triple Trouble*, but there's no reason to conclude any of those outtakes were "intended" to be included in anything.

# Mutual Appreciation Society

Over the last several chapters I have dug into the details and consequences of Chaplin's leaving Essanay in 1916—what we haven't touched on yet, is what he left it *for*.

Money, yes, in part. Chaplin joined Mutual Film Corporation on terms that stagger the mind: he was contracted to make 12 short comedies, one a month. In return, he would be paid the staggering amount of $10,000 a week, plus a onetime signing bonus of $150,000. To put these numbers into perspective: he'd parted with Keystone when Sennett balked at paying him $1,000 a week.

Such a salary was unprecedented. Mutual's publicity guys gushed, "Next to the war in Europe, Chaplin is the most expensive item in contemporaneous history." It was the first salvo in the star-salary arms race that continues to this day.

To give their prize the best possible working condition, Mutual bought him a studio. It had once been Climax Studios, and when Charlie was done with it, the place would be home to Buster Keaton. Mutual then established a subsidiary company whose sole function was to administer Chaplin's product: the Lone Star Company.

He might have been the Lone Star of the company, but Chaplin did not work alone. He needed a reliable stock company of supporting players whose skills, rhythms, and loyalty was never in doubt. Edna Purviance he brought with him from Essanay; from the ranks of Karno he poached Albert Austin, John Rand, and Eric Campbell. Henry Bergman arrived midway into the Mutual series but would stay on in Chaplin's retinue until *Modern Times* in 1936.

Chaplin also required an equally dependable crew. His films were about performance—especially his own pantomiming. The last thing he needed was to fret about technical issues when his mind should be on the comedy—his films were only "scripted" in the roughest sense. Improvisation and inspiration ruled. What Chaplin wanted was someone to set up a camera that could capture the action without fussy camerawork, and then stay out of his way while he did his stuff. This he got in Rollie Totheroh—who, like Henry Bergman, continued to work for Charlie until 1936 and *Modern Times*. He also got it in William C. Foster, who worked literally alongside Totheroh, on a second camera (and was replaced later by George Zalibra, a minor-league ballplayer Chaplin met at Essanay). With two cameras, photographing from essentially the same vantage point, Chaplin could get two negatives of every shot. The practice has since resulted in some debate as to which of these two similar but not quite identical negatives is the "true" or "best" one, but it also doubled the odds of Chaplin's movies survival over the years.

In front of these handcranked boxes, Charlie used his skills as a pantomimist to work his magic. Other comedians (Snub Pollard, I'm looking at you) had an anything-for-a-joke mentality, but Chaplin never strayed outside the possible. He would stray outside the *likely*, sure, but he would never pull an impossible gag.

This became no small part of Chaplin's universal appeal. He could play a drunk, a hobo, an itinerant, an immigrant, an ex-con, a genius, an acrobat, a saint, a hero—he earned his Everyman status by virtue of collating traits of every man.

Thus it all came together at Mutual. Chaplin could enjoy creative freedom, financial reward, the comforts of fame, a loyal team, and the joys of discovering the outer limits of what silent comedy could do. Future endeavors might find Charlie chafing against those limits, pushing the envelope ever outward, but his stint at Mutual was unmarred—nothing less than the glorious sensation of limitless opportunity and unchecked horizons.

It begins with *The Floorwalker*, a short memorable chiefly for Chaplin's losing battle with an escalator. This also features a self-referential gag in which Charlie and another

**Charlie (left) and Albert Austin face seasickness on the way to Ellis Island in 1917's *The Immigrant*.**

character manage to trade places simply by swapping clothes—a direct dig at the likes of Billie Ritchie and Billy West who were making a living as off-brand Chaplins sold to less-discriminating audiences. Chaplin was aware of their threat, a constant reminder that he could not afford to rest on his laurels. He had to stay one step ahead of such mimics—and to do so had more to do with the man inside the clothes than the clothes themselves.

The third Mutual, *The Vagabond*, found Chaplin in full "serious artist" mode. *The Vagabond* eschews jokes for "serious" cinematic values—character, story, setting. Edna Purviance plays an abused gypsy girl rescued by a wandering musician (Chaplin). Aside from a funny bit where Charlie sets a table using a shirt, folding its sleeves into passable imitations of napkins, there is scarcely a joke in it. It would take time for Chaplin to reconcile his competing impulses, and bring pathos and laughs together in the same work.

*The Vagabond* is also notable for introducing the notion of art as salvation. Class politics are ever-present in Chaplin's films. The underclass are destitute and only occasionally noble; the rich are foolish and often drunk. What then can help lift the poor out of the wretchedness of poverty? Here, and in *The Immigrant*, Charlie's answer is: they will be recognized as artists and suddenly enriched. Don't laugh—remember the axiom: unlikely but never impossible. Charlie Chaplin went from dirt poor beggar to highest paid entertainer in the world solely because somebody recognized *him* as an artist.

Which brings us to *One A.M.*, a slapstick classic that amply proves why they paid him the big bucks. Aside from an Albert Austin cameo in the first scene, this really is a "lone star" production, in which Charlie plays a rich drunk at war with his own furniture.

Very soon Chaplin hit his stride, and almost everything he made would be an unqualified masterpiece. From December 1916 through June 1917 they came: *The Rink, Easy Street, The Cure, The Immigrant*. Each one phenomenal—any one of them has an equal claim to being The Greatest Short Comedy Of All Time. Descriptions of these films would be pointless— words cannot capture the full extent of what Chaplin did with these moving pictures, and serve only to cheapen them into recitations of gags: this is the one where Charlie stows his hat and coat in an oven, here's the one where Charlie pulls a gun, here's the bit where Charlie falls down the stairs. These are quite simply as good as silent comedy would ever be.

The final Mutual short was *The Adventurer*, in which Charlie plays an escaped convict who passes himself off as a heroic and wealthy man, only to realize he's doing so in the house of the judge who convicted him. It was not the stellar blend of emotion, social conscience, slapstick, and wit that enervated the brilliant run of films immediately preceding it, but was the most popular of the entire Mutual run and a superb encore.

*The Adventurer* appeared in theaters in October 1917, 18 months out from the start of Chaplin's supposed 12-month contract. So much for a movie a month. Given total creative autonomy, Chaplin found that if he was not happy with any particular scene he could reshoot it, revise it, rethink it—endlessly—until he was satisfied. Hours turned into days turned into weeks, deadlines collapsed. As long as it was worth waiting for (and, hoo boy, it was), Mutual had no objections.

Chaplin's policy was to destroy outtakes. Only the finished end product of all these fits and starts was what mattered. However, policies are not always scrupulously carried out, and a treasure trove from these Mutual days survived. The discarded footage revealed the often tortuous process by which ideas were honed to perfection on the anvil of the Chaplin lot. These trims formed the basis for the documentary *Unknown Chaplin*.

Charlie Chaplin was a comedian of the first order. And in his day, there was plenty of competition. In the silent era there were lots of slapstick clowns—and most don't even come close. The true extent of his genius is obscured by our modern focus on the so-called Three Geniuses: Chaplin, Keaton, Lloyd. But sift through the countless hours of silent comedy by … Ford Sterling, Mabel Normand, Roscoe Arbuckle, Billy Bevan, Harry Langdon, Ben Turpin, Charley Chase, Larry Semon, and on and on—some of them were gifted, some had flashes of brilliance, but none of them touched the same heights as Chaplin. To use a word too often misused, he was unique.

There is quibbling to be done over solitary gags—did Roscoe Arbuckle do the bun dance first?—but no one pulled it all together the way he did. He was the Elvis of silent comedy—and the Mutual years were his Sun Sessions.

# Serious Business

*A Woman of Paris*. Not a title that stirs your soul, is it? Maybe you've never even heard of it. Or you've heard of it but just never cared. Or like me you cared but still avoided it because you thought it was the movie equivalent of broccoli—something good for you, but not fun. Well, I'm here to testify. Brothers and sisters, I was once like you, but then I saw the light. I'm here to tell you, you need to put this movie high on your to-watch list. And I'm gonna tell you why. If you want to watch Charlie Chaplin's funniest features, you could sit down with the Mutual shorts and call it a day. But, if you wanted to watch his most important features, you need to focus on *The Kid* and *Woman of Paris*.

I'm defining "important" as "influential," and the influential aspect of *The Kid* is evident: that was the line in the sand between all those comedians who made two-reelers, and those who would join Chaplin as feature comedians. There had been feature comedies before *The Kid*, but now a feature comedy was taken seriously as a movie, not just a really long short. Feature comedies were to be coherent stories with emotional depth—and not every comedian could follow Chaplin into that realm.

It could be argued that was not necessarily a good transition. Comedies often work best in short bursts. In the grand history of movies there have been relatively few truly great feature comedies, and there has always been a tension between being a good movie and being a funny movie. By contrast, television comedies (operating with a running time comparable to a two-reeler) have consistently found ways to be simultaneously well made and funny.

*A Woman of Paris*, though, earns its importance by different means. For one thing, it isn't a comedy. It opens with this disclaimer (just in case you were inclined to complain to the theater management): "TO THE PUBLIC: In order to avoid any misunderstanding, I wish to announce that I do not appear in this picture. It is the first serious drama written and directed by myself. CHARLES CHAPLIN."

It was a singular foray by a great comedian out of his comfort zone into the realm of drama that in turn inspired a great dramatist to transform into a great comedian. Sorry, that is an unfair oversimplification. The "great dramatist" I'm referring to is Ernst Lubitsch, and by calling him that I'm grossly distorting his history just to fit a clever turn of phrase. Lubitsch's early work can't be summed up so curtly as his being a "great dramatist." He was a slapstick clown in two-reelers, then he became the master of Cecil B. DeMille-style opulent spectacles, then he took to making absurdist sex comedies. In short, his early work is muddle of mismatched styles. Each individual work is terrific in its own right, but there's no sense of order.

Then, he sees *Woman of Paris*, and suddenly it all snaps into place. From that point on, he was the Ernst Lubitsch we know today. Without *Woman of Paris*, there would be no Lubitsch as we know him, and without Lubitsch I doubt we'd have had the rise of the romantic comedy in the 1930s.

So, let's get to the movie itself. According to David Robinson, the term "gold digger" had been coined specifically to describe one Peggy Hopkins Joyce, a young lady with whom Chaplin had a brief affair in 1922. Apparently she alternated between boasting of her sexual conquests and painting a picture of herself as a naive country girl. Evidently Chaplin wrote the lead character of Marie St. Claire in *Woman of Paris* in reaction to Joyce. Whatever psychological games Chaplin may have been playing, he structured *Woman of Paris* as a vehicle for Edna Purviance. I'll leave it up to someone else to comment on the awkwardness of casting one ex-lover in a role written about a different ex-lover.

Prior to seeing this film, I had developed the impression that Chaplin's reputation rested entirely on his admittedly peerless physical comedy—as a director he was prone to lapses of judgement. His films can sometimes display seemingly poor editorial choices, continuity errors, and cinematic glitches—which really just reflect Chaplin's priorities. The point of his comedies are his performances, and every cinematic choice is predicated on how to get the best physical performance on screen. If a sloppy cut is needed to get the joke right, the joke wins every time.

But *Woman of Paris* is a beautiful piece of work, flawless in every frame. Much of it looks like it could have been made by F. W. Murnau or Fritz Lang (and I'm not sure I can give any higher praise). This time he doesn't have to worry about directing himself, so he can give undistracted attention to all the other details. He can at last afford to indulge in a level of visual perfectionism unimpeded by the dictates of physical comedy.

Part of the attention to visual detail evident in *Woman* is the efficient use of expressive elements. Consider for example one famous and influential scene. A young man from Edna's past has tracked her down in the Big City and is meeting with her in her apartment. As Edna looks over various dresses, her maid opens a dresser drawer and a man's shirt collar falls to the floor. The maid casually places the collar back in the drawer and continues on her business.

A single prop, shown once, a knowing look, and bingo! Chaplin has made his point: the boy knows she has a lover. That took, what, six seconds? And yet it is a pivotal plot point that drives the whole second half of the film. It is in many ways a Lubitsch touch— that seemingly effortless association of complex ideas with simple props that enables the storyteller to convey massive amounts of information with subtle gestures.

Chaplin and Lubitsch were buddies at this point, and Charlie treated Ernst to a private screening of the film as an unfinished work in progress. Lubitsch emerged from the screening gushing, "I like it because I feel that an intelligent man speaks to me and nobody's intelligence is insulted."

Hollywood producer Henry Blanke would later remark that *Woman of Paris* "influenced Lubitsch's entire life from then on." Where he had once been the master of massive epic spectacle, Lubitsch would from then on narrow his focus to the domestic and the subtle.

Lubitsch wore his admiration for *Woman* plainly on his sleeve. When caught in arguments with pretentious European intellectuals about whether Chaplin deserved to be called an artist, he routinely touted *Woman* as his go-to evidence (and let's face it, he is one of the very few who would choose *Woman* first in such a debate, as opposed to, I dunno, *The Gold Rush*?) Almost immediately, Lubitsch hired Adolphe Menjou, the charismatic cad of *Woman of Paris*, and cast him as, well, a charismatic cad in *The Marriage Circle*.

That's not to say Lubitsch was all about imitating *Woman*. In fact, the differences between Chaplin's movie and Lubitsch's works are crucial. For one thing, Chaplin's is not a comedy. It has the pace of a comedy, and has touches that feel so very Chaplinesque, but there are few if any intentional chuckles. By contrast, Lubitsch adopted the same stylish veneer, the same ironic distance and dry wit, but in his hands this, in and of itself, was the comedy.

The fundamental difference in stance between Chaplin and Lubitsch surfaces as well in the content. To explore this, I need to describe something of the plot of *Woman*. The film revolves around the idea that the only way a woman can make her way in the world is in relation to a man. The socially approved mechanism for this has a virginal girl conveyed from the house of her father to the house of her husband on the night of her family-sanctioned wedding. But, when Edna's character Marie finds this avenue foreclosed due to a set of cruel circumstances out of her control, she opts for Plan B, in which she trades sexual favors to powerful men in return for a comfortable but empty life.

At no point in the movie does Chaplin present a single female character who does not conform to one or another of these two paths, and at no point does anyone ever challenge the social assumptions at play. When Lubitsch took to copying Chaplin's technique, he dropped all that Victorian nonsense and happily depicted emancipated and uninhibited women.

It isn't just that Lubitsch saw a different kind of world, even Chaplin's own slapstick peers did. Just a few short years after this film came out, the folks at Hal Roach Studios were churning out two-reelers with Thelma Todd and Anita Garvin as single girls living on their own, maintaining apartments, holding down jobs, paying their own bills.

Chaplin was very stubbornly a 19th-century kind of thinker. Throughout his films, when he depicted work, it was manual labor—while competitors like Harold Lloyd and Charley Chase depicted a world of white-collar office-drone employment that was actually more in line with the experience of the audience. Even his supposedly forward-thinking *Modern Times* clung to a sense of robber barons vs. alienated laborers that wouldn't have been at all out of place

**Adolphe Menjou romances the woman of Paris herself, Edna Purviance.**

in a movie made 10 or even 15 years earlier, but which would have seemed utterly passé 10 or so years later.

As a result of this anachronistic stance, even at his most eloquent, Chaplin seems to be arguing a point that's already been made. In *Woman of Paris* he sets out to condemn a restrictive Victorian attitude, and does so to an audience of flappers and suffragettes.

Because contemporary audiences have lost touch with the specificity of the historical moment, and merely encounter a film like this as something old, this anachronism gets swept under the carpet. We can just sit and marvel at those very same qualities that thrilled and inspired Lubitsch—a film of visual poetry and efficient expressivity, a work of ironic detachment and intellectual confidence, a masterpiece.

# The Other Chaplin

Once upon a time, there was a comedian who got his start with Fred Karno, came to Hollywood to work for Mack Sennett, made the transition from short films to features, was one of Hollywood's highest paid comedians, and left his mark in some of the most important and beloved classics of silent cinema. And did I mention his name was Chaplin?

Syd Chaplin, that is.

To the extent he is remembered today outside of nutjobs like myself, he's thought of mostly as a supporting player in Charlie's films. He was certainly a tremendous asset to his famous brother, in films such as *A Dog's Life*. But to focus on stuff like this devalues Syd, and reduces him to an also-ran, when he was a full-fledged top-billed comedy star in his own right.

During the 1910s, when Charlie was making his seminal short comedies at Essanay and Mutual, Syd was working with Mack Sennett on a series of shorts in which he played a character called "Gussle." Gussle, for want of a better description, was a self-conscious Chaplin-alike. Syd made the necessary tweaks to accommodate his heavier girth, and didn't attempt to copy Charlie's costume and mannerisms in the slavish way that professional Chaplin mimics did—he just took the general idea and adapted it to his own idiom.

In the end, Gussle looks like the unholy love child of Charlie Chaplin and Shemp Howard—he combines Shemp's appearance with Charlie's physical grace, and fuses both of their more violent traits. Charlie's early shorts at Keystone were often startlingly violent—and Syd's Gussle shorts leaned heavily on the knockabout form of slapstick havoc.

Reggie Gussle—with his oil-slicked hair parted in the middle, a mustache apparently swiped off Snub Pollard's face and stuck on upside down, a drunkard's swagger—was consistent with the character he'd started playing on the Music Hall stage for Fred Karno, and simply ported over to films when he joined Sennett.

Now as any decently informed Chaplin buff can tell you, Charlie started his career in the English Music Halls with the Fred Karno Company. But, and here's the secret history that isn't often mentioned, he was there thanks to his older brother Syd. Actually, half brother, if we want to be technical. But Charlie considered Syd a full and true brother, so who are we to split hairs?

To trace the proper history of Charlie and Karno, we start with Syd—although exactly how to start with Syd is a bit of a mystery.

As it happens, where on the planet Syd was born is a question mark for historians and genealogists, who think but are not sure that he was born Sydney Hawkes, in 1885, in South Africa to a pair of traveling British actors. A year later, mama Lily Harley divorced her husband to pair off with Charles Chaplin. In 1889, they had a boy named Charlie. Papa Chaplin died, Mama Chaplin underwent a nervous breakdown and suddenly Syd and Charlie were on the streets, bereft and alone. They were shipped off to an orphanage, and Syd had no choice but to step into the surrogate father role.

Syd was a natural entertainer, and he made pocket change as a street performer. In 1905, this landed him a better paying gig (yup, better paying than pocket change) as a comedian with Fred Karno's troupe. And it was then and there that Syd started lobbying Karno to open up a slot in the cast for Syd's younger brother Charlie.

If Syd stopped there and did nothing else, he'd have already earned a place in film history for the momentous act of introducing Charlie to the stage.

In 1914, Charlie made the leap away from Karno to join Mack Sennett's Keystone Pictures—and within a year he was on his way to being the biggest movie star in the world. By August 1914, Charlie wrote letters back to Syd in England urging him to come to America and get a job at Keystone—and furthermore, recommending that his brother play hardball with Sennett in his salary negotiations.

You could say one good turn deserves another—Syd got Charlie a job at Karno, Charlie got Syd a job at Keystone. But there's more to it than that: Charlie was at that point already scheming to leave Keystone—he needed greater creative freedom than the omnipresent Sennett would ever give him. Charlie knew that his leverage with Sennett was as great as it would ever be, and if he was ever going to do anything with it, now's the time, so why not use that power to maneuver his brother into a plum job?

This is indeed how it played out. Sennett hired Syd, gave him a one-year contract for his own run of top-billed solo shorts, with a better than average starting salary. At which point Charlie quit to join Essanay. Sennett was obliged to keep Syd and treat him well as a bargaining chip in his efforts to woo Charlie back.

Sennett had forged a secret alliance with D.W. Griffith and Thomas Ince. Between them they were the three most powerful and significant figures of American film in 1914. This triangle of talent (nudge nudge) also roped in some bankers and movie financing types to create a megalithic media conglomerate called Triangle. Their plan was to lock all of the major Hollywood stars into exclusive contracts with Triangle, and then go to theater chains and say, look, if you want any movies with these top marquee names in them, you have to agree to our distribution terms: namely, if you buy one you buy all. If you want to screen any Triangle films, you have to agree to be an exclusive Triangle outlet and buy everything we send you.

It's called "block-booking" and it's such a controversial practice that today various governing bodies have created strictures to prevent it, but in 1915 it was a legal, if unpopular, strategy.

It was also potentially a self-destructive strategy, because it only works if you have something so attractive on offer that exhibitors will agree to accept these terms. If you don't have enough things that the exhibitors want, then you've just locked your own self out of competition altogether and put yourself out of business, because block-booking also means, if you don't take one, you don't take any.

Which meant in simple practical terms, Mack Sennett was under extraordinary pressure to get Charlie Chaplin back. He'd hire Syd and give Syd just about anything he asked for if it gave him any better odds of getting Charlie back.

Of course, it didn't actually change his odds of getting Charlie back, but Sennett didn't really understand that. He, and moreso the money men at Triangle, believed Charlie's departure was all about money. Offer Chaplin enough cash and he'll come back. The fact was, Charlie was seeking something Mack Sennett could never give him: creative autonomy, but Sennett selectively remembered only Charlie's salary demands.

Charlie did leave Essanay, but not to return to Sennett. Instead, he went to Mutual where he was paid exponentially more than Sennett and Triangle could afford.

Mack Sennett still had Syd, though—and a Chaplin is better than no Chaplin. Keystone had been swallowed by Triangle, but Sennett wisely retained his own studio, Mack Sennett Productions, as a separate entity whose product would be distributed by Triangle. Sennett could see where this was headed: without Charlie Chaplin, Triangle's monopoly would fail, and Sennett made sure he'd ride it out safely, capable of distributing his comedies through other chains when and if the need arose.

**Syd Chaplin and a simian costar in *The Missing Link* (1927), a silent comedy with synchronized music and sound effects.**

By the end of Syd's year-long contract with Sennett, it was obvious Charlie wasn't coming back, and while the Gussle comedies had been popular enough and reasonably profitable, Sennett let Syd go. It was by no means the end of his solo career. However, Syd did put his solo work aside repeatedly from time to time to support his brother in whatever capacity he was needed most. Some of the time, this meant playing alongside Charlie onscreen. For example, in Charlie's *Shoulder Arms*.

Syd also handled Charlie's business affairs, and negotiated Charlie's first million dollar contract in 1917.

This is how history remembers Syd—as Charlie's shadow. But there was that time, way back when, when Syd was a top billed movie comedian all by himself. A top-billed comedian, at that. Syd's solo career relaunched in large measure thanks his starring role in the 1925 Al Christie-produced feature film *Charley's Aunt*. This led to Syd's own million-dollar contract, making big-budget features like *Man on the Box*, *Oh, What a Nurse* and others for Warner Brothers.

By this point, Syd had retired the Gussle character and moved on to something new— if Gussle was a sort of Charlie Chaplin-meets-Shemp Howard hybrid, the new Syd played a Harold Lloyd-meets-Shemp figure, allowing his own fairly handsome face to be seen without funny haircuts or silly mustaches.

In 1926, Syd made *The Better 'Ole*, a World War I farce distinguished by its pioneering application of new technology—the Vitaphone synchronized sound system. This wasn't talkie technology, mind you, but a way to synchronize music and sound effects to silent films—and a crucial transitional step towards talkies. As the talkie era dawned, Syd was ready for the bracing changes: "I can see a time a coming when we shall have colored films, not only with dialogue, but third dimensions." Syd said this in the 1920s, mind you.

He also said, "What is going to happen to us wretched comedians is more than I can say. Until now people like my brother, Harold Lloyd, and myself have worked almost entirely without script, depending on the inspiration of the moment for our greatest gags."

So, Syd realized he'd need to start thinking about writing scripts for this brave new world of talkie comedies. Thus, in 1929, Syd was busy writing a feature based on the *Mumming Birds* music hall sketch he and Charlie had performed on Fred Karno's stage back in 1906. Charlie had already raided this act for his silent film *A Night in the Show*, but Syd had ambitions to flesh it out to a larger canvas.

At the time, Syd was contracted to MGM, and working out of Elstree Studios in England. And then, kablammo, suddenly Syd left England, and quit MGM. The *Mumming Birds* movie was never made—Syd never made another movie at all, silent or talkie. He settled into a vagabond lifestyle, slumming around the world living off the mountains of cash he'd stockpiled during his brief stint of fame.

A lot of great silent comedians hit hard times with the advent of talkies. Some weathered the change better than others, many vanished into obscurity. But Syd's precipitous departure from the screen is something else altogether. It's not that he had trouble adapting to talkies, or audiences didn't like his voice, or his physical comedy seemed odd when weighted down by sound effects, or that the studio bosses shoehorned him into the wrong kind of material—he never even had the chance to have any of that happen, never had the chance to fail. He was eager to embrace the new sound technology, had an idea, had a studio backer, had creative freedom, had money, he lacked for nothing—but nothing came of it.

He plummeted off the screen so completely that when Syd died in 1965, Charlie Chaplin's kids were gobsmacked to read in the obits that their uncle had once made movies of his own. Decades had elapsed and nobody had breathed word one about Syd's solo career—it was if it never happened.

What gives?

Or phrased differently, the same question: what happened at Elstree in 1929 that Syd spent the rest of his life running away from?

If you're a fan of Roscoe Arbuckle you've already guessed the punchline. It was a sex scandal.

This had more than a little to do with class politics of the 1920s. Prior to 1914, serious and commercially viable motion picture production was largely situated in France. Hollywood started to take over beginning in 1914, thanks in large measure to the international popularity of Mack Sennett's wildly anarchic comedies. The sudden economic boom in Hollywood took a lot of country bumpkins, immigrants, and other undesirables and made them rich and famous, more or less overnight. Sennett once said that "pioneers are seldom from the nobility; there were no dukes on the Mayflower." These are wise words—pioneers take risks, brave new frontiers, face unfamiliar dangers—not the sort of thing you do when you've already got something to protect. So the movie colony of Hollywood was populated with outcasts and misfits, finding a novel form of success. The Chaplin boys were dirt poor in England—they crossed an ocean and got million-dollar contracts to make people laugh.

There was an old guard, of old money, represented in, among other things, the world of publishing. Many of these old money types were horrified by the new money Beverly Hillbillies. Movie stars and slapstick comedians were the rappers of the 1920s—a bunch of people whose lives and heritage knew nothing about money suddenly enriched beyond all reason, and tending to spend that money in ostentatious ways. You want to put yourself into the mindset of the time, when you think of Roscoe Arbuckle, think of the Notorious B.I.G., 50 Cent, Ja-Rule and Murder Incorporated.

So from 1914 onwards, Hollywood faced a massive influx of once paupers getting rich, buying absurd houses and flashy cars, and partying hard all the time. The old money types were offended by the boorish habits, and to continue the parallels to today there was a contingency of moralists and Bible-thumpers who were aghast at the loose morals of these Hollywood types. These were the same self-important moralists who got the country to ban alcohol outright, so naturally they had no love lost with the hard-partying movie folk.

For a long time coming, the moralists and the old money guys in the publishing business had been looking for a way to go after Hollywood, and the Roscoe Arbuckle affair—whether trumped up for the purpose or an accidental coincidence—was practically a gift from the gods. It ruined Arbuckle's career and sent shock waves through the film business. A scandal stirred up around Mabel Normand, another Mack Sennett find, nearly scotching her comedy career. And Syd had already, in his capacity as Charlie's business manager, helped his brother navigate his way through a few scandals attending the Little Tramp's sexual proclivities.

Which is a long way round to saying that come 1929, Syd knew the score: sex scandals ruin movie careers and destroy comedians. The moment he was accused of sexual improprieties, he knew he had but two choices: do everything in his power to suppress the story and quietly retire from movies—or allow himself to become the target of a hungry press and angry public and be forcibly, ignominiously retired from the movies. Either way his life as a screen comedian was over, it was simply a question of how much privacy and dignity Syd would be able to maintain.

As Roscoe Arbuckle had himself discovered, there is a risk in playing an onscreen roué—people start to think it's true. And in one of Syd's very last films, *The Missing Link*, made for Warner Brothers in 1927, a disgruntled dame chuffs, "It is very evident that a lady isn't safe near you."

As it happened, this wasn't just Syd's onscreen persona. Darryl Zanuck called Syd "the greatest ladies' man in Hollywood history—better even than Errol Flynn."

Exactly what transpired in England is unknown—Syd did a good job of burying the facts, because that was the point after all. His strategy of removing himself from the public eye had its intended effect of keeping the salacious details safely concealed. To a certain extent, all we know is what we don't know—it was alleged at the time he'd assaulted a 19-year-old girl. Perhaps people were mixing him up with his more famous brother, whose habit of robbing the cradle is the stuff of legend. The girl in Syd's case was no child—birth records firmly establish her age as 22 at the time of the incident—which we know because she was sufficiently aggrieved to get her case heard in a British court.

Somehow, Syd injured her breast—whatever that means, and this is as far as the facts can take us, and none of the parties are around to defend themselves against further speculation. Writing for *The Independent*, journalist Matthew Sweet put in legwork worthy of an old-school private eye, but got no further than this: the young woman took her case to court, and Syd went on the lam, more or less the rest of his life.

What was once a vast and bustling enterprise of American slapstick has been narrowed by our pop cultural myopia to a singular focus on the Big Three. No longer do we have the memory or attention for the dozens of comedians who once populated the screen—and it has gotten so bad that now there's a rambunctious competition for the honor of the fourth slot—advocates of Roscoe Arbuckle or Harry Langdon or Charley Chase all vie for their guy to be recognized as the Fourth Genius. Anything less than that is total obscurity. Because we feel compelled to compare everybody back against the Big Three, we tend to be overly indulgent of those comics whose personas are distinct and decently original, even if they're not as funny. Billy West or Billie Ritchie—these guys are hilarious, and their films absolutely retain the power to hold an audience's attention today, but they rarely get the chance because they are inescapably seen as second to the man they mimic, Charlie Chaplin. They don't get judged on their raw comedy merits. This is also true of Syd, destined by that name to be always compared to his more famous brother.

The 1915 *New York Times* piece also had this to say about Syd: "He affects his kinsman's mannerism, even to the mustache, but he is not so good a comedian. Charles can kick twice as often and as hard as Syd, which means he elicits twice as many laughs." The Chaplin name was both boon and burden—it opened doors for him surely but kept him forever in comparison to his brother.

But what if he was called Sydney Hawkes? What would you have thought of him then? Would you even have read this?

# Buster Keaton vs. the History of Comedy

This is the story of a custard pie, a movie camera, and the very origins of American slapstick.

In the 1940s and '50s, American popular culture took to nostalgic reflection on the bygone age of silent comedy, much like modern pop culture pines for the 1980s. If there'd been a VH1 in 1945, it would have feasted on the likes of *I Love the 20s*! And, like the '80s nostalgia of today, the simplest and cheapest way to look back was with a compilation of clips. Eventually the most sophisticated of clip jobs would come along in the form of Robert Youngson and Paul Killiam's movie collages, but many years before that, the industry was already leaning in that direction.

Another way to indulge nostalgic reveries was to bring back the superstars of the lost form to strut their stuff in cameos intended to pay homage to their art. Arguably the most prominent example of this approach was 1939's *Hollywood Cavalcade*, directed by Irving Cummings.

Made the year after Mack Sennett received his honorary Oscar, *Cavalcade* is essentially a fictionalized version of Mack's life story. Set aside the fact that Mack Sennett actually appears in the film, as himself—that is but a weirdly recursive moment of meta-textual loopiness in what is otherwise a sort of bio-pic with Don Ameche playing Mack. The film takes us through the broad strokes of Mack's life, hitting all of the beats and in the right order.

With one important exception—the moment when Don Ameche becomes the King of Comedy and anoints his girlfriend Alice Faye (the Mabel Normand figure of the film) as the queen of slapstick. It involves Buster Keaton and it goes like this.

The film crew is set up to shoot a romantic drama starring "Molly Adair" (Alice Faye), and the assistant director calls out over the bullhorn that the scene will also feature *"Buster Keaton as the Romantic Lover!"* The scene starts to unfold, and Buster is supposed to step into a jewelry store to buy his sweetie a ring, and while he is away the villainous "Claude" (George Givot) sets his rapacious eyes on "Molly." According to the script and the directions shouted at him by "Mike Linnett" (the Mack Sennett figure played by Ameche), Buster is supposed to swan out of the jewelry store and slug Claude. Except this goes awry fast. Buster struggles with the fake scenery, and staggers around looking for some prop with which to hit his rival. The director is going apoplectic: *"C'mon Buster! We're running out of film!"* Meanwhile, Mike Linnett's valet is sitting nearby with Mike's lunch, including a large custard pie. *"Well, needs must,"* Buster apparently reasons, as he grabs the pie and flings it—straight into Alice Faye's face.

The crew erupt in laughter, the starlet erupts in fury, and Buster looks around in *"What, me?"* confusion.

That is one of the most potent scenes in all of film history, in my opinion. First, let's look at the pie itself. It's always hard to pinpoint when the first of anything was—and the spotty survival of silent films makes exhaustive research impossible. So, with that caveat, I can report that I have in my notes that the earliest recorded pie thrown in a screen comedy was in 1913, in a Mabel Normand, Roscoe Arbuckle short called *Noise from the Deep.* I

**"This fellow Keaton seems to be the whole show." As this undated publicity still shows, Buster did many things. Throwing pies was one of them.**

invite anyone who disputes this to correct me—please, if you know of an earlier pie, I want to see it.

In the pitch of slapstick nostalgia in the 1940s and '50s, certain aspects of silent comedy would be exaggerated as defining characteristics—shorthand signifiers of the genre. Actual silent comedies were never as flickery as their mid-century copycats, nor were they ever as fixated on pies. Some comedians took to snooty objections that they had never thrown a pie. (*How insulting, to be thought of as a lowly pie-throwing clown*, said people who spent their screen careers throwing bricks instead.) But not Buster Keaton. He happily threw pies throughout these mid-century throwbacks, and set himself up as an expert on the art of pie slinging.

The most significant thing about Buster's scene in *Hollywood Cavalcade*, though, is not that he throws a pie, but that it suggests his comic slapstick is an accident.

Buster took to the role of the accidental comedian and made it his own. Consider the made-for-television *The Silent Partner* from 1955, produced by Hal Roach. In it, Keaton plays a comedy has-been, beloved by die-hard fans but forgotten by the masses. It is a vaguely biographical sketch of Keaton himself (and made two years prior to the equally vaguely biographical sketch of Keaton that purported to be *The Buster Keaton Story*). Like *Hollywood Cavalcade*, it casts Buster as the bumbler whose accidental slapstick unwittingly created screen comedy.

This idea turned out to be a stubborn meme. That same year, 1955, found Mack Sennett making another cameo as himself in *Abbott and Costello Meet the Keystone Kops* (asked to identify himself, Mack throws a pie). The film involves Bud and Lou scammed into buying a bogus movie studio. This leads, inevitably, to that same idea that bumbling fools stumble unwittingly onto a movie set and accidentally create comic art. In a key scene, the boys stumble into the middle of a B-Western, and as a reward for ruining the shoot are given a contract as comedy stars.

There is something almost perverse at work here. Mack Sennett was a natural born anarchist who was drawn to the slapstick form through his own sense of the ridiculous; Buster Keaton was a gifted acrobat and vaudeville veteran who cultivated keenly developed philosophies of comedy. These two men worked hard at the business of comedy—yet time and again allowed their hard work to be lampooned on screen as the by-product of simple ineptitude.

It could be argued that Sennett and Keaton and their contemporaries were indeed uneducated, and that their comedy was unsophisticated stuff as compared to the screwball comedies that had by that point taken over Hollywood, and the depiction of slapstick pioneers as accidental artists merely reflects this state of affairs. But the prevalence of the accidental comedian archetype throughout silent comedy begs for some more coherent explanation.

And so we dial back to 1909, and find *Those Awful Hats*, a Biograph comedy directed by DW Griffith starring Mack Sennett (in costume and appearance, at least, replaying his role from *The Curtain Pole*). Mack and his wife elbow their way through a crowded movie theater and take their seats, rudely unconcerned with how their oversized hats block the view of the patrons seated behind them. But this creates a recursive loop—what happens if, while watching this movie, there happens to be someone in front of you wearing a giant hat? Which part is funnier—the thing happening to you, or the simulacrum of it on the screen?

Mack must have gotten this stuck in his head, because the same scenario starts to show up in his own films. The 1913 short *Mabel's Dramatic Career* is a variation on the theme, with Sennett again in the audience of a film, this time becoming way too involved in the events of the Mabel Normand movie he's come to see. This was a crucial twist—now the joke wasn't just about disruptive patrons at a movie, but about rubes who had trouble distinguishing fact from fiction. In *A Film Johnnie*, Charlie Chaplin duplicates the premise of *Mabel's Dramatic Career*, this time taking Mack Sennett's role as the fool in the audience who can't tell the onscreen action is fictional. Later in the same film, he bumbles onto the Keystone set and interrupts the filming of another comedy, mistaking staged action for a real damsel in distress. By 1916, the recursive loop closed tighter, with Mack Swain attending his own film in *A Movie Star*, triggering the same fact vs. fiction confusions.

Slapstick violence is inherently accidental—that's key to what makes it funny as opposed to horrifying. The havoc in *The Curtain Pole* isn't the result of a maniac maliciously smacking everyone in the head, it's the consequence of a clumsy person who isn't paying attention. It follows quite naturally that comedians who had built their careers on that kind of thoughtless chaos would continue the notion in all settings. Put them on a movie set and they will cause disaster, because that's what they do, and since audiences do indeed pay to watch that kind of disaster, the characters in those movies recognize the results of this havoc as commercially viable comedy.

In the case of Buster Keaton, what we are talking about is a comic whose professional career was rooted in an audience's enjoyment of unintentional havoc. It was what made him a star in the first place.

Back in the turn of the century vaudeville days of Joe and Myra Keaton, the two weary performers were shuffling from one ramshackle theater to another, putting on their show. The had a little kid in tow, a tyke named Joseph, whom they called "Buster" in honor of his rough-and-tumble ways. Other families divided childcare responsibilities such that the mother would tend to the little ones while the father went off to work. But Papa Keaton's "job" was entertaining people on a stage, and it required Mama Keaton to be along his side. There was nowhere else for little Buster to go, so he ended up in the act, where his natural childish curiosity and immature misunderstandings caused problems. These problems were incorporated into the act, treated as jokes, and made into the centerpiece of the act.

In 1956, Buster told an interviewer that his family's act consisted of a simple fact: "I'd simply get in my father's way all the time and get kicked all over the stage." Which meant that from Buster's very earliest memories were about creating accidental comedy—and he never let go of the idea.

Here are just a few of the many instances in Keaton's body of work where he played a character whose mere presence on a stage or in front of a camera resulted in accidental comedy: *The Garage*, *The Playhouse*, *The Cameraman*, *Free and Easy*, *Speak Easily*, *The King of the Champs-Elysees*, *Mixed Magic*, and *War Italian Style*. That's an awful lot of "accidental" jokes, from a man who obviously knew exactly what he was doing.

# Out the Window Backwards

The legend of Buster Keaton has been passed down from generation to generation, until he has become the film world's equivalent of Paul Bunyan—the mythic hero of tall tales.

*They say* a cyclone carried him out of his window when he was an infant. *They say* he got his name from Harry Houdini himself. *They say* he walked out of his place in one of vaudeville's top comedy acts to become a Broadway star—and then walked out of *that* contract to be a low-paid second banana to film comic Roscoe Arbuckle. *They say* the first thing he did on Arbuckle's set was to disassemble the camera to see how it worked.

None of these is strictly true, mind you, but neither are they wholly false. A myth always travels better when packaged with nuggets of truth.

What is indisputably true is that Buster Keaton was a visionary artist in two different media. He was at once a peerless physical comedian and a pioneering cineaste, who happened to reach the height of his powers in both of these forms at a propitious moment in history when audiences were hungry for both. Critics routinely compared his films to the works of Rene Magritte, Samuel Beckett, to James Joyce's *Ulysses*, and T.S. Eliot's *The Wasteland*. He was a genius.

You wouldn't catch him agreeing with that statement. "You can't be a genius in slapshoes," was Buster's routine retort to such claims. But a look at any one of his 19 silent two-reel shorts made between 1920 and 1923 proves him wrong: here is proof that geniuses do come in slapshoes after all. Each short is a miracle of comic invention, and while some are better remembered than others, there isn't a clinker in the bunch. Each one exemplifies in different ways what made Keaton the artist that he was.

Although Buster is remembered as an acrobatic comic who did his own stunts (Jackie Chan has openly acknowledged the debt he owes to Keaton), his films are even more a statement of metaphysical preoccupations. The world depicted in a Keaton movie is a deceptive landscape of surrealistic transformations, misunderstandings, and implacable tricks of Fate. In some of these films, Buster is caught in a dreamscape, in others he is living a waking nightmare. Throughout it all, he struggles to stay afloat.

Buster is spry, quick-witted, and adaptive—but the universe around him is inconstant, unpredictable and hostile. These are fables of Man vs. World, and the gamesmanship between Keaton's endlessly inventive mind against the machinations of the physical world are addictively entertaining.

*Convict 13* was the second of Buster's shorts to reach theaters, but the third he made—he was dissatisfied with *The High Sign* and shelved it for a later release, once his reputation was more firmly established and its defects would be of reduced consequence. That we can enjoy *Convict 13* today is something of a minor miracle—the ravages of time had eaten away at available copies until only fragments remained. Then, in the 1970s, Raymond Rohauer pieced together copies unearthed around the world to reassemble a nearly complete reconstruction. Such an act of reconstitution befits a film that is itself about metamorphosis and death. The transformations of the film begin from the very start, as Buster's game of golf starts to devolve into a fishing expedition. Buster's handicap is so extreme, he manages to ricochet a simple putt off a nearby barn and knock himself unconscious with the rebound (the stunt is an act of absolute magic, born of such unlikely precision it must have taken ages to shoot).

The sleeping Buster is then discovered by an escaped convict, who swaps clothes with him. When Buster awakes, he finds that literally the clothes make the man. He is now, for all intents and purposes, Convict 13—chased by swarms of angry prison guards for a crime committed by another. As a sign of the unlikely irony of his situation, Buster finds he can successfully elude his pursuers by ducking inside a nearby complex—the prison itself. But Buster has absorbed an important lesson in all of this—if changing clothes is tantamount to identity theft, then a well-timed costume change can transform him from prisoner to warder, or back again. The trick will be to figure out when is the right time to change identities—because in the cruel logic of this film, the prison can change its rules faster than Buster can change clothes.

There are grim jokes aplenty here—one key sequence involves the intended execution of Buster Keaton. It takes an especially dark comic imagination to seek laughs in the hanging of an innocent man. Buster Keaton, though, finds a way to make that hangman's noose his ally.

Transformations abound in Keaton's movies. Even the *titles* can misdirect you. *The Goat* is not about a goat—at least not a cloven-footed mammal. But then *The Love Nest* isn't about a love nest, *The Navigator* isn't about a navigator, *The General* isn't about a general, and while there is a butler in *Battling Butler*, the butler isn't the one who battles.

**Buster Keaton and costar Virginia Fox are spooked by *The Haunted House* (1921).**

*The Goat* is a two-reel study in deception and transformation, in the gap between reality and what gets filmed in the place of reality. They say the camera never lies, but in Buster's world this isn't so. This camera did lie, and its lie sparks the creation of an alternate universe where innocent Buster is a wanted murderer haunted by his victim—ironically, the theme of a man wrongly accused of a monstrous crime would be Roscoe Arbuckle's real-life fate within the year. *The Goat* is a miasma of misdirection—dummies for people, a live Indian for a dime store statue, a carpenter for a surgeon, a phone booth for an elevator. The mistaken identity that drives the plot—if "plot" is the right word, or should we say that drives the chase—is when luckless Buster is mistaken for Dead Shot Dan the escaped murderer.

Several sources claim that Dead Shot Dan was played by Malcolm St. Clair, the man who shares directing credit on this film with Buster. It makes for a good story—as if they were interchangeable after all. Film scholars have studied photographs of St. Clair and concluded that this was just another tall tale—which is too bad, since the film does feature Buster's other co-director from his silent shorts, Eddie Cline, playing the policeman by the telephone pole. Buster had a high regard for St. Clair, whom he called "a great director," and placed alongside Frank Capra and Leo McCarey as examples of great comedy directors who learned their craft working for Mack Sennett. That's some high praise—especially considering that *The Goat* marked Keaton's first credited collaboration with Mal St. Clair, and one of his last—evidently Mal made a big impression on Buster.

Buster needed the services of a good co-director on something as ambitious and complicated as *The Goat*. Filming a two-reel-long chase sequence took its toll on the man—in one stunt fall Keaton missed his target and badly injured his hips, knees, and elbows. Keaton was out of commission for three days to recover—and then he was back at it, running and jumping and hanging off the sides of speeding cars.

Throughout this film, Buster is racing—but getting nowhere. It takes all his skill and speed and ingenuity just to stay in place, as the cogs of the universe click methodically around him. At times there is a bleak, fatalistic tone to all this—but at the same time, Buster's keyed into that mechanistic fate just well enough to spy the escape routes no one else sees. Speeding trains, amazing stunts, breathless chases, special effects, and armies of angry coppers—if you were in a crazy hurry and only had 20 minutes to fully digest the entirety of Buster Keaton's work, this might be the movie to watch.

Where *The Goat* is a representative example of Keaton's silent shorts, *The Playhouse* is as marvelous as it is atypical and singular. The opening reel of *The Playhouse* is as sustained a sequence of comic innovation and cinematic craftsmanship as anything ever filmed. There is not one Buster Keaton cavorting here, but many. The double- and triple-exposures were challenging enough, but familiar. Keaton was not the first comedian to play two roles on screen at once. By the time he appears ninefold in the same frame, though, we know we're in the presence of something extraordinary.

Georges Méliès had done such a thing, back at the dawn of movies, in films like *The Melomaniac*, but no one before Keaton had attempted something so audacious yet achieved results so seamlessly perfect. Fellow slapstick comedian Charley Chase tried his hand at something similar, playing four versions of himself at once in the Hal Roach talkie short *Four Parts*, but his duplicates shimmered and vanished at the edges of their overlapping domains. Miraculously, Keaton and his cameraman Elgin Lessley achieved superior results, despite working more than 10 years before Chase, in a substantially more primitive environment, with hand-cranked cameras and custom-made equipment designed by Buster himself and given life by newly hired technical wizard Fred Gabourie. No wonder he told his crew, "Keep this quiet, you lugs!" No point sharing your secrets.

The project had its roots in an accident and an in-joke. The accident: Buster had broken his ankle on the set of *The Electric House*, and had to suspend production on that short while he healed. Worried about falling behind schedule with his monthly releases, he realized he needed to make a film that found its laughs in something other than his typical pratfalls and physical stunts. Which brings us to the in-joke: Silent era dramatist Thomas Ince was fabled for taking excessive credits for himself ("Thomas H. Ince presents a Thomas H. Ince production, supervised by Thomas H. Ince"). Keaton poked fun at this egotism by filling the screen with himself, and chuckling, "This fellow Keaton seems to be the whole show!"

The result was mesmerizing surrealism. While that first reel tends to get all the glory and attention, it is in the second reel that things become more personal. The concept of duplicates follows Buster out of his dreamscape and into a waking dream, where one woman appears to be two, and two men act as one. Mirrors abound, and identity seems to melt like salt in the rain. Buster turns into a monkey—even his humanity is subject to transformation. The monkey is an homage to one of Buster's onetime vaudeville peers, a performing chimp named Peter the Great. Throughout *The Playhouse*, Buster makes little nods to his vaudeville past—recreating a few of his old routines in a new medium for a new audience.

But the deepest tribute is not in any single gag, but the concept overall: Buster made his vaudeville debut as a toddler. His parents had an established act, but no babysitter, so they let their baby boy join them on stage, where he proceeded to do what all children do: create havoc. This became the new act for the Three Keatons—Papa Keaton would gamely try to perform some given act, and Buster would unwittingly undermine it. This idea wormed its way deep into Keaton's comic imagination, and throughout his life he returned to it. *The Playhouse* is one of the better expressions of that idea, already hashed out once before in a film he made with Roscoe Arbuckle, *Backstage*. Time and again Buster would find ways to disrupt someone else's show and bring his unique brand of chaos to the stage: *Free and Easy*, *Speak Easily*, *The King of the Champs-Elysees*, *The Silent Partner*, *Hollywood Cavalcade*, even to *War Italian Style* one of his last feature appearances in 1966.

*The Playhouse* was the fulfillment of Buster's original eight-picture contract. It was such a hit that he was hastily and enthusiastically signed for another dozen. Once his injured ankle recovered, Keaton set out to complete *The Electric House*.

Many of Keaton's films involve crazy houses—*One Week*, *The Haunted House*, *The Scarecrow*—but Keaton's Rube Goldbergian innovations reach their peak in *The Electric House*. The premise kicks off with a confusion of identities: when his diploma gets accidentally swapped with a fellow graduate's, the botanist Buster Keaton is mistaken for an electrical engineer, and hired by a millionaire to wire his house. "I want to be amazed," the rich man commands.

"I want to be amazed" is perhaps the wrong thing to say Buster Keaton, who sets out to do just that. The result is genuinely amazing, and utterly singular in conception. Other comedies had riffed on the idea of modern marvels—and 15 years later, Charlie Chaplin would stuff some similar jokes into his *Modern Times*, but the gimmick here is that the absurd electrical contraptions are not the malevolent machinations of a heartless society bent on dehumanizing efficiency. Buster is a whimsical Frankenstein, whose well-intentioned genius goes awry only when sabotage is brought into the equation. That angry colleague, whose misplaced diploma cost him a job that was rightfully his, tracks Buster down and sets out to rewire the house to expose Buster's incompetence.

The thing is, botany-student Buster really wasn't incompetent. The set-up in *The Electric House* resembles that of *One Week*, but with the punchline reversed: both films find Buster unwittingly constructing a surrealistic homestead after mistakenly swapping documents with a rival. The difference here is that without the mean-spirited interference of his rival, Buster's Electric House might actually have worked. Of course, installing a superpowered indoor escalator that deposits passengers at a second floor balcony overlooking a swimming pool is just asking for trouble.

That electric staircase leads to the film's best, and most Keatonish, gag: Buster is doubled over, carrying a heavy trunk that, unbeknownst to him, contains a person, but he makes only Sisyphean progress up the stairs because they are running the opposite direction, at exactly the same pace. In one image, Buster is performing an impressive physical stunt, involving imaginative mechanical design, with a metaphysical fatalism. Who needs to make two-reel shorts when you can express everything you want to say in just one frame?

*The Love Nest* would be Buster Keaton's de facto swan song in silent shorts. He had not yet fulfilled his contract, and still owed the studio one remaining short. But in November of 1923, the board of directors of Buster Keaton Productions met in New York to discuss the fate of the man whose name adorned their company. His run of silent shorts had been modestly successful—and while both Harold Lloyd and Charlie Chaplin outstripped him at the box office it was nonetheless obvious his star was on the rise. Both Lloyd and Chaplin were making features—and the board was thinking that it was high time for Buster to join them. For the businessmen who were to make the final decision, one fact loomed above all others: features made more money. A dollar invested in a comedy feature returned a vastly higher profit than the same dollar invested in a short. The Board voted to leave Buster's 20th and final short unmade and ordered Keaton to turn his attentions to his feature debut, *The Three Ages*, instead.

As a farewell to the format of two-reel silent shorts, *The Love Nest* would prove to be as bizarre and distinctive as anything he made. Somber, elegiac, and full of dark humor, it also had the narrative and thematic focus he would need in the world of feature films. *The Love Nest* is the only of Keaton's shorts for which he took sole credit as writer and director. At least, this is how it has appeared to scholars. It is just one of the questions asked by the damaged state of the surviving materials—studio records indicate Eddie Cline co-directed this, as he did practically all of the shorts, and the existing titles may just be an inaccurate reconstruction.

Another such question concerns Virginia Fox, Buster's leading lady through many of these shorts. *The Love Nest* marked her final collaboration with Buster—and in the film as it stands today, that collaboration is nothing more than a fleeting glimpse in the opening shot, and her appearance in a photograph. However it's hard to say what her contribution to the film originally constituted. For decades *The Love Nest* was considered a lost film, until Raymond Rohauer recompiled it in the 1970s from materials found overseas, primarily a print recovered from the then-Czechoslovakia. Since then, additional discoveries of material in France and the Netherlands have helped restore additional fragments, but it is safe to conclude that the original ending was not so abrupt, and the original beginning included more of Virginia Fox rejecting Buster.

That rejection propels Buster to sea—just as it would do later in the feature film *The Navigator*. Where *The Navigator* involves Buster's travails with a cantankerous ship, Buster's principal nemesis in *The Love Nest* is decidedly human. The tyrannical captain of the ship is burly Joe Roberts, Keaton's longstanding foil and a friend of the Keaton family. He played the heavy in 16 of Buster's shorts, and continued alongside Keaton in *The Three Ages* and *Our Hospitality*. During production of *Our Hospitality*, he suffered complications from a stroke and died at the age of 52.

Death hangs heavy over *The Love Nest*, which is saying something, given Keaton's penchant for macabre humor. Buster had always shown a mordant streak—yet few of his gags are as bitterly funny as the one where he sinks an entire ship, drowning its crew, in order to escape in a lifeboat. Brilliantly conceived and played with patient deadpan perfection, the joke is as close to the line as Buster would dare. Meanwhile, the recurring gag of Captain Joe Roberts crossing the names of his mates off a list and tossing a wreath into the sea to commemorate their execution becomes almost a Lubitschean touch.

Speaking of running gags, some of them spill out beyond the boundaries of this film and invade his other works. *The Love Nest* joins *Convict 13*, *The Playhouse*, *The Frozen North*, and later features like *Sherlock Jr.* in its dream-setting. In *The Paleface*, Buster had a gag where a title card alleged that two years had elapsed, with no change in his position or behavior in the frame. In *The Love Nest*, he reverses the gag—we see time elapse by having him reappear with a ludicrously fake drawn-on beard. Buster ran a variation on this joke in his later talkie short *Ditto*, in which the passing of time is conveyed to the audience by Buster's sudden acquisition of an absurdly fake beard.

Buster copied himself because no one else could. Other comedians could do great stunts, or eye-popping special effects, but no one quite copied Buster's worldview. Here is a man of a mechanical mind and a quick wit, but also clumsy and naïve. Who but Buster Keaton could pull off an effortless yet wholly unintentional mutiny? And who but Buster Keaton would see that triumph unmade in an instant? This is Buster Keaton in a nutshell: he needed the legendary Great Stone Face, because a man who openly expressed emotion could only face such reversals of Fate with endless tears, not stoic resolve.

# Eureka

Buster Keaton has a problem.

Working backwards: (5) he'd very much like to get an audience with a certain general, so he can present his latest invention—a gun fitted with a headlight, for improved aim; (4) the general is inside a swanky casino; (3) the casino's dress code requires formal attire; (2) renting a tuxedo costs money; (1) Buster's broke. But Buster has recently made the acquaintance of a loudmouth (Jimmy Durante) who has explained that casinos are naturally jumpy around men with guns—they're worried about bad publicity when people commit suicide.

If a dead body is found near a casino, the house has a habit of stuffing money in the corpse's pockets so it won't look like he killed himself after losing.

You can see the light bulb go off behind Buster's sparkling eyes. He needs money, he's outside a casino, he has a gun...

And there, ladies and gentlemen, is why I love *The Passionate Plumber*. Keaton's first four talkie features at MGM were hit-or-miss affairs even at their best. And while conventional wisdom would have you believe that the addition of Jimmy Durante marked the beginning of the end, in fact it was a decided improvement. I'm going to work through this thesis in more detail below, but for those of you in a hurry who just want the gist of it, just copy and paste the following formula into your head and be done with it: *The Passionate Plumber* = funny + stylishly made + smart Buster + appropriate use of Jimmy Durante = good movie.

That may be a bold assertion. I know I'm in direct contradiction to a bunch of Keaton fans to even speak kindly about any of the talkie era stuff. I own a few (otherwise wonderful) books on Keaton that come to abrupt stop after *Spite Marriage*, as if Buster dropped dead after his last silent film. Other books compact discussion of his talkie career into as little space, and as dismissive a discussion, as possible.

When silent comedy scholar and Slapsticon co-founder Richard Roberts was asked to appear in a documentary about the history of Hollywood, the producers asked him to explain why Keaton's career was such a profound disappointment once sound came in. Richard objected. He didn't agree it was a disappointment, and wanted instead to talk about how Buster—alone among his contemporaries—remained active, inventive, and fresh until the late 1960s. How he continued to perform terrific comedy while remaining culturally relevant, extremely busy, and quite happy—while also exploring new media. All while the likes of Harold Lloyd and Charlie Chaplin retired and faded away. The producers of the documentary didn't want to hear any of that—it didn't fit their narrative. Buster was destroyed by sound—everybody knows that!

In its meandering and stuttering way, this book sets forth the argument that the shift away from the slapstick comedy of the 1920s and towards the dialog-based screwball comedies of the 1930s was more a result of cultural transformations than it was technological transformations. This is not a consensus viewpoint at all. For many critics and historians, the assumption is that the advent of sound set the language of film back about 10 years. To that, I'd say, go watch Ernst Lubitsch's first talkie, *The Love Parade* (discussed more fully later in this book). It is as spry and visually inventive as anything made 10 years later—or for that matter, 10 years earlier. If bolting his cameras to the floor inside a soundproof baffle and aiming them at an immobile microphone was a hindrance to technique, Lubitsch didn't let it show.

Nor did Fritz Lang, whose first experiments in sound, *M* and *The Testament of Dr. Mabuse*, make his silent films seem inexpressive and limited, not the other way around.

While I'd agree that sound technology in those first few years of the 1930s imposed some technical limitations on filmmakers, the evidence shows that especially inventive and ambitious filmmakers found ways around those limitations and showed the promise of the new form. And if anyone was an inventive and ambitious filmmaker, it was Buster Keaton.

And Buster Keaton was eager to make talkies. MGM had to hold him back for about a year. When he did start working with sound, he showed how his kind of silent-era slapstick could work with a soundtrack. Consider a key gag from *Parlor, Bedroom, and Bath*. For now, don't worry about whether this was representative of the rest of the film (it's not) or his MGM talkie output generally (ditto, not)—I'm just offering it up as a sign that his style of comedy did not, on any fundamental ground, mismatch with sound.

Buster and his girl are going for a drive. Suddenly, one of the wheels pops off the rear of the car and it skids to a halt. Buster steps out of the car to inspect the problem, when he hears the approaching whistle of a train. He turns, and realizes in alarm that the car is sitting, dead, right on the tracks. Urgently he helps pull his girl from the car, barely getting her to safety as the train thunders across the tracks from the right of the frame to the left … completely missing the car, which is only straddling one set of tracks. Phew! Then, of course, another train approaching from left to right immediately ploughs across and destroys the car.

It is in all respects a repeat of a gag first seen in the short *One Week*, and adapted in *The General*—both of which are silent-era classics of Keaton's beloved by posterity. Yet this talkie-era version is no second-rate knock-off. It is a perfect example of how Keaton could still perform silent-style slapstick gags in a sound film. His comedy was capable of working with a soundtrack, he was eager to explore the new medium, and he had the visionary talents to go beyond the limitations imposed by the technology.

Coulda, but didna, and therein lies our problem. The problem wasn't that Buster and sound didn't mix—it was the fact that poor Buster had the misfortune to work for MGM—where comedy went to die. It was a top-down corporate structure of strict control and airlessness. Not a place conducive to comedy. Not like, say, Paramount. I get the feeling that if you were to have walked out onto the floor at Paramount in those days and said in a loud voice, "I don't believe this is a real movie studio!" the whole place would have suddenly vanished in a puff of smoke. Apparently, it had never occurred to anyone at Paramount that it was possible, not to say desirable, to check up on what anyone was doing with the company's money. And so, anarchic comedians thrived there, as they were essentially without adult supervision: W.C. Fields, the Marx Brothers, Mae West. I mean, c'mon, they put Ernst Lubitsch in charge of the place! Lunatics in charge of the asylum!

The upside was comedians at Paramount made terrific movies that have stood the test of time. The downside was they lost money catastrophically and nearly sank the whole studio. An axiom: what's good for comedy isn't always good for business.

MGM was the antithesis of that. It was an exceptionally well-run corporation that kept scrupulous track of every dime. They had vast resources and knew how to use them, and the results spoke for themselves. So, let's be big Keaton fans and own up to the dirty little secret—*The Passionate Plumber* outgrossed every one of the superlative classics he made in the silent era save for *The Navigator*. MGM had nothing to complain about in the box office returns of these much-derided talkies—they were profitable, they were hits.

But we're not here to talk about commercial success in the 1930s. What matters to us today is aesthetic quality. Fans of Buster Keaton's classic silents bristle at the MGM talkies—that's why they get such bad press—but clearly some are better than others. And when I say *The Passionate Plumber* is one of the good ones, I'm flying in the face of almost everything ever written about Keaton.

Edward McPherson spends much of his book *Tempest in a Flat Hat* giving a full chapter to each of Keaton's major silents, but dispenses with *The Passionate Plumber* in a single, slim paragraph, dripping with contempt. Of co-star Jimmy Durante, McPherson says he provided "an insidious torrent of mugging, catchphrases, and malapropos."

In his autobiography, *My Wonderful World of Slapstick*, Keaton himself barely addresses his MGM films, and makes only a passing reference to *The Passionate Plumber*. To the extent he talks about those days, it is with regret that he looks back on the decision to team him with Durante in the first place. "There is no one in the world like Durante, bless him, but in my opinion we just did not belong in the same movie."

Notice two things about that quote. One—he calls him "Durante." Not Jimmy. And then there's that oddly phrased not-quite-a-compliment "no one in the world" bit, softened a little by the "bless him" addition.

Buster hated Jimmy Durante. When he articulated this dislike in public, it was always couched in terms of how their comic styles clashed, how they did not function as a comedy team. But that was for public consumption: the real problem was that Buster just didn't like him personally. He found Durante's personality abrasive.

Now, let's pile on: Buster was going through hell with his soon-to-be-ex-wife Natalie, he rankled at the conditions of his employment at MGM and specifically butted heads with Lawrence Weingarten, and he was drinking a full bottle of whiskey a day. So, Buster was under stress personally and professionally, had a drunkard's natural paranoia—and didn't like Durante as a person.

Few Keaton fans today would argue that that the pairing was a good idea—but that doesn't mean it was inherently a bad idea either.

Here's what Lawrence Weingarten himself has to say on the matter (as interviewed by Tom Dardis for the book *The Man Who Wouldn't Lie Down*): "Keaton was doing a certain amount of business. And we thought that Durante … in this particular role [in *The Passionate Plumber*] would be fine, that's all. We weren't thinking about bolstering [Keaton]. There were a number of pictures made, we tried our best. If it wasn't good enough, that's another thing. But we didn't set out to destroy Buster."

Keaton had signed a two-year contract in June of 1930. *The Passionate Plumber* came out in February 1932, with the contract nearly up. If MGM wanted to get out of the Keaton business, the simplest solution would have been to just not re-sign him.

The conspiracy theories proffered by some fans and critics (e.g., MGM used Keaton to build up Durante's career) mask what actually happened.

At MGM, Keaton had been stripped of his usual colleagues and collaborators. Gone were Clyde Bruckman, Elgin Lessley, and Fred Gabourie. In their place, he was now stuck with as many as 22 writers (!), all scribbling away to think up wacky dialogue.

Between 1930 and 1933, Buster starred in seven full-length sound features at MGM. There are bright spots: *Doughboys, Parlor, Bedroom, and Bath, The Passionate Plumber*, and *Speak Easily* all have much to recommend them. But they have no cohesive comic identity—nothing that makes these four movies seem "of a piece." And with the exception of *The Passionate Plumber*, they have little in common with any idea you may have of what Buster Keaton was about.

Much has been made of MGM's refusal to let Buster perform risky stunts—a decision that removed a key component of Keaton's persona. But this was in fact the least of it. Lawrence Weingarten, the studio exec with the most direct influence over Keaton's films, thought of Buster as interchangeable with just about any of the comedy players on the lot.

He went around buying the rights to various stage plays that tickled him, and plunked Buster into the film adaptations without ever considering that, maybe, Buster might shine if left to think up his own ideas.

MGM had hired Keaton as an actor. He had been, in his silent films, a writer-director-star-auteur, but this was a concept fairly foreign to studios at the time (and not much appreciated even today). Keaton had rarely taken screen credit for anything other than acting, and in fact he may not have been aware at the time of how weird his production method was—how much directorial responsibility he was exercising even when he didn't claim the credit.

At MGM, Keaton tried to lobby for the right to work on his own, but he didn't have a contractual right to it, and the studio hadn't granted it to anyone else, ever (if you would like to argue that Marion Davies' private production unit had independence, that's a fair point, but she was funded by Hearst, not MGM, and so was a decided exception). Thus, when I noted above that visionary filmmakers like Lubitsch could make talkies that had the cinematic invention of silents, Keaton was denied the chance to flex his own muscles in that regard because he wasn't the director, Eddie Sedgwick was.

Sedgwick wasn't bad, and you can kind of gauge what he brought to the table by seeing what happened when he briefly left. Sedgwick was busy with another gig when talkie #4, *Sidewalks of New York* was made, and so Jules White and Zion Myers took over.[1] One early sequence in the film was later copied by White almost word for word into the Three Stooges' *Disorder in the Court*, with Curly ably substituting for Buster. When Curly Howard can do the gag better than Buster Keaton, that's a pretty sure sign that the material wasn't suited to Keaton in the first place. But that didn't stop Weingarten, heedlessly plucking stage plays from Broadway in which to drop Buster as a dim-witted Curly-wanna-be.

Mind you, the results weren't always bad. *Parlor, Bedroom and Bath* is a fairly crappy Keaton movie, but it's not a crappy movie overall. If you didn't know who Keaton was and could just watch it on its own terms, it is actually quite charming. Compared to other farce comedies of its time, it holds up very well. If it had starred, say, Robert Young (then on the earliest end of his break into movies), we'd probably be celebrating it as a minor gem.

The first four Keaton talkies all made money, whatever fans might say about them today. But the fourth, *Sidewalks of New York*, had problems. MGM's exhibitors wired back to the home office to complain about how unfunny it was. It was one thing for Keaton to grouse and moan, but Weingarten had to listen to the exhibitors. So concrete steps were taken to make the next one, *The Passionate Plumber*, an improvement.

As ever, it was a play that caught Weingarten's eye. This time it was Jacques Deval's *Her Cardboard Lover*, but mindful of the exhibitors' complaints about *Sidewalks*, Weingarten spent half again as much as he had to buy the play as he did on "three scenes" for Buster. Sorry—the documentation is not clear about what those "three scenes" are, but we can guess.

The core of the plot involves a romantic triangle, which with the addition of an extra pole turns into a romantic polygon. Tony (Gilbert Roland) loves both Patricia (Irene Purcell) and Nina (Mona Maris)—and they both love him. But Tony's a scamp—pretending to Nina that he's married to Patricia, pretending to Patricia he's married to Nina—and who knows how many other women orbit him beyond the view of the cameras. Patricia has enough self-respect to know this is wrong, and that she should break it off. But she doesn't have enough self-respect to actually go and do that. So, she hires Elmer Tuttle (guess who) to play her lover—to drive away Tony—and to keep her from caving in to Tony's entreaties. Along the way, her gigolo-for-hire starts to inspire genuine love in her (this is similar to the plot used by Ginger Rogers and Fred Astaire in the brilliant romantic comedy musical *The Gay Divorcee*, and we will encounter variants of it in the likes of *Fifth Avenue Girl* later in this book).

That's probably what the play was. But there's a lot of extraneous stuff cluttering the front of the movie before we get anywhere near that plotline—and I'm pretty confident that those "three scenes" occupy the front half of the picture. It is in the front half of the movie—and nearly only the front—that we find Jimmy Durante.

He is pretty grating. I'll give you that. But look at how Buster is being presented. Buster is not just a gigolo—or a plumber—he's also an inventor. His introductory scene finds him methodically deploying a giant clamp, a welding torch, hammers, and a handsaw in a Rube Goldberg-ish approach to fixing a broken cigarette lighter. This is the Buster Keaton I know and love from the past.

Bizarrely, Edward McPherson wrote that in *Plumber*, Buster played "a brain-dead beret-wearing gun-toting plumber." Well, he's right about the beret and the gun. But what I love about this film is that, finally, Buster is no longer brain-dead. He's certainly out of step from other people—but it's the geek hero's place to be socially maladroit. His eyes are always scanning, looking for the escape no one else sees (again, this is classic Buster).

Consider what almost certainly is one of our three added scenes: Buster has provoked Tony into a duel. Keaton recycled some of this duel stuff for later films—a similar sequence appears in *An Old Spanish Custom*, and then recycled again into *Pest From the West* (produced by Jules White, no less). What's striking here is how the filmmakers use Durante. *He* gets saddled with the village idiot stuff, while Buster gets to play the scene mostly silent. When he speaks, it's a doozy—his perfectly delivered suggestion "*Let him use a sword, I'll use a pistol*" is one of the best laughs in the film. But Buster isn't there to do one-liners, he's looking for the way out (which is what that one-liner is really about).

Look at his eyes throughout the scene—it's the look of a man who is calculating how to cheat to win. They are the same eyes that glimmer in Keaton's most inventive silent classics.

The duel is minor stuff, really, when compared to the standout sequence at the casino. You could pull the casino sequence out of context, give it a freestanding title, and it would rank as one of Keaton's best comedy shorts. It nimbly mixes visual gags, cinematic style, character development, some wicked Keaton one-liners, and coherent storytelling. And to get it started, we get a hint of why the movie needs Jimmy Durante. Somehow you have to explain to the audience that the casino will shove money in Buster's pockets if they think he's committed suicide outside. Either he has to say it to someone, or someone has to say it to him. So, for this scene at least, Buster needs a friend to talk to—enter Jimmy Durante.

This is generally how the film uses Durante—as a means to get across verbal information so as to keep Buster from having to talk too much. Instead, Buster gets only crackerjack one-liners to say, because he no longer has to explain any plot (Buster's dialogue in *Passionate Plumber* is the best and funniest of any of his sound films).

And once the film settles into its second half, it's the Buster-and-Patricia show, with almost no further use for Jimmy Durante. He fades into the background, all but forgotten. Meanwhile, Buster tackles this romantic plot with incredible aplomb. Buster behaves strangely throughout the latter half of the movie, but it isn't because he's stupid—it's because he's single-minded. He has been given a mission to play Patricia's lover, and he carries it out with ruthless attention, and occasional physical agility as needed.

It's the vaguely autistic practicality of the true geek hero: the Buster in *The Passionate Plumber* and the Buster in *The General* would get along with each other just fine.

**Buster Keaton and Polly Moran in *The Passionate Plumber* (1932).**

It all leads to a clever finale, in which Buster gets to be smart and brave and in charge. No wonder Patricia swoons—he's Buster F'in Keaton! The sexual awkwardness of *Parlor, Bedroom and Bath* is gone—we can credibly believe that Patricia would eventually warm to Buster, to find him a worthy lover. In fact, the hostile combat of their interaction, gradually melting into true love, is the template of screwball comedy.

It isn't screwball yet, not fully, not yet. And the film descends into silly slapstick towards the end that undercuts some of the better humor of earlier—Buster is mistaken for a doctor who has to "examine" her with his plumbing tools (the film skirts around rude plumbing jokes, planting them in the audience's minds without saying them openly). Buster then gets to perform another variation on the carry-an-unconscious-woman gag that he first performed in *The Navigator*, embellished in *Spite Marriage*, adapted into *Parlor, Bedroom and Bath*, and would continue to perform until his death. The ubiquity of this routine however points to a problem at the heart of Keaton's comedy—he has no real use for a female costar, and functions at his best when his leading lady is passed out. This would never do in the age of screwball.

The last film on Keaton's existing contract was *Speak Easily*. The studio rightly concluded there was no reason to tamper with success—*The Passionate Plumber* seemed to work just right, so everybody was back in place. Including Jimmy Durante. And in the end, *Speak Easily* was a bright spot. Even Buster himself admired it, and considered it his best MGM talkie—an opinion shared by many Keaton fans.

But, while the onscreen quality was there, Buster was an offscreen mess, and his unreliability cost the studio enormous sums. His drinking was out of control, he fought, he misbehaved, he got troubling coverage by the gossip press. MGM signed him to just one year this time, one film (*What, No Beer?*)—they were reluctant to hitch themselves to a sinking ship.

I'd rather have my eyeballs sandpapered than sit through *What, No Beer?* again, so I can't recommend you watch it. But in case you find yourself accused of terrorism, and in Gitmo or some overseas CIA-funded Black Ops prison your torturer happens to put the thing on for you, before you cave in and confess to whatever they've charged you with, take a note of how Buster and Jimmy in that film share a single narrative role. They have different "personalities" but there's really only one function being served. You could remake the film with a single actor replacing both of them and not have to juggle the plot at all. And this wasn't because MGM wanted to team them–it was because Buster couldn't be counted on to come in to work anymore.

But he got better. Sobered up, replaced ex-wife Natalie with new love Eleanor, and kept on working—and while they don't get written about in the books very often, he bequeathed to posterity a wealth of talkie shorts, TV shows, industrial training films, and sundry oddities that almost defy cataloging.

# What, What No Beer?

*What, No Beer?* is just about as unloved as a movie can be. If all the hatred and invective thrown at this 65-minute-long 1933 comedy were somehow bottled up and concentrated, it could power a small city. (And ladies and gentlemen, that's my modest proposal to solve the energy crisis—wean us off foreign oil and start using movie criticism as an alternative fuel source.)

There are several things worth noting about this film, and strangely these things tend not to be noted, even though they're pretty much right on the surface, as easy pickings.

The first of these is the observation that Edward Sedgwick is actually directing this cheapie comedy programmer with a fair bit of panache. The camera setups are carefully arranged, the editing is spritely, and on the whole there has been a sincere attempt to do this well.

The second noteworthy aspect is that, on paper at least, this is just about the most Keatony of Keaton's MGM features. One of the distinctive characteristics of Keaton's silent cinema is the way he mines reality for his comedy. From *Our Hospitality* to *The General*, from *Steamboat Bill, Jr.* to *The Cameraman*, Keaton spent as much time depicting the social and environmental milieu of each film as he did conjuring up the visual gags and stunts.

Consider *Cops*—the film is a 20-minute chase scene in which Buster is pursued by an infinite mob of lawmen. All he needed was an excuse to get the chase started, and then its own internal logic would take over and drive the rest of the film. He could've used any old MacGuffin to start the chase—and when competitors tried to rip him off, that's what they did (for example, see Billy Bevan's *Be Reasonable*, Bevan's attempt to knock-off *Cops* which indeed relies on any old nonsense to get the chase started). But instead of opting for any cheap expediency, Keaton connects his slapstick mayhem to real-world traumas of anarchist terrorism (and makes a passing reference to the fad of goat gland cures, as well). Keaton's comedy didn't just trade in existential angst and slapstick artistry, he always kept it tethered to real history.

Poster for *What, No Beer?* (1933). This is enough, you don't need to watch the movie too.

Of all his MGM talkies, *What, No Beer?* is the only one to connect so palpably to the real world. In 1933, President Roosevelt signed the repeal of Prohibition, specifically lifting the ban on beer first—and famously quipped, "Now would be a good time for a beer!" (Anheuser-Busch obliged, with a highly ceremonious delivery of some beer to the White House, thanks to a fleet of corporate Clydesdales.) Inevitably there would be an awkward transition—a moment when suddenly it was legal to make, import, and sell alcohol again, and there would be demand *on that day*, but that demand could only be met if alcohol had been made, imported, and prepared for sale *prior* to that moment—in other words, illegally.

In *What, No Beer?* this visionary role is Jimmy Durante's. He plays Jimmy Potts, a barber, who realizes that the repeal of Prohibition opens up a market for legal beer—and he wants to be one of the first entrepreneurs to fill that role. He has a plan, a beer-making recipe, and an eternal never-say-die, never-shut-the-hell-up attitude that marks many a successful capitalist. What he doesn't have is any seed money for his startup.

Enter Buster Keaton, as Elmer J. Butts, taxidermist.[1] Elmer has been socking away nest eggs inside his stuffed animals, and has 10 grand he can use to help buy a brewery.

As it happens, their first attempt at beer-making misfires terribly, and results only in non-alcoholic near-beer, but this is fortuitous. The law hasn't changed yet, and so they are raided for flaunting Prohibition—only to be released when the police realize the brew isn't alcoholic. They then go back to the brewery, fix their recipe, and return to business, safely off the cops' radar. Angry gangsters try to muscle in, miffed at these upstarts stealing their carefully honed market, only to mistake Buster's blithe ignorance for supreme self-confidence, and decide to follow him as "The Mastermind."

OK, enough plot synopsis—the big takeaway here is that in addition to the properly Keatony real-world vibe of the premise, there are also numerous sequences tailor-made to exploit Keaton's physical comedy. Now, admittedly, each of these is designed merely as a rip-off of one of his famous routines from earlier films: Keaton trying to mix up a five gallon batch of beer inside a brewery vat designed for 500 gallons could have happily riffed on similar scenes in *The Navigator*, in which Keaton tried to make breakfast for two in a kitchen designed to feed dozens. Later, a rival gangster's moll tries to seduce Buster, leading to another variation on Keaton's "trying to move an unconscious woman" routine. And the film climaxes with Keaton unleashing an army of beer barrels down a steep street, in an echo of his famous chase scene from *Seven Chances*.

On top of all of this, there's Jimmy Durante himself. Conventional wisdom has it that Durante was a terrible choice of screen partner for Buster, and mired the films in talk-oriented comedy at the expense of the visual comedy for which Keaton was known. But that's just it—Durante was there to shoulder the puns and silly wordplay that the MGM gag writers apparently couldn't get enough of, and thereby took that burden off of Keaton's shoulders. In any given scene, one of them could serve as the straight man for the other, alternating the kind of comedy being performed as they go. This is not so far off how comedy teams like Laurel and Hardy or The Three Stooges work. If you want to be reminded of what would happen to poor Buster if it weren't for Durante, go force yourself to sit through *Free and Easy* where one of America's greatest comedians was forced to repeat the line "The Quoon has sweened" over and over, thanks to the dialogue writers' mistaken apprehension this was funny.

I mean, sure, it would have been best if MGM's writers hadn't felt compelled to put such idiotic verbal nonsense in the films in the first place, but apparently that was too much to ask. At least in the Keaton-Durante films, Buster gets room to do his physical gags (which are largely absent from *Free and Easy*) while Durante handles the dialog comedy. There is more physical comedy in the Durante-pairings, not less (compared to the other MGM talkies, that is).

And so, in theory, *What, No Beer?* had the potential to be the greatest film Keaton made for MGM. It had a premise worthy of Keaton's style, it had Durante as a buffer zone allowing Keaton room to develop physical gags without worrying about wordplay, and it had three comedy sequences intended as showcases for Keaton's comedy wherein he had the opportunity to riff on and build upon past glories. And behind the camera was Eddie Sedgwick, directing his heart out and trying to make it all look good.

Of course anyone who's seen the finished product knows how far off that mark they landed, but it wasn't doomed from the start. The opportunity was there for this to be great—or at least pretty good. It could even have been adequate.

Wanna see why it failed? Don't blame MGM, don't blame Durante. Just look at Buster—the thousand-yard stare in his eyes, the sunken flesh sagging around his famous Stone Face, the gargling noise that passes for his voice, the looping swagger of his body where once there was acrobatic grace. This is a broken man. He just phoned it in. Every time the film gives him space to innovate and improvise, he just goes through the motions necessary to get the scene over with.

The fact of the matter is that Durante wasn't brought in to handle the dialog comedy, he was brought in as insurance. Keaton was so drunk by this point he sometimes didn't make it to work at all—causing expensive delays. But if he and Durante occupied the same narrative position, then anytime Keaton wasn't available or able to do a scene, here was Durante to take over and keep the cameras rolling.

The uncomfortable irony watching *What, No Beer?* is that its depiction of Keaton as an accidental beer baron (who believes himself to be presiding over an empire of near-beer) was made by a man so drunk he got himself fired. The Keaton-Durante team was a top-money-maker for MGM, highly rated in popularity polls and responsible for a string of nicely profitable inexpensive comedies.

Louis B. Mayer didn't fire Keaton lightly—but his unreliability was now a serious issue. In 1933, on the heels of completing *What, No Beer?*, Keaton's contract expired without renewal.

To understand why Keaton allowed himself to be consumed by drink in this way, we have to skip back in time to 1921. This was the year that Buster married the wrong girl.

Her name was Natalie Talmadge. She came from a family of successful actresses such that her family name lent a certain degree of prestige to Keaton's own up-and-coming career, but beyond that their pairing made no sense. They didn't really love each other, and it's hard to tell if Natalie even ever much liked him. Inevitably, as loveless marriages do, it unwound into divorce—but it unwound slowly and painfully. And instead of unwinding in a sensible, adult way, in which the two partners separated amicably, it just frayed apart stupidly.

Natalie took Buster's sons, James and Robert, from him. Let me rephrase that—she didn't just take them out of his life, she took him out of their lives as well. She changed their names, to remove that offending "Keaton" brand. And as a result there are direct descendants of Buster Keaton walking the Earth today—grandchildren, great-grandchildren, and great-great-grandchildren—who are denied the most basic and obvious link to one of the few true geniuses of cinema. The name Keaton was erased. Keaton lost his children, just as much as if they had died. And this happened in 1932.

No wonder the man drank. Of course he tried to find escape in oblivion—and maybe the alcohol helped soothe the pain, for a while. But if he was using booze as an escape from the wreck his life had become, it was only wrecking it further. He drowned the pain of one divorce in enough alcohol to blot out his own memory—and he awoke from a proverbial "lost weekend" in Mexico, married to a gold-digger named Mae Scribbens. How's that for irony?

Buster bottomed out then, and he got better. He dried up, and returned to work—and died old, happy, loved, and well off. Alcohol helped him escape, and then he escaped from alcohol.

Which brings us back to *What, No Beer?* Jimmy Durante's dream is to open a legal brewery that puts Americans back to work, making something of value for American consumption. He sees it as an all-American economic cure-all—but he then finds it's a business dominated by gangsters and crooks. Prohibition itself was an attempt to ameliorate the perceived dangers of alcohol, which only ended up creating the Mafia and vastly increasing the number of alcohol-related crimes. There's a weird balance at work in all of these interrelated anecdotes, which is perhaps best summed up by this quote from *The Simpsons*: "*To alcohol—the cause of, and solution to, all of life's problems!*"

# Keaton International

There are two things Buster Keaton could have done in the talkie era that would have been successful in terms of screen comedy. Option #1 was to transition away from the kind of physical comedy for which he was known and become a more generic dialog-based comedian. This is what MGM expected of him, and by and large this was successful. His MGM talkies were profitable and popular. Films like *Speak Easily* and *Parlor, Bedroom and Bath* are excellent on their own terms. They are not what we've come to expect from Keaton, or what most fans want from Keaton, but these are nonetheless funny movies that function exceptionally well and Buster Keaton is funny in them.

The alternative to being a dialog comedian in the MGM mode, option #2, was something Keaton came to realize later: "When sound came, we found this out—we found this out from our own pictures—that sound didn't bother us at all. There was only one thing I wanted at all times, and insisted on: that you go ahead and let me talk in the most natural way, in your situations. Don't give me puns. Don't give me jokes. No wisecracks. Give that to Abbott and Costello. Give that to the Marx Brothers. Because as soon as out plot is set and everything is going smooth, I'm going to find places in the story where dialogue is not called for. There can be two or three people working at jobs—well they work at them without talking. That's the way I want it. So you get those stretches in your picture of six, seven, eight, nine minutes where there isn't a word of dialogue. In those, we did our old routines."

This idea is illustrated by that scene in *Parlor, Bedroom and Bath* which recreated a bit from *One Week* but did so with a soundtrack. For that matter, Buster's use of the Carry-an-Unconscious-Lady gag later in the same film is another example of successfully adapting silent-era gags into talkie films more or less intact. Buster did not get much opportunity to develop this alternate approach during his time at MGM, but it flowered more fully in the years to come.

In some ways, Buster's flameout at MGM was the best thing that could have happened to him. For one thing, it forced him to sober up. Other slapstick comedians of his generation

**Buster Keaton had a full and lively career in the sound era in both movies and television.**

with similar substance abuse problems died young (cf Charley Chase!)—Buster hit rock bottom, rehabilitated, and got back to work. Secondly, because he didn't have a nest egg of riches to retire on, he had to keep working—which, combined with a powerful Midwestern work ethic, meant he continued to make movies—features, shorts, industrial films, commercials, live TV appearances, television serials … he enlivened everything from *The Twilight Zone* to *The Donna Reed Show* to *Candid Camera*.

Other silent comedy stars, if they continued to the sound era at all, eventually gave up on their old personas. Charlie Chaplin took the Tramp into *Modern Times* in 1936 but went no further. When he lampooned Hitler in 1940's *The Great Dictator*, he couldn't help but acknowledge that his own longstanding appearance happened to share a mustache with the world's most hated villain, but beyond that it is hard to see *The Great Dictator* as a true "Tramp" comedy. Still, let's grant that it is—and say that Chaplin took his silent era persona all the way to 1940, and *then* stopped.

Harold Lloyd made it farther—reviving his "glasses" character in 1947's *The Sin of Harold Diddlebock* with screwball maestro Preston Sturges. Yet this was a diminution of both men—lesser Lloyd and lesser Sturges, a whole less than the sum of its parts.

Chaplin and Lloyd, being brilliant businessmen who controlled their own creations, knew when to call it quits, and let themselves fade gracefully into retirement. Buster Keaton did not. He already had *What, No Beer?* on his resume, which meant he pretty much had no dignity left to maintain.

Two things about Keaton in this post-silent world.

#1. He kept wearing his old costume. There was no attempt to moderate it for the modern world, or even to acknowledge that there were once the clothes of a much younger man. Keaton remained Keaton, a stubborn and welcome intrusion of the past into the present.

#2. He shut up.

He didn't just decide to hand over the puns and dialog gags to costars while he found moments of silent action to do his thing—he just stopped talking altogether. There was little effort expended to make his silence plausible or coherent—like his clothes, it meant he was a living relic of a bygone age still adhering to rules of a game no one else was playing.

Singlehandedly, Buster Keaton continued to fly the flag of a silent era comedy aesthetic long after his peers had retired and/or died, on deep into the swinging sixties. Because he took work wherever he found it, he ended up appearing in a number of foreign-made films. And because these are foreign films that had virtually no distribution in the United States, they are almost never discussed.

The first came in 1934, following Buster's ouster from MGM. *Le Roi de Champs-Elysees* ("The King of the Champs-Elysees") was made in France for producer Seymour Nebenzal, the man who produced Fritz Lang's *M* and *The Testament of Dr. Mabuse*. In fact, weirdly, some footage from *The Testament of Dr. Mabuse* was reused in *Le Roi*. (It's as close as I'll ever get to having Buster Keaton vs. Dr. Mabuse.) Buster plays two roles in this film. One is a dangerous gangster, recently escaped from prison and ready to retake his criminal empire. The other is an aspiring but inept actor.

This second role leads to some "disrupt the performance" gags that Keaton seemed drawn to (skip back a few chapters for more detail). For example, in one key scene Actor-

Buster has been mistaken for Gangster-Buster and taken back to the gang's HQ, where legions of armed thugs surround him—some of them hoping to kill and usurp him. Naturally, Actor-Buster wants to sneak out of the place before his true identity is discovered, but that's harder than it sounds.

This was still early in the talkie era, and Keaton is still trying to find his voice—pun intended. He is dubbed for the most part throughout this picture, which gives him more dialog than he was comfortable with. As the years wore on, he gravitated away from dialog and into the weirdly mute mode described above.

For example, consider his appearance in the Italian film *L'incantevole Nemica* ("The Charming Enemy"). This 1953 farce was directed by Claudio Gora, a man better known as an actor, and whose acting credits tend towards the bloody end of the cult movie spectrum: *Mad Dog Killer*, *Seven Blood-Stained Orchids*, *The Death Ray of Dr. Mabuse*…. This was one of his rare outings as a director, and the film is intended as a social satire. According to the plot synopsis on IMDB, the story involves "a cheese factory owner [who] fears communists and mistakes a meek youth who works for him for one of them. He invites the young man to his house where the youth falls in love with the factory owner's daughter." I don't understand Italian, so after watching the film I can't dispute that description, but it doesn't really matter for our purposes because Buster Keaton only appears in one scene and he has literally nothing to do with the rest of the story. In that scene he performs a stage act, derived from old silent comedy routines, that seems to comment on the workplace-related stuff of the story—union organizers, communists, and capitalist barons provide a satirical backdrop for this scene of a worker struggling with the means of production. But, really, you could snip this out of context and watch it all alone and it would make as much sense as it does in the movie.

Buster's last feature film ever was the 1966 Italian comedy *Due Marines E Une Generale* ("2 Marines and 1 General," also known as *War Italian Style*). Shot before *A Funny Thing Happened on the Way to the Forum* but released after, *War Italian Style* was the last feature film to include Keaton—and he looks ghastly pale in it. I can't be sure if this is a sign of his failing health or a poor attempt to evoke his old silent-era whiteface makeup that misfired terribly. So many things misfire in this movie I wouldn't put it past them. This is one of those cases where so much went so wrong that it ended up making something genuinely interesting. Maybe not entertaining—I wouldn't go that far—but definitely interesting.

Unlike Keaton's cameo in *L'incantevole Nemica*, Buster has a prominent co-starring role here—which I'll get to in a moment—alongside the top-billed comedy team of "Franco & Ciccio." Franco Franchi and Ciccio Ingrasia had teamed up as a stage comedy duo and become so popular in that mode they ported their act over to movies, where they cranked out some 114 films together. They're like an Italian hybrid of Abbott and Costello mixed with Martin and Lewis, but the worst parts of each. Ciccio Ingrasia, the one who looks like Kramer from *Seinfeld*, was the Bud Abbott–styled straight man. Franco Franchi was the pair's Jerry Lewis imitator, always mugging and contorting for the most grotesque of gags. Franchi, however, idolized Buster Keaton. He considered it one of the highlights of their 114-film career to have made one with Buster Keaton.

Franco & Ciccio play a pair of American GIs (!) whose incompetence so enrages their superior officers that rather than punishing the pair they are ordered onto a suicide mission deep in Nazi Germany. It's a premise that has cropped up in a handful of strange little war movies, like Enzo Castellari's original version of *Inglorious Bastards*. In this case, the two bumblers have to get far enough behind enemy lines that they can capture high-ranking Nazi strategist General von Kassler—guess who.

Yup. Somehow it's come to this. Buster Keaton, in his final feature film, plays a Nazi General. That's the world we live in.

But the film doesn't paint Von Kessler as a villain. He's somewhere between too-incompetent-to-be-dangerous and secretly-sympathizing-with-the-good-guys (in other words, he's Buster Keaton!). So, along the way, he and the Americans forge a wary alliance—but not before the movie has suffered whiplash-inducing tonal shifts, irrational plotting, sloppy filmmaking, bad acting, and increasingly bizarre black humor.

Getting weirded out by the sight of Buster wearing a swastika and doing the "heil Hitler" salute? Well, this is one strange movie. This is all about forgiving and freeing a Nazi General–compare it to the finale of Quentin Tarantino's version of *Inglourious Basterds* which is basically a reverse image of this idea. But for as strange, and incoherent, and annoying as this movie is, I dare you—I literally dare you—to watch the end and not smile. The General escapes Nazi Germany and changes out of his uniform into a very familiar ill-fitting suit and flat porkpie hat, and he walks off into the sunset in that getup.

That's where our story ends. Buster did survive in the sound era—he wormed his way into a strange little niche that no one else was even trying, and for about 40 years after silent movies ended, he maintained his screen persona, his comedy aesthetic, and his flat hat all the way to the end.

# Fake News

*Too Hot to Handle* is a fairly forgotten romantic comedy from 1938. It is passable entertainment for most viewers, and no more. But this unassuming distraction is a rumination on how movies lie, and how people who lie tend to make movies. Like Georges Méliès's faked coronation of King Edward VII, these are newsreels that lie—documentaries that are secretly fictional (which is the sort of thing we had on our minds at that very first film show in 1895, with the Lumière Brothers' very first film being a staged "documentary"). The film in question is by Jack Conway, and is a quasi-remake of a Buster Keaton silent classic—one that calls into question the conventional wisdom of what happened to the silent clowns when the movies started to talk.

The thing you have to know going in, though, is that while *Too Hot to Handle* is a solidly entertaining action-comedy from Hollywood's Golden Age, in which two top movie stars (Clark Gable and Myrna Loy) frolic their way through some expensive stunt-addled set pieces, I'm not necessarily calling your attention to this film purely for its own modest merits. Now, *Arsene Lupin, Next Time I Marry, Modern Love, The Window*—those are movies to climb mountains for. If you miss those films when they come along, that's when you have to seriously question whether watching classic movies is really your thing. If you miss *Too Hot to Handle*, what you're really missing is a chance to wrestle with the curious legacy of Buster Keaton. But that's going to take a while to explain.

OK, now the first place to start with 1938's *Too Hot to Handle* is actually 1950's *Watch the Birdie*, but it won't make sense to start there so instead let's go to 1928's *The Cameraman* instead and work our way out logically.

*The Cameraman* is a silent classic by Buster Keaton in which a bunch of wonderful things happen, all of them gorgeous and thrilling. But to boil that film down to a plot summary we can say this about it: Buster wants to impress a girl, so he takes up filming newsreels. During his escapades, he unwittingly and accidentally films something secret and powerful, but he does so while also screwing up a bunch of things he was supposed to get right—and it is during a screening of his screw-ups that his other, secret footage is also shown.

*The Cameraman* was arguably Buster's biggest commercial hit in its day—but I have to put an emphasis on the word "arguably." For people who track these things, the data is a bit of a mess. *The Cameraman* was Buster's first film for MGM, a professional outfit that knew what it was doing, as compared to Keaton's own former indie venture which made great movies and then fumbled their distribution. Comparing apples to apples is hard here, because part of what MGM a more professionally run company was that it kept better records—and another part of what MGM a professionally run company was that it strangled artistry, which gives Keaton's fans an incentive to try to interpret the imperfect distribution data in ways that make his solo efforts look better.

Either way, this was a high-water mark in Keaton's career. He followed it up with *Spite Marriage*, which was the title of a movie. But Buster was also suffering in the throes of a real-life spite marriage—one that was headed to divorce, scandal, and heartbreak. Losing his wife was one thing (they hadn't been close in years) but when she left she took the kids, and renamed them so they were no longer Keatons. Buster spiraled into depression and alcoholism—

OK, you've heard this story before. Fine. It has a happy ending—Keaton lived a long and happy life in which he ended up richer, more beloved, and busier than he had ever been back in the glory days of the silent era. So there.

But along the way, Keaton's alcoholic slide cost him his stardom, but he found other employment with MGM, wherein he migrated behind the scenes to serve as a comedy consultant and gag writer on other projects. This resulted in some legendarily misguided gigs, like his begotten stint working with the Marx Brothers. They were each brilliant, genius comedians—but as different as chalk and cheese. And so it went, until Buster started working with Red Skelton. Red was a true physical clown with an elastic body and a willingness to do anything for a laugh. And between 1943 and 1950 he collaborated with Buster Keaton on three remakes of Keaton comedies. *Spite Marriage* became 1943's *I Dood It*; *The General* became 1948's *A Southern Yankee*; and *The Cameraman* became 1950's *Watch the Birdie*.

Keaton readily admits that the films were adapted so comprehensively that "if you sat through them back to back you wouldn't know it was the same picture." Of the three, *Watch the Birdie* is the strongest, and the most Keaton-y.

And, for that matter, I bet if you watched them back to back, you would peg the similarity in plot: Red Skelton takes up movie cinematography to impress a girl; he unwittingly and accidentally films a nefarious plot by the bad guys; that footage is screened in a surreal mishmash of filmic screw-ups…

That's not to say that the Skelton version isn't substantially different, but the source material is recognizable underneath. Keaton said of the three remakes, "in every case, in those three remakes, the second picture didn't compare to the original for laughs or enter-tainment. Now, all for one reason: the writers there today and the producers insisted on improving the originals. So, all three pictures died of improvement."

That's not to say Keaton had a low opinion of Red Skelton—in fact, he always went out of his way to praise Skel-ton as a natural clown, and someone who could have thrived in the silent era (that was Keaton's highest praise). He called Skelton his "pet."

Which is actually a trifle odd—Skel-ton was indeed a physical clown capable of Keatonish slapstick, but the similarity ends there. Buster Keaton's comedy was as dry as a martini, and Skelton is wet like a slobbery dog kiss. That's not a normative judgment—different strokes for different folks. Slobbery dog kisses aren't for me, I prefer Keaton's intellectual, existentialist comedy, but your mileage may vary.

Which at last brings us to 1938—you thought we'd never get there. In fact we've already been here. This was the point when Keaton's bad slide turned around—

Red Skelton starred in a series of 1950s comedies remade from Buster Keaton's silent classics.

his divorce was final, his run of sound shorts for Educational Pictures had ended, his alco-holism had bottomed out, and he had returned to MGM to accept a lowly uncredited job as a gag writer.

And one of the first projects to which he was assigned as a consultant was a film about a newsreel photographer who unwittingly and accidentally films some compromising footage, which is later screened by mistake … wait a minute!

*Too Hot to Handle* follows the adventures of a roguish and unprincipled newsreel jockey named Chris Hunter (played by Clark Gable), whose reputation for snagging the most iconic images of any situations rests almost entirely on his habit of just faking them. In an effort to entrap him, Hunter's competition (Walter Pidgeon) sets up an even bigger fake, involving the intrepid pilot Alma (Myrna Loy), daringly flying medical supplies into a war-zone. Things go wrong, and Chris ends up crashing Alma's plane and nearly killing her in the process—but this disaster produces multiple alternate realities as a result.

Alma misunderstands the incident as Chris saving her from certain death, and it serves as their "meet cute" for an intense romance to follow. But … Chris filmed the whole thing, and that filmed record not only clearly shows his culpability in causing the plane wreck, but also records Alma's confession as being involved in a staged event that never involved any real medical supplies at all.

Just to make things more complicated, this film clip is then edited in such a way as to create one version that makes the two of them seem like heroes, and an uncut "director's edition" version that smears them. (The consequence of the eventual public screening of that uncut version is the source of the movie's title.)

We're barely 20 minutes into the movie and already we've got some heady stuff going on—the rest of the movie has a lot to live up to. But one thing should be obvious already—this isn't a strict remake of *The Cameraman*.

What connects it most strongly to *The Cameraman* is Keaton himself, who worked on *Too Hot to Handle* as a gagman. However, we aren't entirely sure what parts Keaton shaped or not. Educated guesswork is all we have. Complicating the matter is that even though Buster was just a lowly uncredited MGM gagman at one the lowest points in his life, which would strongly suggest his contribution to the project would have been minor, the resulting production feels informed by Keaton on a great many levels.

For example, the complex recursions of that "rescue" footage, which shift in meaning throughout the film as the context changes. *Too Hot to Handle* could have treated its film-within-a-film aspects as a mere gimmick—but instead the cinematic nature of film is never far from view.

In 1958, Buster Keaton sat down with Christopher Bishop of *Film Quarterly*, and clarified his idea of how the tradition of silent comedy ought to have progressed into the talkie age:

Q: You felt that you could function just as well in sound?

BK: Why sure. The only thing we did in laying out our material was to deliberately look for action laughs, not dialogue laughs. That has always been my fight with the brass. There were all these writers, and all these writers could think about was funny sayings and puns.

Q: I wonder how you feel about making a sound comedy—whether they are silent comedies with music and sound effects added.

BK: I wouldn't want to do that today.... [H]ere's what I'm going to do. We go ahead and talk—put all the dialogue in the first fifteen minutes—let 'em try for little laughs as we go—but for the second fifteen minutes deliberately go for places that just don't call for dialogue. In other words, we don't go out of our way to avoid them, but it is just a natural thing that two people busy building something—there's no reason to talk, you just go ahead and build.

Setting aside the delicious irony that Keaton became one of those teams of MGM writers he so excoriated (and as one he sat around cooking up physical gags for films while his fellow gag writers thought up "funny sayings and puns"), the thing that interests us today is the fact that *Too Hot to Handle* actually follows Keaton's paradigm—it is a film that is in places a rapid-fire dialogue comedy of the screwball tradition which also comfortably lets the dialogue stop to give room to elaborately choreographed and awe-inspiring set-pieces.

This is an A-list production from MGM starring two of their top stars. Money was spilled on this thing—it is proof that MGM was willing to adopt Keaton's model. This is important to remember in terms of the debate over how silent clowns fared into the talkie age—the story is usually told of the great geniuses of silent comedy like Keaton facing unrelenting intransigence from studio brass in the 1930s, and being unable to function as physical comedians in an age dedicated to "funny sayings and puns." But the thing is, *Too Hot to Handle* isn't a slapstick comedy. It may be reminiscent in places of a Keaton comedy, contain comedy sequences invented by Keaton, and reflect Keaton's philosophy of comedy filmmaking over-all—but it isn't the kind of movie Keaton himself would ever have made. There is something else in its DNA.

If you were to go looking for this film's closest relatives, you wouldn't look among the works of Keaton and Lloyd—you'd look at screwball. The closest relatives are *His Girl Friday* and *Nothing Sacred*—films about unscrupulous journalists and the not-entirely-upstanding women they love. Well, for that matter, why stretch things? Clark Gable played a similarly roguish reporter in the movie that put screwball on the map—Frank Capra's *It Happened One Night*, the film that allegedly "invented" screwball.

Here is where we pause to note that the so-called inventor of screwball, Frank Capra, got his start at Mack Sennett making movies with Harry Langdon. Who are the other key directors of screwball? Well, there's Leo McCarey— who got his start at Hal Roach making movies with Charley Chase. Ernst Lubitsch was himself

**Clark Gable plays the rugged but unethical lead in *Too Hot to Handle* (1938), a loose remake of Keaton's *The Cameraman* (1928).**

a silent clown in two-reelers before switching over to romantic comedy.

But how much of a switch was that, really? The vast majority of silent comedies are at least nominally romantic comedies—they have a base-level plot about boy-meets-girl and then a bunch of absurd physical gags are layered on top of that. What separates slapstick from screwball isn't silence versus speech—there are silent romantic comedies in the proto-screwball mode and there are talkie-era slapstick throwbacks. What distinguishes one species from the next is the extent to which they took their respective romantic aspects seriously.

Or, put more precisely, the extent to which they took their female characters seriously.

I'm not just talking about Buster Keaton treating his female co-stars as props to be thrown around. I mean it across the board—the slapstick clowns rarely left much room for any co-stars, male or female, to compete for screen time or audience affection. Even Harold Lloyd, the most conventionally handsome of the silent clowns and a filmmaker whose movies are most overtly about boy-meets-girl, did not allow his female leads to develop meaningful personalities or characteristics. They were objects to be won, interchangeable all.

One of the few silent comedians to give priority to his costars was Charley Chase— and if he'd been allowed to have his way, his plan was to permanently bring on Thelma Todd as a co-star. Thelma Todd, mind you, was a bankable comedy star in her own right— in fact, her stardom was the reason Hal Roach refused Chase's idea. Roach wasn't keen on paying two stars to make just one set of films. In their few co-starring films, they are true co-stars—Thelma is allowed to be funny, interesting, and distinctive.

Even without Thelma Todd, Chase was atypically generous to his co-stars—at times his shorts seem more like ensemble comedies. It is therefore not coincidental that Chase survived into the talkie era unbruised by the transition. This is the point where we should be talking about Charley Chase's *Modern Love*. If we want to identify a "missing link" between slapstick and screwball, it is a better candidate than *Too Hot to Handle*—*Too Hot to Handle* was made in 1938, long after even Charlie Chaplin gave up the ghost and abandoned the old model. But *Modern Love* emerged in 1929.

*Modern Love* is a hybrid in several senses: it is a silent film retrofitted with talkie scenes, and it is a screwball romantic comedy made out of the raw stuff of slapstick. When silent comedy fans talk of Charley Chase's career, they grumble about how he never got to make a starring feature—and they can say this in flagrant denial of *Modern Love* because, to be precise, *Modern Love* is not a Charley Chase vehicle—he shares the stage fully with Kathryn Crawford, just as you'd expect from a romantic comedy. It is a signpost of how Chase could have survived into the screwball era, had his life turned out differently. Wouldn't you have paid to see Charley Chase and Claudette Colbert in something (anything) directed by Preston Sturges? I know I would.

The key, though, is that in that above hypothetical the presence of Claudette Colbert is at least as important as Chase or Sturges. The screwball comedies that took over from slapstick let their female leads be as nutty, sexy, and unruly as the men. The biggest flaw of *Too Hot to Handle* is its failure to fully utilize Myrna Loy. She's capable of playing a wilder sort of woman than the script lets her—and as such, she fails to come across as a worthy adversary/love interest for the wily Clark Gable. And perhaps this is the last vestige of Buster Keaton's handiwork, still haunting the edges of the film. The stray references to *The Cameraman*, the Keatonish action set-pieces, the Keaton commitment to physical action over dialog ... and the Keaton habit of sidelining the female costars. Tut tut.

Frank Capra, Leo McCarey, Ernst Lubitsch, and the other leading lights behind the transition to screwball and romantic comedy all proved their mettle in the days of physical comedy, but they saw room for improvement. They took the existing structure—a rudimentary romantic plot on top of which sits a bunch of looney stuff—and allowed the understructure to become more fully developed. The looney stuff on top was now held up by a more substantial foundation. The fact that the looney stuff started to drift away from elaborate physical comedy into situational comedy needn't distract us—*Modern Love* and *Too Hot to Handle* can serve as examples that the slapstick traditions could be maintained within a screwball context, at least in theory.

# Why Don't You Say
# Something to Help Me?

Laurel and Hardy's first talking picture, 1929's *Unaccustomed as We Are*, may not be their best or most representative or most important or best remembered short. As such it disappears too easily into the shadows of such bigger triumphs as *The Music Box* or *Helpmates*. But on closer examination, this unpretentious little film has a lot to offer. For one thing, *Unaccustomed as We Are* happens to mark the very first time that American movie audiences had ever heard *any* of their favorite comedians speak on screen.

Charley Chase was a close second with *The Big Squawk* later the same month, the Marx Brothers had *The Cocoanuts* in theaters by the summer of 1929. Harry Langdon's *Hotter Than Hot* followed soon thereafter, and Harold Lloyd reshot *Welcome Danger* as a talkie for release in the fall. Buster Keaton and W.C. Fields started talking onscreen the following year. Charlie Chaplin didn't make any onscreen vocalization until *Modern Times* in 1936.

It is of course obvious that sound replaced silent film generally. With the exception of the odd experimental film or gimmick, silent films are no longer manufactured. Several factors are said to be at fault. Some performers had developed screen personalities that were at odds with their actual speaking voices. Some filmmakers were accustomed to giving directions to their cast while shooting, shaping performances as the camera rolled—or in other cases, playing music on the set to establish a rhythm or mood. Such techniques had to be aborted when microphones were present. For that matter, those microphones were notoriously finicky. Scenes had to be staged to group the actors close to the microphones, which had to be somehow hidden from the camera. In turn, the camera's own noise had to be blocked from the microphones by some kind of baffling apparatus. The result was an imposition of stodgy, stagy film techniques. Where cameras had once roamed according to the whims of the directors, they were now slaved to the limitations of the sound recording equipment. All-new studios had to be built to the needs of the new technology, at a time when the stock market was crashing and America was entering the worst economic crisis of its existence. The investment in sound was therefore precious, and to protect that investment the studio heads were reluctant to wait while silent filmmakers adapted. Instead they brought in staff from Broadway and the stage, and subordinated the silent era technicians to these new arrivals who "knew" how to handle dialogue. The aesthetics of sound film shifted in order to emphasize the new attribute: films came to prioritize talk and song. The likes of Buster Keaton and Charlie Chaplin and Harold Lloyd had been kings of a particular environment. Sound completely changed the production environment, aesthetics, and economics of their business. Like dinosaurs facing the havoc wrought by a crashing asteroid, they had to adapt or die.

At least, that's how the story is usually told. When the subject of Laurel and Hardy's transition to sound comes up, it is excused as an anomaly—the exception that proves the rule.

As it happens, Laurel and Hardy made the transition to sound handily. The reduced production schedule of short comedies meant it was far easier for the makers of shorts to change over than it was for comedians working in features. On May 4, 1929, American audiences enjoyed the opening day of the Laurel and Hardy two-reel short *Unaccustomed as We Are*.

Originally, it was to have been titled "Their Last Word," an ironic defiance of the fact that these are their *first* words. From the beginning, no special pride of place is given to their first words. You can imagine the publicity guys at Hal Roach Studios desperate to bill this as "Laurel and Hardy SPEAK!" but when the moment comes the boys get no privileged entrance. The film fades up on the hallway of an apartment building as Stan and Ollie stride into the frame in the middle of a conversation. It is as is they have always been talking.

**Stan Laurel (left) and Oliver Hardy (as seen in the 1933 short *Busy Bodies*).**

Ollie looks like a man who's enjoyed many a meal, and the words he uses are rapturous, almost lustful, as he describes his wife's cooking. Stan listens to all of this, but his mouth isn't watering yet. "*Any nuts?*" he wants to know. Ollie's build up is deflated, and not for the last time.

Ollie stops in the hallway to exchange pleasantries with his neighbor Thelma Todd. Their conversation is immediately derailed by their mutual insistence on formality. Ollie can't just ask how her husband is; he has to ask, "*And how is Mr. Kennedy, Mrs. Kennedy?*" Thelma's responses are every bit as ridiculously mannered: "*Oh, he's very well, thank you, Mr. Hardy.*" After what feels like an eternity of this, Ollie notes to Stan, "*That was Mrs. Kennedy.*" Stan's bewildering response—"*I was wondering who it was.*"

Ollie is concerned with social propriety, to the extent that he often misses how far out of alignment appearances can get from reality. Stan, too simple-minded to be under any illusions, is the one to break the spell. Ollie can't have a normal conversation with Thelma, because he's so distracted by formalities that he has no mental energy left to think of anything worth saying. He introduces "Mrs. Kennedy" to Stan because that's what etiquette demands in such a situation—and is then annoyed to learn that Stan actually needed that tidbit of information. Ollie is satisfied by the surface of things—and this is his downfall, every time.

It is not an especially good joke, but it is a kind of joke they had never before been able to do. Stan and Ollie have punctured social graces throughout their silent films, but did so by tearing buildings to their foundations or dragging live horses into the middle of tony mansions. Now they can work on a smaller scale.

They are now at Ollie's door. Inside, he promises, is the sweetest girl Stan could ever hope to meet. To hear Oliver describe her, she must be the very definition of American femininity. Ollie calls to her in a sickly-sweet coo: "*Yoooo-hooo.*" From off camera comes the growling reply of some rabid animal: "*Whaddya mean, yoo-hoo?*"

It is a priceless moment. Mae Busch's bleating delivery of the line sells the gag beautifully. She looks like Barbara Stanwyck but has the temperament of Jimmy Cagney. She's the sort of dame you wouldn't want to meet in a dark alley. She storms onto screen with a look of fury so intense it's a wonder Oliver doesn't burst into flames on the spot.

We understand Stan's befuddlement at the turn of things ("*Are we in the right apartment?*") but the real joke is in Oliver's confusion. How could Oliver live with this woman, day in and day out, and have described her the way he did? How could he have honestly expected any other response from her than the torrent of abuse she starts to spew upon sight of Stan? Somewhere in his mind, Oliver Hardy has constructed the world he believes he ought to live in. It's a place where his best friend is a competent and trustworthy figure, his wife is a loving and supportive partner, and he comports himself as if these things were true, despite all the evidence to the contrary.

Oliver and Mae are screaming at each other now, with Stan looking vaguely awkward beside them. He clearly hasn't figured out that they are arguing about him, and is embarrassed for his friend to have such a private spat in front of him. With both performers screaming, the dialogue is completely obscured. It is as confident a moment as Ollie's initial appearance, walking into the frame in mid-sentence. This is a film specifically designed as a vehicle for Laurel and Hardy to talk, and they are willing to let that descend into inchoate noise.

During the row, Ollie absent-mindedly turns on the record player, and Mae equally absent-mindedly finds her rant settling into the rhythm established by the music. Once she realizes how silly she sounds, more or less "singing" to the backing track, her fury burns even hotter and she storms out. We are barely five minutes into the film, and Laurel and Hardy have shown themselves to be supremely comfortable with the new medium.

Hal Roach had a separate print of *Unaccustomed as We Are* prepared for those markets that were not yet equipped for sound. This alternate silent version of the film is exactly the same footage, but with the soundtrack removed and title cards inserted where necessary to make sense of it. The silent version of the film quickly becomes mired in intrusive title cards that disrupt the flow of the action and fail to serve the jokes. For example, Stan's line "*Will there be any nuts?*" is funnier when it actually punctuates and punctures the full description of the upcoming banquet. The abbreviated description offered by the title card is an inadequate set up to the punchline. Similarly, Stan's improbable reaction to the endless "*How are you, Mrs. Kennedy?*" routine is diminished when it is cut back to a mere handful of cards—which are themselves more of an interruption than a joke.

However, writer Bernie Walker and director Lewis Foster are in a jam. If they don't interrupt the scene with title cards, they are left with a lengthy sequence of Laurel and Hardy standing in a hallway without any interesting action. The *only* jokes here are verbal. In theory, you could start the film at the moment that they enter the Hardy's apartment, but that would remove the introduction of Thelma Todd, a vital character to the remainder of the plot. Almost immediately after Mrs. Hardy storms out, the plot has contrived to have Thelma end up in Ollie's apartment, virtually nude, and hunted by her ruthlessly jealous husband—*this* is what the film is really about. Short of reshooting the opening sequence entirely, the silent version has no choice but to surrender to an awkward and unsatisfying approach.

Laurel and Hardy's first talkie is confidently and completely constructed as a talkie. It isn't a silent film with dialogue added; removing the dialogue diminishes it. Far from robbing them of their power as comedians, the addition of sound has given them a new dimension with which to make their jokes. They even make the first utterance of a line that would become a running gag and trademark: "*Why don't you do something to help me?*"

Prior to seeing *Unaccustomed as We Are*, it is hard to imagine what voices audiences may have imagined belonged to these two characters. Laurel and Hardy had experimented successfully with a few domestic comedies in the style of *Unaccustomed as We Are—Their Purple Moment, Should Married Men Go Home, We Faw Down*, and *That's My Wife*—but most of their silent shorts find the boys as rough, down and out figures. They are escaped convicts (twice!), hard laborers, unemployed vagrants, sailors, street musicians, boxers.... When we finally hear them speak, it is with a surprising hint of erudition and gentility. Oliver Hardy speaks with a soft Southern accent—not a twangy drawl, but a gentle lilt atop a deep, honeyed voice. Stan Laurel has a British accent (he hailed from the same place as Charlie Chaplin and came through the same career channels). Rightly or wrongly, an accent like Stan's has been associated with education and sophistication. These two men speak with voices that seem utterly at odds with their physical rowdiness and mental ineptitude. However, this is no *Singin' in the Rain*-style scenario where their misfit voices undermined their characters. Instead, it is essential to the joke. These voices imply a certain pretension, a reach for social grace that we also find in Ollie's awkward formality and misapplied etiquette. These voices belong to men who want to think of themselves as gentlemen.

The Three Stooges made their prolific career in much the same comic milieu as Laurel and Hardy. Several Stooges shorts are outright remakes of Laurel and Hardy films. Yet there was a crucial difference in personality. A typical Stooge gag went like this: the three of them have devolved into mayhem, and some figure of authority or social superiority tries to get their attention by calling, "*Gentlemen! Gentlemen!*" The Stooges look around in confusion, wondering who the poor chap might be talking to. Laurel and Hardy would never make such a joke—no matter how decrepit their circumstances, they always just assumed they *were* gentlemen. As with everything else, Oliver Hardy happily glossed over any discrepancy between the world he wanted to live in and the one he actually did.

Sound did not kill Laurel and Hardy's career—if anything it propelled them to new comic heights. They continued making films together until 1951, without much changing their act along the way.

# Harold Lloyd 101

Even if you've never seen his films, you've seen him dangling from a clock face a dozen stories high. That image, from the climax of Harold Lloyd's 1923 feature comedy *Safety Last!*, is arguably the most iconic of the entire silent era.

Lloyd's character could climb tall buildings with his bare hands—but Lloyd the film-maker climbed Hollywood. Barely five years after arriving in Los Angeles, Lloyd had rock-eted from a penniless nobody to becoming one of the most popular and beloved screen comedians of all time. That famous image is just one relic of his legacy, one marker among many of Lloyd's impressive reach.

Ironically, Lloyd wasn't all that keen on being remembered as a "thrill comedian," which was only one facet of a long and illustrious career. He was that, true, but also a striver, an optimist, a winner, who sometimes stumbled haphazardly into unexpected suc-cess—in short, much like his screen persona.

Lloyd's original ambition was to become a serious actor. Lurking about studio lots, taking low-paying jobs as a movie extra, Lloyd met fellow aspirant Hal Roach. They shared the same frustration at struggling in Hollywood's margins, the same dreams of making it big in show biz, the same entrepreneurial drive. And they shared a realization: In those ramshackle early days of movies, a clever person with nothing to lose might as well make their own opportunities rather than wait to be discovered. Together they would make movies—once Roach had learned directing at Essanay and Lloyd had been seasoned at Mack Sennett's Keystone factory.

Roach cobbled together the resources necessary to produce and distribute a series of one-reel comedy shorts starring Harold Lloyd. But Lloyd was no fool—if everything else about their venture was the personification of insane risk, the only sensible thing to do was to make as commercial a product as they could manage. So he stuck close to the Keystone formula, and played a Charlie Chaplin knock-off called Lonesome Luke.

To their surprised relief, audiences loved Luke—enough to pay the bills and keep the lights on, at least. But as their enterprise stabilized, Lloyd's creative energies yearned for something more challenging and personal than the Chaplin-alike Lonesome Luke. Both Lloyd and Roach felt they could compete with Keystone slapstick by offering a very different aesthetic, grounded in everyday reality and domestic concerns. Lloyd was a conventionally handsome leading man; if he took off the comedy mustache and abandoned the self-consciously zany costume, he could play Everyman. The only trick was how to trademark that Everyman, how to turn himself into a marketable brand.

In 1917, Lloyd experimented with wearing a pair of wide-rimmed glasses. Nothing more to it than that. He put on a pair of glasses and played his role straight. Instead of a comic grotesque making jokes out of his inability to function in normal society, Lloyd inverted the formula: He would play an ordinary fellow, thrust by circumstance into out-landish situations. Lloyd's comedies piled thrills upon thrills, chases upon chases, going as big and as absurd as physically possible while keeping the mayhem rooted in everyday reality.

Exactly who came up with the glasses, and when, is the subject of enduring contro-versy—everybody wants a piece of success. And success it was—even in faraway Imperial Japan, Lloyd fandom took hold and "Roido" style glasses became the height of fashion ("Roido" being more or less what "Lloyd" sounds like spoken in Japanese). He was making cheap-jack one-reel programmers for an undercapitalized start-up, but he was becoming a household name.

In 1919, Lloyd and Roach made the crucial transition away from one-reelers to the more prestigious and profitable world of two-reel shorts. The inaugural two-reeler was

*Bumping into Broadway*. Lloyd and his team started assembling the promotional campaign to publicize this new series of comedies, starting with *Bumping into Broadway*. It was a propitious moment: Although the most famous image of Harold Lloyd would be that frame from *Safety Last!*, the most important photograph ever taken of Lloyd would be one taken to promote *Bumping into Broadway*—and this photograph would never be seen.

The photographer asked Harold to pose with a prop bomb, one of those cartoony round black anarchist's balls with a sparkling fuse, and pretend he was using it to light a cigarette. Thanks to a terrible mix-up, the "prop" bomb held real explosives. The fuse ran out, it blew up, and Lloyd awoke in the hospital—blind, his face scarred, and his right hand a mangled snarl of flesh.

Roach assumed he had just lost his star, and by extension his studio. But like the indomitable young upstart he played on screen, Lloyd was not easily stopped. He recovered. He regained his sight, his face healed, and he took to wearing a trim pair of white gloves, to hide his prosthetic fingers (it would be hard to get audiences to laugh at his outrageous stunts if they had reason to believe there were serious consequences). Only his closest friends and coworkers knew the secret.

Harold Lloyd returned to work, and continued crafting elaborate stunt-filled spectaculars that were as breath-taking as they were funny. Following an amicable split with Roach,

**Harold Lloyd gives himself a pep talk in *The Freshman* (1925).**

Lloyd established his own studio, and maintained ownership of his films—which were plentiful: He was more prolific than Chaplin and Keaton combined. Harold Lloyd is credited with inventing the preview system, recutting and reshooting films based on audience reactions to test screenings. Lloyd also embraced the coming of talkies, and was the first major comedian to start working in sound.

Despite his enthusiasm for talkies, Lloyd's sound comedies were not as popular as his silents. Unlike his peers, he could not blame the bumpy transition on studio interference or problems with his speaking voice. It has been suggested that the problem was simply that his role as an earnest go-getter was out of step with Depression-era attitudes. Whatever the reason, Lloyd sensed something was off, and retreated from the spotlight following the disastrous 1938 flop *Professor Beware*. A real bomb couldn't slow him down, but a figurative bomb ended his career.

Except that's not quite true. In 1941, Lloyd produced one of Lucille Ball's earliest comedies, *A Girl, a Guy, and a Gob*, and collaborated with Preston Sturges on 1947's *The Sin of Harold Diddlebock*. And he took control of his back catalog, buying up the rights to his movies. In 1962 and 1963 he produced a set of retrospectives of his own work, assembling clips of his "greatest hits" into the showreel features *Harold Lloyd's Harold Lloyd's World of Comedy* and *The Funny Side of Life*.

Other comedians of his generation had faded into obscurity or struggled to remain relevant. Lloyd could look back on a prolific and prodigious body of work. He succumbed to cancer in 1971, but never really left. The Harold Lloyd Trust has maintained his back catalogue and kept his classics in circulation to thrill new generations.

The films made before *Bumping into Broadway*, however, were left to vanish. There was something about that exploding bomb that seemed to cleave his personal history cleanly in two: On the one side were the films he embraced, curated, and bequeathed to posterity; on the other were the vestiges of the Lloyd before Lloyd—his Chaplin copies, his pre-glasses films, his hardscrabble one-reelers. Lloyd left these behind and never looked back. Even if he'd showed an interest, they were out of copyright, and widely believed to have burned to ash long ago. Richard Schickel's major biography of Lloyd in 1971 claimed that even identifying the titles of all those pre–1919 Lloyd films was beyond hope.

Let me direct your attention once again to the man dangling from the clock. Look at him—he's holding onto the hands of time, he's literally turning back the clock. Many of those movies once lost have been found. What didn't exist in 1971 has now been returned to us. Harold Lloyd can cavort on our screens as if time means nothing. But here's the deal: it's not enough for us to know Harold Lloyd. We gotta spread the word. Each one teach one, as the saying goes. If you ever find yourself answering the question, "Who's Harold Lloyd?," here are some talking points.

## He Was the Everyman Comedian

Silent slapstick was overrun by the Funny Mustache Brigade. But in a field crowded by buffoons in awkward costumes and silly facial hair, Harold Lloyd skipped the grotesqueries to focus on playing an ordinary, boyishly-handsome fellow. His one nod to the prevailing style was a set of tortoise-shell glasses—to brand his image and create a recognizable silhouette, but one that was real-looking. And his persona followed the image—an ordinary young man of recognizable ambitions.

Consider an early scene from the feature *Speedy*. Harold (temporarily) has a (fake) house with a wife and a dog. A comfortable middle-class idyll. In reality, the kid is dirt-poor ex-soda-jerk, hitching a ride on the back of a passing furniture van with his sweetie after a day at Coney Island. But for a moment his dreams are tangible, and we connect— his dreams are our dreams.

In the 1960s, a new generation of slapstick fans found Lloyd's middle-class aspirations to be troublingly conservative, and downgraded him in favor of the vagabond hero Charlie Chaplin or the Kafka-esque existentialism of Buster Keaton—better suited to the counter-cultural sensitivities of the day. But time marches on, and maybe today's audiences are ready to sympathize with Harold's ambitions.

## He Gave Good Chase

Lloyd's films often revolve around chases, and as his canvas expanded from one reel to two, from two to five, from five to 10, his chases grew more ambitious.

Consider a climactic scene from the feature *Girl Shy*. The clock is ticking and our hero has to get to the church in time to stop his sweetie from marrying a bigamist. The massive, sprawling, epic chase includes a terrific moment when Harold's car is stopped on a winding mountain road by a junker running the opposite direction. Unable to get around the blocking vehicle, and unable to convince the other driver to back up, Lloyd simply trades cars(!) and drives off (in reverse) in the junk car as the flummoxed other driver realizes how much he has traded up. Problem solved.

## Thrill Comedy

A fair bit of Harold's comedy isn't jokes per se, but absurd, farcical situations contrived to provoke death-defying stunts. These stunts tend to elicit gasps, or shrieks, more than laughs.

South California is full of steep hills—some of them can produce optical illusions of you frame them just right. Lloyd started playing with this effect, setting up perfectly safe situations framed against the hills in such a way as to suggest that a distant street in the valley below was actually the street below a skyscraper, turning safe heights into what the camera saw as impossibly dangerous ones. He experimented with different ways of exploiting this illusion, with various contrived reasons to get him out onto the ledge of a "skyscraper" in various short films.

In *Safety Last!* he hit upon the prefect formula to exploit the effect. It took patient plotting—spending several reels doing nothing but establishing a series of premises, assumptions, and conflicts that in the finale all lock into place to force Harold to climb a tall building with his bare hands. The soul of the movie is the climb itself, but it works because of the skillful way in which Lloyd and his gagwriters made sure the absurdity was grounded in logic (and the logic grounded in absurdity).

There are other things to celebrate about Lloyd, of course—he pioneered preview screenings! He was the first silent comedian to make a talkie feature! He shot 3-D nudes in color! But if you need to indoctrinate a newbie, just grab any of the features I mentioned here (*Speedy, Girl Shy, Safety Last!*) and you can't go wrong.

# Mustache, Glasses and Suit

Most histories of silent comedy tend to focus on two major turning points in the lives of each of the major slapstick comedians: (a) the moment when they transitioned out of two-reel shorts and into features, and (b) the moment they transitioned out of silent films and into talkies. Our understanding of Chaplin and Keaton has largely drawn from how they navigated these crucial turning points. But in the case of Harold Lloyd, there are actually two major artistic turning points that eclipse those more familiar ones, but which have been largely ignored by history. As it happened, Harold Lloyd handled the leap to features and then to talkies fairly effortlessly. He'd already taken his knocks long ago. If we want to grapple with Lloyd's artistic evolution, the real things to pay attention to are a) when he stopped playing Lonesome Luke and put on his trademark glasses instead, and b) when he transitioned from one-reel shorts to two. The only problem is, these turning points occurred in a cycle of films that have been largely unavailable, and so even if scholars recognized that these turning points mattered hugely, they just weren't things anyone was in a position to actually comment on.

Chronology is important here, so let's start at the beginning: If you have my DVD of *American Slapstick Volume 1*, put on *A Submarine Pirate* and listen to my commentary. Wait until the bit where I say I don't think Harold Lloyd is even in the movie, then pause it and look at the cook in the background: that's Harold Lloyd (it wasn't my finest moment in the history of audio commentaries).

Before Harold Lloyd became one of the country's most beloved comedy stars, he was a struggling actor living hand to mouth in the margins of Hollywood. He found work with legendary comedy producer Mack Sennett as a bit player, where he quickly distinguished himself as something other than a mere upright actor. In case you don't know the special lingo, at Sennett's lot, actors were cataloged by their abilities with slapstick action and stunts. Some actors were just "stand-up actors," but the valuable ones could do things like "Brodies" (a particular kind of fall named for a man who leapt off the Brooklyn Bridge), or "108s" (a fall preceded by a leap). Lloyd was a Brodie master and an adept 108-man, which made him especially useful. In 1915 he got the rare chance to show his stuff in a Sennett film. *Courthouse Crooks* concerns the villainous machinations of leading man Ford Sterling and his attempts to hide his affair with the judge's wife, Minta Durfee. Along the way, Lloyd gets framed for stealing a necklace. On the run for a crime he didn't commit, Lloyd takes flight in a chase scene that dominates the middle stretch of the film and shows what Lloyd would be capable of, as soon as he was in the starring role.

If that augured a new place for Lloyd on the Keystone lot, it was too late: he and Hal Roach decamped to start their own company, Rolin. But since the startup venture was undercapitalized and fraught with financial risk, Harold had the good sense to take few creative risks.

This is where the Lonesome Luke era starts—a cycle of 62 one-reel shorts Lloyd made between 1915 and 1917. In Lloyd's own description, the Luke character was designed to riff on Chaplin: "The cunning thought behind all this was to reverse the Chaplin outfit. All his clothes were too large. Mine were going to be too small. My shoes were funny but different. My mustache was funny but different, as well. Despite the fact that my costume was a direct reversal of Chaplin's, it was purely imitative."

With so little of the Luke era available for viewing, this is the part that commentators latched onto to have something to say about it. When Tom Dardis wrote Lloyd's biography in 1983, at that time only four Luke films were known to survive. But what everyone "knew" about them were that they were Chaplin imitations.

Which is sort of true. Thirty years after Dardis made his count, we now know 14 Luke films to have survived (at least that's the current count as I write this). I've only seen a handful (*Luke Joins the Navy*, *Luke's Movie Muddle*, and *Lonesome Luke, Messenger*) but what I see in them is mostly consistent with the way they've been described.

Take *Lonesome Luke, Messenger* for example. Luke wants to finagle his way into a girls' boarding school by posing as an electrician. He is neither a competent electrician nor a competent bike messenger (his earlier attempt to deliver a package to the school—*which*

**Harold Lloyd (fourth from left, second row) and Hal Roach (immediately behind him in the third row) launched the Rolin Film Company in 1915.**

*was actually his job*—failed, which is what led him to grab a pile of wires and try again). The Chaplinesque elements include the costume (as noted), his laconic attitude and balletic slapstick as he swans in, towing chaos in his wake, and his status as an outsider crashing the party. But there's something missing. In film after film, Chaplin was the rambling outsider tramp, caught up in slapstick mayhem, but he tended to be able to function in these alien situations anyway. That was part of the comedy. He never failed to do things correctly—instead he succeeded at doing things he just wasn't supposed to have been doing in the first place. It's a subtle thing, and a lot of Chaplin mimics missed it.

So for all the Chaplinesque trappings around Luke, he couldn't actually do Chaplinesque comedy because Luke was designed as a failure. Here's a guy who can't even deliver a package. If this was a Chaplin film, Charlie would stagger in with fistfuls of random wires, and then somehow miraculously actually wire up the house after all. (See also Buster Keaton's *The Electric House* where that's exactly what he does.)

But within months of that film came the "glasses character." That's what all the books call it—the "glasses character." Lloyd took off the anti–Chaplin costume and put on a pair of wide-rimmed glasses and found fame and success. Except, now that we can see these early glasses films rather than just make assumptions about them, there's something else going on. In some of the earliest glasses character films like *Bashful*, *A Gasoline Wedding*, and *Take a Chance*, he didn't just put on glasses. He had a whole costume that went along with them, a fancy dress three-piece suit and top hat! He abandoned that outfit after a while, and no one's really talked about it since, but it helps mark the transition for us: although he's dressed like a rich man, that's not how the character is written. He's living hand-to-mouth, just trying to get by. In *Take a Chance*, he starts off wondering how to spend his last quarter: he can either have a meal or get a haircut. One or the other. Then he loses his quarter and can't have either. He does all this while wearing that suit.

So what we have is a character depicted as a striver, a yearner. Instead of being an outsider because of his inability to conform, he is an outsider by circumstance, struggling to get in and succeed. He's dressed for the job he wants to have (rich guy). And whenever opportunity knocks, he's prepared to go to extreme lengths to seize it. His business strategies are dishonest, he's quick to shove another out of his way to get what he wants, he's pushy—but he's endearing because he is defined in affirmative terms. He wants something. In contemporary parlance, that makes him *proactive*.

The comedy is still made up of chase scenes and Keystone-inflected knockabout. Some of these early "glasses" shorts feel like off-brand Keystone films in every detail—*Take a Chance* is a prime offender in the Let's-Rip-Off-Mack-Sennett Sweepstakes. But what changed was the underlying structure of that slapstick: he swapped out a comedy of failure for one of success, and gave the audience a character they could root for. He stepped away from the most recognizable superficial aspects of Chaplin mimicry but surreptitiously stepped closer to Chaplin's secret formula.

From 1917 to 1919 he churned through endless variations of this material, refining and improving as he went. If you watch the entire block of shorts in a row, you'll risk tiring of seeing the same gags over and over—but the obsessive focus on refinement paid off. He moved away from the top hat and tails; he abandoned the Keystone approach of simply choosing an interesting location and hoping for the best; he gradually allowed his supporting cast to stop playing grotesques and start playing realistic human beings; and he redirected the slapstick away from violence for violence's sake.

Then in 1919 he stopped making one-reel shorts, and with *Bumping into Broadway* started making two-reelers. This was a gargantuan leap for the Hal Roach Studio, which had been so ramshackle and amateur a company that managing to make two-reelers was a technical and logistical challenge they hadn't cracked for years. But the real money was in two-reelers, and if the studio was going to survive they needed to make that leap.

Eventually, Lloyd broke with Roach and started his own studio. And afterwards, he came back to his old boss and partner and negotiated to buy the rights to a package of his back catalog, to preserve and maintain. The Harold Lloyd estate has since kept care of those films and helped keep them in circulation in various media. But there was a catch: when Lloyd made that deal, he bought the rights from *Bumping into Broadway* forward. He left the one-reelers on the other side of the divide, orphaned, destined to be forgotten. Fire eventually consumed most of them, hence our lingering uncertainty over what survives.

The Harold Lloyd estate has since gone back and acquired as much of the pre–*Bumping into Broadway* material as possible. But it is very telling that Harold Lloyd made the choice he did, to orphan those older films. By 1919 he'd worked out what he was doing, and all traces of the earlier experimentation were gone. He could start from there, and present to the world a coherent back catalog of films for which he need make no excuses or explanations.

But for the scholars and fans who want to see how he became the Lloyd we know and love, those early experiments are absolutely mission critical.

# The Sin of Harold Lloyd

Alone among the great silent comics, Harold Lloyd stood at the exact intersection of slapstick and screwball, at the intersection of physical comedy and dialogue. Harold Lloyd, you see, made a film with Preston Sturges. It was neither man's greatest hour, but the mere fact of its existence is breathtaking. It's like finding Ernst Lubitsch directing Charlie Chaplin, or Blake Edwards directing Laurel and Hardy.

Let's take stock of this for a minute: we have one of the greatest physical comedians of the entire silent era, yet who is also preternaturally comfortable with the world of talkies. He is paired with a visionary of the new dialogue school of comedy, yet one who has an enduring appreciation of the values of silent comedy. They are going to collaborate as equals on a film that will be made without studio interference. If there is ever going to be a moment when the old guard of silent comedians are going to function without compromise in this new world of screwball, then there could be no better opportunity than this.

Harold Lloyd was the first feature comedian to release a talkie.[1] Lloyd yanked his already completed feature *Welcome Danger* from theaters to reshoot it with dialogue. From a contemporary viewpoint *Welcome Danger* is hardly remembered fondly in either form, but it was in its day one of Lloyd's biggest commercial hits.

Emboldened by his first success in the brave new world of sound, Lloyd followed it

**Harold Lloyd yanked his already completed feature *Welcome Danger (1929)* from theaters to reshoot it with dialogue.**

with several more talkies—including the frankly marvelous *Movie Crazy*—all of which he produced under complete artistic freedom.

Lloyd viewed these talkies with deserved pride, and when he put together his own retrospective Greatest Hits compilation film *Harold Lloyd's World of Comedy* in 1962, he mixed and matched clips from his silent classics and talkies in equal measure.

In his biography of Lloyd, Richard Schickel put forth the assertion that Lloyd had a speech defect that impaired his ability to function in sound films—but I'm unpersuaded by the evidence. What evidence even is there, you ask? This: Lloyd used a dialogue coach for a couple of days on the *Welcome Danger* set, but that's about the extent of it. If anything, Lloyd's speaking voice seemed perfectly suited to his screen persona to a degree not shared by Keaton's or Chaplin's voices.

In fact, come the early 1940s, Lloyd was performing on the radio. On the radio! A silent comedian on the radio!

None of this supports the idea that Harold Lloyd was out of place in a world ruled by talking pictures.

But … then there's Lloyd's own words, in which he complained about battling with a director regarding what Harold saw as a ruinous over-reliance on dialogue, to the exclusion of physical comedy, or "business." "He didn't want gags to come into it, he wanted this dialogue. But this called for business, and he said, 'Well, the business is too good for my dialogue ... it'll kill the dialogue.' I said, 'Let it kill the dialogue, what are we after? We're after entertainment, laughs."

Sadly, and oddly, the circumstances behind that quote are the film that brings us here today: Preston Sturges' *The Sin of Harold Diddlebock*. I'm a bit leery of citing a year for this movie—the bulk of it was shot in 1946, it was released in 1947, then pulled from theaters for re-editing and reissued in 1951 as *Mad Wednesday*.

Sturges had always shown a great predilection for slapstick pratfalls in his films, and frequently cited the influence of the great physical comedians of the preceding generation. Sturges had just completed cinema's equivalent of a homerun streak: between 1940 and 1944 he made: *The Great McGinty, Christmas in July, The Lady Eve, Sullivan's Travels, Palm Beach Story, Miracle of Morgan's Creek*, and *Hail the Conquering Hero*. The man was a visionary genius, and the output of just those four years alone is enough to cement a legend as one of filmdom's finest comic minds.

Feeling unappreciated at Paramount and tired of making some of history's greatest comedies in an atmosphere of perpetual institutional combat, he left to forge an ill-advised partnership with Howard Hughes. This was a dumb move in several respects—not least of which the fact that battling Paramount executives was a minor and prosaic annoyance compared to battling the impossible Mr. Hughes, and the fact that Preston was now obliged to create a movie studio from scratch.

As his first act under this new professional agreement, Sturges sought out Harold Lloyd and convinced him to return to the screen in a pseudo-sequel to Lloyd's silent *The Freshman*. Sturges was so firmly convinced of the unassailable rightness of this idea that he didn't even bother to negotiate a salary with Lloyd—if the aging comedian felt that his fabulous personal wealth wasn't enough and he deserved to be paid a Clark Gable–style star's ransom, that was fine by Preston. Whatever. And if he had to pay half again on top of that to secure permission to reuse footage from *The Freshman*, that too he accepted without blinking.

Furthermore, Sturges decided to afford Lloyd the same working conditions he used to enjoy on the silent films of yore: a lackadaisical production schedule that assumed large swaths of the film would be improvised or improved upon as they went.

So what went wrong?

Well, for one thing, it didn't really go all that wrong. The reputation of *The Sin of Harold Diddlebock* is more dire than is deserved—it opened to decent reviews and strong business. True, box office returns started to piffle and it played better in some regions than others. Hughes withdrew it from release to spend a couple of years tinkering with it, but that had much more to do with Hughes' egomania than any actual demerit of the film itself. And say what you will against Hughes' recut version *Mad Wednesday* (now sporting a better title, one fewer reels, and a talking horse)—it scored a Grand Prize nomination at Cannes in that form.

In fact, a fair bit of *Sin's* poor reputation these days is the fault of its wretched presentation—not since the 1940s has anyone seen this thing in the form Sturges intended in anything other than a dilapidated and run down print. I hunted down multiple copies in various film and video formats from several different countries and every one of them was the same public domain detritus.

Of course, even if someone like the Criterion Collection were to come along and polish this back up to its original glory, it would still look cheap compared to Sturges' Paramount classics. As I noted above, his partnership with Hughes was a business agreement, not an actual functioning movie studio. Whatever skills Sturges had in the screenwriting and directing departments didn't necessarily imply an administrative aptitude—in fact, he may well have had ADHD. He needed some institutional resources to back him up, and Hughes did not supply any.

On top of all that, Sturges allowed the situation to become a right mess. His carrying on with the female lead, Francis Ramsden, provoked Mrs. Sturges to file for divorce, and the ensuing litigation was an ugly distraction (the way I phrased that may have implied that Sturges took a shine to the starlet and started up an affair—in fact he took a shine to Ramsden, a model with no pretension towards being an actress, and cast her in the film as a way of keeping her close). The gradually deteriorating relationship with Hughes was another ugly distraction.

Be that as it may, that's not enough of an explanation. I've come out swinging on behalf of any number of shoddily-made films or decrepit relics of once-lost movies that have spoken deeply to me—the crummy appearance of *Sin of Harold Diddlebock* is no excuse. So let's dig into the movie and see where it works and where it doesn't.

Sturges has a history of toying with audience expectations. *Palm Beach Story* (a close contender with *The General* for the greatest comedy of all time) behaves as if it is a sequel to a non-existent film, and *Sullivan's Travels* recursively folds details of its own making into the film's plot. *Miracle of Morgan's Creek* concludes by bringing in the characters of *Great McGinty*—suddenly and unexpectedly recasting the proceedings as having taken place in that same filmic universe. So his decision to open *Sin of Harold Diddlebock* with the finale of another movie, *The Freshman*, is in some ways the next logical step.

What follows though is perhaps not the sequel we would have expected. The brash young go-getter of *The Freshman* has turned into a grey, worn-out office drone, all ambition drained of him. On his cubicle walls are vapid slogans consistent with the earnest all-American character we saw in 1925, but living a decent life doesn't seem to have paid off for him.

Now here is where it gets interesting—and where the relative approaches of Lloyd and Sturges first start to meaningfully diverge. When Harold's boss Mr. Waggleberry (Raymond Walburn) fires him, he ostensibly does so because Harold has fallen into a stale rut and allowed his former fire to die out. Later, Harold voices his belief that his boss was right to do this—that the security of a 9-to-5 job allowed him to stagnate, and only the chaos of "mad Wednesday" provided the adrenaline rush necessary to rekindle his ambition and innovative thinking.

In interviews about the film, Harold Lloyd highlighted this theme as part of what excited him about the project. Lloyd called it "a lovely story. The theme of the story—the fight against smugness which comes from security—is a very fine theme." That quote goes on to find Lloyd complaining about how the finished film came out, but my interest is in the suggestion that this is the theme of the movie. Because I am not at all sure that it is.

Sturges' films generally function by saying one thing and meaning another. In most cases, the most reasonable person's position is made to sound foolish, and the most foolish position is treated as the obvious truth. So, while it is true that Harold Diddlebock goes around saying he is a better man for being pushed into extremity, since when has a Preston Sturges hero ever been right about anything?

Reading between the lines of Waggleberry's firing of Harold, we can pick up on a few important details: He doesn't actually remember much about Harold at all, and has a habit of plucking sports stars out of their lives to give them menial entry level jobs. He makes big noises about upward mobility in his firm, but there is no evidence apart from his own self-serving statements that any of this is true. In particular, we can see that the Depression hit these people hard, and largely wiped out Harold's savings, while his wealthy boss genuinely believes they shared that sacrifice equally.

In other words, the job Diddlebock loses was an unfair system that tended to blame its victims. And now all of a sudden we're in a very different world than anything Lloyd ever created. As good as Lloyd's films are—and they are sublime—they are not what you would call ironic. He traded on shared assumptions of American values and work ethics that were exceedingly popular in the Jazz Age.

During the mid-century slapstick revival, Walter Kerr's book *The Silent Clowns* took a jaundiced eye towards Lloyd's legacy. In general, Kerr seemed suspicious of Lloyd's value system—and he critiqued Lloyd's comedies from that political perspective. In an age where the Establishment was allied with the Vietnam War and the Watergate break-in, turning fire hoses on peaceful protestors or opening fire on college students, Lloyd's conservative pro–Establishment value system rang the wrong bells.

I have to bring myself into this conversation here: when I was a kid, I was enthralled by Keaton, and to a lesser extent Chaplin. I adored Laurel and Hardy. But the only Harold Lloyd film I had access to was *Safety Last!* Until I was an adult, that was the only Lloyd film I had ever seen, and had ever had the opportunity to see. But I got a copy of Walter Kerr's book when I was a pre-teen and I memorized it. I read that thing 'til the glue failed and the pages fell out. So I internalized this critique of Lloyd from Kerr's book when that was my only exposure to the man.

Eventually the home video boom opened up my access to other Lloyd films—and the day would come that I helped restore a few myself.[2] Despite the late exposure to Harold Lloyd, I fell in love with his films. I struggled to reconcile that with this image that had been built up in my head from reading Kerr—the preconceived idea that Lloyd would feel like some reactionary thug, that my most personal values would feel attacked by his films. Nope. Looking back, I realize Kerr was influenced by the zeitgeist of his day, and probably would have felt differently had he been writing in, say, the 1990s.

But what this shows is how Lloyd's local-boy-makes-good aesthetic can potentially run aground in eras in which those values are not as widely agreed upon as in the 1920s.

The 1930s, the Depression era, was a time in which the country was full of Harold Diddlebocks—hard-working people who couldn't get ahead. People whose ambition was stunted because of outside factors. People who lost their jobs at the whims of the 1 percenters who dared claimed they all shared the same sacrifices. If Harold Lloyd's comedies lost some of their allure in the 1930s, it may have been due to this larger cultural shift more than anything else—because as we can see in Lloyd's quote about the theme of *Diddlebock* is that he didn't get the joke. Lloyd believed in the very values his films espoused (and why shouldn't he?) and missed any ironic commentary on those values. Sturges crafted a satire that subtly played off Lloyd's established persona, and Lloyd took it at face value.

Note also that the latter half of the film finds Diddlebock rampaging through Wall Street trying to threaten the mavens of high finance into running a circus that is guaranteed to lose money because admission will be free to the poor—his sales pitch, shouted at top volume while he wields a live lion, consists of "*Hello! Everybody hates bankers!*" It's not as if any of this is, y'know, subtle—but apparently as far as Lloyd was concerned, the theme was "the fight against the smugness which comes from security." Lloyd and Sturges were speaking the same words but they weren't talking the same language.

And so the movie barrels on, thundering riotously through its comedy set-pieces *as if* these incidents are meant to prove the point that risk taking is a good thing. Risk taking may well be a good thing—sure, why not?—but this film is not really making that point at all, and these comedy set-pieces are working off a different agenda anyway.

What we get in the movie are four different Harold Lloyds (or is that four different Harolds Lloyd?) The first is the "classic" model, represented by the *Freshman* footage. The fourth is his 1940s analogue—a middle-aged Harold Lloyd clambering across a skyscraper's ledges dangling from a lion. Between these bookends are two other variations on the character: the defeated office monkey we met above, and his drunken Jekyll and Hyde counterpart. Or maybe Jekyll and Hyde is the wrong reference—this is a comedy, and it's about the liberating effect of alcohol—perhaps the better reference is *The Nutty Professor*'s Buddy Love.

In one sequence, Harold is accosted by a rummy gambler, Wormy (Jimmy Conlin). Wormy starts out trying to wrestle some spare change from Harold (who just happens to have $2,000 in cash on him). It quickly turns into a battle of aphorisms, in which familiar phrases are bandied about as if they were actual arguments. Schickel's bizarre comments about Lloyd's speech impediment notwithstanding, Lloyd shows himself here to be a first rate dialogue comedian. Throughout the film he lasers in on exactly where Sturges' dialogue has its greatest punch, and then softens his delivery around it. He never oversells the jokes. Lloyd pitches every line with the right wry sensibility. Compared to the over-broad mugging of Eddie Bracken in Sturges' last couple of pictures, this is a revelation.

Inspired by the idea of helping a virgin drinker discover his inner rummy, bartender Edgar Kennedy invents a concoction he calls the Diddlebock, whose potency turns mild Harold temporarily into a Buddy Love-ish lunatic. In anticipation of *The Hangover* over 60 years later, the rest of the film consists of Harold trying to reconstruct his memories of what he did while he was drunk—and like *The Hangover*, it entailed jungle cats and life-changing decisions.

That the Diddlebocked version of Diddlebock would end up with his own personal lion with which to wreak wild havoc across Wall Street was an aspect of the film that Lloyd was reportedly wary of—but which was consistent with comic trends of the time. Less than 10 years earlier, Cary Grant and Katharine Hepburn's slapstick antics with a mountain lion made *Bringing Up Baby* one of the keystone comedy hits of its era. (That's keystone with a little k, mind you, not a capital K.)

If anything, the problem with this middle stretch of the movie is that Sturges is calling upon Lloyd to carry too much of the movie. That was the paradigm of the old silent classics, in which "hero" comics like Lloyd dominated the screen in vehicles designed to highlight their personalities. But the dialogue comedies of the 1930s and '40s, of which Sturges was a master, were built on double acts—usually a romantic couple. You could have a staid, repressed, normal like Cary Grant and a wild, uninhibited sprite like Katharine Hepburn, toss in a leopard, and let the lunatic havoc fly.

The "screwball" in screwball comedies referred to the nutty behavior that, more often than not, the *female* lead unleashed during a combative relationship with the male lead. But the pattern was flexible—in *Hail the Conquering Hero*, Eddie Bracken tries to be the reasonable wet blanket but he's pulled along into screwball antics thanks to the soldiers around him.

The problem here is that Harold Lloyd has to be both parts of the double act, the straight man and the comic. In his Diddlebock phase he wears a loud suit and a crazy hat and invades bankers' offices with a lion to tell them how much people hate bankers, and then he comes down off his alcoholic high to wonder what he's been up to.

There's a lot to like about *The Sin of Harold Diddlebock*. It is not a failure by any means—and it is due for a reappraisal. Neither is it a success. In the end, the disappointment of finding such a train wreck at the intersection of slapstick and screwball has to be tempered by understanding that the fault maybe didn't lie in the premise, but in something simpler.

Wouldn't this movie have worked a lot better if Lloyd had enjoyed a proper co-star? What if he got to do his Diddlebock routine and let somebody else play straight man to him—or better yet, since he's more entertaining as the straight man, what if you put the loud suit and the lion's leash on a pretty girl and had her lead Harold into predicament after predicament?

You know who I would have nominated as that co-star? Lucille Ball. This was 1946, a few years before her breakout on TV in *I Love Lucy*, but she was already a solid performer seasoned by working alongside the Three Stooges, The Marx Brothers, Edgar Bergen and Charlie McCarthy, and had made a truly wonderful screwball gem for director Garson Kanin called *Next Time I Marry*.

You know, it's too bad she didn't work with Harold Lloyd during this period. Because just imagine how splendid it would have been if Harold Lloyd had directed Lucille Ball in a screwball comedy in, I dunno, let's say 1941 ... wouldn't it be awesome if that turned out to be true?

# When Harold Met Lucy

Fans of Lucille Ball almost certainly are familiar with the moment in *I Love Lucy* where she recreates the "mirror routine" with guest star Harpo Marx. And even casual film buffs may have seen Lucy with all three Marx Brothers in *Room Service*. Her performance alongside the Three Stooges in *Three Little Pigskins* may disappoint viewers by wasting her comic talents in a thankless role, but it serves as yet another notch in Lucy's belt, another fixture of American comedy that she touched. She spent her early years as an under-appreciated foil to Ginger Rogers, until she started to graduate into Ginger-ish roles of her own. There she is with Edgar Bergen and Charlie McCarthy in *Look Who's Laughing*, not to mention her wonderful screwball comedy *Next Time I Marry*, directed by Garson Kanin. Late in her career she performed with Buster Keaton in a televised tribute to Stan Laurel.

But buried in Lucy's overstuffed CV is a comedy crossover rarely mentioned. Her appearances with the Marxes, the Stooges, Keaton, or Ginger—we know those. But what of the film she made with Harold Lloyd? Why is that so poorly remembered and rarely seen? This, then, is the story of when Harold met Lucy.

To be fair, Harold Lloyd's onscreen appearance in this film is limited to a title card in the opening credits, and nothing about the actual content of the more would lead anyone to think, "Gee, I betcha Harold Lloyd had a hand in this."

Lloyd had decided that his advancing age and the American public's shifting tastes were reason enough to stop making the kind of slapstick-oriented starring vehicles for which he was known. But he remained a brilliant filmmaker with a powerful business mind, so he parlayed his skills into producing films for others. He set up shop at RKO and started writing checks out of his own accounts to back a couple of features, of which *A Girl, a Guy, and a Gob* was the first.

Oh, that title. This may be the worst movie title I've ever encountered. What were they thinking? The intention seems to be to signal a love triangle—a girl (Lucy), a boy (Edmond O'Brien before he turned into a puffy mess), and a juvenile man-child in a state of arrested development (George Murphy). But the word "gob" never really staked out much of a space in American slang. I tried looking it up in a slang dictionary to see where it came from, and I couldn't identify the usage intended by this woeful title (I identified other usages–it would make a fine title for an Australian porn movie.)

The love triangle puts us in the territory of romantic comedies of the period. As a broadly defined genre, romantic comedies of the 1930s and '40s predominantly adhered to a narrow formula, perhaps best exemplified by *It Happened One Night*: nutty rich girl on the run, betrothed to a perfectly fine but dull man, gets into crazy misadventures with a commoner, and their culture-clash combat serves as high-octane romantic attraction.

They didn't all follow this template, of course, and those that hewed most closely were often self-conscious ripoffs of *It Happened One Night*. But if you sit down to a marathon of 1930s and 1940s rom-coms, be prepared for a smorgasbord of crazy heiresses, farcical shenanigans, and a lot of economic dislocation.

As a rule, screwball elevated female comedians to a position of equality if not superiority over their male costars. The vast majority of these are stories of love triangles, and the majority of those are girl-boy-boy stories rather than boy-girl-girl stories, so what we're talking about is a two-decade run of comic actresses being able to dominate the screen when paired with two male costars. But the economic subtext deserves some mention too. It is really striking just how much these films hammer on the Us-Versus-Them divide.

Hollywood had always been in the business of selling depictions of glamour to mass audiences—and it comes as no great surprise that the Great Depression imbued those depictions of glamour with unpleasant new dimensions. Audiences still wanted to see the luxury and opulence, they just now felt a new ambivalence. How Hollywood navigated that ambivalence, though, is very curious. One can imagine that there might have been a Depression-era appetite for Cinderella tales. But instead of selling fantasies about poor people plucked from their hardscrabble lives into the dreamy comfort of wealth, screwball comedies are about rich folk rescued from their dreary airless existence by the earthiness of poverty. Screwball heroes will always sacrifice money for freedom, will always choose true love over comfort.

And this brings us to *A Girl, a Guy, and a Gob*. Edmond O'Brien plays a man sentenced to a life of comfort. He was born wealthy, he has an undemanding job as the head of a ship-

**Harold Lloyd entertains British World War II evacuees on the RKO set of *A Girl, a Guy, and a Gob* (1940).**

ping company (it isn't even an interesting company to be head of!), he is engaged to an ice-cold princess, and his fiancées mother is as shrewish as they come. He has every reason to believe that his life will consist of nothing but known contours, every detail conformed to the socially expected norms. No day will surprise him, the future is a known quantity.

Then here comes Lucy, and with her, a whirlwind of chaos and nonsense. She brings joy and life into the dreary life of a rich boy. No wonder he falls for her.

There's a third wheel in this love triangle, but before we meet him, a few words about the role Lucille Ball plays here. She is the focal point of slapstick antics, but not really the instigator of them. Aside from a klutzy fall off a step ladder in one scene, there's little of the Lucy we would come to know from TV. (If you're looking for an early Lucy flick full of crazy antics, seek out *Next Time I Marry*.)

With the slapstick largely the province of her supporting cast, Lucille Ball instead takes over a leading role much closer to the kind of role that Ginger Rogers might take, were this a bigger budgeted and more prestigious picture. She's a shopworn angel, buffeted by life but not beaten down. Unlike O'Brien's character, her world is one of unknowns and risk. She has no reason to believe the future will be bright—might as well live for today and hope for the best. They would make each other so happy.

But there's that third person, the "gob." George Murphy plays a wayward soul with a wandering eye. He loves Lucy and she loves him, but he is chronically incapable of making the kind of responsible choices one would need to be able to settle down. Any kind of future with him will be nothing but trouble.

So we have our triangle: the man she should be with versus the man she ought to be with, or vice versa. The choice is between the wrong mate, who comes from her world, and the right one, who does not. Clearly she should end up with O'Brien—every muscle in this picture is straining towards that goal—but that finale will have nothing to do with rescuing Lucy from a life of chaos, but rather about bringing O'Brien into that chaos. The point of the story is about saving *him*.

That being said, O'Brien doesn't have the chops to carry the picture. It may be his character arc driving the plot, but the movie is at its most interesting when Lucille Ball is on screen. Ball was an amazingly physical comedian, but not in the sense of being a wrecking ball prop for big slapstick set pieces. Harold Lloyd was a physical comedian, and he literally climbed walls. Lucy's physicality is much more intimate. She uses every aspect of her physicality—her eyes, her posture, her body language, inflections in her voice—to convey the maximum amount of information in any given scene. She is playing an entirely different game from her costars, and shows them up so thoroughly it's astonishing how long she languished in B-movies before ultimately deciding to take matters into her own hands and turning herself into a star. This movie comes so very close to being a Lucille Ball vehicle, but stops short—because to be a Lucille Ball vehicle people would need to be coming to the theater to see her, and she wasn't yet at that level of stardom.

The pieces are close, though. The film is attributed to several writers, one of whom was Bert Granet, who wrote an earlier Lucy flick, *Go Chase Yourself* and would return to Lucy's orbit years later as producer of *The Lucy-Desi Comedy Hour*. The other top billed writer was Grover Jones, who wrote *Trouble in Paradise* for Ernst Lubitsch and *The Milky Way* for Harold Lloyd. The director was Richard Wallace, a veteran of comedy shorts for Mack Sennett and Hal Roach who had previously directed Stan Laurel and Clyde Cook, and would go on to make romantic comedies written by Nora Ephron's parents, Henry and Phoebe.

In other words, the production team here were experienced hands at comedy, steeped in both the slapstick and screwball traditions, and both Lloyd's past sensibility and Ball's future one were well represented. I am not stretching the facts to call this a Harold Lloyd/Lucille Ball crossover, that properly belongs to the screwball tradition. Strangely, though, the result is hard to recognize as a Harold Lloyd picture.

Take for example the finale. Lucy's two suitors chase each other across the city—but let's look at how this sequence is actually staged. Both men love her; she loves them both. In *Design for Living*, Ernst Lubitsch got away with letting the girl go home with *both* her suitors at once, but only Ernie had the gall to try to promote three-ways to mainstream audiences. We know Lucy will end up with just one of these men, and there's no real doubt which one it will be. The drama is in seeing how we get to that conclusion.

Earlier on, Lucy advised O'Brien that women respond to forceful displays of love. But Chekov would be disappointed, this is one gun that never gets fired: you'll grow old waiting for O'Brien to pull that caveman stuff on Lucy. He has too much admiration and friendship for Murphy, and too much respect for Lucy to do anything to bust up her relationship.

Recognizing that his rival won't make a move towards Lucy as long as he's in the picture, and realizing that he's not marriage material, Murphy takes a runner—hoping to precipitate the Happily Ever After ending that everyone's been waiting for. But O'Brien is too noble to take advantage of the situation, and goes chasing after Murphy to reunite him with Lucy.

And so the chase. The dramatic and comic tension of the sequence lies in the complicated emotions of these two men, how both are driven to an act of self-sacrifice in the name of the woman they love. The rushing through traffic is the circumstance surrounding a scene that is about something else.

Aaaaand that chase is filmed using an astonishing number off process shots and other "cheats." The conventional reading of *Sin of Harold Diddlebock* is that Lloyd's daredevil sequence on the skyscraper ledge was a pale shadow of his thrill comedy work in the likes of *Safety Last!*, that Lloyd had been compromised by Sturges' decision to film that stunt sequence in front of back projection and process screens, that Lloyd did his best work when he did his stunts "for real."

This is of course supremely silly. Lloyd had always relied on trickery for his stunts—he was missing most of the fingers of his right hand, and he was no fool. He'd figured out how to exploit an optical illusion created by Hollywood's steep hills in order to create a forced perspective suggesting great height. Once, on a promotional tour, Lloyd arrived in a town to discover to his chagrin that the local authorities had evidently promised to the crowd that the famous comedian Harold Lloyd was going to show up and climb one of their buildings! Lloyd had to sheepishly explain that just because you see him do it on film doesn't mean it really happened.

And here, at the climax of *A Girl, a Guy, and a Gob*, the big thrill sequence is all process shots and fast cuts. Lloyd is the producer here, answerable to no one, and if he wanted to shoot any of these stunts with greater verisimilitude, no one was there to tell him no.

This is just a footnote in Harold Lloyd's career. It would be foolish to argue otherwise. That this is such an obscurity in Lucille Ball's history is harder to explain, and touches on the great mystery of Lucy. For approximately 15 years, she waited in Hollywood while her talents were underused. She moved up the ladder from being wasted in supporting roles to being wasted in leading roles, but then progressed no farther. Around the time this film was made, RKO executives commissioned a survey of their various prospects. The research on Ball came back with grim news: scarcely half the audience even recognized her name at all, she was considered unlikely to ever be a star.

When Lucy and Desi Arnaz pitched their idea for a sitcom, CBS brass and advertising representatives alike resisted it. *I Love Lucy* only got made because Lucy and her husband invested their own money and did it themselves—a move which gave them ownership and creative autonomy.

For 15 years, Hollywood's producers and talent scouts had Lucy's extraordinary talent sitting right in front of them. It doesn't take any special faculty to be able to watch something like *A Girl, a Guy, and a Gob* and see that this woman is operating on a whole different level than any of her costars. But not once during all this time did anyone rush in to sign her up and give her a better platform.

That's why these early RKO films play such a minor role in any biography of Ball, why even her fans rarely speak of them. Films like this are residue of a complete professional dead end. When the time came, she had to make things happen for herself.

It has been said that two-reel theatrical shorts were a superior venue for comedy than long form features because the 20-minute running time more closely matched the average length of a vaudeville set. I have to take that on faith—I've never met anyone who actually saw vaudeville first hand. But it is striking how the world of two-reel shorts leads into television sitcoms. Roughly 20 minutes or so of entertainment, plus commercials, fits a TV half hour slot. Laurel and Hardy and the Three Stooges both saw their theatrical two-reelers repurposed as television "episodes."

And how did Lucy fill that half hour slot? With venerable comedy routines like "Slowly I Turned" and the mirror gag, with the stuff of slapstick. Lucy repackaged the form and content of slapstick for a new generation, but with a crucial adjustment. Much of silent slapstick had trended towards the epic misadventures of extraordinary men. Lucy scaled everything down for television, and pitched her slapstick not as the extraordinary but as the quotidian. Lucy was an exaggerated version of a person you may already know, or be.

# Lucy vs. Lucille Ball

Arguably Lucille Ball's most characteristic screen appearances was in the underrated screwball gem *Next Time I Marry*. This fun B-movie is a thinly-disguised knock-off of *It Happened One Night*, directed by the great Garson Kanin. There's no good excuse for this treasure to be so little known. Admittedly, the parallels to *It Happened One Night* are easy enough to catalog: a screwy heiress on the run, trying to engineer her wedding to a smarmy European count against her family's opposition; she spends the film on a cross-country road trip with an earthy American man, as their shared adventures spark a genuine romance between them. Some moments come so close as to be near clones: a hitch-hiking gag, a camping scene, the bride takes a runner during her own wedding, etc., etc.

Lucille Ball makes a ditzier and more energetic lead than Claudette Colbert did—she seems less interested in being glamorous and loved, and simply throws herself fully into being funny. I haven't seen every one of Lucy's films, so I'm hesitant to throw out superlatives like "the best" this or "the first" that, but I'd be surprised if there were many movies that come as close as this does to rivaling her *I Love Lucy* excesses. Throughout the film she concocts hair-brained, poorly-thought-out schemes that inevitably backfire on her, provoking increasingly frantic yelps and cries. That she also spends most of the film locked in a trailer doing combat with her "husband" also invokes fond memories of *The Long Long Trailer*. But listing the ways in which this film resembles other works of popular culture grossly undersells its charms, and largely misses the point. Sure, this is a brazen attempt to cash in on the success of *It Happened One Night*, but what makes it work so well aren't the similarities but the idiosyncratic differences.

The crux of the plot is the inheritance of socialite Nancy Crocker Fleming (Lucille Ball): her father has encumbered her wealth with the proviso that she must marry an ordinary American, so as to protect her from the clutches of gold-diggers like Count Georgi (Lee Bowman). Lucy's great scheme to circumvent this problem is to go marry some schmuck (she finds one at a ditch-digging project and pays him to marry her), then she can scurry off to Reno to divorce him and marry the Count with all her money intact.

The problem is that the schmuck she cons into marrying her, Anthony J. Anthony (James Ellison, trying very hard to be Joel McCrea) didn't do it for the money. He didn't do it for love either—he sees Lucy for the scatterbrained human tornado she is right away. He did it to buy his freedom—Lucy offers him $1,000, but he bargains her down to $793 because that's what he needs for a specific purpose (I won't say what that is—that'd be a spoiler, and some of the film turns on Lucy's attempts to figure out what that money is needed for). So, in a sense, he did do it for money—but he's not a gold-digger, and he has his pride. When Lucy tells the press that he was just a Cinderella Man trying to get at her money, James Ellison decides to race to Reno first to divorce her and prove his point.

At this point the film jumps into some new territory unlike that of any comparable *It Happened One Night*-alike. As Lucy and James race each other to Reno (with the Count in hot pursuit), the clichés of chase movies start to fall apart. The antagonists camp together, take their meals together, and plot their next moves in tandem—and then when the sun rises they get right back to chasing each other! It's like those *Looney Tunes* cartoons in which the sheepdog and the wolf socialize during their off-hours, and return to comic antagonism only when on the clock.

*Next Time I Marry* is almost half as long as *It Happened One Night*, yet is packed with something like twice as many comic incidents and set pieces. For a low-budget B-quickie, it's very handsomely appointed: Garson Kanin ponied up for some expensive special effects and some dicey stunts, and keeps the whole thing zippy and refreshing.

The one place where you might see the low budget evident is in the cast. There's Lucy, natch, and an underused but nevertheless brilliant Mantan Moreland (whose increasingly exasperated reactions to the Count are fantastic—the guy had expert comic timing, and was routinely wasted in racist supporting roles). Granville Bates plays Lucy's guardian, in a role that was seemingly written with a Charles Coburn or a Walter Connolly in mind. As noted above, James Ellison tries his mightiest to channel Joel McCrea, and Warren William would have brought even more greasiness to the role of the Count. But all I'm really doing there is just listing better known actors who would have done exactly the same thing—there's no knocking the solid work of Granville Bates, James Ellison, or Lee Bowman here, whose only failing is not being more famous. Why do you even need a more famous supporting cast when you have Lucy in the lead? What more do you need?

Which brings us to the central question in all of this: how could a movie this good, so thoroughly in tune with its zeitgeist and with the pedigree of Lucy and Garson Kanin, be so little known?

In James Harvey's exhaustive, loving survey of *Romantic Comedies in Hollywood*, he never even mentions this movie. William K. Everson's *Hollywood Bedlam* devotes a whole chapter to knock-offs of *It Happened One Night*, and skips this entirely—he even stops to do a tour of Lucille Ball's screwballs, and even there he misses it. Even weirder, biography after biography of Lucille Ball herself manage to mention this only in passing, if at all. What gives?

Ironically, the answer lies in Lucy's fame. This movie was eclipsed by the fame of its star, believe it or not.

Some years ago I took a trip through wine country in California, and we made a point of stopping at the Raymond Burr Winery. I didn't expect the wine to be very good (and it wasn't), but we had so many great wineries already on the schedule (Quivira, Unti, etc.) that we could afford to visit one for reasons other than viticulture. The grounds of the Burr winery were gorgeous, and the main building was something of a Raymond Burr museum. I bounced in and struck up a conversation with the staff—noting that I admired Raymond Burr as that rare Hollywood figure who did it all: he managed to work with Fritz Lang and Alfred Hitchcock, Godzilla and the Muppets, Natalie Wood and Grace Kelly, Tarzan and William Cameron Menzies. The breadth of it all is staggering. (Sound of crickets chirping.) The staff at the Raymond Burr museum had no idea what I was talking about. The place was a shrine to *Perry Mason* and nothing else. The walls were lined with framed copies of every *Perry Mason TV Guide* cover. I was the first person who'd ever shown up wanting to talk about anything but *Perry Mason*.

Lucille Ball and Desi Arnaz in *I Love Lucy*, **the role that eclipsed Lucy's movie career.**

The same phenomenon occurred during my research on *To Be or Not to Be*. As it happened, most of the cast and crew of that classic died within 15 years of its release, and so much of the information about its production that a researcher might otherwise find in film texts written in the 1960s and '70s was just absent. However, Benny survived long enough to write memoirs and be interviewed, and to have his reminiscences downloaded for posterity in various ways. Yet for all that material on Benny, 99.9 percent of it concerns his radio and TV shows, with a few scattered anecdotes about his mostly misfired film career.

Which brings us to Lucy. There is no shortage of written material about Lucy's remarkable career, but most of it concerns her Desilu days, not her 1930s B-movie career. Add to that the fact that the likes of *Next Time I Marry* are hardly ever screened on TV, and there simply hasn't been an opportunity for it to emerge from the shadows of her domineering TV career.

All the more reason for you to fight the power, seek it out for yourself, and enjoy.

# Artists and Models

There is a fairly well-regarded American comedy called *Artists and Models*. It has Jerry Lewis, Dean Martin and Shirley MacLaine in it, and was directed by Frank Tashlin. This chapter is not about that film at all, but rather a wholly unrelated comedy from about 20 years previously that just happens to have the same name. Raoul Walsh's 1937 *Artists and Models* is strictly filler stuff, the kind of thing independent TV stations used to jam into the late-night hours to avoid having to broadcast dead air.

Which is unfair. *Artists and Models* is quite enjoyable, if you know how to approach it. Problem is, knowing how to approach it requires a bit of context—and that context is generally lacking for contemporary audiences. Encountered cold, it just looks like a crazy mess. Which it *is*, but there's a world of difference between a sloppy incompetent mess and a deliberate anarchic mess. But to make the case for why this is the latter and not the former, let's pick apart what it is first.

Jack Benny is the obvious place to start—he's the headliner, after all. The conventional wisdom is that Jack Benny's cinema career was a non-starter except for Ernst Lubitsch's *To Be or Not to Be*, but he's got a few great bits here—and if anything, this seems to have had some vague influence on Lubitsch. For one thing, there's a scene where Benny thinks he's been shot that is recreated gesture for gesture in *To Be or Not to Be*. The finale finds Benny in Renaissance gear exceedingly like his Hamlet costume from *To Be or Not to Be*.

While we're listing funny Benny bits, there's also the moment where he stops to listen to Jack Benny on the radio, or when he carries on a non-sequitur-laced conversation with Rube Goldberg. I mention all these because the cumulative effect is to signal that this is going to be an absurdist star-driven comedy vehicle.

As far as Benny's part of the proceedings go, that holds true: he plays a promoter named Mac Brewster, who's in charge of the Artists and Models Ball (a big gala event of some kind). He's also arranging models for various advertising accounts, including Townsend Silver—the commercial imprimatur of the blue-blooded Townsend family. Jet-setting Alan Townsend (doughy Richard Arlen) believes that the right ad campaign behind his line of silverware will bring urbane well-bred sophistication to the masses—and to that end he wants the Queen of the Artists and Models Ball to be the same person as the Townsend Silver girl.

Benny's long-suffering girlfriend is Paula Sewell, played by Ida Lupino, and she wants that gig. Benny wants it for her, too, but Alan Townsend shoots the idea down without even laying eyes on her—he wants to use a true socialite. So Paula cooks up a scheme: pretend to be a socialite and get Alan's attention, so he hires her without realizing it's the same girl he already rejected. Off she goes to Miami to infiltrate his vacation, and…

Well, here's where it gets complicated. This plot should play like a screwball comedy—it has all the ingredients: the mistaken identities, antagonists falling in love while traveling together, love triangles, love crossing class barriers. All the boxes are ticked. But while Jack Benny's comedy chops are not in doubt, there's a reason nobody hails Ida Lupino as a great comedienne.

She doesn't even try. She plays her scenes straight, and it shows what a slender reed separates screwball comedy from romantic drama. With her no-nonsense portrayal of what are, in fact, all-nonsense scenes, the film develops a severe case of schizophrenia as it wobbles between Benny and Lupino's separate plotlines.

If that's all there was to it, we could just chalk this up to some poor casting or maybe Raoul Walsh not effectively integrating his two stars into the same style. But if you add up all of Jack Benny's and Ida Lupino's scenes, you barely get half this film's running time. In terms of tonal shifts, whipsawing between Benny and Lupino is just the beginning.

Instead, the film skips madly between Jack Benny's absurdist bits, Ida Lupino's not-

**Nineteen thirty-seven magazine ad for *Artists and Models*.**

quite-screwball stuff, and various vaudeville routines featuring guest performers. There's a scene where Martha Raye staggers around like a drunken sailor while Louis Armstrong plays "Public Melody Number 1," or another scene where Russell Patterson's marionettes stage a massive musical number that mutates from a *Fantasia*-style orchestral performance into a Busby Berkeley-esque revue.

Some of these vaudeville intrusions are incorporated into the logic of the plot: for example, the opening sequence is a grand spectacle of "let's do everything we possibly can, all at the same time, for no reason at all" that introduces us to the idea of Jack Benny as an entertainment promoter (here's another connection to *To Be or Not to Be*, which opens with a similar rug-pulling gimmick). Similarly, the climax finds Richard Arlen proposing to Ida Lupino, and her Cinderella moment actually happens while the two of them are dressed in Cinderella costumes, plus he actually has a glass slipper—but all that makes "sense" because it's supposedly part of the big Artists and Models Ball gala finale.

Meanwhile, some of the musical interruptions just happen, suddenly and without explanation, as if the filmmakers grew bored with their plot and decided to do something else for a while.

Let's take Judy Canova and Ben Blue as a case study.

There are two ways to explain why Judy Canova is even in this movie—(a) the thoughtful way, and (b) the correct way. The thoughtful way would involve the observation that she serves a crucial narrative function in Ida Lupino's "screwball" story. Like *It Happened One Night* (which came out two years before this film, and directly influenced the screwball components of *Artists and Models*), the romance between Lupino and Arlen is threatened at the 11th hour by some stubbornness and hurt pride. Arlen has gotten into his head that Lupino played him for a fool—just because she lied to him about who she was, and manipulated her way both into his affections and into his employ. Consequently the film heads towards its conclusion with the various parties lined up with the wrong romantic partners—someone needs to go convince Arlen to get his head out of his butt and realize that he genuinely loves Lupino and she genuinely loved him. In *It Happened One Night* this role is played by Walter Connolly as Claudette Colbert's dad—the plain-speaking guy who cuts through all the nonsense and says the obvious. Judy Canova has that role here.

But that's just happenstance. The real reason Judy Canova's in this movie is she was a middlingly popular performer who gets trotted out to do her shtick—which in Canova's case is loud, brassy, hillbilly comedy.

Canova comes barreling into the movie like a force of nature, right after Ida Lupino has had way too much time to pretend this is a sensitive piece of serious drama. Fast on Canova's heels is Ben Blue, an annoying comic who tended to play man-baby roles in the Harry Langdon mode, but without Langdon's penchant for sly transgressive mischief. Blue mostly just twitches and gapes.

Words just don't do justice to Canova's and Blue's big scene together. Bear in mind, neither of these characters have any real connection to the rest of the plot, except for Canova having one useful and relevant line of dialogue later on. They just show up and completely sidetrack everything—seconds ago we were wondering who will be the Queen of the Artists and Models Ball and who will model for Townsend Silver, and now we get (a) an inventor of artificial rain, (b) a boy and girl smacking each other like the Three Stooges, (c) is it love?, and (d) why not sing a song while you're at it? If you squint, you can sort of force their scene into making sense. As I already mentioned, Judy Canova has a role to play in the denouement, and since both Jack Benny and Ida Lupino end up finding true love at the end, it sort of fits that Judy would also get paired off with a boyfriend. It's weird for them to sidetrack everything so thoroughly with a digression into artificial rain as a career, and a such a strange song, but there's no law that says subplots have to be related to the main plot very closely. OK, it's an oddity, but not yet an incomprehensible digression. *But then the puppets start playing.*

How?

The puppets are even introduced—they get their own title card, fer crissakes! And they're clearly on a stage—they'd have to be! They're puppets! But what stage??? Who's the audience for this??? Where is this taking place??? The person in the story who stages shows like this is Jack Benny, and he is back in New York. Judy Canova and Ben Blue are down in Miami with Ida Lupino.

And then Ben Blue wanders into the puppet show, dazed and confused. He plays it like a child, unaware of social boundaries, entranced by the spectacle, going where he shouldn't. He's invaded the stage. You're waiting for the stage hands to hook him off the stage before he gets tangled up in the marionette's wires. But Ben starts interacting with the puppets—he's part of the show.

Stop.

This is where any flimsy remaining pretense to logic shatters. Ben Blue was introduced to us as a retailer of rain, he's not an entertainer. He's a dim bulb—I can buy him getting excited by the puppets and rushing the stage, but then he gets incorporated into the show. However in the real world Ben Blue is a professional entertainer, and he's in a movie full of professional entertainers—each of whom gets to do their act. Russell Patterson gets to have his puppets perform not because it has anything to do with anything, but because it's interesting.

This is the key: *Artists and Models* is primarily a vehicle for vaudeville comics and other performers to do various comedy and musical numbers. There is a loose narrative structure that more or less ties all these bits together, but not completely. The movie isn't a comedy plot that is variously interrupted, but more like the 1930s equivalent of a sketch variety show like *Laugh-In*, or *Saturday Night Live*.

You should keep your eyes out for it because it's quite fun (Jack Benny's reaction to being proposed to by Gail Patrick is terrific). More to the point, though, keep your eyes open for similar 1930s comedies that use the structure of vaudeville and variety reviews instead of narrative logic to hold themselves together. As discussed in Henry Jenkins' excellent but densely written text *What Made Pistachio Nuts*, the 1930s were full of these anarchic comedies. In fact, a small handful of them broke out and went big, so big they became massive hits remembered for generations even as the context that spawned them was forgotten … but that's a story for the next chapter.

# Duck Soup

The 1930s were chock-a-block with movies like *Artists and Models*, closer to a variety revue than a narrative experience. These kinds of movies jumble together a bunch of entertainers—mostly comedians, but not necessarily—and then drape the flimsiest of plots over them to provide some sort of rudimentary structure, and then just sit back and let them go every which way. Which, as you may have suspected, leads us straight to *Duck Soup*.

It's not hard to fall in love with *Duck Soup*, the most gloriously anarchic of the most anarchic comedy troupe. Whether this is your first Marx Brothers experience or not, chances are once you've fallen in love, you'll want more—and the most sensible way of slaking that thirst is to go looking for more Marx Brothers films, right? And as you obsessively track down and consume the rest of the Marx catalog, you'll find as everyone before you has that *Duck Soup* represents a pinnacle of that anything-goes aesthetic, and that as you move out to the farthest periphery of the edge their films are less unbounded.

There's an easily diagnosed and marked difference between *Duck Soup* and the film they made after it, *A Night at the Opera*. *Duck Soup* is an unruly thing, and the Marxes' trademark anarchy extends to the structure and style of the film itself: in one celebrated scene, Groucho and Harpo perform an extended silent comedy vaudeville routine (the fabled mirror gag), which is immediately followed by a trial scene. But Groucho changes sides during the trial, hiring the accused traitor as his Minister of War, only to have the whole scene devolve into a musical number ("All God's Chillun Got Guns"). Which is bizarre enough, were it not for the fact that the depiction of the onset of war involves such non-sequiturs as Harpo getting into bed with a horse, and stock footage of monkeys rampaging. When Groucho gets his head stuck in a vase (how?), and the response is not to break the vase and free him but to draw his face onto the vase and leave it there, that's almost the most sensible thing that happens in the movie.

By (sharp) contrast, *A Night at the Opera* includes the Marx Brothers as wacky characters in a decidedly generic plot. The other non–Marx characters have clearly defined motivations that inform their actions, as opposed to cyphers whose sole purpose is to set up jokes. The Marxes do crazy things, but those crazy things are clearly motivated and tied to the ongoing plot.

According to every history of the Marx Brothers I've ever read, this transition is universally understood as a consequence of their moving from the poorly managed wilderness of Paramount to the button-down corporate world of MGM. Not only was MGM infinitely more professional, but their producer at MGM, Irving Thalberg, was a no-nonsense mogul who consciously molded the Marx style to fit the conventional, traditionalist approach of the more august studio.

OK. All of that is true. But … there's something missing. The wild anarchy of *Duck Soup* may be the most unhinged the Marxes ever got on film, but when you compare it to some of the other anarchic comedies of the era its actually fairly tame. Consider *Hollywood Party* from 1934. Here's the Wikipedia description of this thing: "*Hollywood Party* (1934) is a musical film starring Jimmy Durante and distributed by Metro-Goldwyn-Mayer. The film is notable for several disconnected sequences that have little connection with each other. Each sequence featured a different star with a separate scriptwriter and director assigned, not unlike Paramount's *If I Had a Million*. However young Roy Rowland at 23 is given sole credit by IMDb for the entire production, this film marking his directorial debut which may explain why scenes don't match or are not correlated to one another."

What happens in it? Well, Jimmy Durante is apparently the star of a series of Tarzan-like movies, whose box office appeal is faltering because his lions aren't energetic enough.

That's the plot.

The film is mostly remembered for Laurel and Hardy's scene in which they crack eggs on Lupe Velez. There is also a scene with the Three Stooges—that's right, it's a movie that includes both Laurel and Hardy *and* the Three Stooges. But wait, there's more—Mickey Mouse is in it, too, because apparently cartoon characters can interact fully with live actors in this particular world—Mickey introduces a bizarre animated sequence renowned for its sexual imagery (!). In a film that barely cracks an hour's running time there are no fewer than eight musical numbers, including Durante's catch-phrase "Inka Dinka Doo" turned into a song. Mind you, the whole Durante-as-Tarzan thing was a last-minute addition to the movie, somehow, even though it's the main narrative thread. Which tells you something about how highly the filmmakers rated narrative coherence.

Basically, *Hollywood Party* is a wild anarchic mess that makes *Duck Soup* seem sensible by comparison—and we should compare them, because they emerge from the same tradition. It's harder to see when you focus on watching just Marx Brothers movies, but when you broaden the lens to encompass all of 1930s comedy, you can see that the 1930s had a thriving sub-genre of movies that disregarded narrative in favor of vaudeville-inflected spectacle: *here's some funny people, watch them do their thing. And maybe have some songs, too.*

For that matter, consider this: *Hollywood Party* was produced by … (wait for it) Irving Thalberg! He was perfectly capable of indulging in such unrestrained anarchy when he felt like it. *Duck Soup* belongs to a bigger family of 1930s vaudeville-inspired absurdities that

**Lobby card for *Duck Soup* (1933).**

flourished for several years and then faded away. Coming along in 1937, *Artists and Models* is already a late-period entry of the form. By the time the Marxes were ensconced in MGM, that mode of comedy filmmaking was no longer in vogue. Thalberg's *Hollywood Party* days were well behind him. The Marx Brothers' films start taking a more consciously narrative bend because that's where comedy was going overall. 1935 was the key transition year when screwball comedy came into its own.

Or, put this way: in 1933, *Duck Soup* shared the screen with the everything-but-the-kitchen-sink version of *Alice in Wonderland, Dinner at Eight, Dancing Lady* (Joan Crawford and Clark Gable vs. the Three Stooges), *Footlight Parade, Gold Diggers of 1933, Hallelujah I'm a Bum,* and *International House*—which all scurry in various ways around the vaudeville revue aesthetic. Whereas in 1935 *A Night at the Opera* shared the screen with *Hands Across the Table, Ruggles of Red Gap, Top Hat, Twentieth Century,* and *It Happened One Night*— all films which married screwy comic behavior to carefully worked out stories.

Watching only Marx Brothers films limits one's ability to observe how Marx Brothers films related to the culture at large—and distort our understanding. Moving the Marxes from Paramount to MGM wasn't the most important detail in explaining the difference between *Duck Soup* and *A Night at the Opera.* It's just the one that pops out when all you have is the filmography of the Marxes to work with, and go looking for answers within their personal and professional history.

# Eat Your Apple After Now

Walter Kerr's book *The Silent Clowns* is quite possibly the best book ever written about movies. It is certainly my personal favorite. That being said, it sets forth an argument about the legacy of silent clown Harry Langdon that I absolutely reject—namely, that Langdon was dependent on his collaborators, and after Frank Capra left him, Langdon spun out. Mind you, this is also the claim of Frank Capra himself, and has been repeated by other luminaries in the field such as Leonard Maltin. Anyone who argues otherwise is going up against giants.

Before we get into the merits of the claim, there are a couple of important details to note. The first is that Kerr and so many of the writers on silent comedy subjects throughout the 20th century were working from a limited menu of available films from which to draw conclusions. A great number of Langdon's films were not readily accessible. This didn't seem at the time to be a severe hinderance, because the ones that could be viewed were the ones most popular and successful, which had emerged from his most productive period. But that logic only gets you so far—you would be on shaky ground trying to draw grandiose conclusions about the totality of Charlie Chaplin's career on the basis of just his Mutual shorts.

In Langdon's case, the problem is that if you only review those films that Capra most strongly influenced, you will inevitably come away with an inflated sense of Capra's importance. Capra, and Kerr and Maltin, put forth an interpretation of Langdon's screen persona that is fully consistent with his work in *Saturday Afternoon* and *The Strong Man,* two films that are indeed strongly influenced by Capra, and then claim that his earlier and later works are the outliers. But if you sit down and watch his entire output, what becomes clear is that he had a consistent set of comic ideas that remained in place throughout his 20-odd years of films, and that if anything the Capra material is the outlier.

Now, you can still say you *prefer* the Capra iteration of Langdon. That's a matter of opinion and a popular one at that. But that is a very different position than claiming that Capra created Langdon's persona for a comedian unable to articulate his own comic identity effectively.

Before we dig too much farther into this, perhaps we need to establish, for the benefit of the newcomers in the audience, just who this Harry Langdon fellow is. According to Frank Capra, Charlie Chaplin said the one comedian he felt intimidated by was Harry Langdon. You always have to be skeptical of hearsay, but it is an interesting thought. According to Mack Sennett, Langdon was a greater artist than Chaplin. Sennett said this in 1928, mind you—years after he and Langdon had parted company, after Sennett had already distributed the last of his stockpiled Langdon back catalog, and long after he had anything left to gain or lose by association with the now-washed up star. And this from the man who had launched Chaplin's career. (Sennett was also the man who pushed Chaplin away by refusing to meet his salary demands. Sennett balked at paying Chaplin $3,000 a week—that was too rich for him, more than he thought Charlie was worth. Then Sennett signed Langdon for $7,500 a week. That's more than twice what Sennett refused to pay Chaplin, more than he ever paid anyone else.)

And whether or not Chaplin felt Langdon snapping at his heels, Harry definitely had a fan in Harold Lloyd, and later in Stan Laurel as well. This is the comedian other comedians came to see.

In an interview, Langdon talked about the lessons he learned during his long years—decades—on the vaudeville stage. He said: "One valuable little thing I learned in vaudeville is that you can pretty well control the laughter of your crowd. If things were going well, I'd play along at a fairly slow tempo and keep my voice well down. If the laughs were too few and quiet, I'd increase my speed and raise my voice."

There's a cliché about the difference between stage acting and screen acting—that on the stage you have to make everything broader and louder and more expansive so it "reads" to spectators in the back of the theater. When Langdon was on top of his game and everything was clicking, he could turn it all down to the lowest possible setting—he only had to speed up or speak louder when something was wrong in his relationship with the audience. This was how he performed on the *vaudeville* stage, the lowest, broadest, crudest form of theatrical entertainment. When he ported that aesthetic to the movies, where the camera demands a smaller, more intimate performance, his style of comedy was dialed down to a whisper. Langdon boasted privately of how much pride he took in being able to drag out a gag longer than anyone else.

Most of the big comedians of that era worked with almost no script—they'd show up with little more than a bare-bones premise and ad-lib the rest. *Charlie at a health spa. Buster works at a garage. Lloyd at an amusement park. Now, go!* That didn't work so well with Langdon. His world of comedy was a palette of vacant stares and running in circles that only had significance when in some other context—he needed something to play against. Dogs, skunks, monkeys, herds of sheep, exploding cows … and mannequins, wax statues, empty suits of armor, telephone poles, glasses of beer, invisible insects—anything inhuman or inanimate he could inexplicably treat as sentient.

To illustrate this difference, consider a short film Chaplin did for the U.S. government to promote Liberty Bonds for the war effort in World War I. The short is around 10 minutes long and Charlie does it against a black backdrop with only the most abstracted props. His mastery of expressive mime was such that he could make a film that consisted of Charlie and almost nothing else, and have it be meaningful, even funny. But put Langdon in an empty room by himself and you've got nothing.

I don't mean that as a criticism of Harry Langdon, just a descriptive statement of fact. Because, given the right context, Langdon's bizarre world of inappropriate reactions became sublime.

Here's another Langdon quote: "There should be a breathing space between laughs, with a gradual development leading up to a laugh. A picture that is one laugh from start to finish becomes tedious. Relief is necessary."

That's a bold statement, and it could so easily have been said by Chaplin. There were so many of the silent comedians of the age desperately mugging—*Look at me! Look at me!!*—especially so at speed-addicted Sennett, that Langdon's steadfast stubborn insistence on the low-key and subtle is remarkable.

You can see the echoes of Harry Langdon's legacy in the likes of Jerry Seinfeld and Larry David, Ricky Gervais, the Kids in the Hall, and David Cross—comedians who confidently disregard the conventional rules, deliberately make the audience uncomfortable, and revel in the performance of things not readily identifiable as jokes.

It was a truly unprecedented approach to screen comedy. Not only was he disregarding the usual standard-issue Sennett formula of violence and mayhem, he was flying in the face of every other silent comedian as well.

In her extraordinary study of Langdon's comic style, film scholar Joyce Rheuban cites Sigmund Freud's definition of humor. Seems Dr. Freud says comedy is when someone expends an inordinate amount of energy on physical functions but not enough on mental functions. Now, what Freud's supposed to know from funny is beyond me, but man, did he nail it with Langdon or what?

So, with that as our background, let's cycle back to Walter Kerr's take on Frank Capra's take on Langdon's comedy. According to their line of thinking, Langdon was a sort of baby-man, a fully grown toddler with all the sexlessness that implies. Kerr in particular asserts that much of Langdon's comedy came out of this sexual confusion. His prime examples for this are *Saturday Afternoon* and *The Strong Man*—two exceptional films, but still just two films. Buster Keaton played a rich man in two exceptional films, *The Navigator* and *Battling Butler*, but I wouldn't go around saying that was essential to his Keatonness.

In fact, far more prevalent in the films of Harry Langdon is an *aggressive* sexuality. His kisses cause women to swoon in *Soldier Man* and *The King*; he is a skirt-chasing womanizer in *Picking Peaches*, *His First Flame*, and *The Chaser*; sexual misadventures on his part drive *The Hansom Cabman*; and in the vast majority of his films (including *Saturday Afternoon*) he is a married man. The central gag of *Tied For Life* is a blue-balls joke about a man unable to get his wife alone on their wedding night—when he finally does get some privacy with her, he's so potent she gives birth to quadruplets!

I'll admit that Langdon's portrayal of this Lothario is absurdly asexual and childlike, but that fits his overall comic approach of inappropriate juxtapositions. In Langdon's films the simple act of cross-dressing, no matter how poorly done, is treated as a fully effective gender-role-reversing disguise. The implausible womanizer is another joke in the same vein. The idea that his character had no business showing interest in women is simply unsupportable.

The Kerr analysis of Langdon placed such priority on his sexlessness as perceived in *Saturday Afternoon* and *The Strong Man*, that the central premise of *The Chaser* (Harry's faithless wandering is punished by a judicially imposed gender role reversal) seemed to come out of nowhere. But seen in the larger context of his whole career, *The Chaser* is the one that more easily belongs, and it's *The Strong Man* that seems a misfit.

*The Strong Man* is also the film that most obviously depicts what Capra said was his intention with Langdon. Capra claimed that Harry needed to be a decent soul in a corrupt world, whose essential goodness saw him through hard times. In other words, Capra described the very basis of more or less all of his subsequent work—he would shape Gary Cooper and Jimmy Stewart into identically-shaped characters in films like *Meet John Doe*, *Mr. Deeds Goes to Town*, *It's a Wonderful Life*, and so on.

Capra was an artist who believed in a "genuine" America, a small town realm of values threatened by the cynicism of city slickers and intellectual phonies. The problem was that Harry Langdon *was* one of those cynical phonies! He was a merry prankster who took great joy in sending up the very infrastructure of the movie comedy form in which he worked.

Note that when Langdon was allowed to both write and direct his own short films later in the sound era, he had an attraction to stories about actors trying to perform in a poorly made play: *Goodness a Ghost* and *The Stage Hand* are good examples. He was drawn to that extra layer of artificiality, the meta-meanings of inept poseurs struggling to fit in amongst other phonies. But what sells these shorts are small, isolated moments in which Harry's bizarre, inhuman line delivery makes a joke of something that shouldn't be funny. There is nothing about the line "*I like beer*" that is recognizable as a joke, but in *The Stage Hand* Harry's out-of-left-field line reading turns it into one.

Or, for another example, in *Goodness a Ghost* Harry is an aspiring actor struggling to rehearse the line "*Did anybody call an officer?*" Each subsequent attempt is farther off the mark than the one before—the more he rehearses, the worse it gets.

This is not the kind of stuff Capra was ever going to find funny. But it was where Harry excelled. The two men were fundamentally different in their conception of what made a movie work. Capra built great stories, with carefully drawn characters intended to illustrate his moral principles; Langdon thought ridiculousness was its own virtue and frequently indulged in the 1920s and '30s equivalents of "blue" material.

To my mind, the defining characteristic of Harry Langdon, the thread that ties him together across the decades, is his indecisiveness. Give him a task, and he runs in every possible direction. If you ever wondered what "going nowhere fast" looks like, check out a Langdon picture.

There is a scene from the Hal Roach short *The Head Guy* that shows how in the sound era, he found a way to turn that from a visual into a verbal gag. Thanks to some awkward and implausible sitcom style shenanigans, Harry's girlfriend mistakenly believes he was flirting with some chorus girls and dumped him (there's that sexual side of Harry again!). In despair, he "cries." I had to put that in quotation marks because his sobbing isn't real, or realistic, it is a simulacrum. He knows he is supposed to cry in this situation, but isn't sure how, so he imitates, poorly, what he thinks it's supposed to sound like (and there's that phoniness aspect again!). He starts babbling. "*If Nancy don't want me, then I want to die.*" As soon as the words are out of his mouth, his eyes widen in fear. Someone has just threatened his life!

Now, of course it was *him*, but he spends the rest of the film acting as if he is two people, arguing with himself. He even tries to explain his tortured logic to himself: *if Nancy doesn't want me, then I don't want to live....* But he gets tangled up in his own words and can't quite make it to the end of the sentence. So, it's back to "sobbing" because that's a simpler expression of despondency.

He tries again, and this time manages to express himself more succinctly: "*I scrub for Nancy, and I work hard for Nancy. Nobody else would I work hard for. Nobody but her. And if she don't want me, then I'm gonna die. I will die, I will die!*"

And he pounds the table for emphasis, but ... you see, just before launching this speech, he picked up a nail file and started cleaning his fingernails. It's possible that this physical distraction was what enabled him to marshal his thoughts into such coherence. Without the nail file he couldn't finish the sentence. But now when he wants to pound his

**Harry Langdon surrounded by dancing girls in the bizarre comedy short *The Head Guy* (1930) which swapped visual gags for verbal illogic.**

fist on the table as a rhetorical flourish, he has to first set the nail file aside, and that fumbling act causes his fist-pounding to miss punctuating his words by a few crucial seconds.

He resumes cleaning his nails, but the interruption completely derailed his thoughts. He keeps talking about suicide, but now his tone of voice is wrong, his emphasis skewed. The idea of suicide was evidently too terrible to contemplate, so now when he talks about dying it's more like he's come to think of himself as terminally ill. But this puzzles him (*when did I get sick, exactly?*) and he tries some more "sobbing" while he tries to retrace his thoughts.

This leads to a sudden change in mood. He looks up brightly and tries to snap his fingers nonchalantly (emphasis on "tries"). He puffs himself up as if putting on a show to impress onlookers. But he's the only person in the room. Who is he trying to fool?

"*Ha ha!*" (the laugh is as fake as his cry) and he boasts of getting a pretty girl (which he then changes to "bigger girl" for some reason) and again tries unsuccessfully to snap his fingers, a gesture that doesn't oblige him to give up the nail file but ends up just as poorly timed. Now he's expanded his description of his new, better girl to include the fact that she will smoke. But this reminds him of Nancy (because she doesn't smoke) and his phony bravado is undone.

The rest of his speech—and there is a fair bit of it yet to go—is incomprehensible because during the preceding part he opened his lunchbox and took out a sandwich, and the rest of his rant is delivered while he eats. The act of crying and eating simultaneously initiates a coughing fit, and to clear his throat he pulls an apple from the lunchbox.

"*I could jump in the lake I will I don't want my apple now I don't want no apple now I don't want no apple now I'll eat my apple after now.*"

End of scene.

?!?!?!?!

This is verbal surrealism. It is a purely dialogue-based joke, unique to Langdon's character. No other comedian could have delivered a scene like that, and none would have tried. The effect is more worrisome than funny. It is profoundly off-putting and weird, and I love it.

I haven't even said anything about *Three's a Crowd* yet. It's been said it's a great film, just not a comedy. I absolutely consider it a masterpiece, and say so in my audio commentary to the DVD edition, but I've never once felt a compunction to laugh in it.

But so what? I don't laugh during Chaplin's *A Woman of Paris*, nor Ernst Lubitsch's *The Man I Killed*, nor Leo McCarey's *Make Way for Tomorrow*. And if you think any of those films reflect poorly on their makers, well, then we're going to have to take this outside and settle it.

# The Back of Joan Crawford's Head

There is a moment when the back of Joan Crawford's head became a potent symbol in the history of American screen comedy. Most historians, if asked to demonstrate why screen comedy changed so radically in the 1930s, point to a blackface Al Jolson singing his heart out and say, "There ya go." Not me. I point to the back of Joan Crawford's head. "There ya go."

I'm not saying that the technological transformation wasn't real, or wasn't significant.

It was clearly a profound shift in Hollywood's gravity: theaters invested heavily in the new equipment and needed to justify that expense by switching over to showing talkies instead of silents; the sound-recording technology imposed clunky limitations on filmmaking technique; some former movie stars were vexed by how their voices did not fit their screen personas ... true, true, true.

But the question I posed isn't whether *The Jazz Singer* was a big deal, it was why the decades-long international dominance of silent slapstick suddenly gave out and was replaced by a brand new genre of romantic comedies? If that's the question, then the whole *Jazz Singer* thing becomes a noisy variable. Take it out of the equation—for example, by imaging a world where the advent of sound happened much later, or much earlier—and you'll see the same transition taking place anyway.

If we want to understand why the dinosaurs died off, let's start by looking at the dinosaurs. Silent slapstick flourished from basically the dawn of cinema (*L'Arroseur arrose*, 1897) and throughout the first two decades of the 20th century. In its purest form, it was a cinematic form that prioritized the "hero" comedian—Charlie Chaplin, Buster Keaton, Harold Lloyd. Their movie adventures were designed as vehicles in which these great men would perform their physical comedy and visual gags. There were exceptions to the rule— lady slapsticians like Alice Howell, or comedians like Sidney Drew who de-emphasized visual comedy. But in the main, when we talk about silent slapstick, we're talking about a tradition derived from live vaudeville in which a male solo performer would command the attention of his audience by doing funny things with his body.

Harry Langdon entered Hollywood in the mid–1920s, when this format had cohered into formula. He was himself a mature adult, approaching middle age, joining a mature medium. His brand of comedy depended on audience familiarity with the formula—he played off existing audience expectations, specifically by screwing with the timing of familiar jokes and defying genre norms. Langdon was decidedly a second generation screen comic— he exemplified Slapstick 2.0.

Other practitioners of Slapstick 2.0, who similarly made their careers out of playing off variations of what had gone before, included Laurel and Hardy, Our Gang, and the Three Stooges—comics who are remembered at least as much, if not exclusively for their work in sound films. To the extent slapstick was going to continue into the 1930s, this was to be its direction. Harry Langdon was the spearhead of the future.

And by 1926, Harry Langdon pretty much owned the screen. His run of short comedies at Mack Sennett's studio had been an unprecedented hit, and he was fast eclipsing the better-established comedians who'd blazed the trail before him. He'd left Sennett (who was more Slapstick 1.0 than Sennett?) to start making feature length pictures for First National, the same studio that ushered Charlie Chaplin from shorts into features. The first of these was to be *Tramp, Tramp, Tramp*.

*Tramp, Tramp, Tramp* concerns a cross-country foot race into which Langdon has been improbably and inappropriately registered. You see, he is smitten by a billboard model, and since the foot race is sponsored by the company she advertises, he's all but compelled to do it (it makes sense to *him*). And the movie therefore contrives to put Langdon face to face with the billboard model. Whereupon he goes into fits of both mental and physical gymnastics trying to work out how his angel can be *both* on the billboard *and* standing next to him.

**Harry Langdon's first released feature film, *Tramp, Tramp, Tramp* (1926), unwittingly found the limits of silent slapstick with back of costar Joan Crawford's head.**

And it's here that we find Ms. Joan Crawford. She was only 22 years old—and that's if we believe her birthdate was in 1904. There's some controversy about that date, and it's possible she's actually still a teenager in 1926. She's certainly still quite green—she's little more than a glorified extra at this point in her career. In the years to come, she will become one of the enduring stars of Golden Age Hollywood. But first she has to finish this take.

In *Tramp, Tramp, Tramp* she has the chance to be the leading lady. That's a bit of a misuse of the term—she doesn't get much screen time nor much characterization, since Langdon's solo act dominates the proceedings, but she is the top-billed actress in a film by one of Hollywood's hottest comedians. That's a career boost no matter how you cut it.

But she cannot get through a single take without giggling uncontrollably. Langdon is going into spasmic fits, and as he does his shtick, Crawford does what everybody in the audience will do—she laughs.

Exasperated and exhausted, director Harry Edwards offers a solution: we don't have to do this in one take. We'll frame it so we see Langdon and the back of your head. You can laugh—as long as you hold your head still. Then, when we go to do your close-ups, Harry can go back to his trailer and take a break, and you don't have to try to keep a straight face while looking at him.

It was a fine solution. But it only worked because the film didn't require Harry and Joan to actually interact at all. Her character is just a cipher, a prop. You don't need to see anything but the back of her head. It worked because the movie was about Harry Langdon, and everything else was secondary.

In other words, the real problem was that the strength—and weakness—of the film depended wholly on Langdon. This was the hidden fault line in all classic slapstick. Get a great comedian working at the height of his powers and relatively unfettered creative freedom and you could get a masterpiece. But the added value of great collaborators was always going to be limited. There was a wellspring of talent in Hollywood—they were pouring into the city by the bus load, and some of them were geniuses. The working method and style of the great slapstick auteurs had little use for these talents, whose skills were being wasted.

Or, put another way, neither Slapstick 1.0 nor Slapstick 2.0 had much room for women. Go back and take a look at my list above—Langdon, Laurel and Hardy, Our Gang, the Stooges. It's a Guy's Club. It's not that Hollywood didn't have any funny women—they just didn't have much of a place at the slapstick table.

It's also worth noting that the funny women coming into movies weren't generally coming from that vaudeville stage tradition that had minted the likes of Harry Langdon. Instead, Carole Lombard, Claudette Colbert, Jean Arthur, and so on were glamour queens who demonstrated awesome comic chops and started getting opportunities to explore those skills because the filmmakers they worked with saw something special.

For several years leading into this great transitional moment, there had been a new generation of great comedians rising to prominence as writers and directors, but not necessarily as performers themselves. They made comedies to be enacted by others. These writers and directors had come up the ranks during the Slapstick era—Leo McCarey, Ernst Lubitsch, Gregory La Cava, George Stevens, Frank Capra. They'd seen the old model at work, and they'd mastered it. Now they were building something new.

And that something new, Slapstick 3.0, would be a more ensemble-based style of comedy, which gave pride of place to these funny ladies. They would be comedies which would derive as much comic pleasure out of how they were written and directed as how they were performed. And put together, these factors meant that this new comic form would emphasize social criticism—deriving laughs from how these funny ladies defied social norms. People would come to call it "screwball."

And Capra? He was there, standing alongside Harry Edwards, telling poor Joan Crawford to keep her back to the camera. The only reason we even know this story is because Capra told it.

Of course that right there makes it suspect. Capra told many stories about his time with Langdon and few of them were strictly true. The staging of Crawford's scene with Langdon is perfect as it is—it's actually tough to imagine a superior setup in which her face would have been visible during the take.

But the fact this anecdote, however exaggerated, stuck with Capra long enough to make it into his memoir means that it says something about Capra, regardless of whether it accurately describes anything about Crawford. And what it says about Capra can be best understood by watching what he did in the years following his break from Langdon.

Roughly 10 years later, with *It Happened One Night*, Capra bottled lightning. The pieces of screwball had been swirling about Hollywood's orbit for years. In other words, *It Happened One Night* wasn't precisely the first screwball comedy, but it makes for an easy to identify moment when all the ingredients appeared in the same recipe. It wasn't that the new formula emerged fully formed in 1935—more that these ex-Masters of Slapstick had all been rowing in the same direction for several years, and the blockbuster success of *It Happened One Night* was a very public proof of concept to the new aesthetic.

Capra never directed Crawford in one of these newfangled screwballs, but his use of the likes of Jean Arthur and Claudette Colbert shows the lesson learned from *Tramp, Tramp, Tramp*: if you've got a great actress in your film and all you can think of for her to do is stand with her back to the camera, you're doing it wrong.

# Downton Valley, or Ruggles Conquers the West

*Ruggles of Red Gap* is an odd duck. It is a crucial turning point into the formative genre of screwball comedy, but it isn't easily recognizable as a romantic comedy nor is it especially female driven. It was Charles Laughton's favorite screen role, but he is not known for comedy, and his performance here consists substantially of standing still and trying to suppress an awkward smile. It's a 1930s Hollywood comedy for the Downton Abbey set, whose most famous scene involves a British valet reciting the Gettysburg Address to a bar full of Wild West toughs. In other words, it's a movie that calls for some unpacking. So let's get started!

In the previous chapter, I put forth the postulate that there were talented writers and directors working in silent slapstick who were incentivized to move away from the slapstick model because the focus on solo stars a) limited the extent of their own contributions and b) squandered the plentiful resources of Hollywood's many comically-gifted performers. My metaphor for this argument was that if all your movie could think to do with Joan Crawford was show the back of her head, you're doing it wrong. This was a clumsy metaphor, of course—for one thing, Joan Crawford was the least suited to comedy of practically any Hollywood starlet in history. For another thing, I don't want to be misconstrued as slinging any mud on *Tramp, Tramp, Tramp*. Harry Langdon was a bona fide genius and his (sorta) debut feature is side-splittingly funny. I just meant that Hollywood's eco-system wasn't going to thrive on the specialty flavors of Harry Langdon, and needed to cultivate more robust cash crops.

We can actually see this process in action with *Ruggles of Red Gap*. The story (which had actually been filmed once before, as a silent comedy!) involves a proper "gentleman's gentleman" (Laughton, as the titular "Ruggles") whose employment contract is lost in a card game to a loudmouth American rancher (played by Charlie Ruggles, but don't get distracted by his last name—that's just an unfortunately confusing coincidence). The American's social-climbing wife (Mary Boland) thinks having a British valet is just the thing to rub in the noses of her equally snooty friends back in Red Gap.

At first, the valet is horrified by this turn of events. To be torn from his employer (Roland Young) and sent off to the untamed Wild West is unnerving, and his new employer is uncouth and ignorant of social custom. But once in Red Gap, the valet starts to realize the benefit of his employer's resistance to Old World social mores. The rancher accepts his valet as an equal, and introduces him to his friends not as a servant but a person. America's classlessness might be its greatest saving grace.

Laughton insisted on getting Leo McCarey as his director, for what was launched as practically a Laughton-vanity project. McCarey had been one of the creative forces behind Laurel and Hardy, and from there had gone on to direct other slapstick icons in star-driven vehicles: *Six of a Kind* (Burns & Allen); *The Milky Way* (Harold Lloyd); *Duck Soup* (The Marx Brothers). In other words, the resume of a gifted comedy mastermind, but one whose own auteurist vision was at least partially obscured by the personalities of his stars. But *after* this film McCarey's career looked like this: *The Awful Truth, Make Way for Tomorrow, Going My Way*.... Movies that not only mark out McCarey's unique personal territory but also cause us to retroactively reevaluate his earlier works and find the irreducible McCarey in them. *Ruggles of Red Gap* is where McCarey becomes McCarey.

And so what is the McCarey touch? Part of it is the ensemble nature of his works, where every supporting player is given the space to command the screen/steal the scene, where the effect of the film is magnified by the collaboration of a deep bench of onscreen talent.

I said that Laughton's performance includes a lot of standing still and trying to avoid smiling—which opens up a lot of space for other actors to take center stage. There's Charlie

**From left to right: Mary Boland, Charles Ruggles, Charles Laughton, Lucien Littlefield, and Leota Lorraine.**

Ruggles, a blunderbuss of loud checkered suits and unfaltering enthusiasm (and a George Bush-y habit of nicknamification). There's Mary Boland, a shrill onslaught of self-aggrandizing social climbing. There's Roland Young, marble-mouthed and meek. And there's Thelma Todd's erstwhile costar Zasu Pitts as Laughton's love interest—a rare opportunity for Pitts to be the leading lady in a Hollywood blockbuster.

In addition to the appealingly quirky romance between Laughton and Pitts, a second romance blossoms late in the film between Roland Young and Leila Hyams. Weirdly, and significantly, their romance, which plays out in just a handful of scenes between minor supporting characters, is a key plot point. This is what I mean about McCarey's approach to ensemble-based storytelling. These subsidiary characters' actions have more direct consequences to the resolution of the story than the primary romance between the leads.

In short, this is how the New Comedy differed from slapstick. You could make a movie that depended entirely on, say, Harry Langdon to sell each and every one of the jokes—or you could generate laughs from a good dozen actors, and summon all their disparate plot-lines and character attributes to contribute to the finale.

# The $30,000 Question

*The Jazz Singer* has persisted in posterity and popular memory far in excess of the merits of its actual content—it is however remembered as a revolutionary picture, one that precipitated a sudden reorientation of the industry. But the real story behind the switch to talkies is messier—and doesn't have much of anything to do with *The Jazz Singer*. It is instead a story about the dynamics of format wars.

Readers of a certain age may remember the VHS vs. Betamax war of the 1980s; perhaps some of you were early adopters of camcorders and struggled to compare VHS-C to Hi8. There were two kinds of laserdiscs—one was foolish and the other expensive. When DVD was rolled out, it was the product of a consortium of manufacturers who had hoped to work together to avoid another format war, only to face a competitor product called DivX on the format's debut. Blu-Ray beat out HD, but then failed to capture the market share it had anticipated because streaming video beat out physical media. Go back in time and you can find Pathex 9.5mm versus Kodak 8mm in the 1920s.[1]

You could even go back to the very beginning, where motion picture technology itself was a scrum of competing formats—was film a celluloid product or paper-based, was it recorded on glass, did the sprockets run down the sides or the middle, how wide was the gauge…. I once met a man who maintained an astounding personal museum of archival movie equipment, including the camera used to film Lilian Gish's first ever appearance. The number of different film formats from the late 19th century he had on display would have choked a horse.

But the format war of interest here is the battle between Vitaphone and Movietone. I set the story up by invoking format wars with which I hope you are familiar, because the more you understand the dynamics of those battles the more you can understand how this particular process played out. And that in turn matters, because the popular reception of

*The Jazz Singer* was not what pushed talkies into American theaters. The movies started to talk because William Fox had his back against the wall trying to compete with Jack Warner.

William Fox is one of those classically American rags-to-riches success stories, who built a movie empire through true grit and personal endurance. He had an infrastructure of nationwide chains of theaters through which he could release productions starring some of the country's most popular stars. But even at the height of his success he was running behind Paramount and MGM, and by the mid–1920s he was losing ground.

So in 1925, he sat down with his closest advisors—Saul Rogers and Winfield Sheehan—and formulated a strategy to get back on top. The central element of this strategy was to invest heavily in the development of sound recording technology. He had an engineer already, by the name of Theodore W. Case, and Fox also bought the patents of inventor Lee DeForest. This was the foundation of Movietone, a sound-on-film process that by 1927 Fox started to roll out, principally in short subjects like two-reel comedies or newsreels.

Whereas Movietone was a sound-on-film process, its chief competitor, Vitaphone, involved recording sound on discs and playing the platters while the film unspooled. Remarkably, Vitaphone didn't have nearly as many synchronization problems as you'd expect, but as a technology it was inferior to the Movietone approach—so the fact that sound-on-film eventually became the default industry standard and sound-on-disc became a museum piece makes sense. Back in 1927, though, this was nowhere near a certain outcome.

The very first ever Movietone program was the premiere of F. W. Murnau's *Sunrise*, at Fox's Times Square theater in New York on September 23, 1927. There was a Movietone newsreel and then *Sunrise* was shown with synchronized music and sound effects—the first ever feature film to have a synchronized soundtrack.

Meanwhile, Fox's top competitor in the race to sound was Warner Brothers, whose Vitaphone process was similarly used initially on short subjects, and was rolled out as a synchronized music-and-effects accompaniment to an otherwise silent feature, *Don Juan*. The entire industry still eyed sound warily as a novelty. In order to equip themselves to even screen sound films, theaters had to undertake costly retrofitting that could run upwards of $30,000—per screen—and to make the sound films in the first place, studios needed to abandon their existing plants and invest in entirely new soundproof stages.

Theater owners are famously conservative businessmen. They don't, as a rule, even bother paying to clean their sticky floors until a health inspector demands it. (Yes. I've worked at movie theaters. I speak from experience.) So why write a $30k check? They did it because sales people from Fox and Warners convinced them they had to in order to keep apace with their competitors–and having spent that money (in 1930s dollars mind you) they weren't about to let those speakers go idle.

Nobody was eager to go spend that kind of money until they had to—and Fox and Warner Brothers were spending that kind of money only because they were jockeying for position in a future market whose existence they were only speculating.

Fox was winning that race, hands down. And he was winning it by using sound sparingly, and making mostly silent features. Warner Brothers decided on a desperate but bold ploy—

They made an all-talkie feature film, with big musical numbers, starring one of the country's top singing stars. This was of course *The Jazz Singer*, and the gamble worked. In 1926, Warners was losing millions of dollars a year—after *The Jazz Singer* they were seeing profits of millions.

For the industry as a whole, it was the tipping point. Now, all of a sudden, theaters that had been reluctant to switch over to sound did so in droves—which in turn pushed down the costs, making it easier for other smaller theaters to do so too, which created a spiral effect that quickly retrofitted the entire exhibition industry. Having made these investments in new screening technology, those theater owners wanted to make sure they got the benefit of the investment—they wanted to be able to advertise that they had this sparkly new fad, and they wanted to prioritize talkie screenings. Theaters started to refuse to book silent films.

Please note that their refusal to book silent films was not a response to audience demand for talkies, it was an attempt to *create* audience demand for talkies—any theater that spent the equivalent of a quarter of a million dollars in 1928 money to hook up some speakers and then let that equipment idle while they paid a piano player to accompany silent films was a chump.

Fox's Movietone process was now the second-runner. To regain his status, he needed to aggressively push Movietone—bear in mind Movietone and Vitaphone were not compatible formats, so if a theater equipped for one it couldn't play the other. Every theater that signed up for the opposing side's format was a lost sale, a vanished customer. Once you buy a VHS player you won't be buying any Betamax tapes. This was war.

So Fox invested major sums in a new studio complex called Movietone City.

To finance this expansion, Fox took out loans of $30 Million—and that was just for Movietone City. Fox was also buying up theater chains like they were going out of style. All these debts were to come due at the end of 1929 and the start of 1930. His plan was to repay those loans by selling new shares of stock, whose value would be pumped up by the newly expanded production facilities, shiny new technology, and new theater outlets. It was a risky plan. And it was while he was arranging this new round of stock issuance he was injured in a car crash and hospitalized.

His creditors seized the moment of his incapacitation to claim he was in default—it was a hostile takeover. Suits were filed, old friends stabbed each other in the back, the press ate up the juicy gossip, and when the dust settled William Fox had lost control of his company and was no longer in the movie business. Winfield Sheehan stepped up and took the reins—Fox no longer had any role in the company that bore his name.

Sheehan was a ruthless player, and he sided with the hostile takeover against Fox. Sheehan felt that with all the money going into Movietone, and with the obvious direction the market was going, that it was imperative for the studio to turn out sound pictures and nothing but.

It is ironic that the first feature film to have a synchronized soundtrack was F. W. Murnau's *Sunrise*. The Movietone process used on *Sunrise* forced Fox to aggressively push Movietone to compete with Vitaphone, and led to theaters stopping booking silent films altogether. So, in other words, the movie at the heart of this transition from silents to talkies isn't really *The Jazz Singer* at all, it's *Sunrise*.

# F. W. Murnau's Comedy Masterpiece

F. W. Murnau's *Sunrise: A Song of Two Humans* is the dictionary definition of a classic film. It won (for all intents and purposes) the first ever Academy Award, has been placed on the National Registry, and was the first silent film put out on Blu-Ray. It routinely places in "Best Of" lists, it's a picture whose artistry is intended to be accessible to mass audiences. It is conventionally beautiful, conventionally narrative, conventionally stirring. It needs no apologies or excuses, it's just excellent in every way.

But did you know it was a comedy?

Consider the basic premise: *Sunrise* presents a sexy, vampish "Woman of the City" who invades a rural idyll where her very presence corrupts a naïve young man. In order to pursue this temptress, the young man comes to believe his only escape from his existing small-town romance is to kill his girl, which he utterly fails to accomplish, and thereby sets in motion the plot developments of the rest of the film.

And just six months before *Sunrise* hit theaters, American audiences saw the exact same plot in Harry Langdon's comedy *Long Pants*!

My point isn't that Murnau played as drama what Langdon mined for giggles—not by a long shot. For one thing, Langdon's film crossed enough taboos (or do I mean *tabus*?) that some audiences didn't find it funny at all. More to the point, Murnau does play *Sunrise* like a comedy, and its contents are not very much distinguishable from what constituted comedies of the same period.

*Long Pants* preceded *Sunrise* by half a year, but we can find more reference points coming out around half a year *after Sunrise*. *Sunrise*'s main characters go on a date to a carnival, where they run into money problems and an out-of-control animal (see Harold Lloyd's *Speedy*), and the film climaxes with a catastrophic storm (see Buster Keaton's *Steamboat Bill, Jr.*)

It isn't just that the film is structured like a comedy, it is absolutely jam-packed with comedy actors, too. Janet Gaynor, the female lead, was a fairly inexperienced young actress whose resume before showing up here largely consisted of comedy work—Laurel and Hardy's *45 Minutes from Hollywood*, Syd Chaplin's *Oh, What a Nurse*, Clara Bow's *The Plastic Age*, Charley Chase's *All Wet*, various and sundry Hal Roach one-offs. Once she and her hubby/attempted murderer George O'Brien make their way into the city, they spend the rest of the film encountering comic actors. Ralph Sipperly, the Barber, came from Fox's own comedy shorts division. Jane Winton, the Manicure Girl, came from such comedies as *Footloose Widows*, *Why Girls Go Back Home*, and *Millionaires*. And then there's the Obtrusive Gentleman (Arthur Housman) and the Obliging Gentleman (Eddie Boland). Both Housman and Boland were small-time comedy stars who were brand names in their own right, having top-lined their own respective series of comedy shorts.

On top of all the comic actors, there are actual jokes: the wedding reception mistaking the peasant couple for the bride and groom, the business at the photographer's and the headless statue, the comic misunderstandings at the salon, and a drunken pig!

This is a "silent film" in that no dialogue is spoken, but it has a synchronized soundtrack that includes sound effects and music, and sure enough the various slapstick punchlines get their little "boing!" and "wah-wah" music cues just like you'd expect. They are supposed to be laugh getters.

Murnau's allegiance with the world of comedy continued in the follow-up feature to *Sunrise*, *City Girl* (whose title, a riff on "Woman of the City," signals from the outset its agenda *vis-à-vis Sunrise*. *City Girl* opens with a scene in which a rube on a train unwisely reveals a fat bankroll and his own unwary attitude towards his money, rendering him an easy mark for the attention of a grafter. And once again we find Murnau pulling plot points from the films of Harry Langdon—in this case, the short *Lucky Stars*.

Murnau stuffed the cast of *City Girl* with comedy veterans, too: Eddie Boland is back (briefly); Guinn "Big Boy" Williams was a regular supporting actor in silent and talkie comedies (including the brilliant *Ladies Night in a Turkish Bath* with Jimmy Finlayson); David Torrence earned his slapstick comedy credentials a few years after working with Murnau, in the Laurel and Hardy film *Bonnie Scotland*; and Richard Alexander was on the front end of what would prove to be a wildly varied career that would range from *All Quiet On The Western Front* to playing Prince Barin in the Flash Gordon cliffhanger serials. His slapstick credentials? He's in Harry Langdon's *See America Thirst*, as well as Laurel and Hardy 's *Them Thar Hills* and *Babes In Toyland*.

Finding such comedy references in a Murnau film may be jarring to those who think of him only in terms of *Nosferatu* and other grim fables. And that may be a sizeable con-

**After a botched murder attempt, George O'Brien takes his wife Janet Gaynor on a comic tour of the big city. Don't think that's what *Sunrise* (1927) is about? Go watch it again.**

tingent, I realize. It is generally the tendency of critics who write about Murnau's films to identify the comic elements as something imposed on Murnau against his wishes by the studio in an effort to Americanize and popularize his films. The primary English language text on Murnau is Lotte Eisner's *Haunted Screen*—the very title of which signals its preoccupations and prejudices when it comes to Murnau. And so in her fealty to those prejudices, Eisner skips over, dismisses, or otherwise brushes under the rug any of Murnau's works that don't fit the bill.

Lotte Eisner suggests that all these tawdry jokes were inserted into *Sunrise* by Fox gag men and Murnau was obliged to go along with them. Hey, but wait a minute—*Sunrise* was famously made without studio interference, and even after his falling out with Fox, Murnau never said that *Sunrise* was anything other than a work of total creative freedom. The thing is, you can't have your cake and eat it too—you can't say Murnau had total creative freedom but he also had to tolerate jokes inserted into the script against his will. If *Sunrise* was Murnau's vision, his vision was prone to flirt with comedy.

Now might be the time to note, ahem, that *The Last Laugh* too has its own comic elements, in which a bleak story comes to a tragic end, and then reboots itself as a comedy for its final reel—inspiring the English language title. For that matter, Murnau made *Finances of the Grand Duke*, a mild action-comedy about a master thief that in many ways anticipates similar lighthearted fare along the lines of *Arsene Lupin* or *To Catch a Thief* or a fair chunk of Steven Soderburgh's back catalog.

I've long been of the opinion that comedy and horror are very similar modes of entertainment and expression. You exaggerate something to an extreme, and you provoke a reaction—that reaction may be a scream or a laugh. People can laugh when they're scared (a common enough response to John Carpenter's *The Thing*) or scream at a comedy (a common enough reaction to Buster Keaton's *Sherlock Jr.*). It doesn't much surprise me that Murnau would dabble in both.

Let's break it down: The young man (George O'Brien) rows out to the middle of the lake with his trusting wife (Janet Gaynor) where he intends to drown her. But when push comes to shove, as it were, he loses his resolve and rows mindlessly to the opposite shore, where they board a trolley car. And in one of the most astonishing sequences in all of cinema, the shell-shocked couple gather their wits as they are transported from what might as well be a medieval village straight out of *Nosferatu* through a forest to an industrial patch (is that a factory, then a mill?) and finally arriving in a futuristic Metropolis that you half expect to be populated by sentient robots. All in the span of a couple of minutes. There is no such trolley ride anywhere in the world—this thing might as well be a time machine.

The transformation is absolute. The opening scenes take place in a silent movie world of exaggerated gestures and portentous symbolism. The scenes set in the city exhibit more naturalistic acting, and are more observational in tone. The city scenes are obsessed with the details of the setting—the cars, the clothes, the architecture, the store fronts, the people-watching, the traffic. Dramas do not often get bogged down in such observational fascination with their setting. It happens sometimes—as with the semi-documentary approach of Billy Wilder's *People on Sunday*, or perhaps Robert Wise's *Star Trek: The Motion Picture*. But it happens a lot in comedies, where the observational detail is part of establishing the ironic commentary. Think Jacques Tati's *Playtime*, Chaplin's *City Lights*, Jean Renoir's *Boudou Saved from Drowning*, or just about anything by Harold Lloyd.

Murnau has introduced two outsiders into this cityscape—scraggly, haggard refugees from a horror film who have stumbled into this world in a state of high emotional dudgeon and will encounter it as if they are visitors from another planet. Again, the parallel is to a comedy's structure, with the outsider hero(es) providing for a commentary on the world around them. Charlie Chaplin rarely stumbled into any of his adventures after a botched murder attempt, but all Murnau has done is to provide a context for his protagonists' alienation where someone like Chaplin uses his costume as a shortcut to the same ends. Like Boudou or Mr. Hulot, George and Janet are outsiders invading this space. We will witness its familiar contours through their eyes.

It isn't just that the preoccupations with location prefigure the themes of so many comedies, it's that the specific juxtaposition of Old versus New in terms of location has been so resonant a factor in such important comedies (*Steamboat Bill, Jr.*, *Mon Oncle*, *Modern Times*, *Yo-Yo*) and also specifically places *Sunrise* squarely in the zeitgeist of late '20s comedy.

For example, consider what happens once George and Janet arrive in the city. They proceed to stumble from one episodic set-piece to another. In one of these, they crash a wedding ceremony and are overwhelmed by the moment. Wedding vows take on an eerie significance when juxtaposed with trying to kill your wife. George breaks down, begs for forgiveness, and the two stagger into the street in a romantic haze. In another transformation of setting not unlike the trolly-car ride that brought them here in the first place, they lose track of where they are and see themselves in the fields of home—until car horns bring them back to reality. And what ensues? Slapstick havoc, that's what—a punchline, just like you'd expect. Traffic-based gags abound in comedies of this era. But what exactly is the root of the gag? Is the traffic there to underscore the joke, or is the joke there to draw attention to the traffic? If we think it's the former, then what's the joke? Well, it's that traffic is a bear, right? Either way, the scene emphasizes the modern tribulation of city streets packed with noisy cars going every which way.

But as an observation, that is at once universal and also rather banal. In other words, the sort of observation that one might find in a standup act today. It is fundamentally the stuff of comedy, and back in the 1920s it was fundamentally the stuff of movie comedy. Thanks to the coincidence of the age of movies and the age of cars, there wouldn't have been much to say about traffic prior to the dawn of film. And it doesn't really belong in any other medium. Paintings can't capture the movement well; theatrical performances can hardly stage this indoors; no one would write a book about traffic because it isn't a literary subject. But 1920s comedians, working in film because standup wasn't yet really a thing, put such material into movies all the time.

*Sunrise* is a rumination on modernity—with a vaguely European old world giving way to a new American urbana—just as post–World War I Europe post was giving way to new American century. At the same time, the film industry was maturing (the arrival of sound technology upending the old order and bringing new sophistication). Pointedly, *Sunrise* does not view this transformation as a bad thing. It seems to be tilting that way in its early scenes, the way the evil vamp is called "Woman of the City," as if her corruption is connected to her sophistication, as if City=Evil. Once George and Janet arrive in that city, though, what they find is wonder, fun, and welcoming strangers. The city folk are sometimes a little perplexed by the two rubes, but never in a mean way—and no matter what George and Janet do or break or misunderstand, they are greeted by smiles and tolerance.

*Sunrise* shows how the new world, threatening as it is to the old, doesn't have to lead exclusively to corruption—it is possible to navigate your way through this modern world and still come out morally whole. And as such, *Sunrise* is about hope in the face of wrenching change—and this is what comedy was going through at the time, tossing out the familiar old world of slapstick chaos and replacing it with sophisticated screwball. It could be a destructive transformation, to be sure, but not exclusively so.

On one side of that divide would sit the likes of Charlie Chaplin, artists with a sensibility forged in the remnants of the 19th century, and they would be more threatened by the coming maturity of the film industry, no matter how central they had been to nurturing that maturity. And on the other would sit the likes of Cary Grant, a fundamentally 20th-century sensibility. And between those poles are the Charley Chases of the comedy world—the pioneers who emerged from silent comedy's slapstick era to point the way to what was next.

But I get ahead of myself.

I'm not spoiling the next couple of chapters to note that the primary transformation would be a recalibration of male and female gender roles, at least as far as their onscreen gender roles went—I've said this here before. The solo comedians of slapstick's Golden Age had to make way for a new breed of female stars, who took equal footing with their male costars. And what came of that transformation would be the screwball comedy, whose genre conventions presuppose flirtation as a form of combat, or vice versa. The stars of 1930s romantic comedies meet cute and engage in reel after reel of open combat, before discovering that hate is just a variation on love; you have to really care for somebody deeply to want to fight them that badly. And so, fists give way to embraces and the former opponents end up in each other's arms.

A template, by the way, that you'll find in F. W. Murnau's seminal comedy, *Sunrise*—in which the couple starts off as opposed to one another as humanly possible, and end up as tightly allied as conceivable.

# Jean, Clara, Bombshell and It

*Bombshell* is a delightful pre–Code screwball comedy. It is at once a zippy, aggressively paced comedy with one of early film's most glamorous comediennes, while also being a sharp-edged and angry satire about Hollywood power dynamics and women's sexuality. It is also an M.C. Escher-like knot of in-jokes and life-imitating-art-imitating life self-referential whorls. It is a bubbly, bitter comedy emerging from the intersection of two great comediennes, whose earthy sexuality was both their ticket to stardom and their downfall; two women whose careers were tragically destroyed before they reached the age of 30 but who managed in that short window of time to permanently etch their names and memories into pop culture posterity. You'll be hard-pressed to identify 90 minutes of celluloid that accomplishes more than this.

The story begins with Clara Bow—we can summarize her key biographical details swiftly: the hardscrabble beginnings, the breakthrough moment when her natural charisma was discovered, the struggle to hold together a stable sense of self with such a poor support structure. Her mother institutionalized for mental illness, her father an overbearing stage dad leeching off her success.

And then comes British romance novelist Elinor Glynn and her book *It* which coined a euphemism for sex appeal—the 1927 movie version cast Clara Bow in the lead and permanently identified her as "the It Girl." But here's the thing about "It": like being cool, the key is the unselfconscious nature of it. Try too hard to have "It" and you won't. Having "It" does not mean being beautiful or handsome—there are plenty of beautiful people who seem to belong to another species altogether. That's an unattainable beauty. The "It Girl" is real, tangible, available. To quote *Playboy*'s tagline from a subsequent generation: The Girl Next Door.

This had consequences. Becoming the "It Girl" made Bow's sex life part of her public image, made it public property. With it came the slut-shaming rumors: that she slept with men, women, and dogs, she did it in public, she did it with multiple partners, she did it with the entire football team. Some of the people who spread these salacious lies went to jail for it—her secretary was convicted of blackmail, the editor of a tabloid paper was jailed for printing lies. But the problem was not all of it was lies—she did replace her partners the way some women changed their shoes, she was friendly with an entire football team—and those fragments of truth within the lies kept them alive.

The scandals destroyed her career. By the age of 28 she was forced into retirement and never made a film again.

Playwrights Caroline Francke and Mack Crane were fascinated by this American tragedy, and the irony of a woman whose sex appeal was specifically cultivated by Hollywood as a marketing hook, and then she was punished for it. A lot of people made a lot of money off of the very traits in Bow they criticized in her. The writers turned this into a thinly-veiled play, which they called *Bombshell*.

The play was never produced, but it was picked up by director Victor Fleming to be adapted into a film. Fleming had a special interest in the material—he had been through the revolving door of Bow's affections and recognized the "Lola Burns" of the play. But he rejected the dramatic emphasis of the play in favor of a comic treatment—you could sell the anger much better, he figured, by packaging it within satire.

Enter Jean Harlow. She too had some personal insight into the subject matter—her first speaking role was in Clara Bow's *The Saturday Night Kid*. Moreover, she lived the life herself: she had the same hardscrabble roots, the same parasitic family leeching off her hard work, the same scandal-laden sex life.

Harlow had started off as a bit-player in slapstick comedies—appearing briefly with the likes of Laurel and Hardy or Charlie Chaplin, a bit part in an early Lubitsch film, and struggling to get taken seriously. *Variety* rudely summed up her prospects: "It doesn't matter what degree of talent she's got—nobody ever starved possessing what she's got."

**Jean Harlow's real-life experiences became the background for screwball antics in *Bombshell* (1933).**

Starting up a relationship with MGM executive Paul Bern was a good career move for a while, and led to an MGM contract and better-appointed films. But when Bern was found shot in her home, the questions started flying: had she killed him? Did he kill himself? Had some other ex-lover killed him and then MGM fussed with the crime scene to make it look like a suicide?

Together, Fleming and Harlow turned *Bombshell* into a sharp-witted and breezy comedy, that went beyond the contours of satirizing the rise and fall of Clara Bow. Early in the film, Lola is told she has to report to the set for retakes on *Red Dust*, an actual film that Harlow had just finished shooting. Her love/hate interest, smarmy PR guy "Space" Hanlon, was played by Lee Tracy in a spoof of actual MGM publicity chief Howard Strickling.

Behind the scenes, poor Jean Harlow couldn't help but slip into mimicking her on-screen character. During post-production, she married her cinematographer Hal Rosson—a marriage that lasted only a year. During production, MGM script clerk Morris Abrams rolled his eyes at the way Harlow's lazy, indolent family fatted themselves off her money while she worked a grueling schedule—just like the scenes she played in the film. "They were parasites," he clucked.

Both Bow and Harlow had a sex appeal that relied in part of their earthy, unrefined ordinariness. Just as *It* turned Bow into the It Girl, *Bombshell* branded Jean Harlow with a lasting nickname—The Blonde Bombshell. And, like Bow, Harlow's career burned out not long after—Harlow succumbed to kidney failure and died at age 26.

It's unclear what would have happened to Harlow's career had she lived. She was a top box office draw in the early 1930s, but the onset of the Production Code posed a problem for her. The kind of movies in which she had excelled were now forbidden, the public persona she developed was on the outs. Before the moralists came along to claim this independent and talented young woman was a threat simply for being who she was, her sexuality had made a lot of men very rich. She made blockbuster after blockbuster, she was a top marquee name for years—and she was such a role model for young women that sales of hair dye spiked as millions of fans tried to mimic her signature look.

Harlow glows in *Bombshell*—true to the screwball template, she anchors a comic ensemble wherein she holds her own against a large number of male (and some female) costars. For a film made two years before *It Happened One Night*, *Bombshell* surprisingly fits in almost all of the requisite screwball ingredients. For example, Harlow's character is trying to get together with a smarmy European count that everyone else can see is wrong for her.[1] There are various and sundry slapstick ex-pats in supporting roles—such as Three Stooges founder Ted Healy as Harlow's belligerent brother, or former Harry Langdon-copycat Billy Dooley as an obsessive stalker fan. Most of all, this is an aggressively paced barrage of fast-talking and lies, fast thinking and schemes, as a boy and a girl attack each other over the course of 90 minutes as a form of combat-laden courtship ... except...

That's not quite accurate.

There is something missing, an element of true screwball that is isn't fully developed here. Most of the best screwballs involve a crazy lady unleashing havoc on the men around her, and the consequence of her chaos is happiness. Here, for all that Harlow does to anchor and dominate the film, she is the *recipient* of the chaos whipped up by unethical PR man Space Hanlon (played by Lee Tracy). He either directly instigates every chaotic surge or he pours fuel on a fire set by someone else to ensure it blazes out of control. And all this abuse is to deny Harlow her happiness. The film ends where it began, with her and Lee Tracy back at square one, in a perpetual hamster wheel of comic cruelty.

The world of screwball comedy will eventually perfect this tricky formula, and deliver a comedy film about a "romantic" couple incapable of being together and incapable of being with anyone else either because of their irredeemable cruelty and selfish oblivion—and it will be one of the greatest comedies of all time. But we're not there yet.

# Miscasting for Fun and Profit

"You are sitting on top of the world!" So read the telegram Ernst Lubitsch sent Maurice Chevalier shortly after the release of *The Love Parade* in 1929. He was right—and more, Ernst was the one who put him there.

Just two years earlier, Maurice lived in a different country and had a different job. He had been an exceedingly popular cabaret star in France. Silent movies didn't have much use for a singer, but as Hollywood switched over to talkies, various movie moguls went shopping in Europe for bargain talent. There were multiple bids for Chevalier's services, and Paramount won. For all that, Chevalier's first American film was a lackluster thing now forgotten: *Innocents of Paris* was an inauspicious start for a career.

Chevalier didn't just have a thick French accent, it was a rough-n-tumble French accent. One biographer called it the "French equivalent of Cockney." As such, Maurice had gotten it into his head that he was a working-class hero type. He didn't yet realize that to untrained American ears, *any* French accent conveyed worldly sophistication and high class.

But then there was Ernst Lubitsch. He was an outsider, too, a German among Americans, and he knew a thing or two about reinvention. The son of a Jewish tailor, Ernst had first gotten into movies as a slapstick clown in silent shorts. As his popularity grew, he earned the right to direct his own movies—and started to develop a reputation as a first-rate director of massive epics. This is not how he is remembered today, but at the time he was called the Griffith of Germany. Hollywood headhunted him, and in 1922 he came to America, on the leading edge of the exodus of Teutonic talent that would only escalate as the Nazis came to power. Once in Hollywood, Lubitsch started to scale things down, replacing spectacle with subtlety. By the time he was ready to make his first sound picture, Lubitsch had crafted a new reputation as a master of romantic comedy.

Perhaps "romantic" is the wrong word for it. Lubitsch comedies were sex comedies. He'd figured out how to tell the dirtiest of jokes in a seemingly tasteful fashion, such that people who would otherwise pretend to be horrified at such raunch would hail him as a genius. For his first sound film, *The Love Parade*, Lubitsch was planning a musical based on the play "The Prince Consort," set in a fictional European fantasyland. Lubitsch wanted Chevalier to play the rogue Count Alfred, a diplomat whose relentless skirt-chasing scandalized his homeland to the point they recall him from France. Chevalier objected, saying the stiff uniforms and upper-crust characterization didn't fit his persona.

Chevalier apparently wasn't listening. Whatever this role looked like on paper had no relation to what Lubitsch was actually putting together. He had no intention of creating a *convincing* foreign land of European potentates and palace intrigue. He was determined to cast every role against type. Rather than try to conceal the gulf between reality and expectations, his plan was to do everything in his power to emphasize those misfits. He brought in former silent comedians, his old comrades—folks like Lupino Lane and cross-eyed Ben Turpin. He cast gravel-voiced Eugene Pallette as a cabinet minister—because his pugnacious voice would make every single line he said into a punchline. It took a fair bit of cajoling to convince Chevalier to take the part, and the return on that investment of trust was fantastic: Chevalier was rewarded with a nomination for Best Actor—one of six Academy Award nominations received by the film, which was Paramount's highest grossing blockbuster hit to date. Lubitsch was named by Film Daily on the Top Ten Film Directors—his fifth time on that list, more than any other moviemaker. Top of the world, indeed.

Lubitsch gave Chevalier an impressive, if unconventional, entrance scene. Chevalier doesn't even get to sing the first song—that honor goes to Lupino Lane, as Chevalier's valet. In fact, Chevalier doesn't sing for some time into the film, and once he does enter the film he is shoved to the margins as other characters—unnamed supporting players who appear only this once—provide what we need to know about him.

*The Love Parade* opens on the valet singing as he sets a table for two—and then yanks the tablecloth out from under the champagne glasses in a magical flourish (there's no point to this gag—just putting the viewer on notice that expectations are likely to be violated without notice).

Count Alfred is heard, but not seen, and he's not even heard very well. He and a woman are arguing behind closed doors—and Lubitsch lets the camera linger on that door for some time before Chevalier walks through it to directly address the audience! The woman follows him, venting raw fury. Why? Because while she was getting dressed, she found her garters didn't fit. They weren't her garters. Before Alfred can explain the origins of these bonus garters, her husband storms in. Her infidelity exposed, she grabs a gun and shoots herself dead. Blazing with jealousy and vengeance, her husband takes the gun from her corpse and fires it at Alfred. Who doesn't move. Alfred taps his chest, checking for some kind of bloody wound, then shrugs. The gun wasn't loaded with real bullets—and the lady's ruse has been exposed. The faux-suicide has been enough to shock her husband into forgiving her. Reconciled, he helps her get dressed to leave. Or, he tries to: her dress clasp is stubborn. She grows impatient with his incompetent fumbling and walks over to Alfred, who clasps it with an effortless grace born of familiarity.

This all takes place in under five minutes. Chevalier has barely moved, hardly spoken, yet

**Maurice Chevalier got a nomination for Best Actor for his role in *The Love Parade* (1930), then Paramount's highest-ever grossing blockbuster.**

we now understand him thoroughly. The sheer volume of intimate characterization, intricate backstory, and impeccable comic timing packed into those five minutes has left the audience whiplashed.

But with all that's happened, we almost overlooked the most important thing: Lupino Lane's song. From a contemporary perspective, it doesn't stand out. But this is 1929, when movie musicals were haphazard things called "revues." Hollywood had collectively assumed that movie audiences wanted their movies to be realistic, and since people don't just burst into song during their daily lives, the only way to work a song into a movie scene would be to have it be a self-contained and self-conscious performance. Lubitsch figured this reasoning was asinine. Operas mix dialogue and singing all the time, and nobody complains. Who says a movie couldn't tell a coherent story in which the characters sometimes sang their lines?

That *The Love Parade* arguably marks the birth of the movie musical becomes an even stranger achievement when you consider the technical challenges facing Lubitsch in 1929. You don't even have to be a film pro today to be equipped with editing tools on your phone superior to anything Lubitsch had. Cutting sound recordings in those early days was just this side of impossible. Typically, when a song would be sung onscreen in 1929, the camera stayed focused on the singer, without cutting away, while the performer sang along live to a real orchestra, playing off-screen. In one show-stopping sequence of outrageous ambition, Lubitsch not only cuts *during* a song, he cuts back and forth between two different couples singing the same song in two different locations. To even do this at all, he had to have the two sets built side-by-side, alongside a single off-camera orchestra, and two separate soundproofed camera baffles aimed at the two sets. Ernst sat on a stool between the two sets and directed both scenes simultaneously. The soundtrack was recorded intact in a single pass—no cutting of it was required, and the synchronized images could be cut back and forth with technical impunity. Other filmmakers were still dipping tentative toes into the new talkie medium; Lubitsch was already rewriting its rules.

He felt so confident about the new opportunities afforded by working with sound, he was already playing games with the technology. A key scene is not shown to the audience at all, but instead Lubitsch shows us the reactions of eavesdropping busybodies, who narrate it to us. The joke is in the way their descriptions clearly reveal more about what they hope is happening than what they actually witness, but to get that joke the audience needs to have a visual impression of things they cannot see, and an understanding of the psychology of the various narrators. It's a multidimensional approach to storytelling, a conviction that no single frame of the film would ever be just what it appears.

If you're going to make an operetta on film, casting a beloved singer like Maurice Chevalier makes a lot of sense. The problem was, who to cast opposite him? Ernst set to interviewing actresses, and found his pickings unexpectedly slim. "Those who are attractive often have poor voices and those who can act and have good voices are not so pleasing in their appearance," he complained impolitely to the press. "The screen now demands a girl who looks well, can act well, and speak well."

According to some reports, he briefly considered Lillian Roth for the lead, but was dissuaded by her strident Brooklyn drawl and wrote a supporting role for her instead: she plays Lupino Lane's love interest, and she's one of the singers in the two-way duet described above. The anecdote has a strong whiff of the apocryphal to it—Lubitsch was not the kind of director to be put off by someone's classless accent. What is known, though, is that his discovery of Jeanette MacDonald was awkward, delayed, and unlikely. He was discouraged by the crop of talent he'd been shown, and was debating signing Bebe Daniels to the role, when he was shown an old screen test that an unknown aspiring actress had made a year earlier for a different project. At first, the thing was shown to him with the wrong soundtrack, and only after some slapstick-style bungling did the projectionist finally locate the correct voice to go along with the film. There on the screen was a bug-eyed blonde, skinny and unsure of herself, projecting an air of assumed and artificial authority. She was perfect, and her name was Jeanette MacDonald.

Ernst started calling her "Mac" as a term of endearment. She reciprocated the gesture, and called him "Lu." Then he took to calling her "Donald," and rather than call him "Bitsch," she surrendered. He thought she was too thin, and gave her milkshakes between takes to give her more feminine curves. He wanted her to fill out her negligee better because she was going to spend a lot of time in it.

The first time we see Jeanette she's in her lingerie. By 1920s standards, she's essentially nude. But that's just the start of the scene. As it goes on, she takes off the nightie and hops in a bath—she spends the rest of her first scene actually nude. The movie's still only warming up—she'll be back in her underwear several more times. This would become the hallmark of her career—rare would be the movie in which Jeanette MacDonald kept her clothes on.

Here she plays Queen Louise, a wise and patient ruler of a country that cannot rest until she's wed. There's only so long she can be expected to put up with sexual frustration, but finding a mate has been tough. Whoever she marries will be "Prince Consort," a glorified pet, and finding a man willing to take on such an emasculated position is a tall order. It doesn't help that, at least as Lubitsch portrays it, the entire country is one enormous small town, parochial and small-minded, populated by rubes and gossips. But then, who should appear in the Queen's chambers but Count Alfred? He's gorgeous and manly—not to mention rakish and defiant. He's everything she wants and nothing that she needs. She stares with desire and confusion—who *is* this guy, and why is he here? Alfred can't even make a proper accounting of himself—he's apparently there for punishment, but neither he nor the Queen can quite figure out why, or what sort of punishment is called for. The more she stares, the more she wants. Love at first sight (or at least lust at first sight), and utter catastrophe in the making. The rascally qualities she loves in him also make him a terrible choice. Can she hope to domesticate him without destroying him?

For some critics, *Love Parade* unfolds a typical example of Hollywood's anti-feminist attitudes. Why should this strong woman have to surrender to her husband's domination at the end? That's one way of reading it—but let's not forget that there is a recurring joke of describing Alfred as the Queen's "wife." The things that threaten to drive them apart aren't his sexual urges—there is no "other woman," no love triangle of any kind. The problem is the limited life afforded any "wife," male or female. The larger moral of the picture is: if you love somebody, don't make them your wife.

Lubitsch needed to learn that lesson himself. His wife Leni Sonnet, married since 1922, had been carrying on with his best friend. Everyone close to him knew; no one told. Divorce followed—Ernst was the victim of the very sophisticated permissiveness he depicted in his films.

Better days were ahead, though, both personally and professionally. The most impressive aspect of all the critical accolades and artistic achievements that attended *The Love Parade* is that, in the fuller context of Lubitsch's career, it is not even remembered as one of his best films. You can't claim to be at the top of the world if you're still climbing.

# Girls! Girls! Girls!

Two lovers, locked in a room—the future of the state itself depends on whether their roiling lust for each other will override their other emotions and compel them into a marriage. The last time these two saw each other, Danilo (Maurice Chevalier) thought Sonia (Jeanette MacDonald) was a whore. The first time they saw each other, Sonia knew Danilo was a gigolo. And if all this talk of prostitution sounds tawdry, just remember that is in fact what this is all about: the King has ordered Danilo to seduce Sonia because unless she has a compelling reason to stick around in the Ruritanian kingdom of "Marshovia" she'll take her wealth with her, crippling the economy. This is about trading money for sex, and sex for money.

Fans of high culture of course know this story as the beloved *Merry Widow*. Franz Lehar's opera had been entertaining audiences around the world since its Vienna premiere in 1905. But the prudish censors who governed Hollywood in 1934 weren't what you'd call fans of high culture. For them, Ernst Lubitsch's film version of *The Merry Widow* was just a piece of smut.

So how exactly did this thing get made in the first place? And what did it have to do with the Marx Brothers?

We start with a man returning home. He removes his hat, he climbs the stairs to the bedroom, he opens the door—and there is his wife, in bed, startled and a little guilty. She's talking fast, like she's nervous, trying to cover for something, a distraction. The man opens his closet to put away his coat and tie—and there is Groucho! "*Believe it or not, I'm waiting for a streetcar.*" Before the husband even has a chance to properly stoke his jealousy, a clanging streetcar actually arrives in the bedroom! Groucho boards and rides away!

Don't worry if you don't recall which movie this scene is from, because it was never filmed. Ernst Lubitsch cooked the idea up for his proposed contribution to the omnibus film *If I Had a Million*. Exactly why the pieces never came together, I don't know—some facts get lost to the ages, you know—but this was as close as the greatest comedy director of all time came to working with the greatest comedy team of all time. That being said, let's also note that a variation on that scene, a little less absurd and Marxian but still recognizably the same idea, does appear in *The Merry Widow*. Why waste a good idea?

Ernst was feeling his O's at the time. He'd made masterpieces like *Trouble in Paradise* and *Design for Living*—daring, provocative comedies that all but spat in the faces of the self-appointed censors trying to impose their Puritan preoccupations on the nation's popular culture. He was hitting these heights against a backdrop of utter desolation in Hollywood. Not a single film released in 1932 made good money. The years 1932–1934 were the very pits of the Great Depression. Hollywood was a desperate wounded animal, bleeding money and frantic to make safe, crowd-pleasing cost-conscious choices. Yet improbably, here was this funky little immigrant who made expensive movies about sex. There was nothing safe about a man whose idea of a romantic comedy was one in which the leading lady doesn't chose between her two suitors, but happily shacks up with them both. Lubitsch got away with such shenanigans because of economics. His prestige films were hits—the studio bosses had a hard time saying "no" to a man who made them boatloads of money. And when he did hit a rough patch, his money-losing films were critical darlings and international hits that justified their losses with good PR.

Lubitsch was known for his oblique, indirect touch—often mistaken for "subtlety." But there's a difference. Lubitsch lobbed bawdy joke after bawdy joke at his audience, but in ways designed to just barely miss the target cleanly, and instead not fully register as dirty. The viewer is inundated by these off-target gags to the point they know they've seen something ribald, even if they can't quite put their finger on what.

For a long time, censors had a problem censoring Lubitsch—he didn't just scatter sex references into his films where they could be easily cut out; he made films so fundamentally about sex that the censors' only viable option was to ban them outright. But the censors weren't a government body—they were an industry body created to insulate the filmmaking community from government action. In other words, they were there to protect the industry and its profits. So when Lubitsch confronted them with sex-obsessed films that cost a shocking amount of money to make the censors tended to throw up their hands in defeat and let his stuff slide rather than risk telling his studios that they couldn't release them at all.

**Ernst Lubitsch's take on *The Merry Widow* (1934), starring Jeanette MacDonald and Maurice Chevalier, ran afoul of the censors.**

This didn't last forever.

Meanwhile, let's bring Irving Thalberg into the story. He wanted to make a film version of *The Merry Widow*. His studio MGM had already made one 10 years earlier (by Erich von Stroheim—everyone's go-to guy for frothy sex comedies, right?) and he figured the market was ripe for a second go-round. Lubitsch was not on contract to MGM, but surely he could be had on a loan-out agreement, and who would be better for such a thing?

Lubitsch in turn had his own idea about who was best suited to play the leads—why Maurice Chevalier and Jeanette MacDonald, of course! They had been his muses for several years now, even if both players were starting to tire of that arrangement.

Anita Loos took the first pass at writing a new scenario—Thalberg wanted to make sure the new film was different enough from Von Stroheim's version that he didn't have to pay any royalties. In my opinion, Loos was the perfect screenwriter for the gig, and it's a real shame that she and Lubitsch never properly collaborated, because they seem to have such similar sensibilities.[1] But if you get Lubitsch, you get his entourage, so he had his regular writers Ernest Vajda and Samson Raphaelson take another couple of drafts.

This hints at something worth noting about this entire production: Lubitsch had the authority to bring in the cast and crew he wanted rather than be obligated to MGM's roster of talents. He also had the right of final cut, a rarity in those days. Hell, the right of final cut remained a rarity for decades. But such was the power of the Lubitsch brand name.

But the power of Lubitsch's name no longer extended to the censors, not in 1934. The newly emboldened Production Code office under Joseph Breen and Will Hays' Legion of Decency were scandalized by Lubitsch's utter disregard and contempt for their idea of decency, and they were no longer intimidated by his stature. *The Merry Widow* was MGM's most expensive film to date, but that no longer swayed them. Their offices demanded various cuts—*after* the prints were made—at tremendous cost.

That's right—some poor sod had to unspool each and every release print and individually splice out the bits these two prudes couldn't abide. And MGM had to eat that cost, and then stand by while audiences and critics treated the latest Lubitsch film as so much chopped liver. It lost money, it got poor notices. Ernst Lubitsch didn't make another film for three years…

But … let's rewind and tell that story again, from a slightly different perspective. Everything I just said is true, but there's another story, buried in the first.

That poor MGM intern stuck in the editing bay manually censoring every release print? That meant that the cuts were made "downstream" from the negative after it had been locked. Which means that the subsequent TV screenings and DVD releases came from the uncensored negative—Joe Breen and Will Hays cost MGM some money and heartburn in 1934, but their cuts were isolated in time and forgotten by posterity. *The Merry Widow* lived on, and has since been recognized as a proper masterpiece, unencumbered by their foolishness. And Lubitsch's three-year hiatus? Well, on February 4, 1935, he was appointed head of production at Paramount! If the censors wanted to marginalize his worldview, he just gained the ability to propagate it far wider than he ever would have been able to on his own.

Ernst Lubitsch conquered Hollywood.

# I Won't Back Down

The repetition of certain lines of dialogue is one of the defining characteristics of Ernst Lubitsch's cinema. Lubitschean characters repeat certain lines as a way of creating double-entendres on the spot. Audiences are expected to recognize the repetition, and to remember the context of the original lines, so that those memories get overlaid on top of the repeat, imbuing the words with a weight of additional meaning beyond the literal significance of the words themselves.

To single out an especially piquant example from *To Be or Not to Be*, consider what Lubitsch does to the phrase "Heil Hitler." Over the course of 90 minutes it is yawned by Jack Benny, treated like an Abbott and Costello routine by most of the rest of the cast—*Heil Hitler! No, I Heiled Hitler first!*—there is a fake Hitler who says "Heil myself," and of course Carole Lombard's orgasmic moan of the line.

The central conceit of the movie isn't about making fun of what the Nazis took from Poland, it's about creating a fictional space where the Poles take everything from the Nazis. This isn't a movie about the German invasion of Poland—it's about a Polish invasion of Germans. During the course of the film, our heroes subversively appropriate the Nazis' uniforms, their identities, even their salute—and as these icons of Nazi terror are systematically taken over by the Polish actors it simply serves to undercut the power of those totems. They turn "Heil Hitler" into a punchline before the first German troops set foot in Poland. By the time the real Nazis show up and try to say this salute seriously, the words have been completely deracinated and redefined by the heroes so that you can't help but chuckle. Name one other movie where the phrase "Heil Hitler" is used as a joke.

Well, I can name one—*Ninotchka*, by Ernst Lubitsch in 1939. That's right, the year that World War II began is when we find Lubitsch's first ever "Heil Hitler" joke.

*Ninotchka* concerns the efforts of the Soviet government to raise money by selling some of the jewels confiscated from the former Russian royalty. A group of Soviet emissaries have been bumbling around Paris enjoying Western decadence without ever coming even remotely close to selling any jewels. So Stalin sends a new emissary to take over their misfired mission and get the job done right. So, the Soviet Three Stooges come to the train station, nervously awaiting the imminent arrival of this new agent.

They scan the faces of the people disembarking from the train, trying to spot which one is their newly arrived comrade. They see a little man with a scraggly beard and an Eastern European mien about him—this fellow is certainly Russian, they agree. But as they approach, he salutes, "*Heil Hitler!*" and embraces an Aryan blonde. Ooops.

So right away, the very first use of a Heil Hitler joke in the Lubitsch canon is about the danger of relying on stereotypes to judge people, about the difficulty in distinguishing Us Versus Them. The guy you think is a communist turns out to be a Nazi.

And then here comes Greta Garbo as Ninotchka—*she's* the one they're supposed to be meeting. She is a hard-edged, no-nonsense Bolshevik firebrand—a Communist Leslie Knope. Practically the very first words she speaks, uttered within seconds of the Heil Hitler gag, is to note approvingly that Stalin has just overseen a new round of mass trials—"*There will be fewer, but better, Russians.*"

Which is about as black a joke as you can get. Here is a joke about mass murder and state-sponsored terror that is intended to be our introduction to the title character, the heroine, Greta freaking Garbo—the person we've bought our tickets to see, the character whose triumph we are here to root for. Over the course of the movie, Ninotchka never backs down from that position or recants it. To the end she remains a committed Soviet, genuinely committed to the cause and determined to do her part to advance Stalin's government's agenda. Not only that, but the movie stands in her corner, too. She gets to spread her propaganda to other characters in the film—and to us in the audience—and she is persuasive, too, getting Melvyn Douglas to join her team. Although she is reciprocally corrupted by him in turn, as we'll discuss in just a second, it is not in any way that implies that she was wrong to believe as she does.

Just ruminate on that. In 1939, Ernst Lubitsch made a comedy about communism that didn't universally condemn it, and it was a mainstream blockbuster hit. This, from the director who brought you *Design for Living*, a romantic comedy that endorses three-ways as the solution to love triangles. Lubitsch was in the business of defying conventional wisdom and prevailing social mores and doing so in ways audiences enthusiastically endorsed.

How does Melvyn Douglas' character corrupt Ninotchka? By getting Great Garbo to laugh. That was the selling point of the movie, you know—Garbo laughs! But more than just a one-off gimmick, it's the heart of the movie.

Melvyn Douglas seduces her with silly jokes—most of them told horribly, none of them very good. In the end he has to abandon the wordplay and go for a slapstick pratfall, but once she laughs she's hooked. Life is better when you laugh, and a society that rejects laughter isn't a society that is worth fighting for. The ultimate contest between Capitalism and Communism won't be won by ideology, it comes down to who has the best jokes. It's all about the liberating—and revolutionary—power of laughter. For that matter, it's about the power of silly jokes and dumb slapstick, not sophisticated humor.

Which brings us to *Cluny Brown*. Because *Ninotchka*, with its first stab at a Heil Hitler joke, came out in 1939, the eve of war. *Cluny Brown* also handles Nazism, in 1946, the end of the war. They are Lubitsch's bookends to World War II, and they frame the themes of *To Be or Not to Be* very nicely. My big question about *Cluny Brown* is … where are the Nazis?

I know this isn't a question that's probably been burning inside much of anyone else besides me, but I suffered my way through the awkward and disappointing biography of Ernst Lubitsch by Scott Eyman, a book I'd only bought because I wanted to see how a scholar steeped in Lubitsch would address this very question. As far as I'm concerned, it's a question that cuts to the very heart of what Lubitsch was all about. And Eyman missed the point entirely.

I could build a time machine and travel back to 1993 to write an angry letter to Eyman, but that seems a misuse of resources. Once I finish work on my time machine the first thing I want to do is go back to the 1920s and collect some prints of films like *Heart Trouble* and *Hats Off*, so I'm not wasting any of my time machine's battery power just to berate some poor biographer, even if he did fluff the shot something awful. So, instead I'll just unload my rant here—and maybe we can have some fun digesting what made Lubitsch the genius that he was.

First things first. As of this writing, *Cluny Brown* is one of the least accessible and hardest to see of Lubitsch's films, so it's worthwhile to catch everyone else up so we're on the same page. Lubitsch was riding the crest of a creative wave that is almost incomprehensible. If we forgive the aberration of *That Uncertain Feeling* sandwiched in the middle, from 1939 to 1943 Lubitsch was making hit after hit: *Ninotchka*, *The Shop Around the Corner*, *To Be or Not to Be*, and *Heaven Can Wait*. It's even more astounding to us now in retrospect because we can appreciate *To Be or Not to Be* as a masterpiece, whereas audiences in 1942 were too horrified to get it.

And then this wave came crashing down, with Lubitsch's abrupt heart attack in 1943. At the very height of his creative powers, he was forbidden by his doctors to work. At best, he was permitted to produce—only to watch feebly from the sidelines as his inept protégés Otto Preminger and Joseph Mankiewicz fumbled *A Royal Scandal* and *Dragonwyck*, respectively. Preminger never understood Lubitsch's comedy at all, and while Mank was a better student, his work on *Dragonwyck* was so far off the mark Lubitsch had his name removed from the film. Which was awkward, seeing that the posters had already been made: the studio had to affix stickers over his name to redact it from the one-sheets.

Finally, he got the go-ahead from his doctors that he could get back to work. Naturally, he jumped hungrily at the first available project—*Cluny Brown*, adapted from Margery Sharp's 1944 novel of the same name. The Fox writers had already hashed out a couple of screenplay treatments of the book, none of which Lubitsch liked. He started anew, and wrote the script exceedingly quickly (for Lubitsch, that is) and got it approved by the studio with almost no changes or notes (for studio exec Darryl F. Zanuck, that is).

Speaking of anomalies—I'm told that Lubitsch made fairly few alterations to the source. I have not read the novel myself to confirm this, but see no reason to doubt it. The man who dared rewrite Noel Coward's *Design for Living* ("I was only interested in the premise of it," sniffed Lubitsch) didn't see much in Sharp's novel he needed to change—that, or he was in such a rush to make it, he didn't feel like wasting time.

Before we proceed to talk about the movie itself, one more note about its origins: when the studio bought the rights to the book, it was with a stipulation that Jennifer Jones play the lead. (What was Sharp thinking?) She would eventually join the production straight from the embattled set of David O. Selznick's *Duel in the Sun*. How embattled was it? So embattled that *Duel in the Sun* didn't even make it to theaters until *after Cluny Brown*.

So, we have a recovering and weakened Lubitsch, desperate to get back on top after losing three of his best years to his heart troubles. And it's built around a miscast star arriving in a flurry of distraction. OK, well, I don't really mean "miscast," because that's one of the Essential Traits of Lubitsch (ETL for short) that I wanted to discuss here. If you were going to argue that Jones was miscast as Cluny Brown, you might point up that the role calls for a rowdy, brash, assertive young woman—the kind of role that typically went to Betty Grable. But Lubitsch cast Betty Grable in the next film, *That Lady in Ermine*, as a Queen—the kind of role that Jennifer Jones should've gotten. It seems backwards.

Instead, we get Jones, full of neurotic energy and frostiness, in a role written for a Betty Grable—and thus she infuses it with an additional dimension, a layer of inner life that the film does not make explicit. Grable would've played a cartoon—Jones turns the cartoon into a woman. And then *That Lady in Ermine* reverses the trick—with Grable providing an unexpected degree of earthiness and tawdriness to a role that could otherwise seem too aloof.

So ETL #1 is a deliberate and consistent policy of "miscasting." In his day, critics accused him of not understanding American accents properly, and seemed to believe that if Ernie really knew what connotations these actors brought with them, he wouldn't be casting them as Kings and Queens and society folk. Balderdash! Meanwhile, Eyman, my *bête noir*, occasionally makes excuses for Lubitsch's odd casting choices by saying these were the only people he could get access to at this studio or that. Who says you need to make excuses? Consistently, Lubitsch made the most of actors and actresses who seemed profoundly out of place in what he asked them to do: Miriam Hopkins, Gary Cooper, Greta Garbo—and Jack Benny for crissakes! Not for nothing did these performers reminisce about their work with Lubitsch as having been their best.

The point though is not to get mired in arguments about where *Cluny Brown* came from, but rather what's in it—and what's conspicuously missing—and what conclusions we can draw from that odd recipe.

There are two concurrent parallel storylines to this film. The first one follows the titular Miss Brown, who has the misfortune to want, to dearly want most in all the world, to be a plumber. But she lives in 1938 England, where rigid class roles and gender restrictions have placed that aspiration permanently out of her reach. "*I wish I could roll up my sleeves and roll down my stockings and unloosen the joint. BANG BANG BANG!*" Jokes about plumbing as a metaphor for sex are already familiar double entendres, but by the time this absurd scene of Cluny Brown deliriously pounding on pipes with her hammer is over, that surface layer of entendre has been sufficiently battered to leave just the single dirty entendre underneath.

"*You wouldn't have thought I was out of place.*" Poor Cluny is perpetually out of place—in large part because she doesn't care, and her desired place is (allegedly) unattainable. Let's be clear that being a "plumber" is a metaphor—what she wants is to be free, sexually and spiritually, in a world that allows for no such thing.

It is instead her fate to be employed as a parlor maid in the English countryside. Thanks to some complications upon her arrival at her new post, the family mistakes her for a guest, instead of their new maid. They proceed to treat her as a guest, until the shattering truth is discovered. The breach of etiquette is unimaginable. As the new maid, she has no right to sit at their table, to eat their scones, to speak to them at all.

This scene may be the most significant in the entire picture—it's certainly the linchpin of my analysis. The house is pretty, the family is decent and kind, the village is quaint—it's not a bad fate, as these things go. But as pretty as the house is, it will never be her *home*. As decent as the family is, they will never be her friends (nor her family). And the village—well, here's the thing about the village: Cluny gets one day off every week, and that day is the one day the village cinema is closed. She can look forward to never seeing a movie. Ever.

It is a suffocating life. There is only one escape route for her: to marry some nice boy and quit. But she can't just grab any eligible male. The house she works in is full of handsome strapping young lads, smart and rich, full of energy and passion (we'll come to them in just a bit), but they're off-limits. She's a servant, and can only go shopping for a mate among other working class blokes, which does limit her options severely.

Her eyes eventually alight on Mr. Wilson, the local chemist. There are scarecrows with more personality, there are executioners who are more humane, there are trolls who are more attractive. But her choices are few, and she can learn to make do. His mother, though, is a different story—she's a passive-aggressive battle-ax, she's the mom from *Psycho* while still alive, she's the embodiment of the suffocating lifestyle Cluny has ahead of her.

Suffice to say, Cluny's romance with Mr. Wilson is short-lived. She has the audacity to fix his plumbing—in the presence of his mother!—and that as they say is that.

And before you grumble that plumbing doesn't have anything to do with hammering violently on pipes (*BANG BANG BANG!* indeed), let me just say that this is, like ETL #1, all part of the joke. Realistic depictions of plumbing aren't as funny as slapstick, so Ernie opts for the funnier version. This is where Otto Preminger goes wrong in his Lubitsch-lite efforts—given the choice, Otto would go for a realistic depiction of plumbing, and lose most of the laughs.

Now, you're probably wondering what any of this has to do with Nazis. Indeed—that's why we're here.

So, let's meet the other protagonist of this tale, Adam Belinski, played by Charles Boyer. He falls in love with the free-spirited manic pixie dream girl Cluny Brown, and they bond over silly jokes. The repeated line in *Cluny Brown* is Belinski's reference to defying conformity by choosing to throw "squirrels to nuts," instead of the (more sensible) other way round. The two of them quote this back and forth to each other, and to other characters, throughout the film as a way of distinguishing which people have a proper love of silliness or are agents of conformist stuffiness. Belinski is a fugitive Czech humanist fleeing the Nazis. It is said the power of his ideas and his eloquence in expressing them is a greater threat to fascism than any weapon. He's skulking around incognito, until Andrew Carmel, John Fruin and the luscious Betty Cream recognize him and sweep him away into hiding at the Carmel estate (the same place where Cluny is working).

Yup. Betty Cream. That's her name. It's like she was supposed to be a Bond girl but ended up on the wrong set. As played by Helen Walker, she's a potent concoction of sexpot packaged inside a deeply intellectual and hard-headed activist. She's the female equivalent of a Swiss Army Knife—12 different women in one. She's more woman than Andrew can handle—but he's not even going to get a chance to try as long as the two of them are too busy being Earnest with a capital E to get their freak on. It takes some sly (and utterly unasked for) interference by Belinski to hook them up properly.

Now wait a minute. What exactly is going on here? Belinski has been secreted away to the Carmel estate because he's a prominent anti–Nazi. But he consistently misses opportunities to engage his hosts on political discussions. If they're expecting to experience the gifted oratory and wisdom of a Great Man, he's sorely letting down his side. He spends most of time tinkering with people's love lives and making caustic ironic comments. The only change he really seems to care about is spare change.

The first time I saw this, I assumed the story was heading to a third act twist in which it would be revealed that "Belinski" was in fact a conman posing as the Czech dissident in order to bum lodgings, food, and cash off of unsuspecting do-gooders. I felt justified in this assumption because throughout the film he *acts* like a con-man—and I do mean throughout. I don't wish to spoil the final punchline, but let me just say that at no point does he behave like similar figures in other movies.

As a foil for contrast, consider *To Be or Not to Be*'s villain, Professor Siletsky—an intellectual whose speeches and radio broadcasts are key to whipping up anti-fascist sentiment in the West, but who turns out to be a traitor helping the Third Reich.

Had *Cluny Brown* been building to this unmasking of the conman "Belinski," it would have been a clever mirror of how Cluny was mistaken for a guest. You'd have had a grand satirical theme of how society treats people not for who they are but for who they appear to be. If you think a charming young lady is a house guest, you feed her tea and crumpets. If you think she's a servant, you expect her to vanish into the background and shut her yap. If you think a handsome foreigner is a fugitive philosopher, you feed and house him. If he turns out to be some schmo with a silver tongue ... then what?

Weirdly, this isn't where the movie is headed. There is an unaccountable gap between what we are told about Belinski, and how he actually behaves. Taking the movie at its word that this man is the legendary anti-fascist scholar Adam Belinski, then we really do have to ask, "where are the Nazis?" The movie spends all this time telling us that he's threatened by Nazis—yet not once does anything happen to verify this. It's set in 1938, with England on the verge of going to war with Germany—yet nothing happens to put this in context. We never see any Nazis or see any of their cruel handiwork, and Belinski then never talks about any of it, either.

Scott Eyman writes, "Belinski's achievements—which we have to take on faith—seem incidental to the simple sybaritic pleasure he takes in his own company."

*Yes. This is true. C'mon, Eyman, ask why this is true. Please, it matters—*

Eyman also notes, "the obliviousness of the English is never really germane to the story; neither is Belinski's anti–Nazi past."

*Oh, sorry, Eyman, you were getting hot there for a moment, and now you went cold again. Don't you get it, man? The two are the same thing.*

What are Nazis? Don't say German fascists in the 1930s and '40s—that's too specific. Belinski is an intellectual, a philosopher—he's opposed to ideologies, not to individual people. The ideology of Nazism is one that elevated a certain class of people as legitimate and desirable, and considered everyone else below them, worthy of persecution or even annihilation. People were consigned to concentration camps or gas chambers based not on their actions but on accidents of their birth—and this inhuman system was defended as the natural order of things.

There are "Nazis" in this film. They are the Carmels, they are the Wilsons. Ordinary Englishmen and women who reflexively accept the idea that social caste defines a person's fate. Lubitsch implies an analogy between the English class system and German concentration camps. It's enough to make your jaw drop.

English audiences took it as a slap in the face. The English press excoriated the film—and while their reviews tended to be couched in terms of how the details of the movie were inauthentic, this was hollow deflection. Seriously, are you going to complain that the clothes worn by the characters seemed like Hollywood approximations of English garb, in a movie where Jennifer Jones *fixes toilets by hammering on them*? Those critics were stung by the fact they had just sat through a 96-minute-long sustained assault on basic English assumptions about society, and they lashed out at the nearest target, which was the film's alleged inauthenticity.

(Some UK critics noted the film's credits were full of German names and scoffed that the only thing Germans knew about England was how to bomb it.)

*To Be or Not to Be* scandalized audiences in its day because it had the audacity to treat Nazis as human beings, to give them humanizing traits and even jokes. To give the Nazis good jokes! This was unheard of—filmmakers were expected to depict Nazis as irredeemable monsters. Hitchcock's *Lifeboat* is a perfect case in point—the thrust of the film is that there is something so fundamentally wrong about Nazis as people that the rest of the world should show them no mercy. Such films posit that the Allies' greatest weakness was their sense of democratic tolerance and forgiveness—attributes that the Nazis would exploit against us.

Lubitsch never bought that line. Let's be clear—he wasn't *for* Nazis—the Nazis very nearly killed his daughter, they did kill members of his family, and if he'd ever been stupid enough to return to his homeland they'd have happily killed him too. He knew all that, but he just wasn't the kind of person capable of writing anyone off as irredeemable. Twice he tried to make promotional *Why We Fight* or *Know Your Enemy* films for the war effort—and both times they were rejected as unusable. Propaganda wasn't in his nature.

Anyone who saw Lubitsch's *The Man I Killed* already knew this. Smack in the middle of his run of early-30s musical comedies—between *The Smiling Lieutenant* and *One Hour With You*—he made this bitter drama about a World War I vet plagued by guilt over having killed a man in the war. The rest of society doesn't know how to console him, because they don't recognize it as a crime. If anything, they'd like to pin medals on him as a hero. But he—and Lubitsch, and the film—make no distinction between wartime activity and murder, so he trundles off into enemy territory to meet his victim's family and try to make amends.

Audiences stayed away from *The Man I Killed* in droves (really? it has such a marketable title!). It belongs on a triple bill with Harry Langdon's *Three's a Crowd* and Leo McCarey's *Make Way for Tomorrow* as a film that uses the tools of comedy to present a soul-crushing tragedy. It's got ETL #1 in full force—you don't cast Lionel Barrymore as a German if you care about verisimilitude. But what matters to us here is its philosophy of tolerance. Lubitsch doesn't believe in enemies, he doesn't believe in Nazis. His films can't muster enough hatred to come up with real villains—the only thing he finds unforgivable is cruelty, and in *Cluny Brown* the cruel ones are the ordinary English folk that most viewers probably assumed were the good guys.

Sorry, Eyman. *Cluny Brown* is an extraordinary film, rich and dense and demanding of viewer attention. The obliviousness of the English is absolutely germane to the story, and so is Belinski's anti–Nazi past. Lubitsch does nothing by accident. When the man so renowned for directing by indirection leaves something out, all your attention should be on the missing piece.

To swing back to where we were at the start of the chapter, if you come into *To Be or Not to Be* looking for a specific condemnation of Nazism, if you're looking for propaganda, you're in the wrong movie. Because what Lubitsch decries about Nazis, what he opposes, isn't something unique to them—it's the same thing he's been fighting all along. That's because, as we've seen all throughout the movie, the Nazi salutes and Nazi uniforms and all those markers of Nazism don't really mean anything. Anybody can wear that uniform, anybody can say Heil Hitler. That doesn't mean a thing. What matters is the person under-neath—and people are people, the world over.

The thing about propaganda is it defines the enemy in very clean, stark Us Versus Them ways, and then seeks to dehumanize "them" so that it is easier to fight and kill them. But once you've defined your conflict in tribal terms, you've ceded a lot of the argument—by which I mean, if the only thing that makes us better than them is that we're us and we're not them, then the difference between good and evil is largely a matter of circumstance. Admittedly, making some kind of relativist argument that seeks to equate the Allies and

Axis powers as being all brothers under the skin is deeply problematic, but that actually leads us into the aesthetic problem: Once you've started depicting your enemy as the ulti-mate Big Bad, then it follows that you need some kind of extraordinary response to be able to defeat that enemy. If Nazis are the worst manifestation of human depravity in history, the closest thing to the Devil walking on the Earth, then it's going to take the greatest heroes to stop him: you need Great Men like Winston Churchill, General Patton, Douglas MacArthur—you need the Greatest Generation! It's no coin-cidence that World War II is where a num-ber of superheroes were born: Wonder Woman and Captain America, for exam-ple. The earliest iteration of James Bond, as a literary character in books by Ian Fleming, cast him as a World War II vet-eran.

Carole Lombard in *To Be or Not to Be* (1942).

In terms of storytelling, the propa-ganda mode doesn't leave much room for any ordinary people—except as the vic-tims, the people your heroes are going to save. Lubitsch's *To Be or Not to Be* though isn't a contest between Us Versus Them— and Lubitsch is very careful to remind us throughout that we are in no position to even identify which people are on which side. For all you know Hitler's a guy in a costume and Gestapo headquarters might be a theater. And the secret high sign between the Nazis, their passphrase "Heil Hitler," might just be a joke uttered between Poles.

We've already seen in *Ninotchka* how a silly joke can unravel the most deeply held ide-ologies. This is the real reason the Nazis were bound to lose. You can ban jokes all you want, it doesn't stop people telling them—and a society that tries to forbid silly jokes will find itself in perpetual war with its own citizens, while the society that celebrates the silly will find no end of converts and loyalists. If there's one thing we know from watching Lubitsch's films, it's that in a battle between comedians and censors, the comedians always win.

# The Unexpected Comedy Stylings
# of Alfred Hitchcock

It's important to bear in mind that the "World War II era" is not a monolithic thing, but was in fact broken into several discrete phases. For example, there was a period of time, in both the United Kingdom and United States, when war hadn't actually started yet but seemed increasingly likely, and filmmakers like Alfred Hitchcock made "wartime" thrillers before the war as a way of whipping up popular support for the coming fight.

Hitchcock made a number of these in the United Kingdom prior to the outbreak of war in 1939 (*The Lady Vanishes*, *The 39 Steps*, etc.) and then came to America and did the same thing, making *Foreign Correspondent* before Pearl Harbor. The plot of *Foreign Correspondent* is actually about the American press trying to suss out the likelihood of impending war. Then, after the United States joined the war in late 1942, a new phase began where propaganda was no longer about convincing audiences that a war needed to be fought against these Nazi bastards but that now that we were fighting we should keep our morale up—and *To Be or Not to Be* had the misfortune to be made in one propaganda era but released in another. Its farcical vision of Nazism played differently to audiences now that war was no longer just somebody else's problem. But that being said, *Foreign Correspondent* and *To Be or Not to Be* stay weirdly in synch.

Some of the parallels are in personnel: Charles Dobosh is one of the first actors to appear in both films, playing the theater director in Lubitsch's film and the news editor in Hitchcock's. Rudolph Maté was director of photography on both films. Walter Wanger was to have been producer on both, until scheduling conflicts pulled him off the Lubitsch picture.

Some of the parallels involve character types and narrative themes: both films turn on the idea that a prominent intellectual known as an influential voice of peace is actually an enemy agent. Herbert Marshall plays this role for Hitchcock, and Stanley Ridges plays it for Lubitsch. Both films involve a character sent into enemy territory for an intel gathering recon mission. Both films involve the impersonation of a public figure.

The more interesting and revealing parallel is more subtle. Consider for a moment the opening act of *Foreign Correspondent*. It is packed with comedy: it opens with Joel McCrea making paper dolls while his boss muses that his habit of punching policemen makes him a perfect choice for the assignment. Soon McCrea is involved in a silly scene with a Latvian diplomat whose language is hilariously gibberish, a gag he would replay two years later for Preston Sturges in *Palm Beach Story*. There's McCrea's "meet cute" with Laraine Day, which could have come from any screwball comedy. There's every scene with comedian Robert Benchley—McCrea's first contact abroad.

Even after the plot starts to heat up, and a diplomat is apparently assassinated, the film remains in a comic mode for a while. McCrea takes after the assassin, but finds himself in a car with George Sanders, with whom the primary topic of discussion is not "Hey, a major diplomat just got shot in the face" but rather "Gee, your name is spelled funny."

The assassin's getaway car mysteriously vanishes into thin air, and our heroes are stumped. They stand around perplexed, and the authorities arrive—at which point McCrea's response is to make another joke about George Sanders' name.

And then, something interesting happens.

McCrea loses his bowler hat and goes to get it. In and of itself, this is another gag—a Laurel and Hardy routine, a running joke McCrea already did earlier in the film. In retrieving the hat, he has the vantage point to notice that one of the windmills is running backwards. It's such an unlikely sight that not only has no one else noticed, but they don't believe him when he insists on it.

This is where the movie shifts gears—and the literal shifting of gears inside the windmill to cause this anomaly is just a wonderful meta-joke highlighting the way Hitchcock is manipulating the audience. For the last half hour we've been watching a comedy with comedy stars doing things that in any other film would be unambiguously comedy routines. The tone has been light and jaunty. And then, at the moment McCrea goes to pick up his bowler hat out of the mud, as they say, "the shit just got real." The film changes register into thriller. McCrea goes clamoring around inside the windmill, surrounded by baddies,

with the very architecture of the place a threat, every shot moving him into greater danger—and the fact that this nightmare sequence follows so abruptly after being told for half an hour that it's all a joke is what gives it an extra oomph.

Joel McCrea and Laraine Day find the funny side of Nazi spycraft. Don't think that's what *Foreign Correspondent* (1940) is about? Go watch it again.

The windmill scene marks a major transition in tone. The tension is ramped up throughout the scene in part due to the brilliant staging and set design by William Cameron Menzies, but also because McCrea has been catapulted out of one movie and into another.

*To Be or Not to Be* plays the exact same trick—spending its first act in the realm of broad farce and then suddenly dropping the audience unexpectedly into a true wartime thriller where all the jokes have been stripped away. The difference is how Lubitsch uses the structure and tools of a thriller to give teeth to his comedy, where Hitchcock uses the structure and tools of a comedy to give energy to his thriller.

Notice how Hitchcock continues to invoke comedy elements throughout the film—such as Joel McCrea's recreation of the Marx Brothers stateroom gag from *A Night at the Opera*. The latter part of the film involves the kind of romantic mix-ups that dominate screwball comedy: Joel McCrea and Laraine Day have gone off on a pleasure jaunt through the countryside and ended up at an inn, where she mistakenly believes he's trying to get her into bed. She huffs off back to daddy, and Joel has to make amends, but plenty of complications intervene in which it isn't clear who is where. But as much as these scenes fit perfectly with the kind of stuff 1940s romantic comedy did in its sleep, Hitch has twisted it all by mapping this bedroom farce stuff onto the machinations of international intrigue. McCrea wasn't trying to get her into bed—he was trying to fake her kidnapping (!), and when she returns home to pout, she derails their attempt to force a confession from her father and puts everyone's life in even greater danger. For all the seriousness of the situation, the bedroom farce material still functions as comedy. When George Sanders breezes in to try to save the diplomat's life, he does so with a comic's swagger and deadpan flippancy that even Groucho Marx would have been proud of.

Where they differ is that an Ernst Lubitsch film starring Jack Benny and Carole Lombard is expected to be a comedy, and the only surprise is when it shifts gears at the end of act one. An Alfred Hitchcock film is expected to be a thriller, and that expectation drowns out the comedy in the first act to the point that it isn't entirely recognized for what it is.

This is a key difference—*Foreign Correspondent*'s first few reels are not "comic relief"—there's nothing to be relieved from and the entire approach is consistently comic. Even though the first half hour is completely played for laughs, no one was fooled into thinking the film was a comedy.

But what did Hitchcock make immediately after this film? *Mr. and Mrs. Smith*—a screwball comedy with Carole Lombard and no thriller content at all.

# Mr. and Mrs. Smith

Buried in the august accomplishments of Alfred Hitchcock is a film so bizarrely out of place that many scholars of Hitch simply jump over it, as if it didn't even exist. If you see it, and try to place it into some kind of context with the likes of *Psycho* and *Vertigo*, you'll probably find that old *Sesame Street* song shuttling around the back of your mind: *which of these things does not belong? Which of these things is not like the others?* But the sad thing about all this is, while *Mr. and Mrs. Smith* may be a misfit in the life and work of Alfred Hitchcock, it is actually a very fine screwball comedy. But, in a damned-if-ya-do/damned-if-ya-don't catch, *Mr. and Mrs. Smith* is also overlooked by the definitive survey of screwball comedies, James Harvey's essential *Romantic Comedies in Hollywood*.

It's not as if it's easy to overlook this thing—it's the penultimate film by Carole Lombard, just prior to *To Be or Not to Be* in 1942 (after which a stupid and pointless airplane crash robbed the world of her talents).

Carole was a great comedian, but a strange actress—and these are related. She was gorgeous, but she used her face and voice in peculiar, wonderful ways. I hate to use this silly *Inside the Actor's Studio* terminology, but I can't think of any better way to put it than that she had a unique instrument. Not unlike Jim Carrey, Lombard's face appeared to have fashioned out of some combination of rubber and Jell-O instead of flesh and bone. Her eyes widen like saucers, her lips quiver, her head tilts to the side, her voice tremors—all in the span of an instant. Her face is in a constant state of quivering, stretching, trying out different expressions at the speed of thought. Mere frame grabs cannot do justice to her peculiar facial tics, and thanks to that expressiveness she could establish so much character with so little dialog.

It's as if she had attention deficit syndrome of the emotional centers of her brain—any line would be delivered with every possible inflection all at once. The result undermines the possibility of any singular emotion being expressed. As a result, she was best when playing deceptive characters: *Nothing Sacred* and *True Confession*, among her greatest hits, both cast her as someone whose life has become overrun by lies. And the audience forgives her because clearly she doesn't mean it … she doesn't mean *anything*.

This serves her well even when the rest of the film is weak. For example, *The Princess Comes Across* is pretty thin stuff, sloppy and formless. But there she is, once again trapped in a web of lies, her face spasming uncontrollably—and hapless Fred MacMurray inevitably falling in love. It's the second of her pairings with Fred, sandwiched between *True Confession* and *Hands Across the Table*. She has fantastic chemistry with him, but that's no surprise. Her emotional wooziness leaves her naked and vulnerable, more than almost any other actress of her generation, and it made her the perfect pairing for any actor. No matter who she was cast against would appear to have perfect chemistry with her—even Jack Benny.

All those facial tics and vocal gymnastics meant that she was good in any movie, that she could makes even the dumbest script and the poorest direction seem interesting. Although she was always good, she was rarely great. To be great, she needed something external to herself. She needed the support of great screenwriters and great directors, who could find a way to use her weird talents in the service of something resonant and effective.

For example, Ernst Lubitsch. *To Be or Not to Be* is a crazy idea. A Nazi comedy shouldn't work (and a lot of critics at the time were certain that it didn't), but posterity has come to recognize the genius of this masterpiece—and it is one of the only times that Carole actually seems to be a coherent human being as opposed to just a fabulous movie star. Lubitsch worked in irony the way other artists worked in oils, and he realized that if Lombard canceled out everything she said by not seeming to really mean it, then the best approach was to make certain that the only dialog she was given was stuff she's not supposed to mean. She's a human Opposite Day, and in *To Be or Not to Be* she (and Lubitsch) create a complete character out of all the negative space in the shadow behind the screen. That, and she's funny.

That's what she needed—a visionary director who knew how to manipulate the language of cinema to make her great. A visionary director with access to the kind of tools that even the Mitchell Leisens, Wesley Ruggleses, and Gregory La Cavas of the world didn't have. Which is why she asked Alfred Hitchcock to direct *Mr. and Mrs. Smith*. Hollywood didn't have all that many bona fide geniuses wandering around—and Hitchcock was a genius among geniuses.

Sure, comedies weren't his métier, but it was rather unheard of for a director to completely limit himself to a single genre. Even Lubitsch had strayed out of his comfort zone to make the raw drama *The Man I Killed* in 1931. And it's not as if Hitchcock had never played with comedy. Those viewers who want to commit to the idea of Hitchcock as The Master of Suspense can certainly enjoy *Rich and Strange* as a thriller—it has a pervasive atmosphere of tension, and the final reels emphasize peril in a way not out of step with his other thrillers. But in the main, the film plays as a comedy.

Critics have marveled at the elegant storytelling of *Rich and Strange*'s opening sequence—a wordless tableau that establishes the male lead and his urgent need to break out of his routine. But as a fan of silent comedy, I can't lay all that praise at Hitch's feet: its opening sequence could easily have appeared in a Harold Lloyd comedy—in fact, it strongly reminds me of a sequence in Lloyd's *Hot Water*. You can't credit Hitchcock with pioneering cinematic techniques if the same scene could have been made a decade earlier by someone else. The plot involves a married couple who are suddenly freed from their domestic prison by an inheritance. Critic Paul Jensen has noted that the same plot device was used in Hitchcock's silent films *Downhill* and *Juno and the Paycock*—but it is also a venerable slapstick comedy cliché, used several times by Laurel and Hardy to name but one example. The sudden money sets them loose on the world—and much of the film makes sport of their provincial naïveté, while also finding time to lampoon their fellow passengers.

If *Rich and Strange* is a comedy, then it is a romantic one—it deals with their marital disillusionment, mutual infidelity, and ultimate reconciliation. As such, it could stand alongside Leo McCarey's *The Awful Truth* as a film about a couple that flirts with divorce as a way of finding out how much they belong together.

This is just the long way 'round of saying that Carole Lombard wasn't off her rocker when she begged Alfred Hitchcock to direct *Mr. and Mrs. Smith*.

*Mr. and Mrs. Smith* was written by Norman Krasna—one of the more prominent screenwriters of the screwball genre. Krasna had to his credit several gems of romantic comedy: *The Richest Girl in the World*, *Hands Across the Table*, *Wife Versus Secretary*, and (one of my personal faves) *Bachelor Mother*. He knew his stuff, and Carole Lombard could be confident that she was handing Hitch a script by a writer who knew how to use her best. That is to say, it hinges on deception. Only this time, the deception is on the other foot.

The titular Mr. and Mrs. Smith are introduced with the kind of screwy self-consciously zany behavior that gave the screwball its name. She has a rule that they cannot leave the bedroom if they fight until they've made up. This rule causes them to spend days locked in their own room, wreaking havoc with their lives—and it is just one of her various romantic rules which govern their relationship. Another is her determination to always tell the

**Carole Lombard's unique acting style is central to Alfred Hitchcock's *Mr. and Mrs. Smith* (1941).**

truth. Which leads, inevitably, to him admitting that if he had to do it over again, he wouldn't marry her.

Enter a funny little clerk from the town where they did get married to explain that, due to an unlikely bureaucratic complication that only occurs in movies, they aren't legally married after all—so in a sense they do have it to do over again. The clerk also tells Mrs. Smith (if, ahem, that is her real name now)—but Mr. Smith doesn't know she knows, and she doesn't know he doesn't know she knows.

They head out to the restaurant that was their haunt back when they were first falling in love. She expects the night to be a romantic recreation of their wedding night. She stuffs herself into the dress she wore back then (*"I don't understand how it could shrink so much just hanging in the closet!"*) and eagerly anticipates an after-dinner visit to the Justice of the Peace. The problem is, this is no recreation of a fondly remembered night. It is a train wreck. She is furious that he doesn't take her to get married, and that he had no intention of doing so. But the thing is, their romantic recreation had veered off the rails at the start. This isn't the romantic restaurant they remember; she doesn't fit in her dress—in other words, things are different and they've already compromised. It happens quietly, without a word. It isn't fair for her to compare this to her hypothetical situation "if you had it to do over again," because they haven't gone back in time.

No matter. She's angry. The film makes the necessary noises on behalf of the puritanical Production Code that the problem is a couple "living in sin" without the sanctity of marriage, but the real problem is just the emotional one—she asked him if he would do it all over again, and now she's seen that he meant it when he said he wouldn't.

She kicks him out, changes her name back, gets a job, and starts dating. Dating her husband/ex-husband/never-husband's law partner and best friend, at that. If it was just to rub his nose in it, she's had her revenge—he said he wouldn't have married her if he had it to do over again, but in fact once given the chance he sets single-mindedly to winning her back.

By action, he proves his words were lies—there's that ironic distance between what one says and what they mean. But she's now reconsidering her options—maybe she doesn't want him. Or does she? Seeing him date another woman inflames her jealousy in unexpected ways, and there's that conflicted emotion again, as Carole Lombard reveals that maybe even she doesn't know what she means, or wants, or thinks.

The question at the root of all romantic comedy is, to what extent does any couple belong together? What makes a relationship? In Krasna's scripts, he explores this question by stripping away the superficial attributes of a relationship and trying out an alternate. In *Hands Across the Table*, Carole Lombard and Fred MacMurray live together in the same apartment and fall in love, all while trying to marry other people for their money. In *Bachelor Mother*, Ginger Rogers and David Niven find themselves "parents" of a foundling child, and then afterwards start dating and get engaged. And in *Mr. and Mrs. Smith*, Carole Lombard and Robert Montgomery get to experiment with divorce and dating, and still return home to each other—but whereas Hitchcock treated that eventual return to the status quo very cynically in *Rich and Strange*, no such cynicism colors *Mr. And Mrs. Smith*. The *Rich and Strange* protagonists end up together as a sort of failure, but Krasna wants us to understand that Mr. and Mrs. Smith belong together.

Hitchcock himself was as dismissive of the finished film as so many of his fans and critics have been. In Francois Truffaut's career-spanning interview with Hitchcock, he filled two pages dissecting *Rich and Strange* but all he could summon for *Mr. and Mrs. Smith* was an anecdote about Carole Lombard bringing three cows to the set, with name tags for the three leading cast members, as a way of kidding him about the "actors are cattle" crack he'd made.

About that "actors are cattle" remark: Alfred Hitchcock may have been a genius of cinema, but his genius lay in the manipulation of objects, images, sounds. Not so much people. He exploited the existing personas of movie stars like Cary Grant, Jimmy Stewart, Ingrid Bergman, Grace Kelly. In other words, he used their established characteristics to enhance his films. By contrast, Ernst Lubitsch—so derided as "a director of doors"—had a way of using his films to enhance his actors. Lubitsch practically created Maurice Chevalier's American personality all by himself, he rehabilitated Greta Garbo, he made minor stars like Charles Boyer and Miriam Hopkins credible as A-list romantic leads. Lubitsch could give Carole the directorial support she was looking for—while Hitchcock admits he merely shot the script as written without ever getting a personal feel for it.

The musical score by Edward Ward is most unfortunate—silly mickey-mousing behind the action that encourages the audience to dismiss what they are watching. Romantic comedies aren't usually remembered for their music (except for the Fred 'n' Ginger ones), and while Hitchcock's movies are remembered for their music, I wouldn't say that a rich and ominous Bernard Herrmann score would have helped here. As criticisms, go, that's pretty mild—and it's my only serious complaint against this charming trifle.

So, lesser Hitchcock it will always be. But if it represents something of a missed opportunity, that doesn't mean it's a failure—or that being lesser Hitchcock makes it a lesser screwball. This is one case where maybe forgetting that Alfred Hitchcock had anything to do with it might actually make it seem a lot better.

# Divorce American Style

Let's start with a rarely seen 1940 screwball comedy, Roy Del Ruth's *He Married His Wife*. While I won't pretend that this is anything but a minor but somewhat enjoyable trifle, there's something rather weird about it that deserves discussion. A number of social scholars— admittedly some of them film historians, but quite a few of them not film people at all—have written about this movie in a specific context: how Hollywood treats romantic love.

The "he" of the title is horse racing mogul Joel McCrea. His preoccupation with—and incompetence at—the horse trade crowds out any other consideration. Ex-wife Nancy Kelly grew weary of perpetual also-ran status in her husband's life, and divorced him. Ironically, divorce provides her with the opportunity to force her way higher on his list of priorities: as he is now committed to a punishing monthly alimony, he can't help but think of her constantly. McCrea conspires with his lawyer Roland Young to end the alimony by getting Nancy married to someone, anyone—say, their mutual friend Lyle Talbot. The plan goes awry when she snubs poor Lyle for a flashy, oily gigolo Cesar Romero. McCrea starts to realize he cares about something much more than horses or alimony … (there's no real surprise where any of this is heading—just check out the title of the movie if you have any questions).

What makes this interesting to social commentators is that the idea of making a romantic comedy about a divorced couple getting back together didn't just happen the once, or even twice—it's an idea you'll find in: *The Awful Truth*, (1937), *The Philadelphia Story* (1940), *My Favorite Wife* (1940), *His Girl Friday* (1940), *Mr. and Mrs. Smith* (1941), *That Uncertain Feeling* (1942), and *Palm Beach Story* (1942). Add *He Married His Wife* to that list and you have eight such comedies within five years, four of them appearing in 1940 alone.

Stanley Cavell's acclaimed and influential 1984 book *Pursuits of Happiness: The Hollywood Comedy of Remarriage* (derived from a series of scholarly articles he published earlier) posits the suggestion that these films represent an effort by Hollywood to redefine marriage as something driven primarily by romantic love, rather than economic or religious reasons. These films depict couples who have forged deep bonds, that even when tested by separation do not sever.

There's certainly something striking about finding so many of these things all at the same cultural moment—but that very fact gives me pause. The sudden flurry of their appearance suggests that they are actually copying each other. Furthermore, the fact they are all screwball comedies deserves some consideration. Maybe there's something about the nature of how screwball works that led to these, at this specific moment.

The first thing to remember is that screwball comedies are formula-driven film vehicles designed to sell a particular kind of entertainment. Just as silent slapstick would cook up whatever narrative structures allowed the likes of Buster Keaton or Harold Lloyd to then go about and do their acrobatic stunts, screwball plots are there to provide the backdrop for the likes of Cary Grant and Claudette Colbert to fight with each other in silly ways. The tricky balance to be struck is to make sure that the combat is actually good-natured enough to serve as flirtation, because if it veers too far into mean-spirited antagonism then a final-reel reconciliation becomes too difficult to accept. Conversely, if the combat is too good-natured and flirtatious, then how come the couple doesn't just get together right away?

One way of getting a full 90 minutes of entertainment out of comic antagonism is to let it be as flirtatious as possible, and generate as much chemistry as possible between the leading players, but concoct some additional narrative complication that keeps the couple apart. The most venerable, the most commonly seen complication of this sort is to have one or both of the couple already engaged to someone else—and on top of that, to have that pre-existing commitment be between social peers, while the romantic attraction that the film is keeping in abeyance is one that crosses social classes.

The prototypical example is *It Happened One Night*: Claudette Colbert is a spoiled rich girl who's engaged to a smarmy European count. Their relationship, although icky and phony, is between upper crust socialites and European royalty. Colbert may be falling in love with the rogue-ish journalist Clark Gable, but he's not in her league, and that right there provides enough of a barrier that their increasing attraction and intimacy cannnot easily overcome. The entire infrastructure of society has an investment in keeping them apart. There's an added bonus to this narrative structure, too: watching their love overcome that class barrier is cathartic, it's democratic, it's utopian. Films that follow this pattern don't see the lower-class lover of the runaway heiress as a Cinderella man—instead it's the reverse. The poor man saves the rich girl (or poor girl saves the rich man).

Across the catalog of screwballs we see this pattern repeated, with earthy values redeeming the airless rich: *It Happened One Night, My Man Godfrey, A Girl, a Guy, and a Gob, Next Time I Marry, Design for Living, Fifth Avenue Girl, Holiday, Bachelor Mother, Midnight, Slightly Dangerous, Easy Living, Ninotchka, Theodora Goes Wild....* But it couldn't last forever, and the demand for screwball comedy exceeded the audience's patience with variations on the runaway heiress theme. Other recipes were needed—but they needed to be new recipes that delivered the same fundamental flavor: an excuse for an attractive couple to fight for nine or 10 reels before getting together romantically.

The so-called Comedy of Remarriage offered just such a viable twist: the divorced couple could be introduced with the given that they were romantically compatible, but that circumstances drove them apart. We already know they were once in love, and we know that something substantial broke them apart—so their banter can be excessively flirtatious without easily resolving whatever has already separated them. Plus, as an added bonus, it becomes possible to easily expand the cast—films like *He Married His Wife, Palm Beach Story* and *Philadelphia Story* don't just have love triangles, they have love quadrangles. (I liken this to the habit of superhero films of upping the ante by adding villains.)

The Comedy of Remarriage doesn't need to invoke any class differential between the parties (some do, some don't), because the divorce itself is doing the heavy lifting of keeping the lovers apart even as they grow together.

There's something else, too—by their nature, these films begin with the main characters already established as sexually-active adults. They break apart, and experiment with other partners. For films made under the Puritanical restrictions of the Production Code, this was as close as you could get to making movies about adultery. The Comedies of Remarriage have a palpable sexuality to them rarely found in their other screwball peers.

But this brings us back to Stanley Cavell and the concept that these films represented a significant step in establishing the idea of "romance." The structure of these films stack the deck against the main characters as a couple: something has already challenged the integrity of their marriage, and they have viable alternative partners. Isn't adultery supposed to be the thing that dooms a union? How could anyone get back together after such a thing? But no matter how the deck is stacked, our screwball couples are drawn together because of something that defies objective, rational explanation.

In other words, love. Screwball comedies define love as the irrational, ineffable force that brings people together against all odds—and which resists even the most energetic threats. Previous generations had defined marriage in terms of social standing, economic necessity, and religious expectations. The screwball couples tossed all that out the window in favor of crazy, stupid love.

Virtually the entire genre of screwball comedies is predicated on a woman facing two possible life partners, one of whom is an ideal mate in objective terms, the other a total wild card. The so-called "ideal" mate turns out to be dry and uninspiring, while the rogue is a locus of passion. As it happened, Ralph Bellamy became the genre's "go-to" actor to play this sort of role.

Ralph Bellamy had such a massive and sprawling career that you could be a huge Bellamy fan and not actually have seen some of the movies I'm going to talk about—even though Bellamy was a major force in the development of the screwball comedy, and was so singularly associated with it he became a punchline in and of himself.

It starts with *Hands Across the Table* in 1935—which is inexplicably underrated given its significance in the evolution of screwball. Ernst Lubitsch had taken over as chief of Paramount, and one of the first things he did was note that Carole Lombard was being grossly misused in romantic dramas that emphasized her glamour and beauty but ignored her singular comic gifts. *This won't stand,* he said, and promptly orchestrated the production of the giddy farce *Hands Across the Table*, directed by Mitchell Leisen (another underrated comedy force).

The premise of *Hands Across the Table* is that Carole Lombard is looking to marry a rich guy so she can find some economic stability in her life, and while she's trying to engineer this jump in social status, she is living platonically with Fred MacMurray, who is also looking to marry for money for much the same reason. Of course, the thrust of all this is to show how marrying for love is better than marrying for money, and she and Fred MacMurray are truly soul mates who belong together.

That it even makes sense to have a movie that argues people ought to marry for love instead of money speaks to the fact that social attitudes about romance and marriage have really changed over a short period of time. It's almost as odd as running across a story that bothers to argue why child slavery is wrong. You almost feel like saying, "Duh!"

That being said, the movie doesn't make the distinction easy. Fred MacMurray may be obviously the right guy for Carole, but her potential sugar daddy Ralph Bellamy is not obviously the wrong guy. He's a profoundly decent, forgiving, loving, upright gentleman. Rejecting him is hard, and that's what gives the romantic triangle its bite.

Bellamy proved himself excellent at playing such roles, and was quickly typecast as the earnest good guy who the female lead would reject in favor of the dangerous bad boy. As time went on, Bellamy's performance of such roles drifted more and more into comic interpretations of what was originally designed as a straight-man role.

Consider Leo McCarey's *The Awful Truth* from 1937. Cary Grant and Irene Dunne start the thing off by getting divorced, foolishly, and then spending the rest of the film proving that if they aren't good for each other, they're way worse for everyone else. So Irene Dunne has as her new beau that bastion of wrong-right-manliness, Ralph Bellamy—all rich and decent and irksome in every respect.

It was in Stanley Gardner's 1942 *Lady in a Jam* that Bellamy finally

**Irene Dunne and Cary Grant get in each other's hair in *The Awful Truth* (1937).**

became the punchline he was already barreling towards. Because this movie is less well known than the others described above, let me spend a little time setting the stage:

Irene Dunne plays a spoiled rich girl whose irresponsible behavior has bankrupted her, but she is too self-absorbed to even realize the reality of her situation. Patric Knowles plays a psychiatrist who has developed a thing for her and wants to help her, but she can't stand him. Already this is a bit of a deviation from the usual pattern, because Knowles is the "right" guy for her, but he also represents stability and reasonability, where these movies usually push their heroines into unstable and high-risk romantic relationships as their celebration of the power of love. So already the structure of this film means that Knowles' rival for her affections will be a deviation from type.... But look, it's Ralph Bellamy! Or more precisely, it's some bizarro-world counterfeit of Ralph Bellamy, whose over-earnestness has gone over the edge into outright weirdness. He is a ridiculous parody of the uberdecent rural rube, with the added conceit that he's obsessed with composing the perfect "lament" with which to woo her (his first lament wasn't quite sad enough, he thinks).

Ralph Bellamy and the other Right Wrong Men of his ilk always looked good on paper—financially secure, decent, from solid loving families, earnest, respectful, from the right social class. All the boxes were ticked. By contrast, Cary Grant specialized in playing the rogues—misbehaved men who utterly failed to tick any of the boxes, but who were nevertheless clearly the Wrong Right Man.

For all these wacky couples, disregarding social norms and looking for the spark of true love at all costs, it's just a good thing they didn't have any children to get caught up in the shenanigans. Except, of course, when they did...

Ralph Bellamy may have earned an Academy Award nomination in *The Awful Truth* for playing the "Right Wrong Man"—but if you really want to celebrate the best supporting performance in that film, you need to be looking at Asta the Dog. Or to be pedantic— Skippy the Dog. Like all good movie stars, he was born with one name and became a screen icon under another. Norma Jeane Mortenson became Marilyn Monroe, and Skippy the Dog became Asta. According to online legend, Cary Grant got mixed up and calls the dog "Skippy" during *The Awful Truth*—but I'm not so sure. The scene in question finds Grant and his ex-wife Irene Dunne battling in court for custody of their dog Mr. Smith, and the judge asks each of them to call to the dog. Whichever one the dog picks, wins. Grant proceeds to unleash a barrage of variations on "Mr. Smith," including "Smithy" and "Schmitty," all while Dunne is calling out her own variations. I can see how this could sound like "Skippy" but I don't think any mistake was made (perhaps I'm wrong and I just missed it).

The important thing about this scene isn't the dog's name, but his role as the child substitute in their family. This is in fact the role Asta was typecast in. And let's be clear on this—Asta was an icon of screwball comedy with an absolutely impressive resume. In addition to *The Awful Truth* he's in *Topper Takes a Trip* with Roland Young and Constance Bennett, *Bringing Up Baby* with Cary Grant and Katharine Hepburn, *The Thin Man* and *After the Thin Man* with William Powell and Myrna Loy, and *The Big Broadcast of 1936* with George Burns and Gracie Allen, Bing Crosby, and others. And that's just a sampling of his career.

Is career a funny word to use when talking about a dog? We're talking about an individual who was professionally trained specifically to work in films (he was taught to respond to hand signals so he could be cued in his scenes without disrupting the dialog). He had his own fan base: He was one of several animals profiled by the 1936 book *Dog Stars of Hollywood*, not to mention his own puffball promo piece in *The American Magazine* in 1938, "A Dog's Life in Hollywood." He even has a fan site on the web today. And he was paid—handsomely, even. $200 a week in the 1930s (plus another $60 for his trainer) was an order of magnitude above what other dog actors got at the time—which shows what an asset he was in and of himself, because why else pay Asta $200 a week when there are plenty of identical looking dogs available at a fraction of the cost?

Indeed there were plenty of identical looking dogs to choose from—Asta's over-enthusiastic fans went so gaga for wire fox terriers that the breed spiraled into a tragic overbreeding situation. Despite this, however, Asta-alikes only started appearing on screen when the real one retired in 1939, at the age of eight. And you wanna know something? The first time I saw *Another Thin Man*, I just knew that wasn't the same dog. He was billed as "Asta," and sure looked like him, but there was just something off, something missing. This, coming from someone who's never had a dog, and who routinely misidentifies actors (in my commentary track to Syd Chaplin's *A Submarine Pirate*, I openly questioned whether Harold Lloyd even appears in the movie, and said this nonsense *during Lloyd's scene*). If even a schmo like me can tell the real Asta from his copycats (copydogs?), then you know you're talking about an exceptional dog.

Hollywood has had many animal stars, and apparently there were enough canine actors in the 1930s to justify an entire book. But out of this pack, there was just one Asta.

Asta had the distinction of appearing in two films from the curious sub-genre of remarriage comedies, which put him in the same league as other "remarriage" mainstays like Cary Grant, Katharine Hepburn, and Spencer Tracy. As noted above, Comedies of Remarriage are films about married couples who break up, experiment with other romantic partners, and then get back together. Stanley Cavell argues that these films promoted a new conception of marriage as something built on mutual love, rather than religious or economic standards. The thing is, while this is true, it also happens to be true of screwball comedies as a whole. What "remarriage" added to the mix was sexuality—in films like *The Awful Truth*, we have a married, sexually active and experienced couple, who try out alternative partnering arrangements, and then reunite. In other words, a thinly veiled metaphor for adultery, designed to pass the censors.

Remember, though, these are comedies. Frothy, light-hearted things—and they evolved out of silent slapstick, to boot, so they aren't intended to bear much in the way of heavy emotional weight. So, these films needed something to take the sting out of their adulterous themes. If Irene Dunne and Cary Grant are going to sleep around and then decide that, having sampled the alternatives, they really were happier together, that's a potentially explosive and emotionally fraught premise. There's real dramatic risk at the heart of that. So, the couple has a tether to a normal domestic life—a reminder of what's at stake, a totem of the happy home they need to resurrect. Not a child—a child could be traumatized by these shenanigans. Audiences would object to watching Irene Dunne go swanning around in her fancy ball gowns, neglecting her kid. But a dog is enough like a child, without being too much like a child. Asta, as Mr. Smith, is the child stand-in—they even have a custody battle over him—but there's no fear that the romantic adventures of the divorcees will damage him.

In fact, Asta plays this same faux-baby role in most of his screwball comedies. He's the domestic anchor that roots the stars in something recognizable as a family, freeing them to act even more ridiculous and immature during the middle reels.

Which brings me back to *Another Thin Man*, the film where I spotted the low-calorie Asta substitute. This was the third film in the "Thin Man" franchise, and by this point the filmmakers figured having William Powell and Myrna Loy drink their way through an absurdly over-complicated murder mystery wasn't enough, so they added a baby to the mix—Nick Charles, Jr. *Of course* the real Asta had to retire here—putting a real baby into the film by definition forced Asta out. You can't have Asta playing alongside a child because it's like casting Claudette Colbert and Irene Dunne in the same film—they end up playing two versions of the same character and unbalancing the film.

So in 1939, Asta stepped down. His owners and trainers, Henry East and Gale Henry, took him into retirement to enjoy his sunset years, ceding the stage to his knock-offs. Henry and Gale (or do I mean East and Henry? I get confused) kept on training dog actors—they were responsible for most of Hollywood's canine stars—but they never had another hit like Asta. He was a unique combination of talent, charisma, and cultural zeitgeist that all came together in just the right way.

# Magic Pixie Dream Grampa

Let's talk about farces. About romantic comedies, TV sitcoms, and silent slapstick. About Charley Chase, the Marx Brothers, and Charles Coburn. About the lovely 1943 romantic comedy *The More the Merrier*, with Jean Arthur, but also the delirious 1926 Charley Chase delight *Mighty Like a Moose* … but I'm getting ahead of myself.

One dictionary definition of "farce" is "a comic dramatic work using buffoonery and horseplay and typically including crude characterization and ludicrously improbable situations."

Here's another: "a light, humorous play in which the plot depends upon a skillfully exploited situation rather than upon the development of character."

Here's Wikipedia on the subject: "a farce is a comedy that aims at entertaining the audience through situations that are highly exaggerated, extravagant, and thus improbable. Farces are often highly incomprehensible plot-wise (due to the many plot twists and random events that occur), but viewers are encouraged not to try to follow the plot in order to avoid becoming confused and overwhelmed."

Here's my definition (summing above the above): farces are sitcoms. Which is why I'm not all that enamored of the suggestion that farces are about their absurd situations and not their characters, because without a good grounding in character the absurd situations are too ridiculous to register. And it's character that separates the popular sitcoms from the footnotes.

Of all the silent clowns, there was one slapstician who more than any other seemed to be working in a sitcom style decades before TV even existed—Charley Chase. Let's take for example one of Charley Chase's most admired creations, a two-reel silent short from 1926 called *Mighty Like a Moose*. The premise is, at root, as old as they get. One of the classic farce setups involves a husband or a wife setting out to test the fidelity of their partner by engineering a fake affair. One of them takes a disguise, woos the other under false pretenses, and lo and behold an "affair" has begun. Think of the opera *The Merry Widow*. Or that Kate Bush song *Babooshka*. But Chase brings a brilliant, and twisted, twist: in his version, both hubby and wifey are in disguise. How's that you say? Through the magic of plastic surgery! Charley and his wife each "have some work done," but in secret as a surprise for the other. The changes are enough they don't recognize each other. So Charley and his wife are flirting with each other believing themselves to be straying, while also desperately trying to steer clear of their spouse.

The result is 20 minutes of four people rushing around a house, opening and closing doors in an intricate dance of just-missing each other—except it isn't four people, it's actually just two.

This is Chase's forte. The precision timing is peerless. But if you do treat yourself to this gem, watch the doors. Of all the definitions you could offer up of farce, maybe the most practical is: "the comedy of opening and closing doors."

The Marx Brothers boiled the whole genre of farce down to its essence and burned through it in just a handful of minutes in *Horsefeathers*, with the various Marxes and Thelma Todd rampaging through a bunch of doors (and putting on and taking off their "rubbers" as well). But if you really want to have some fun with opening and closing doors in a movie that isn't determined to parody the whole concept, check out the infectiously charming 1943 George Stevens comedy *The More the Merrier*.

To understand all the door slamming going on in *The More the Merrier* we need to step back and take notice of a particular subgenre of screwball comedy. We have discussed the "Comedies of Remarriage" and divorce as a tricky way to tell stories about sexually mature and experienced adults experimenting with other partners, but to do so without falling afoul of the Production Code's prohibitions on depicting adultery. Well, there were other tricks employed by screwball—and one of them was the Roommate Trick.

**Charles Coburn plays a game of musical doors with Jean Arthur in *The More the Merrier* (1943).**

In these films, an unmarried couple would be thrown together into intimate living conditions by circumstance, allowing the filmmakers to explore the ways that enforced intimacy nourished romance, without the censors getting too enraged. Think *Hands Across the Table*, *Rafter Romance*, arguably you could include *It Happened One Night* in this sub-genre—and of course all its clones, like *Next Time I Marry*.

Where *The More the Merrier* riffs on that approach is in numbers. You see, we start with apartment-dweller Jean Arthur. She lives in Washington, D.C., during the pitch of the Second World War. In those days, the sheer volume of people who had to come to D.C. to coordinate the war effort quickly overwhelmed the housing stock leading to epic housing shortages. For example, statesman Charles Coburn, who has come at the behest of the Senate but finds no room at the inn. He blusters and talks his way into getting Jean Arthur to lease out half her apartment to him (he's like that—a go-getter who never takes "no" for an answer).

She's a wee bit worried that people might talk—an unmarried man and a woman sharing a room—and the smile on Coburn's face when he realizes she's concerned that people might mistake him for her lover is one of the sweetest gags in the film. (One of the sharper gags, by contrast, comes in a scene set at Arthur's workplace—dominated by women, with all the men off to war, the ladies wolf-whistle and sexually harass the lone male employee.)

Coburn, meanwhile, sublets half of *his* half of the apartment to airplane engineer Joel McCrea—but keeps this secret as long as he can.

Control-freak Jean works out a meticulous schedule, down to the second, for how she and Charles Coburn will go through their morning routines without accidentally crossing each other in the bathroom. The first iteration of this timetable is a slapstick gem, but it's the second go-round that pays off the gag. Because the second time has all three of them swinging through the doors, with Coburn desperately (and mostly excellently) trying to keep both Jean Arthur and Joel McCrea oblivious as to the other's presence.

If the central joke in *Mighty Like a Moose* was how two people moving in and out of doors could be mistaken for four, *The More the Merrier* takes three people and makes it look like two.

The film was a revelation for Charles Coburn. He'd been a Hollywood mainstay for years, but playing gruff patriarchs and overbearing battle-axes. Films like *Bachelor Mother* and *Vivacious Lady* depended on his comic timing, but barely tapped his potential. By casting him as a lovable old rogue, rather than an insufferable bastard, *The More the Merrier* found the best use for Coburn's talents.

Ernst Lubitsch took his cue from this and cast Coburn in *Heaven Can Wait* in essentially the same role—the magic pixie dream grampa, if you will.

# Ernst Lubitsch Forgives Himself

If you were so inclined, you could convincingly argue that Ernst Lubitsch's *Heaven Can Wait* is a representative example of its time: a costume drama that luxuriates in period detail (playing to the strengths of 20th Century–Fox); a character study told with inventive narrative techniques and non-chronological structure (like Preston Sturges' *The Great*

*McGinty* or Orson Welles' *Citizen Kane*); in glorious Technicolor (surging to popularity in the wake of *Snow White and The Seven Dwarves*). Except … this is Ernst Lubitsch we are talking about. He did not make movies like everyone else.

Although a "character study," *Heaven Can Wait* is the life story of nobody in particular. *Citizen Kane* and *The Great McGinty* fulminate over the accomplishments of Great Men (with capital letters). Lubitsch, as he put it, set forth "a man only interested in good living with no aim of accomplishing anything or doing anything noble." Lubitsch admitted that he faced studio opposition to making a movie that "had no message and made no point whatsoever." He defended his choices, saying, "I hoped to introduce to a motion picture audience a number of people, and if the people should find them likeable—that should be sufficient for its success."

To play those "number of people," Lubitsch was restricted to the roster of somewhat lackluster stars under contract to 20th Century–Fox, instead of the performers with whom he had built his reputation. He reluctantly screen-tested Don Ameche for the lead, and complained to screenwriter Sam Raphaelson, "We are in trouble." Raphaelson was baffled by this—Ameche's screen test was terrific, he thought. Lubitsch agreed—Ameche had nailed it. That was the problem—now he was obliged to use Ameche, in a role he'd written with Fredric March in mind.

Under Lubitsch's direction, Ameche gave one of his career-defining performances, as the lecherous rogue Henry Van Cleve. The film covers Van Cleve's life, from birth to death (not necessarily in that order), by focusing on the women in it—his mother, the French maid who seduced him at 13 (because that makes for great Hollywood movies for the whole family), the various showgirls that invariably caught his eye, and so on. But of these women, one stands apart—his wife and soul-mate Martha (Gene Tierney), with whom he stays married—if not actually very faithful—for 25 years.

Tierney was known for her beauty, but as an actress had a reputation for glassy-eyed diffidence. Lubitsch demanded more from her than she was accustomed to giving—and to inspire a fierier, lustier performance from her, he badgered and berated her to the point of tears. Tierney accused Lubitsch of being a "tyrant," and begged him to stop shouting at her all the time. "I'm paid to shout at you!!!" was his response.

Whatever on-set tension may have existed between the director and his leading lady, the production sailed through on a modest budget and a short, efficient schedule. Lubitsch only spent $1.1 million on the film—remarkable, considering he had the same budget on *To Be or Not to Be*, which wasn't in color and didn't encompass some 70 years' worth of settings and fashions.

Lubitsch felt the key to working so efficiently on-set was in the preparation—specifically in the writing. Having bought the rights to Laszlo Bus-Feketé's 1934 play *Birthdays*, Lubitsch engaged his favorite screenwriter Raphaelson to hunker down with him at Lubitsch's home to adapt the play into a movie. It took Lubitsch and Raphaelson months to craft their screenplay. Raphaelson said that during that time, studio chief Darryl Zanuck asked how things were coming along. "Vell, I tell you—slow but good," Lubitsch replied. Zanuck smiled, "That's fine. The only thing I'd rather hear than that is—slow and great!" Raphaelson marveled at the seeming indulgence from Zanuck, but Lubitsch explained, "Dis time ve are spending here, writing, is de cheapest time ve got. All ve are paying now is your salary and mine. But the minute ve are on de set, ve are paying de stars, de dis, de dat, ve are paying $50,000 a day…" (sorry for the crude ethnic spelling there—that's actually a direct quote from his biography and I'm transcribing it how it's written).

The long gestation period for the script was partly Lubitsch's way of escaping the ugliness and acrimony of his divorce from Vivian Lubitsch, a way of taking the pain of that part of his life and turning it into something positive— Vivian accused Ernst of being a childish kind of man, fixated on his own appetites and unconcerned with the effects of those choices on the people around him, so Ernst went and made a movie celebrating those very characteristics.

The character of Henry van Cleve was conceived as a man "fifteen years ahead of his time, all the time," in terms of sexual mores. In other words, his behavior is only scandalous in terms of the attitudes of the people immediately around him, but not fundamentally scandalous. Time marches on, and forgives him, repeatedly.

Henry van Cleve passes his final hours with a great meal ("*I ate everything the doctor forbade!*") and fantasies of a lovely blonde sneaking into his bed-

Poster for Ernst Lubitsch's *Heaven Can Wait* (1943).

room. Although he had no way to know it at the time, in just four years' time, Ernst Lubitsch would spend his own final hours under strikingly similar circumstances.

Standing in front of the Devil, recounting the long uninterrupted misdemeanor of his life, Henry finds that even Hell isn't interested in his transgressions. His sins don't count as sins. Through the vehicle of this film, Lubitsch presents his own case in its most extreme caricature—a man motivated only by sex and food and pleasure—and granted himself redemption.

## Sturges Before Sturges

Jean Arthur is a writer for *The Boy's Constant Companion*.

No, Jean Arthur is an actress, and in the movie *Easy Living* she plays a writer for *The Boy's Constant Companion*, but let's not get bogged down in such hairsplitting. In any event, she barely holds that job and is fired early in the film. It wasn't much of a job anyway–the harridan spinsters who policed that magazine must have been insufferable coworkers. But it paid the rent.

Well, no it didn't—she's behind in her $7 a week rent when we first meet her, and has only a single dime for her bus fare, so it's not like the job was some fabulous boondoggle. But things are tough all over—haven't you heard there's a Depression on? Of course, if times are so tough, how to explain the fur coat that just dropped out of the sky onto her head?

The good girl thing to do would be to return it. Being a good girl, this is what she does—a dutiful door-to-door tour to find the owner of the prodigal sable. Unaccountably, she finds the rightful owner and it turns out to be her! Or, more precisely, she finds the man who bought the coat and who threw it from his roof, and he insists it's now hers. So … huh.

It's not a total win, though. The sky-fur crushed her hat, and prompted her to get off the bus early, so she's up one fur coat but down a hat and a bus ride. The rich man agrees to make it up to her—his chauffeur will drive her to work, with a detour on the way to a hat shop so he can buy her the most expensive, fabulous chapeau on offer—something to go with her new coat.

This is an improvement for immediate material comforts, but while now she's up a fur coat, a hat, and a ride to work; she is down a job. That's because the harridan spinsters (I did mention them, right?) see her richy new wardrobe and assume the only way some strange man would buy her all that nice stuff was if he was getting something (or rather, getting some) in return. And since that kind of behavior isn't compatible with the moral character of this upstanding Christian magazine, she's out.

Of course it's here that everything goes all wonky. Within 48 hours she will be living a life of unimaginable luxury, wealthy and famous, with a loving husband, a powerful bene-factor, and everything she's ever wanted—all because of the same assumptions that led the harridan spinsters to reject her. One by one, everyone she meets draws the same insulting conclusion about what she's done to get that coat—and then, for their own selfish calculations, proceed to reward her in new ways.

It's *Pretty Woman* in reverse—the good girl, wrongly mistaken for a mistress, who isn't slut-shamed for it, but rewarded.

In other words, what we have here is a film more daring, gutsy, and unpredictable than its age would suggest. For a 1937 screwball farce, this is racy stuff—and convinced it can barrel over any censorial objections through sheer moxie. Which, yes, it could and it did.

But of course this film is a daring, brilliant, hilarious act of moxie—just check out the credits. And no, I don't mean stars Jean Arthur and Ray Milland. They're excellent, but that's not where I want to draw your attention. Nor is it director Mitchell Leisen—then at the apex of his Hollywood

**Jean Arthur in a 1939 publicity photo.**

career and the closest he'd ever come to being called a comedy genius, but not the man of the hour here. No, I mean the real comedy genius, the one who is truly responsible for this bubbly gem—writer Preston Sturges.

Sturges was not yet a name. He hadn't directed a film, and sat on the sidelines burning with jealousy as he watched Leisen. At this point in his career, Preston was a gun for hire, and he'd been hired to turn an existing story by Vera Caspary into a screenplay. Sturges was unimpressed by Caspary's story—some nonsense about a poor girl who steals a fur coat, gets into some farcical situations thanks to the mistaken identities triggered by her new wardrobe, and is eventually judged and punished for her transgressions. Where's the fun in that?

So, jettisoning nearly everything save for the title and the idea of a poor girl wearing an expensive fur coat, he built up a glorious infrastructure of slapstick and sex and glamor and wish fulfillment and romance and wordplay and always breathless pace. Word started to get around Hollywood that Sturges' script was a crackerjack, a comic masterpiece. It wasn't yet enough to win him the directing job he so longed for, but close … one step closer to his prize.

Even with Leisen calling the shots, the Sturges touch was present. For one thing, there are a bevy of supporting players like Franklin Pangborn, Luis Alberni, Olaf Hytten, and William Demarest—they would be regular performers in the Sturges classics yet to come. There's the recurring Sturges trick of a sympathetic character singled out by Fate for unearned benefits (you could play a Sturges film back to back with a Fritz Lang one and their respective attitudes towards Fate would cancel each other out). There's the sense of a madcap universe, in which comic situations and absurdity abound in all directions.

Although, to be true to Preston Sturges, we should say that all of these attributes are one and the same. A Sturges film is about a madcap universe rewarding the innocent and the naive, in which madness and comic intensity comes from all quarters. This approach depends on a reliable company of dependable performers. *Easy Living* is an early example of Sturges' magic, and without his hand at the helm it is necessarily less Sturgesified than say *Christmas in July* or *Palm Beach Story*, but all the symptoms are there to diagnose.

Perhaps the most Sturges touch of them all: watching *Easy Living*, I found myself frequently laughing out loud without being entirely sure what the joke was that triggered it. This is a common experience for me when watching Sturges' films. He builds such comic tension, layering new comic tensions atop old like a Jenga tower of farce, until just about anything—just the right inflection on a line, or a flick of someone's eyes—causes all that tension to escape at once.

Except … can I really credit that to Sturges here? Sure he wrote the brilliant screenplay, but isn't that construction of comic tension at least as much the purview of the director? Can I really hail *Easy Living* as a screwball classic without paying tribute to Mitchell Leisen? (Turn the page and see.)

# The Trouble with Mitchell

Once upon a time there was a Hollywood director at the top of his game. He made movies that were widely popular, influential, critically esteemed, and profitable. He was a visual stylist and a practitioner of high Hollywood glamour. He coaxed great performances from top stars. He was on the short list for producers looking to staff their prestige pictures. Say the name "Mitchell Leisen" today though and be prepared for blank stares.

So what happened? How did someone who flew so high fall into such obscurity? Ironically, the answer is his own success.

Don't fret if you can't rattle off a list of Mitchell Leisen films off the top of your head, let me give you a cheat sheet: *Death Takes a Holiday, Murder at the Vanities, Hands Across the Table, The Big Broadcast of 1937, Swing High Swing Low, Easy Living, The Big Broadcast of 1938, Midnight, Remember the Night, Artists and Models Abroad* (the sequel to the Jack Benny everything-but-the-kitchen-sink blow-out several chapters ago)… This is nowhere near a comprehensive list, but I think it hits most of the highlights.

He was responsible for taking glamour queen Carole Lombard and reinventing her as a comedy star. He directed Jack Benny, Burns & Allen, Zasu Pitts, W.C. Fields, Jean Arthur, Fred MacMurray, Claudette Colbert, Ginger Rogers, Paulette Goddard, Thelma Ritter … the list goes on. And that's just to discuss the films he *directed*. Mitchell Leisen spent decades as a premiere art director and costume designer. In short, we are talking here about an accomplished artist with an outstanding career. But let's take a closer look at some of those highlights and see what happens upon closer scrutiny.

For example, *Hands Across the Table*. This is one of my go-to screwball classics when trying to explain the genre to newcomers. It's not my favorite, nor is it the funniest, but it is by far the most representative. *It Happened One Night* gets all the attention for being the breakout hit that defined the genre, but the cycle of comedies that spun out of its success went pinging off in all kinds of other directions such that it doesn't seem quite like the things it inspired—whereas *Hands Across the Table* manages to pack in practically every ingredient and approach of the genre as a whole. Which sounds a bit like I'm calling it generic, but not at all. I'm saying it's more of a point of inspiration than the Capra film, and if anything about it feels overly familiar today it's because what it did so quickly became standard.

But how much of the credit goes to Leisen? Precious little, because all the attention typically goes to Carole Lombard. This was a mid-career swerve for her, and she demonstrated such peerless comic confidence it was an absolute revelation. To the extent film historians look behind the scenes to understand how Lombard made the switch to comedy, they usually settle on Paramount studio chief Ernst Lubitsch, who apparently was pushing Carole towards comedy and insisted the script be rewritten specifically to write to her strengths.

Now consider *Easy Living*, which is in my opinion a contender for funniest screwball comedy, but is usually thought of a pseudo-Preston Sturges film. Sturges had written the screenplay, which had become something of a cause célèbre around Hollywood before the film was made. Producer Arthur Hornblow knew he had a blockbuster script on his hands, and turned to ace director Leisen to nurture it to the screen. But because Sturges had written something that was self-evidently a hit before a single frame had been filmed, when he started insisting he be allowed to direct his own material, it was hard to refuse him. That's certainly the story Sturges told—that he stood on the sidelines throughout the production of *Easy Living*, fuming at how this journeyman hack was butchering it. Any deviation from his script was like a knife, and he was dying a death of a thousand cuts.

Then we come to *Midnight*. From a script by Billy Wilder and Charles Brackett, *Midnight* stars Claudette Colbert as a down-and-out chorus girl who arrives in Paris one night having lost the last of her money at a Monte Carlo casino. Unable to find a job, she sneaks into a fancy society gala by cooking up a phony identity as a baroness. Weirdly, every time her deception seems due to be discovered, she is spared from humiliation thanks to a variety of supporters who help maintain her disguise, for reasons of their own. It's a Cinderella story in which the princess isn't going to be forced back to her life of poverty—it's a question of whether she will choose that life all on her own.

Like Sturges' backstage agony at *Easy Living*, Billy Wilder raged at what he saw as Leisen's incompetent mishandling of the material. Just as Sturges was motivated by the experience to become a director, Wilder too determined to avoid a repeat of the experience and willed himself into the role of director.

John Barrymore watches over Don Ameche and Claudette Colbert in a publicity still from Mitchell Leisen's *Midnight* (1939).

That was the beginning of the end for Leisen. Not professionally, mind you—he remained an active and respected director through the 1950s. But in terms of posterity, Leisen's memory would now be sullied by the likes of Sturges and Wilder. As their stars rose, they continued to tell of their displeasure at Leisen's directing of their early scripts—and as they became legends, their petty grumblings were preserved and widely distributed.

But did they have a point? How would *Midnight* or *Easy Living* have turned out without Leisen? Well, probably not as good. You see, both films are Cinderella stories (although *Midnight* is more self-conscious about that fact) that drop their heroines into a world of opulence and luxury, contrasting that high life with their humble origins and the rough Depression-era economy outside. In other words, both have a distinctly visual component and a fundamentally human one. These are not characteristics you think of when you think of Preston Sturges or Billy Wilder. Their genius lay in other areas.

Leisen had risen into the world of directing from a background in art design and costuming. Sturges criticized him for worrying about the placement of lamps on the set over the timing of slapstick pratfalls, but this isn't a proper criticism. *Easy Living* gets much of its power from the absurd over-the-top luxury of her new penthouse lifestyle. Getting the lamps right is part of the comedy, as much as the slapstick pratfalls.

It should also be noted that Leisen was also a rare openly gay man in 1930s Hollywood, who knew first-hand what it meant to yearn for acceptance and peace as an outsider (Leisen was nominally married to singer Sondra Gahle, but they lived apart and his relationship with Billy Daniels was not hidden. Daniels had a bit part in *Midnight* and began to appear in and collaborate on Leisen's films from there on). Leisen brought a humanity and a graceful openness to his characters, which might have been at odds with Billy Wilder's harsh cynicism, but that was ultimately to the better of the material.

In both Sturges' and Wilder's self-directed works, the characters tend to come off as programmatic pieces on a comic chessboard, manipulated for specific effect. Leisen brought a warmth to the proceedings, and did so within a context of visual stylization and eye candy that made his films at once earthy and ethereal.

# Ginger Rogers,
# Sad Saks of Fifth Ave.

Gregory La Cava's 1939 comedy *Fifth Avenue Girl* is an excellent example of the 1930s style of romantic comedies, and possibly my favorite Ginger Rogers film of all. It is also a decidedly deviant 1930s romantic comedy that breaks more rules than it follows, and uses Ginger Roger's natural downtrodden deadpan persona to tamp down the usual screwball shenanigans in favor of something altogether more quiet, and bitter. And if that doesn't quite sound like comedy to you, then read on…

*Fifth Avenue Girl* is another Cinderella story, superficially very similar to *Easy Living* and *Midnight*. Like those films, it's about a down-on-her-luck young woman who crosses paths with a deeply unhappy rich man. Turns out the grass isn't greener on the other side after all. Thanks to their chance encounter, the woman becomes the center of a series of mistaken identities and presumed romances, as she is suddenly escalated into a new life of wealth and luxury.

Yes, in broad strokes, it does resemble *Easy Living* and *Midnight*, but let's look past the similarities and focus on where this goes veering off in its own unique direction. First, and crucially, we have to realize that the protagonist of the thing isn't Ginger Rogers, but Walter Connolly. He plays a successful industrialist whose fabulous wealth and life of accomplishment are shaken by a mid-life crisis. He realizes his family is alienated from him and see him only as a money spigot; his wife is actively courting the attentions of younger suitors and living a high life focused on social status; his business is struggling to stay profitable without ruining the lives of his workers. On his birthday, it all comes to a head, when he happens to meet Ginger Rogers in Central Park.

She's unemployed and just a few weeks away from being homeless, but you wouldn't know it from her demeanor. Instead of giving in to fear or despair, she just takes each day as it comes, with the grim stoicism of a condemned woman, maybe, but that's a form of equanimity.

Connolly hires Rogers to pretend to be his mistress—maybe if everyone thinks he's tossing out his family for a pretty young second wife, at least their sense of self-preservation will prompt them to pretend to be nice to the old guy. It's a bit of a cynical plan, and so naturally the cynical Rogers goes along with it.

But here's the thing: the movie gives Connolly's character a purpose to his actions—he has something he wants, and a plan of how to get it. The narrative flow of the movie follows his plan to its conclusion. But there's no such sense of Ginger Rogers' character. She has plenty to lose out of this arrangement, as we shall see, but very little to gain. She can help out a brand-new friend, yes. She can temporarily live the Fifth Avenue life (butler Franklin Pangborn sagely notes that servants get the benefit of living a life of borrowed luxury). She also gets to stave off financial ruin for a while—quite a long while, at that, since her fake sugar daddy has every reason to pay her well for the fake affair. But she has a lot more at risk here than he does. If Connolly's plan goes wrong, he's not likely to be much worse off than when he started. The best case scenario, if *everything* about Connolly's plan goes *perfectly*, is going to end up with Ginger Rogers thrown back into the streets, humiliated and hated. And that's just the end game—along the way she gets the daily drudge of having to live in the same house with people who despise and resent her.

Now that we've identified this peculiar narrative design, let's see its consequences. I called this a "romantic comedy" and it is certainly treated as such, but what exactly is that supposed to mean in practice? You'd probably presume that it means this a comedy in

*Fifth Avenue Girl* (1939) **crams the entire romance between Ginger Rogers and Tim Holt into the final reel.**

which Ginger Rogers falls in love, right? One in which the finale finds her swept off her feet by the love of her life, right?

So let's pause a second and jump back to my other two frames of reference. *Easy Living* got Jean Arthur and Ray Milland together early, and let their romance bloom in the midst of comic chaos spinning out around them. *Midnight* thrust Claudette Colbert into Don Ameche's arms in the opening scene, and then spent the remaining eight reels working out what form their relationship ought to take. But *Fifth Avenue Girl* treats Ginger Rogers' romance as an absolute afterthought.

There's no serious possibility that she and Walter Connolly will end up together—setting aside the awkward May/December aspect of the pairing, the whole point of their fake affair is to provoke his wife into returning to him. So what prospects does Ginger have? Well, there's the old guy's rotten son (Tim Holt). And sure enough, he does sweep her off her feet at the end—but the process of getting there is anything but straightforward, and the emotional effect of that finale is anything but wholly satisfying.

Ginger Rogers and Tim Holt have essentially two and a half meaningful scenes together. That's it. And the first of those occurs a whole hour into the film! The second occurs with the movie 10 minutes away from its conclusion. The final "half" scene is the moment when their hostilities finally give way to ... well, OK, let's address that.

Bear in mind that Ginger Rogers is being paid to pretend to be Connolly's mistress. She plays her part well. Tim Holt believes she is a gold-digging home-wrecking hussy. And she believes him to be a lazy, entitled brat born with a silver spoon in his mouth who doesn't even have the decency to be thankful for that. So, their initial hostility isn't the usual garden variety romantic comedy prickliness. They genuinely hate each other.

The first scene is staged as a mockery of her first encounter with Walter Connolly— they go to the same place and see the same sights, but in place of the gentle humanity and shared appreciation of the absurd that she found with Connolly, Tim Holt just offers up condescension and rudeness.

And that second scene? Well, he plants an unwelcome kiss on her lips—twice—despite her objections. He believes her to be nothing more than his dad's whore, and therefore makes cruel assumptions about her sexual availability. Now, that rapey moment occurs within minutes of the final fade-out. Finally unable to endure any more of this, Ginger breaks character and admits that this has been a ruse. That admission is enough to change Tim's mind—he's apparently been fighting his feelings for this girl while he thought she was loose, but as soon as he learns she isn't, he can admit his love. Why, how gallant of him.

To the movie's great credit, this unsettling undercurrent is part of the point. I said I thought this was arguably Ginger Rogers' best performance, and if it sounds like I've spent a thousand words arguing the opposite, let me clarify: the essential Ginger Rogers character had an earthiness, a world-weary resignation. It's in her smoky voice, her sleepy eyes, her dry Midwestern delivery. This movie is designed to emphasize and exploit those qualities to their best. She starts the movie at a low point, and then with subtle inflections takes us through her additional degradations. But she does it while remaining charming, adorable, lovely. She cracks a bit at the end, but who wouldn't? Here's a person who is a survivor. Pardon me if I choose to stand next to her—when the apocalypse comes, she'll still be standing.

# The Careless Cinderella

*"One of the dullest towns in America is the dreary community of Hotchkiss Falls in the mid-Hudson Valley. The odds are a thousand to one against our finding anyone there with an interesting story. However that's where we are, so let's take a look around."*

Most screwball comedies came in a handful of flavors. The Comedies of Remarriage we've discussed (*The Awful Truth, Mr. and Mrs. Smith, Palm Beach Story, The Philadelphia Story*). Beyond that, there were two main variants—the Vanilla and Chocolate of Screwball. The Heiress on the Run, as the name implies, presented rich girls fleeing their lives of privilege to take up with working-class men (see *It Happened One Night, Next Time I Marry, Lady in a Jam, My Man Godfrey, Holiday*). The Cinderella Story is also self-descriptive: a destitute and desperate girl is mistaken for a rich debutante, pampered by an older Sugar Daddy, and ultimately takes her place among the social set (see *Easy Living, Midnight*, and *Fifth Avenue Girl*, with *Ruggles of Red Gap* as a gender-reversed variant). But once, the world of screwball combined these two flavors: *Slightly Dangerous* is both an Heiress on the Run film *and* a Cinderella Story, and it gives us a chance to dig into what made these two screwball subgenres work.

I'm sure you've spotted the common thread already—both variants involve the crossing of class boundaries, 1 percenters and 99 percenters united by love.

Our ongoing discussion of the origins of screwball has touched on some intertwined threads. One of these factors was the degree to which a genre that prioritized the communal contributions of a deep bench of onscreen performers was better suited to the corporate model of Golden Age Hollywood than the auteurist emphasis behind classic slapstick (the whole "back of Joan Crawford's head" problem). Another key factor was the social condition of the audience. The Great Depression changed the facts on the ground rather substantially. Golden Age Hollywood was remarkably good at crafting sumptuous visions of glamour and excess. Conversely, movies about poverty and grime have never been very popular.

From the beginning, movies have been an affordable source of entertainment, available to mass audiences. Depression-era audiences would be full of people either directly or indirectly touched by the widespread unemployment and economic suffering. Yet the movies were made by wealthy people who had the luxury of being handsomely paid to do soft work. There were a bundle of contradictory impulses that put the whole industry in an awkward place. These screwball comedies got to have their cake and eat it too. They could wallow in the same ole' glamour and excess, while telling stories explicitly critical of the values of the well off. They could simultaneously sell wish-fulfillment fantasies of becoming rich, while sneering at those who are rich.

Notably screwball fell into decline as the Second World War ended. After thriving as America's dominant screen comedy form for over a decade, as soon as GIs started coming home to build a prosperous postwar middle class, the class warfare implicit in screwball lost its allure.

Nineteen forty-three's *Slightly Dangerous* represents a fairly late-period high-point for the genre—things were still tough enough to give the flick an edge. Written by Charlie Lederer and directed by Wesley Ruggles, the ambitions of *Slightly Dangerous* to combine both the Heiress on the Run model and the Cinderella Story were signaled by its working title, "Careless Cinderella." Key to this balancing act is star Lana Turner herself. The role was written especially for her, carefully tailored to give her a career-defining moment. A sad-sack shop-girl in a dead-end job with no romantic prospects and nothing to look forward to except more work, she stages her own death (!) and strikes out for the Big City to reinvent herself. A fortuitous accident gives her the opportunity to effect a complete self-reinvention—specifically the chance to pretend to be the long-lost heiress to curmudgeonly businessman Walter Brennan—and therein fusing the two approaches.

Setting aside the overall high quality of *Slightly Dangerous* and Lana Turner's pitch-perfect performance, there are some historical details worth pointing out. First, we've got the ghosts of old-style slapstick haunting the whole endeavor. Buster Keaton was an uncredited gag writer and allegedly directed a signature scene in which Lana Turner shows how absurdly simple

**Lana Turner strikes a pose in a publicity still for *Slightly Dangerous* (1943).**

her soda-jerk job is by doing it blindfolded. The director of record, Wesley Ruggles, was himself an ex-Keystone Kop and a former Keaton collaborator.

Meanwhile, the picture carries with it seeds of what screwball would become in the postwar era—that is, television sitcoms. Turner's costar is Robert Young, an earnest young fella prone to getting into wacky but innocent mischief. This is the Robert Young of *Father Knows Best*—silly but safe. In other words, postwar prosperity may have pushed screwball off the silver screen, but the form didn't die—it just morphed into the sitcom and kept on truckin.'

# Katharine Hepburn vs. Herself

If you have patience for yet one more Cinderella story, I've got a 1935 romantic comedy with an interesting behind-the-scenes twist.

This Cinderella is *Alice Adams*, a Katharine Hepburn vehicle by ex-Laurel and Hardy cameraman George Stevens, adapted from a Booth Tarkington novel of the same name. It garnered Academy Award nominations for both Best Picture and Best Actress, and revived the moribund career of Hepburn (or at least until the next time her popularity hit the rocks, or the next time after that) and was a breakthrough career moment for Stevens, who reinvented himself as a serious director of significant Hollywood pictures and not just that guy who used to make "Boy Friends" comedies for Hal Roach (never heard of 'em? You're not alone). And yet, both Hepburn and Stevens fought to prevent the film from being as successful as it came to be. And therein lies our story.

Hepburn plays the titular Alice Adams, a poor girl in a nondescript town. The other girls her age cavort at society affairs, showing off their latest tresses and dresses, competing for the attentions of eligible young men. Alice however lives in a shack. Her father is a pharmacy clerk—or he would be, if he wasn't laid up in perpetual bed rest for some unspecified malady. Her brother is a ne'er-do-well, on the slippery slope from petty mischief and gambling problems towards fraud and larceny.

There are no armies of eligible young men vying for her attentions.

There is *one* young man, however—Russell, the most eligible bachelor of them all (Fred MacMurray). Alice thinks that keeping him interested means keeping him ignorant of her true background. Cue the mistaken identities and crazy schemes. In other words, we have once again found ourselves watching a movie about a down-on-her-luck heroine mistaken for a 1 percenter, who successfully penetrates the richy world of society and lands her Prince Charming.

If Hepburn and Stevens had their way, though, that's not where this would have ended—and it's fair to assume that the career boosts the two received from working on such a popular film would not have occurred had they succeeded in making the ending as difficult and prickly and they wanted. But to talk about the ending they preferred we need to first talk about a supreme glue formula. And no, by "glue" I'm not invoking some fancy pants film studies terminology, like "suture." I just mean glue.

Alice's dad (Fred Stone) may presently be an unemployed, sickly former pharmacy clerk, but back in the day he and a colleague at Lamb's Drug Store invented a super glue formula. Or, so we're told by Alice's overbearing mother (Ann Shoemaker), in what feels for all the world like the setup to a punchline that never comes. As far as Mama Adams is concerned, it's a profound failure of character on Papa Adams' part not to try to monetize that formula, especially if their daughter is suffering romantically on account of the family's poverty. She basically bullies him off the bed and into a risky glue startup...

That same story, now told from the point of view of Lamb's Drug Store: Mr. Lamb has kept this useless old man on the payroll indefinitely during his infirmity, out of personal loyalty. Other employers would have cut him loose as dead weight. And now, without even a "thank you" the old fella has stolen the intellectual property that really belongs to the pharmacy where it was developed, and created a rival business. This means war.

From the story's point of view, the irony here is that the whole glue business is the family's attempt to legitimize Alice's deception—instead of pretending to be from a prosperous family, she can actually *be* from one—but it is this very act that most seriously threatens her relationship with Russell. Word gets around that her family has stolen from Mr. Lamb, and whereas Russell has always been amused by and attracted to Alice's pretentious attempts to affect a high-society attitude, this shakes him.

This comes to a head during the film's key comic set piece—a gloriously misbegotten dinner party involving a poorly chosen menu served incompetently by a maid the family has hired for the day to pretend to be their live-in servant (Hattie McDaniel, in what might be her funniest appearance). The central joke of *Alice Adams* is the incongruity of Alice's haughty affectations and her actual lowly station. Key to making that joke land is the famously haughty affectations of the star herself—a set of characteristics so distinctive that it made Katharine Hepburn an easy target for parody both in her own time and for generations after. If you didn't know the character was created in a novel, and already filmed as a silent film once before, you'd be forgiven for assuming it was especially tailored to fit Hepburn alone.

Her assumed air of superiority and singularly independent streak occasionally rubbed audiences the wrong way—Hepburn vacillated between being the greatest female star in Hollywood history and periodic troughs as box office poison. As a general rule, her best screen roles (*Alice Adams*, *Holiday*, *The Philadelphia Story*, *The African Queen*, or just about any of her pairings with Spencer Tracy) swerved into that prickly persona and leveraged it for humanizing effect. Meanwhile her most problematic films lacked that humanizing edge—and watching a tomboyish feminist play rebellious women on screen while treating the Hollywood press rudely and acting as if communicating with her fan base was beneath her, tended to play into the worst stereotypes of the smallest minded people.

Let me be clear I'm not trying to criticize Hepburn at all—I am in awe of her devil-may-care independence. She was unfairly pilloried for making the kinds of quips that Groucho Marx and W.C. Fields were lionized for. It's simply a fact that she worked in a sexist industry in a sexist age, and the very characteristics that made her cool also made her tricky. So the makers of *Alice Adams* had a choice. Producer Pedro S. Berman and his conference room full of writers had put together a script in which Alice's various wacky schemes pay off, true to romantic comedy form, and she wins the undying love of rich boy Russell, who truly loves her for the silly, needy girl she is. Her deceptions are forgiven, even rewarded. Happy ending, cue the house lights. But Hepburn and director Stevens were having none of that. In Booth Tarkington's novel the story ends with Alice and Russell separated—and both director and star preferred the tougher realism of that ending. Together they started rewriting the script, cutting and pasting swaths of the book back into place. In their proposed version, Alice would eventually abandon her desperate social-climbing and get a job as a secretary, to stand on her own two feet without worrying about Prince Charming (a fragment

**Katharine Hepburn battled with producer Pedro S. Berman over the ending of *Alice Adams* (1935).**

of this idea remains in the film, at more or less the halfway mark as Russell catches Alice on her way to apply for a secretarial job).

Producer Berman almost lost his mind. Hepburn was in a slump, taking humiliating pay cuts to appear in flops, and had no star power to leverage. Stevens was a former cameraman whose limited experience directing feature films included making a series of "The Blonde and the Redhead" vehicles for comediennes June Brewster and Carol Tevis such as *The Undie-World* (again, if you haven't heard of this stuff, join the club). And these two were suddenly going to get it into their heads that the public would be expected to pay good money to watch Katharine Hepburn be romantically defeated and then give up on the whole idea?

Berman called George Cukor in to mediate. Cukor was a man whose box office success gave him a certain undeniable authority, and in fact he'd been the original choice to direct *Alice Adams* had his schedule permitted. He reinstated the happy ending—and in fact installed a happy ending for everybody. Berman got his hit and returned a happy profit to RKO for their troubles; Stevens proved himself on a major picture and launched himself into a new role as a director of prominence and not just some slapstick has-been hack; Hepburn turned her fortunes around and almost took home an Oscar.

And we can file this away as yet another case study showing that when directors clash with producers over artistic visions, the director isn't always right.

# Me vs. Capra

Frank Capra is one of the most important figures in this book. While I may take argument with how much of Harry Langdon's success he allegedly created, there is no disputing he played a significant part in the glory years of one of silent comedy's great masters. Then, for an encore, he made *It Happened One Night*, codifying into one film the threads of screwball that had been swirling for years and giving them a commercial imperative. Certainly important things were already developing in the genre thanks to Ernst Lubitsch and others, but the truly glorious *It Happened One Night* was a deserved blockbuster and unleashed scores of crazy heiresses onto the world. If we set out to chart the course from silent slapstick to screwball rom-com, there's no better place to start than Capra.

Unfortunately, I don't care much for the man's films, especially what I consider the execrable *Meet John Doe*. Even though I spend a lot of time in this book defending unloved movies, it isn't the case that I indiscriminately love everything. There are some movies I just can't abide. *Meet John Doe* is one of them. So, to paraphrase Dorothy Parker, I don't intend to say anything nice. Wanna sit by me?

Now you might be wondering: *Meet John Doe* is on an AFI Top 100 something or other list, what's my problem? Well, it starts with the opening sequence—Capra opens the film with a heavy-handed sequence of shots of workers, culminating in an even more heavy-handed shot of the phrase "a free press for a free people" being jackhammered off the façade of a newspaper's office building. So, subtlety is not on the table tonight. Now don't get me wrong—I don't mind if a movie has a point of view, but where is this going?

Capra introduces us to three categories of villains. The first is the paper's owner, who is going to downsize the staff and abandon much of what the paper great just to protect the bottom line. He's a familiar kind of corporate meanie, who only thinks about his own money. He fires Barbara Stanwyck, who finishes off her last day with a big middle finger-ish gesture to her former employer, by writing an "article" that is really just a totally made-up hoax about a down-on-his-luck guy threatening to commit suicide on Christmas Eve as a protest against economic conditions. That story goes viral, in the 1940s sense of the term, and so Barbara is hastily hired back—not because she proved herself to be a valuable journalist, but because the paper needs her to keep the hoax going (and is willing to pay her hush money not to reveal it is a hoax).

Here we meet the other two villains of the piece. One is the powerful political interests (such as the terrible Norton) who decide that the phony "John Doe" would be a useful tool in manipulating public opinion during an election year. These fat cats are basically the same kind of corrupt bad guy as the newspaper publisher, they just operate on a far bigger scale. But on a smaller scale, Barbara also functions as a villain, because she was the orchestrator of the scam. She was willing to sell out her journalistic integrity to save her job—the same unethical selfishness as the bigger bad guys in the story.

So here we have my first objection. Screwball comedy is laudable in large measure for what it did for actresses. During the 1930s and '40s, the prospects for actresses exploded, and instead of being just love interests for the male comedians they became the main show. In many ways, Capra's work on *It Happened One Night* was key to making that new realm of possibility happen. But Capra then suddenly backpedaled from it. He was not comfortable writing for strong women, and his films seem almost designed to force the uppity female stars back into their places.

Stanwyck was an enormously capable comedienne—and in the hands of other directors she could glow in things like *The Mad Miss Manton, Remember the Night,* or *The Lady Eve.* The treatment of Barbara Stanwyck's character isn't just an expression of Capra's sexist discomfort with strong women, it's part and parcel of the movie's Us Versus Them ethos. There is a line of thought that appreciates *Meet John Doe* for its championing of the common man against moneyed interests, a theme as relevant today as in the Depression. The problem is, I don't really see that in *Meet John Doe* at all—I see a feint in that direction, but not the real thing.

For one thing, a huge amount of what comes to be known in the film as the John Doe Philosophy was actually invented by Stanwyck in the first place, and she did it in an effort to protect her job against the moneyed interests—if the movie is serious about these ideas, it should be presenting *her* as the heroine whose triumph we want to cheer. Watching her tearfully apologize to Gary Cooper for failing him (when he was the stooge hired to give voice to her ideas) is just … sad.

More to the point, the thrust of the movie is how the John Doe Philosophy galvanizes, motivates, and inspires "the people." I put "the people" in quote marks because they aren't an actual presence in the film (save for those bits of stock footage at the top). The film agonizes over what words will be given to John Doe to say, predicated on the condescending assumption that "the people" can be so easily brainwashed by a charismatic figure. This isn't just the condescending assumption of the villain Norton—it's the basic premise of the entire movie. In the finale, our hero John Doe succeeds because "the people" latched on to his inspirational words. *"There you are, Norton! The people! Try and lick that!"*

If "the people" are such important figures in the film, why aren't they actually characterized? Neither John Doe nor his hobo friend "The Colonel" are ordinary people, they are insiders in the hoax. However, meanwhile, The Colonel waxes angrily about "heelots," a concept quickly picked up by the rest of the cast to describe how greedy people are constantly looking for payouts from those with money. The film seems to mean that heelots are manifestations of the me-first attitude that is destroying American society. But paired with the film's treatment of Stanwyck, and the Colonel's various diatribes where he praises the simple values of dirt floors and the unstructured freedom that comes from unemployment, the perhaps unintended effect is to imply that what's destroying America is that the uppity have-nots keep lusting after material comforts. If only they'd be happier with their lot, the Depression wouldn't be so depressing.

The whole "heelot" business sounds at times uncomfortably like modern-day prejudices against the poor for "demanding" "handouts" (both concepts there deserve their own scare quotes). That's the problem with Us Versus Them formulations: if you're not careful you can find yourself defining huge swaths of your audience as Them instead of Us. If you come to *Meet John Doe* sympathizing more with Barbara Stanwyck than Gary Cooper, Capra can't do much for ya.

So let me be clear about my own politics: I don't believe in Us Versus Them. I think "the people" is all of us, rich and poor, have and have not, and that the moneyed interests share the same hopes and motivations as the common man. And this is why I love movies: you can watch a movie made almost a hundred years ago, or one made in the very margins of the film industry, or one made on the other side of the world—or if you want to get really outré, go watch one made a hundred years ago by outsider indies on the other side of the world—and you'll find that people are people are people, and always have been. The movies I love most are those that embrace that common humanity and tie us together. That's my biggest problem with Capra—he's an elitist who hates elites. He wants to be perceived as an important and serious artist making Big Pictures about "the people" but he fails to recognize the people in any of his co-workers or the characters he creates. His films draw up Us Versus Them battle lines, but then manages to drop way too many of his own audience into the Them camp.

*Meet John Doe* spends over two hours wagging its finger in admonition at its audience, condemning them for being agents of their own economic victimization, for lacking integrity, for failing to appreciate the simple joys of a dirt floor and an empty pocket. It shames Barbara Stanwyck for being clever and trying to keep her job. And then it whips itself up to a rousing finale to claim that somehow the mass of "people" out there will be inspired by its message to make the world a better place, even though actually depicting what that might look like is beyond the film's imagination.

And the thing of it is, just four years before *Meet John Doe* there was a screwball comedy that dealt with the same premise and ideas and hit it out of the park. It mopped the floor with *Meet John Doe*. Here are some the reasons to like *Nothing Sacred* better: (1) It is a scant 77 minutes long compared to *John Doe*'s patience-straining two-plus-hours bloat. (2) It is in color. (3) It has Carole Lombard in it. (4) It is actually funny. (5) It is also romantic. (6) But most of all—it lands its satiric jabs without being divisive.

**Carole Lombard and Frederic March nurse their injuries as Walter Connolly looks on in *Nothing Sacred* (1937).**

*Nothing Sacred* concerns an ethically-challenged newspaperman (Fredric March) who is involved in a hoax involving a small-town girl (Lombard) whom the public at large has been misled into believing is going to die imminently. As she becomes an increasingly beloved public figure, and the consequences of her hoax grow more tangled, she and the journalist fall in love and find themselves struggling to find a way to restore their sense of integrity without having the scam blow everything up they care about. So—pretty similar in general principles, you have to admit.

Part of *Nothing Sacred*'s success lies in the way it implicates everyone. After introducing Fredric March's sordid schemes in the big city, he is sent out to Small Town America on a mission to find a purer, less made-up story. In other words, the reverse of the *Meet John Doe* set-up, where the reporter can only keep her job by making up the news. What March finds in Small Town, USA, is that the local folk are even *more* corrupt and selfish than he is—a brilliant inversion of the usual stereotypes of small town values versus big city smarminess. Then Lombard arrives in the story—simultaneously spinning a Big Lie while also trying not to. Her internal contradictions are a delight to watch. She gets to be both the cause of the all the problems as well as the victim of those problems at once, and in that way allows us to sympathize with her no matter what happens.

In the end, she and March carry the day because in a world full of liars and cheats, they are supremely better at it than anyone else—it's a victory for smart people (or smart alecks, take your pick).

# Preston Sturges Origin Story

Preston Sturges was a born storyteller, he just didn't know it. For a very long time.

He was also born to make screwball comedies—for a while, he actually lived a screwball plot. He started dating Eleanor Hutton, a proper heiress with a high society family. He dated a lot of girls, but this one struck a nerve. They started thinking seriously about marriage. But when these thoughts were shared with the Hutton clan, there were the usual "*Oh my!*"s and monocles dropping into wineglasses. The Huttons were sure their daughter was acting up to provoke them, certain this roustabout boyfriend of hers was just a gold-digger. But threatening to cut her off did not deter the boyfriend. Instead, the two eloped—while the papers went mad with the story of the runaway heiress and her playwright lover.

For the moment, let's ignore the fact that Sturges' movie-ready romance turned out to be a bust. Instead, let's spend some time luxuriating in this period of Preston's life, when he started to find his way into Hollywood, in the most half-assed way possible.

We start with our hero dating an actress (this was pre–Eleanor, but it doesn't really matter that much. We're not talking about a man for whom monogamy was that big of a thing). He doesn't share the name of this actress in his memoirs, but we do know this: she kept picking fights with him, out of nowhere.

Eventually, she explained to poor befuddled Preston that this was all a gimmick. She was writing a play, and was trying out the dialog on him to see how he responded. It seems she was writing this play about him, and wanted the fictional buffoon on stage to be every bit as numbskulled as the real idiot she'd been dating (or something to this effect—remember, we only got Preston's side of the story).

This triggered Sturges' most primal "anything-you-can-do-I-do-better" instinct, so he holed up in his apartment and hammered out a play. Well, sorta. He wrote the last third of one—then realized that if he was going to be a professional writer he might need to actually finish the thing. So he ground out another two acts, shopped it around town, and eventually got it produced off-off-Broadway for a whole week. It was called *The Guinea Pig*. With enough grit and determination, Sturges leveraged the one-week trial run into a proper entrée to Broadway, where he eventually got a backer and mounted his own production in 1929.

But he was still an international roué, though. He'd been one of those for many long years, and a playwright for only weeks. (Seriously, go check out his autobiography—he is perhaps the biggest comedy director in Hollywood pre–Mel Brooks/pre–Adam McKay, but you'll be at page 267 out of 340 before you get to anything about movies.) So he scuttled off back to Monte Carlo to squander some money pointlessly, and was traveling with a pretty girl (another nameless lass). She wondered, "What are your intentions?" He replied, "Strictly dishonorable."

He realized this clever wordplay was the makings of another hit play (how it actually played out for the night in question he kept to himself).

Six hard days of writing later (what a workaholic!) and he had a script. He posted it to producer Brock Pemberton, and then full of smugness he boasted to his father that by 11:30 a.m. Saturday he'd be getting an offer. Papa hung his head in exhausted desperation. Preston smiled, and explained he'd calculated exactly how much time would elapse between dropping the manuscript at the post office and the earliest moment Pemberton could have finished reading.

And sure enough, at 11:30 a.m. Saturday the doorbell rang—with the postal delivery guy returning the package for insufficient postage. *(waa-waa)*

Yes, Preston Sturges told that story in his memoir. Was it true? Almost certainly not, but he did not become one of Hollywood's greatest comedy directors by worrying too much about what was true.

Eventually, Pemberton did read the manuscript for *Strictly Dishonorable* and did put an offer on it. It opened in September 1929 to sold-out houses, and ran as one of Broadway's hottest tickets for a long, long time. Sturges was now a celebrity. He started writing movies freelance (*The Big Pond, Fast and Loose*) and kept writing plays. But here's the thing: the plays were flops. Audiences apparently enjoyed them, but critics attacked them. And when I say "critics," I am talking about a tight circle of Manhattan writers you can count on the fingers of two hands. Their barbed words were powerful enough to make or break stage shows. They preferred to break them, as if keeping Broadway safe for super-perfection was a noble goal requiring relentless vigilance.

Meanwhile—those films…. Remember them? Probably not. But they made money. Hollywood sent films out across the nation, which meant no single critic was powerful enough to kill even the stupidest film. You could make films, and enjoy making them—films were critic-proof.

So, Preston Sturges—a brilliant, gifted comedy writer the likes of which come along perhaps once every hundred years—was driven out of live theater and into Hollywood, because that was the only place he could avoid bankruptcy (although, being an incompetent businessmen, he drove himself into bankruptcy anyway).

**Preston Sturges, a man of potent words.**

And his first gig in Hollywood? An uncredited rewrite artist on James Whale's *The Invisible Man*. So ... there ya go.

Preston Sturges lived a genuinely preposterous life, such that his own biography was nuttier than any of his films. By the time he started writing comedy he had been: an American ex-pat raised in France; heir to a perfume business; a composer and songwriter; a (stunt) pilot for the World War I American Air Service; an inventor; a kept man…. I think I've lost track of all the things he did.

This list of peripatetic activities is important because unlike most other great comedians, Sturges did not live for comedy—at least not at first. He found himself writing comedy only in middle age, after having failed at a long list of other careers.

Eventually Sturges came to make *Strictly Dishonorable* into a film. More Lubitsch than Sturges, the story inverts a standard cliché plot—this time we get a small-town girl torn between two lovers, one of whom is a European roué phony, but the twist is that the roué phony is the good guy, the all-American boy is a jerk, and the girl is the one with sex on her mind.

For half the running time, we watch as Count Gus (yup, that's his name, Count Gus) maneuvers himself into place to seduce this girl away from her pretentious, abusive, jackass boyfriend—and then, when he's ready to make his move, realizes that (a) she's the one seducing him, and (b) she's a virgin. The gimmick of the thing is that it's the girl with the dishonorable intentions, and when Gus backs out of taking her virginity (*"You are a baby!"*) she is furious. His refusal to have a one-night stand with her very nearly wrecks their nascent relationship and ruins all hope of romance!

There's a lot to like about *Strictly Dishonorable*—it's as impressive as early screen comedy gets. The success of the play had made Sturges into a "name," and catapulted him into Hollywood, where his brilliant comic mind thrived. This success however gave him heart palpitations and soul-searching heartaches. Why? Well, because it was funny—and amusing people by making them laugh has never been treated by critics as being as worthy an artistic pursuit as making them brood over drama. Sturges bought into that prejudice, and fretted that unless he proved himself with something dramatic, he would be dismissed by the critics. In the entire history of the Academy Awards, the number of comedies that have won Best Picture can be counted on one hand; The Golden Globes split out comedies as an entire separate category, and then build up to the grand finale—"Best Picture," not the comedy one, at the end. The implication being that making people laugh is an also-ran kind of achievement.

Charlie Chaplin never worried about this. He flirted with drama—but even *A Woman of Paris* is basically a subtle, muted comedy that only pretends to be a drama. Ernst Lubitsch got his start in drama, making Cecil B. DeMille-ish epics, but he shifted gears into comedy and never turned back—and even when he wanted to take on subjects as grotesque and intense as Nazism, he did it through comedies. I could keep going, but you get the point—most comedy-makers are comfortable in their skin and know the power of laughter needs no apologies.

Sturges would get there, eventually, and by the time of *Sullivan's Travels* he had. But having worked through that fear and doubt in his younger career gave him the necessary fuel to breathe some personal insight into *Sullivan's Travels*. When I first saw the film, I had assumed he was lampooning Frank Capra. Only after learning more about Sturges did I realize he was pulling his own leg—the delusional pretensions that Joel McCrea gets into his head are very much like the ones that haunted Sturges in the aftermath of *Strictly Dishonorable*.

It's easy enough to see why you might think this is about Frank Capra—he's explicitly name-checked, for one thing. And the calamities that befall McCrea as he sets out on his adventure seem culled from Capra movies. But the inflection of these things is off—these are manifestly not how Capra would be doing this stuff. Capra orchestrated everything, characters and situations alike, in a coherent pattern designed to produce a specific moral reaction in the viewer. *Here is what's right, here is what's wrong, here are the goodies, here are the baddies*—Capra lays it all out without shades of gray. Sturges seems to build his films in such a way that all the pieces pull in different directions, for incoherent morals.

What is *Palm Beach Story* about? Is it about the triumph of romance or the futility of it? What's the moral of *Christmas in July*? Are we supposed to celebrate the improbable rise of a dreamer at the hands of capricious Fate, or are we supposed to shudder in horror? Does *Hail the Conquering Hero* advocate deception, or not? Is *The Great McGinty* a heroic figure or a monster? And the sexual politics of *Miracle of Morgan's Creek* don't actually seem to have anything to do with what the characters on screen constantly say they do.

Critic Gerald Mast chalked this schizophrenia up to Sturges' failing as an artist—as far as Mast was concerned, Sturges' insistence on get-out-jail-free endings was a cop-out born of his refusal to fully engage with the politics of the ideas he toyed with. Which is one of the reasons I read Mast mostly to get my blood boiling (my copy of *The Comic Mind* is all dinged up from how many times I've thrown it across the room). By contrast, James Harvey "gets" Sturges and understands the power of ironic ambiguity (my copy of *Romantic Comedies in Hollywood* is all weathered and worn from how many times I've re-read it in joy).

Sturges' version of Capra is aware of its own hypocrisy. And by hypocrisy—this is what I mean: Capra's grand moralistic statements are always taking some abstracted stance about Us vs. Them—for example, in *Mr. Deeds Goes to Town*, where the battle between Mr. Deeds' noble soul and the evil political handlers is played out with the idea that if only "they," the masses, could experience a real politician instead of one all slicked up by machines (another set of "them"), then the country would get back on track. But it's a vaguely fascist depiction of the American electorate—they are sheep, not people. Real people are messy and contradictory, and don't do as they're told. So there's a hidden hypocrisy buried in Capra's films, an unacknowledged assumption that Good and Evil make sense as discrete concepts and they don't overlap.

Sturges sometimes seems like a cynic because he doesn't buy into that worldview. Sturges' film sometimes make grand moralistic statements, but they simultaneously undermine them by populating the screen with messily real people who don't do as they're told.

Consider the bit where McCrea rewards a tramp's humane generosity with an out of nowhere gift—one good turn deserves another, so to speak. Capra would leave it off here, leaving a warm, happy feeling in the audience. Or rather, leaving a superficial and self-satisfied moral superiority in the viewer. Sturges doesn't leave it there, though. He can't help but stage this "milk of human kindness" in a diner in Las Vegas of all places—and McCrea's idea of rewarding the man with a $100 bonus comes with a very wise wisecrack about how this is likely to ruin the very man it's meant to reward. Some good deeds do go punished. Doing the right thing doesn't always help.

Joel McCrea's epiphany that making comedies is at least as worthy as making serious dramas isn't a moral the movie completely commits to. And why should it? Sturges didn't have a moment of epiphany like this—he tried his hand at drama and was simply better at comedy. Sometimes a cigar is just a cigar.

# The Love Song of Captain McGloo

Preston Sturges' *Christmas in July* isn't a Christmas movie. But it is one of Sturges' funniest films, and one where Sturges' somewhat misleading and occasionally inconsistent philosophy really works.

Sturges, you see, was a dreamer. Like his protagonists, he was a restless soul, full of impractical ideas. He was one of Hollywood's true geniuses, yet he often directed his energies away from his extraordinary films and onto less promising, far-fetched business ideas. Sturges lacked the ability to perceive the difference between his good ideas and his bad ones, and so he threw himself with gusto into every venture, no matter how absurd.

This was of course the key to his success, the source of his genius. It didn't just take a visionary artist to make his greatest works, it took a madman who never gave a moment's thought to the possible consequences. A person who played it safe, who shied away from potentially ruinous ideas, would never have made *Miracle of Morgan's Creek*, or *Hail the Conquering Hero*. But there's a balance to be struck between clever risk-taking and recklessness. Not every risky idea is a great one, and a person who stakes everything on *all* of their long-shot fantasies risks losing everything.

Which is where we meet Dick Powell in *Christmas in July*. He's an underemployed file clerk who's in love with co-worker/neighbor Ellen Drew. Marriage isn't on the menu until their can achieve some financial stability—and to that end, Dick has pinned all his hopes on winning a radio contest. Maxford House Coffee is prepared to write a life-changing check to the listener who comes up with the best slogan.

This is as long-shot a long-shot can get. Thousands of people will be entering this contest—and even if you had a brilliant, ad-agency-quality slogan to contribute, the odds are not in your favor. But Dick is certain he has this thing locked.

He doesn't just have a brilliant, ad-agency-quality slogan. He has *the* slogan, one so perfect its perfection will be undeniable.

Here it is: "*If you can't sleep at night, it isn't the coffee, it's the bunk.*"

Mind you, it doesn't undermine his confidence that every time he tells someone this slogan, he is then roped into a protracted and defensive explanation: *You see, it's a myth that coffee keeps you awake. So if you're a coffee drinker and you're having trouble sleeping, it can't be the coffee's fault. That's a myth. And bunk is a slang term for myth. Your sleeping problem must be your crummy bed—your bunk. Get it? It's a pun. Oh, what do you know about quality, you philistine!*

Thanks to some unlikely plot contrivances, he comes to believe that not only *will* he win, but that he *has* won. And the same contrivances cause everyone else to be fooled, too, including the CEO of Maxford House, who dutifully writes the life-changing check. (If you want to see how this happens, see the movie.)

Once Dick gets the check, he goes on a shopping spree to buy gifts for everyone in his life—thus the title of the movie. These fun material goods may make the day-to-day life of his friends and neighbors more pleasant, but that's not "life-changing" in any meaningful sense. What gives this check it's transformative power isn't the dollar value, but what it represents—and the consequent affirmation of Dick's bizarre, misguided creativity.

"*I used to think that maybe I had good ideas and was gonna get somewhere,*" he boasts, "*but now I know it.*"

You can hear Preston Sturges' own plaint buried in the pain of those words. This is a film from a man who was himself unable to distinguish his good ideas from his bad without the external validation of box office receipts and honors that separated the ideas that made him rich and famous from the ones that impoverished and disappointed him.

Sturges had a habit of giving the most sensible, level-headed thoughts to marginalized characters. His flamboyant main characters have dangerous and unstable worldviews, but their craziness is balanced by the characters who speak sense from the sidelines. That way the movies get their cake and eat it too—espousing one crazy viewpoint, while quietly whispering "don't listen to that madness."

Enter Dick's boss, E.L. Waterbury (played by Harry Hayden). When he gets wind that his employee is sacrificing his paid job to spend his mental energies on cooking up a coffee slogan for a radio contest (never mind how nuts the slogan he thought up was), Mr. Waterbury offers these words of advice: "*Ambition is all right if it works. But no system could be right where only half of 1% were successes and the rest were failures. That wouldn't be right. I'm not a failure. I'm a success. And so are you—if you earn your living and pay your bills and look the world in the eye.*"

Of course Dick Powell pays exactly zero heed to this advice, and barrels ahead on his ill-advised path, dragging everyone he knows with him into unintentional deception and certain ruin. Waterbury voiced what I personally believe to be a sensible position—if you earn your living and pay your bills, you're a success. Powell doesn't need to win a contest to validate his ideas, because the fact is his ideas really are terrible.

Back when my kids were younger we used to watch *American Idol*, and I remember being appalled how many people seem to believe they can only validate their existence if they win this singing competition and become a flash-in-the-pan pop-star. But many of them are surrounded by people that love them, bosses who willingly give them time off to pursue their dreams, and enough passable talent that they could probably have a very happy hobby of semi-professional singing or something creative—all of which sounds like a pretty good life to me. But the contestants seem to think all of that is worthless if they don't win—and just was Waterbury says, nearly all of them don't win.

Dick Powell simply will not be told that his slogan is (a) unwieldy and wordy, (b) hard to remember, or (c) factually inaccurate. Far from it, he's argumentative and combative on these points, singularly convinced that coffee actually puts people to sleep (he says a "Viennese doctor" said so). But his conviction is so acute, that when pranksters try to joke with him that despite all odds he did win, the result is that the entire world is warped around him as if this improbable fact was true. It suddenly becomes harder to persuade anyone of the actual facts than to go thoughtlessly along in the craziness unleashed by his "winning" slogan. And then, one solitary sane person emerges in the maelstrom to offer the sage advice that being content with your lot in life is the best way to enduring happiness, as opposed to wishing for miracles. But his advice is laughed off and repeatedly ridiculed—despite the fact that it is plainly correct.

The brilliance of this film is the way it manages to convey the an imminently sensible position while depicting its complete opposite—an attribute it shares with the film Sturges should be most remembered for, if it were up to me, *Palm Beach Story*—a profoundly anarchic comic masterpiece that wholly abdicates any responsibility to make a lick of sense.

The extent to which *Palm Beach Story* abandons all pretense to conventional narrative structure is presented in the opening title sequence. I say "presented" instead of "revealed," because there is no chance whatsoever that anyone viewing this movie for the first time will recognize the significance of what is shown in the titles.

On a second viewing, after you have witnessed the bizarre *deus ex machina* solution Sturges uses in place of a sensible finale, sure, then you can see how Sturges the magician blatantly stuffs his aces up his sleeve right from the opening frames. But I refuse to believe that any human being in all of history has ever watched these opening titles cold, and then said to themselves, "Gee, I wonder when we're gonna see what happened to that other lady?" And if you're reading this without having seen (or remembered) the movie, and that remark made no sense at all, then you're more or less in the position of the people in the audience, watching this movie pretend to be a sequel to a movie that doesn't exist. Because

*Palm Beach Story* (1942) begins where most romantic comedies end, with the wedding (of Joel McCrea and Claudette Colbert).

that's what those opening titles look like—for all the world like a recap of events from a previous adventure. The rapid-fire staccato of images, periodically freeze-framing on a pratfall or slapstick sight gag, comes out of nowhere and barrels along too quickly to fully register. That, and credits are superimposed over it all, further reinforcing the impression that you are expected not to study these images but to gloss over them—they are the to remind you of the highlights of the last film. Of which, of course, there is none. If this is *Palm Beach Story*, then it's prequel must have been something like "New York Story," in which Joel McCrea fell in love with Claudette Colbert. Apparently that faux-quel ended with their wedding (attended by lots of falling and crashing into things), and they lived "happily ever after."

Or did they?

And that's where this movie *begins*. This is something of a bold move by Sturges, for a romantic comedy.

As we've discussed, the rise of romantic screwball comedies marked a rise in the significance of female comedians, specifically an equality between the male and female comedy co-stars. I'm not going to say that the rise of female comedians as equals caused the structure of screwball comedies, or that the structure of screwball comedies caused the rise of female comedians as equals, but I can say with confidence that the two are closely related. Think about it this way: if you've got two comedy leads in a film, one male and one female, and you want to give them more or less equal amounts of screen time and comic business, then there are worse ways to anchor the central dramatic conflict of the story than on their relationship to one another. You have them meet cute, and then combat each other in funny ways for about an hour and a half, until they realize that the things they hate about each other are things they love about each other. Fade out.

We can call this the apart-apart-together model.

There are other ways to pull this off—the Thin Man movies begin with a married couple whose relationship is never in danger, and just puts the two of them into mortal danger instead, tracking down killers and conspiracies. But without Thin Mannish style danger, having your romantic couple start the movie off together is a problematic stance to take. If you choose to have the dramatic conflict be a romantic one, one that puts their relationship at risk, such that you go for a together-apart-together model, you threaten the very structure of your story. For the together-apart-together model to function, you presumably need to make the central dramatic conflict convincing enough to mount a meaningful challenge to the relationship. The more credible the challenge, though, and by extension the more effective the dramatic conflict, the more work the movie has to do to resolve that conflict and reunite the lovers. These two loved each other once, they know what being together is like, and they're seriously considering walking away from that.

By contrast, the apart-apart-together model sets the bar lower. They just need to realize they're in love, not overcome the one barrier that's strong enough to undo that love.

Which brings us back to Sturges and *Palm Beach Story*, which opts for a together-apart-together model but gleefully defies the very storytelling logic I just outlined. The gimmick here is that the force that tears them apart is *exactly* the same force that would keep them together or could reunite them—they never stop loving each other, they never stop wanting to be together.

So what's pulling them apart, you ask? What's pushing this husband and wife toward divorce in Palm Beach?

Joel McCrea is a dreamer, which is a nice way of saying he's down on his luck. His peculiar ambition is to construct an urban airport in the center of New York City by stretching powerful steel nets across the skyscrapers, so that planes can land safely in the middle of a city.

This looney invention encapsulates the Sturges touch. Listening to McCrea describe this plan, it all sounds perfectly reasonable. His scale model is impressive, and you might well sit in the audience nodding your head approvingly, and wondering why, so many decades after this movie was made, why hasn't anyone gone and built this thing yet?

And then, on reflection, realization dawns: the idea is completely bonkers. How would planes safely navigate through the buildings? The noise would be unbearable for the poor citizens of the city, who would have to resign themselves to never seeing the sky again, thanks to the airport that now hovers permanently over their heads. I could keep going with objections to the idea, but why bother? No, wait, one more objection—why does the thing cost exactly $99,000? Even the price tag is ridiculous.

And that's Sturges in a nutshell.

Preston Sturges lived a life so absolutely implausible and so stuffed with absurd events that if someone had set out to make a completely honest bio-pic about him, one that didn't stray from the facts one bit, it would have been laughed off the screen as even nuttier than his comedies. He made screwball farces because he wrote from what he knew—and the weird thing is, *Palm Beach Story* is actually kind of autobiographical in places—just not in the places you might think. The crazy airport scheme, the wastrel rich cougar flitting from man to man, the relationship that tears itself apart because the woman wants to see the man succeed—these are things Preston yanked from deep in his soul and turned into frothy entertainment. He turned pain into laughs, mostly because his pain wasn't recognizable to outsiders as anything real.

In a Sturges movie, the craziest people are made to sound the most becalmed and normal. And, the lone voice of reason in a Sturges film is made to sound foolish. This is the corollary of the proposition that Sturges makes sensible ideas sound foolish and crazy ones sound reasonable: Sturges' movies spend most of their effort advancing ideas and values contrary to what he actually means. His films are jam-packed with slapstick chaos and machine-gun dialogue, but their greatest comic power comes from irony. They are manifestly not about what they are about—as we shall see with *Palm Beach Story*.

McCrea's absurd airport idea is faltering, and the couple can't pay their bills. At which point, Claudette Colbert decides that since she's an attractive and shapely young woman and there are lonely rich guys out there, the best way to help her hubby is divorce him, seek out a sugar daddy, and funnel the cash back to McCrea so he can become a successful entrepreneur. And when Colbert explains her idea to him, it sounds completely sensible, an iron-clad proposition. How could anyone object?

So, off she trundles to Palm Beach to execute this scheme. Within hours she has hooked Rudy Vallee, playing the third richest man in the world. He is utterly delighted to spend money on her, and is so sold on the self-evidently brilliant urban airport idea that he remains committed to it even as Colbert keeps changing her story about whose idea it is— is it the brainchild of her cruel husband, described as a vicious wife-beater, or the intellectual property of her brother, "Captain McGloo?" (Funny names are another Sturges trademark. In the film, Colbert has to come up with a name for her "brother" on the fly, and misremembers his mother's maiden name McGrew.)

In short, Colbert's plan has worked exactly as she said it would. In one scene, she cooks up a crazy scheme, and in the very next scene she pulls it off. What kind of storytelling is that? Where's the conflict?

Well, the conflict is in whether she should be doing this at all. She is successfully executing a very bad idea, that will hurt a lot of people.

Or will it? McCrea has followed his wife to Palm Beach hoping to stop her, which is where the whole McGloo thing came in. Having told Vallee that her husband was a vicious wife-beating lout, she passes her real husband off as her brother, and then *he* finds a sugar momma—Rudy Vallee's sister Mary Astor thinks Captain McGloo is the very picture of desirable manliness, and she is prepared to pay for his companionship.

So what does our dreamer hero really want out of life? Comfort, riches, abundant sex, and professional accolades—or does he want to hang on to his screwball wife and live from hand to mouth instead? So much for happily ever after—the opening titles show us a wedding, and then the movie shows us two possible outcomes. They both have their good points, and they both involve some compromise. You can't have everything—you just have to choose which something you want.

In other words, the movie is a romantic comedy which drives aggressively to this precipice: romance is the bunk. Living happily ever after with your sweetie isn't on the menu—you can have the *living happily ever after* part, or the *with your sweetie* part, but not both together. This is a bleak message for a romantic comedy. The schizophrenic attitude is so bewildering, the audience gets to this point in the story and has no idea what they're rooting to happen now. Do we want Claudette to succeed in her plan—and thereby make this appealing rich dork really happy, and give her (ex-)husband the very success he's aspired to? Or do we want Joel to reveal the truth, and thereby deeply wound everyone and destroy everything?

Sturges gets out of this impasse by suddenly announcing that the rules have changed. It's like playing a game of chess to the brink of checkmate, and then loosing because your opponent hits a home run. What game were you playing?

But Sturges' get-of-jail-free-card of an ending doesn't change the point of the preceding 90 minutes—it just lets you walk out of the theater happy, and maybe unaware that you just watched a deeply romantic story about the impossibility of romance. The plot may be anti-romantic, but this is a Sturges film—and as such, it isn't about what it seems to be about. The tone, the mood, the overall experience is one of love triumphant—a message that somehow comes across despite the abject inability of the rest of the movie to even remotely believe in it.

# Sturges After Sturges (or, the Keystone Pipeline)

Here's where we find ourselves–the proverbial wild west. A shapely blonde dancehall singer, clutching a smoking gun. She's trembling with residual anger, surrounded by friends and allies who are aghast at her latest escapade. She's just shot a judge, in the buttocks, for the second time in as many hours.

That's what's onscreen, in the opening salvo of Preston Sturges' first Technicolor picture. To step out of the screen, though, we must acknowledge the disappointing truth. This was a disastrous flop for all concerned. Preston Sturges had just tossed two million of 20th Century–Fox's money into a hole. Betty Grable had just ruined her streak of profitable hits. Darryl F. Zanuck had just alienated one of Hollywood's true geniuses. No one came out unscathed. None of which is to imply that *The Beautiful Blonde from Bashful Bend* is a waste of your time. Far from it. In fact, set aside that even lesser Sturges is still imminently watchable fun, let's approach this more coldly. Not as a movie to be enjoyed, but as an archeological artifact to help us better understand Sturges' genius, and its limitations.

I'm drawn to the problem films of great moviemakers for this very reason. The "headline classics" are films where everything went right, which hides the inner workings of the machine. But the problem films are ones where something, or multiple somethings, went awry, and diagnosing those glitches provides insight into how that artist worked.

Of course it doesn't take much study to deduce that part of Sturges' winning formula was his comic universe, by which I mean (a) his reliance on his stock company of variously grizzled- and funny-looking character actors, and (b) the furious escalation of comic incidents to the point where just about any and every gesture or utterance turns into a punchline. These are of course two sides of the same coin. Sturges creates escalating comic tension by having jokes come from every direction. Other comedians would be content to drop one funny person into the world and watch the jokes fly—Sturges almost does the reverse. His usual protagonist is an innocent person with some particularly skewed misunderstanding of how the world works, plunked into the middle of a world full of eccentrics—hence the Sturges stock company of players.

Right off the bat we can see that *Beautiful Blonde* is playing by a different set of rules. The stock company is (more or less) in place. Sure, we miss William Demarest—who doesn't? He's awesome—but there are enough other craggy-faced weirdos to populate the screen. But instead of colliding with each other in nuclear comic reactions, their weirdness is tamped down and isolated. The chain reaction never really gets explosive. And then there's the protagonist, our titular Beautiful Blonde (pun intended—it's pretty mild compared to the juvenile 1940s era raunch Sturges indulged in throughout the film). Betty Grable's character is easily one of the most inspired characters in Sturges' entire career, and she's nothing like anyone else he wrote. She's a hyper-sexualized, hyper-violent, hyper-competent sharpshooting jilted lover on the run. In one go, she's a distillation of every Western cliché there was. She's the madonna/whore/love interest/aloof drifter/expert gunslinger/escaped desperado. The satiric possibilities are endless.

Which makes it all the more disappointing that virtually none of those satiric possibilities are even sampled. I mean, that's not really a surprise. Sturges was always more of a farceur than a satirist. Using Grable as a satirical attack on the Western genre would have meant populating her cinematic world with other Western archetypes for her to play off, when Sturges clearly had more interest in giving the supporting cast more specific idiosyncrasies.

Also, to be fair, this is 1947. The Western boom has yet to happen. The so-called "clichés" embodied by Grable haven't yet had a chance to become clichés. Sturges can't be accused of squandering an opportunity so much as failing to recognize he even had it.

Nevertheless it is noteworthy how little momentum is derived from a movie built

**Preston Sturges and Betty Grable on the set of *The Beautiful Blonde from Bashful Bend* (1949).**

around a woman who knows what she wants and knows how to get it. Having shot a judge, in the rump, twice, she's fleeing her inevitable prosecution by assuming the stolen identity of a smalltown schoolmarm. Her number one concern is laying low and not attracting any attention. So you'd think the maximum comic mileage would come out of a series of circumstances designed to attract attention to her. The film briefly feints in that direction—the worldly bombshell is far from the stereotypical schoolteacher, and the film contrives to get a gun into her hand as quickly as possible. But the movie never pursues this line of thought.

A few thoughts on why Preston Sturges' heart may not have been in this: He was concluding his divorce, for one thing. Also, he was pouring most of his time and money into a lunatic plan to develop a new kind of dinner theater—an idea that could be charitably described as an absolute boondoggle. And he was suffocating in his new partnership with Darryl Zanuck, whose micromanaging and second-guessing didn't sit well with Sturges.

Betty Grable lost faith in Sturges and all but disowned the film. It's not that the director and star need to see eye to eye—Sturges and Claudette Colbert made a masterpiece out of *Palm Beach Story* despite his aggravation at what he considered a spoiled and flighty star. But it's clear something wasn't clicking right.

You can see that the filmmakers weren't rowing in the same direction in the fact that Zanuck brought in another director to shoot new footage to impose an alternate ending against Sturges' wishes. Say what you will about Sturges' insufferable qualities, the man always stuck the landing (the aforementioned *Palm Beach Story* ends with arguably the ballsiest go-for-broke punchline in all 1940s cinema). Not letting Sturges decide the ending is just nuts.

But Sturges did slather his attention on one aspect of *Beautiful Blonde*. The gonzo slapstick gunfight at the finale is something Preston seems to have been yearning for all his career.

Sturges, like Blake Edwards after him, worshipped at the Church of Keystone. That is, he was a Mack Sennett acolyte, devoted to the simple joys of pratfalls and custard pies. By virtue of being a "sophisticated" talkie director in the post-slapstick era, he was in the wrong era to work in purely visual comedy. But he deliberately built slapstick set pieces into even his most dialog-driven classics. (Part of his complaint about Mitchell Leisen's alleged mishandling of *Easy Living* was Leisen's lack of gusto when it came to slapstick gags.) And so *The Beautiful Blonde From Bashful Bend* winds itself into a frenzy at last. Everyone grabs a gun, and the laws of physics are briefly suspended to let a cartoon aesthetic take over for several minutes. What Tex Avery did with animated animals, Sturges does with one of the top sex symbols of the 1940s. And for a few precious feet of film, we get a glimpse of what this movie could have been.

# Meet Charley Chase

Charley Chase was one of the funniest, most widely talented, most important, and most influential comedians of the early 20th century. I'm not even going to bother to argue that statement, it is simply a fact—the way that 2 + 2 = 4 is a fact. However, Charley Chase did his work in shorts, not features. With one exception, he did not star in a feature-length comedy, despite a career in movies that spanned over a quarter century. The film critical establishment has historically held a pronounced bias in favor of features, which has meant that by definition Charley Chase's extraordinary accomplishments and legacy are seen as secondary in stature.

This bias has its basis in market realities. Once Chaplin led the charge past the two-reel mark into features, he and his peers who followed reaped more substantial economic rewards and industry prestige. Companies like the Hal Roach Studio that were in the business of making short comedies, or those like Pathé which were in the business of distributing same, were increasingly marginalized by a film industry consolidating itself around a small number of media giants who controlled the production and distribution of movie star-driven feature films.

There is a tendency to view Chase's record of short comedy output, noting the decline in its quality over the later years, and conclude that he didn't make features because Hal Roach didn't let him. Here was the studio responsible for Laurel and Hardy and Our Gang, they knew comedy: They must have seen that Chase's comic personality couldn't support a larger storyline. This is a recurring theme in writings about the era, both scholarly and casual. But it's always struck me as baffling. Sure, Roach was the home to Laurel and Hardy, but he was also behind the Dippy Doo-Dads. As a comedy genius, you can't accuse the man of batting a thousand. The whole idea that Chase was excluded from features because of some defect in his comedy character presupposes the existence of some executive panel of comedy evaluators, who sit around a boardroom and debate the merits of different comedy personas and their abilities to maintain a feature-length storyline. I have never once heard of any such debate actually taking place, and the history of comedy stars from the dawn of movies to this day argues otherwise.

You know what movie executives *do* gather in boardrooms to debate? Money. And the fact is, we can easily understand the rise and fall of Charley Chase's comedy career as a story about movie business economics. The nature of his comedy character doesn't enter into it at all.

As a boy, Charles Parrott (his real name) wanted to entertain. He chose the footlights over school, and became a young vaudeville prodigy. Like many successful vaudeville comics of his generation he soon headed to Hollywood, to the movies. At Mack Sennett's Keystone studio in 1914, the then-20-year-old Charley was working with the likes of Charlie Chaplin and Roscoe Arbuckle. Charley was already a veteran entertainer with versatile talents. He could play supporting roles for legendary comic superstars or if needed take the lead himself. He could play romantic heroes or dastardly villains. And, he could work behind the scenes, directing for others. Before long, he had become one of Sennett's top directors—and that prompted him to ask for a raise. The notoriously skinflinty Mr. Sennett balked at

**Charley Chase (seen here in the 1934 short *Four Parts*) was so prolific in his various roles as writer, director, and actor he might as well have been multiple people.**

upping Charley's pay even by a penny, and so Charley quit. Thus began a tour of the other comedy outfits of the day, with Charley's pedigree and experience growing with every move.

In 1921, Hal Roach hired Charley to serve as supervising director. Charley had creative control over the entirety of Roach's output—except for anything by Harold Lloyd, which was a separate unit under Lloyd's control. In 1923, though, Lloyd split from Roach which left the Roach studio's fortunes resting entirely on one-reel comedy shorts, which were not the biggest revenue generator no matter how good they were. To boost sales, Roach pushed his comics (including Snub Pollard and Charley's younger brother Jimmy Parrott, then performing as "Paul Parrott") to make two-reel shorts instead.

Charley's two and a half year run as the creative director of Roach Studios was a fairly hit-or-miss affair, with the emphasis on the miss. He oversaw the successful launch of the Our Gang series, but that hit was counterbalanced by a painful string of failures: Snub Pollard's frenetic brand of absurdity exhausted audiences at the two-reel length, Stan Laurel's pre–Laurel and Hardy solo shorts did not set the world on fire, Will Rogers did not prove to be a viable silent comedian, and a series of bizarre comedies starring animals billed as the Dippy Doo-Dads were an ill-advised experiment. Necessity being the mother of invention, and with Roach's slate of failed comedy projects being a source of urgent necessity, the studio took their creative director and shoved him in front of the cameras for once. Not wanting to compromise his directorial career if his on-screen work flopped (which, given the recent fortunes of the company, was a good bet), Charley Parrott opted to appear as "Charley Chase" and reserved his real name for his behind-the-scenes work.

Here is where something magical happened.

Because right away from his very first short, Charley Chase was making shining examples of comedy perfection, works of elegantly composed slapstick and satire that took full advantage of all the lessons Charley had learned over the last 10 years of working with nearly every comedian alive.

Roach's publicity for their new star touted his handsome looks and lack of slapsticky exaggeration: "Meet Charley Chase! Pleased to meetcha, Charley! You're a new one but doggone, you sure look like a good one. Don't blush, Charley, but you're a good looking sunamagun. You aren't a cartoon or a caricature. Your face ain't lopsided nor do you sport an Adam's apple the size of a pumpkin; you look like a real human and you act like one. And Charley, you're really funny!"

Set aside the clunky copy writing and the point is clear. What made Chase distinctive was that his comedy had a naturalistic edge.

For roughly the next two or three years, the Roach studio prospered thanks to Chase. He was their top money-maker, and established a prestige to the brand name that accrued value to the other comedians as well. The studio became known for a certain style—an aesthetic of domestic-based comedies more interested in satirical jabs at real life than at ludicrous slapstick havoc, like those of Sennett. Roach's shorts, especially those by Chase, were precursors to television sitcoms, and they were well positioned to benefit from shifting audience tastes away from raw slapstick. Chase started off making one-reelers, the studio's bread and butter product, and by the following year was making two-reelers.

This point needs to be emphasized, because this story is about the economics of the film business. Chase's graduation from one-reels to two was a major, major thing. Up until that point, the Roach studio had failed to launch a successful two-reel series with the exception of Harold Lloyd (who, as noted before, was his own separate business operating under Roach's name, and as such probably doesn't really count) and Our Gang. A one-reel short typically returned about $1,000 to $2,000 in rentals, which then had to be split with Roach's distribution agent, Pathé. But, a Charley Chase two-reeler was bringing in $10,000. Putting Charley Chase in movies meant that the studio's income statements suddenly had an extra zero at the end.

And then came 1926. That was the year when Paramount announced that they would begin distributing two-reel comedies, too. To understand the significance of this development, take note of the fact that Paramount was at the time the biggest movie studio in the world. Their move into the two-reel marketplace was certain to dominate the market and crowd out all the smaller players. Think Walmart coming to a small town and putting the mom-n-pops out of business. In the wake of the news, rumors started to spread that Sennett and Al Christie were going to sign up with Paramount for distribution of their shorts.

Pathé went into panic mode. Pathé's business consisted almost exclusively of selling comedy shorts, and the best case scenario is that they are about to face the most intense competition of their business life; worst case scenario they are about to lose two of their key suppliers to this new behemoth competitor. Hal Roach saw the writing on the wall—the odds of Pathé surviving the coming year were low, and even if they did, they would be a wounded and struggling wreck.

Roach jumped ship to sign with MGM instead—with a 10-year contract promising stability and corporate continuity. As luck would have it, MGM would go on to beat Paramount at their own game and become the film industry's new giant.

For those of you playing at home, you may be thinking, "*OK, I get why Charley Chase didn't appear in any features before 1926. He wasn't even starring in movies at all until 1923, and the Roach studio was barely able to turn out profitable one-reelers for much of its early corporate history. But now they're aligned with MGM they've finally got access to a network equipped to distribute features—now's the time for Charley Chase to follow the example of Keaton, Chaplin, and Lloyd and start making 90-minute-long comedies.*" Right?

MGM took on Roach specifically as a supplier of shorts. MGM had no interest in Roach features. MGM was itself a maker of features, and any MGM-made features they sold returned 100 percent profits to the company. Any features they sold that were supplied by outside vendors like Roach meant they had to share the revenue, and so with a limited number of movie theaters and available screenings, MGM actively opposed any efforts by Roach to branch into features. Roach broke their resistance from time to time—but this was mostly attributable to the runaway popularity of Laurel and Hardy, whose astronomical success set them apart from everything else at the studio.

During the entire 10-year association between Roach and MGM, MGM distributed only 22 features provided by outside vendors. Of those 22, 19 came from Roach's company, and 11 of those were Laurel and Hardy vehicles. One of the handful of non–Roach features MGM agreed to distribute was David O. Selznick's *Gone with the Wind*. In short, MGM was unwilling to even consider an independently-produced feature unless it was something that was already firing on all cylinders, the sorts of things that would become enduring legends of cinema and live forever. If you were making something like *Gone with the Wind*, or a Laurel and Hardy comedy, you had a shot. That was a helluva bar to meet.

Even the top comedy superstars needed transitional features to find their voice—

Keaton's *The Three Ages*, Lloyd's *Grandma's Boy*, Langdon's *His First Flame*. These were malformed, incomplete things. These comedians were afforded a chance to experiment on the feature stage before being expected to be impeccable. Chase was not given the same opportunity. When Roach's contract with MGM ran out in 1936, Hal Roach had decided to call it quits in the short comedy business overall. The market was dying and Roach wanted to transition fully to the more profitable business of making features. If that meant parting company with MGM, so be it. Laurel and Hardy had already moved on successfully to features, the Thelma Todd series had ended with Thelma's tragic death, and Roach's miscellaneous comedies had imploded as unpopular and unsellable. The only two-reelers Roach still had were Charley Chase and Our Gang. And as far as Chase went, this was "up or out time." He had to prove himself viable for features or leave. And by "prove himself viable for features," I don't prove himself to audiences—I mean prove himself to MGM. To win that argument, Chase needed to deliver an impeccable film production.

He had MGM's indulgence to give it a try, with *It Happened One Bank Night* (note the obvious debt of influence owed to *It Happened One Night*—Chase's brand of slapstick was always linked to the development of romantic dialogue comedies). Unfortunately, far from being "something that was already firing on all cylinders," it was plagued by production problems. The fault did not lie with Chase as a comedian, nor really with him as a filmmaker. *Bank Night* was a riot of dumb decisions, yes, but they were legitimate creative decisions that simply proved to be impolitic and ill-timed. He was a victim of circumstance.

The biggest problem was the central conceit of the "Bank Night," which was a common promotion in those olden days, in which movie theaters offered cash prizes to audiences. The real-life Bank Night promoters didn't take kindly to the unauthorized use of their trademarked name and in the legal battle over its use also objected to the satire Chase intended to direct their way. This resulted in wastes of time and money, hasty rewrites, and bad publicity. Compounding this was the fact that Chase used this set-up to lead into a parody of gangster films, at a time when censors were growing increasingly jittery about the use of screen violence. Chase's planned gun-toting gangsters and proto-film-noirish comedy would have been quite at home in the "pre–Code" era a couple of years previous, but the newly empowered film censors decided to throw their weight around. Roach had successfully lobbied MGM to accept his features in the past when he had a strong sell—but *It Happened One Bank Night* collapsed into chaos. It was eventually recut into a two-reel form and retitled *Neighborhood House*, which would turn out to be Chase's final short for Roach.

Chase decamped to Columbia—a ramshackle cheapskate shop that proved a home for many a slapstick refugee. Buster Keaton, Harry Langdon, Andy Clyde—they all ended up at Columbia eventually. And Columbia was also home to the Three Stooges, and as it happened, Chase seemed to understand their slapstick aesthetic better than anyone else. With Chase as their director, the Stooges were never better.

Chase alternated between behind-the-scenes gigs for the Stooges and starring in his own run of shorts (and by now had given up alternating names, he was now proudly taking credit for everything as Charley Chase). Some of Chase's Columbia work is among his best. Directing *Flat Foot Stooges*, starring in *The Heckler*—there's some fine comedy here. The only tragedy is that Chase drank himself to death and died young in 1940—which is horribly tragic, nightmarish, but there's no *career* tragedy here.

Let's summarize: It was only for a sliver of his tenure at Hal Roach that Charley was even in a position to theoretically make features. Chase's unit was hampered by studio priorities that favored Laurel and Hardy. Chase himself avoided confrontation and was temperamentally disinclined to argue effectively on his own behalf. Meanwhile, the bar was set at Laurel and Hardy 's height—in order to get a feature into the MGM pipeline it had to convince MGM executives that it could succeed on the same level of profitability as a Laurel and Hardy feature. Chase's 1936 feature debut suffered from teething troubles not markedly dissimilar to those experienced by his peers during their respective transitions to long-form filmmaking, but under the circumstances of Roach's relationship with MGM Chase would be punished disproportionately for those missteps.

Chase left behind just one example of what he would have been like as a feature movie star. And no, I don't mean *Neighborhood House*. I mean the film I hinted at back at the top of this essay when I noted a singular exception to Chase's "no-feature" legacy. I mean *Modern Love*.

---

# *Modern Love*

*Modern Love* was a 1929 feature comedy from Universal that starred Charley Chase and Kathryn Crawford, produced during the awkward transition into sound filmmaking. It was made as what they called a "part-talkie," in which it was a predominately silent film with talkie sections. If you've seen Charlie Chaplin's *Modern Times*, you've seen the style.

For many years this treasure was believed lost, at least in part. In 2010, intrepid preservationists did the hard work of pulling all the surviving material together to completely restore the film to its original splendor, and premiered it at Slapsticon. I was very fortunate to be in the audience and I am very grateful that I had the presence of mind to fill a notebook with notes while I watched.

Since I have to assume I'm writing to an audience who wasn't with me that evening, let me recount the premise: Charley Chase is married to a working spouse with a better paying and more promising career. It pains his masculine identity to admit that he's "inferior," but any rational economic calculation would conclude that Kathryn Crawford needs to keep her job.

And there's the rub: this was an era when married women weren't expected to work, and without the protections afforded by modern laws, the only way she can be sure of hanging on to that job is by concealing her marriage. And while Charley has several incentives to play along (her salary, for one, and not having to admit to being the lower paid spouse is the other), this is a tough pill to swallow.

Chase and his wife keep separate names (gasp!) and residences. Much of the comedy of the film arises from their efforts to keep their relationship under wraps—they are wed in secret, and concoct bizarre excuses to put forward an alternate explanation for anytime they appear together. In one scene, Charley is forced to play "butler" to Kathryn's dinner party.

If you're getting vibes of Tracy/Hepburn pictures, or Cary Grant's *I Was a Male War Bride*, then go to the head of the class. This was a beachhead for the coming breed of screwball comedies that often premised themselves on gender wars issues. In fact, comedies based on challenging gender roles continue to be a driving force in Hollywood, we've just traded away from a model in which women acting competent is seen as threatening to one in which the norm is the professional, responsible woman playing opposite a juvenile man-child.

In the screwball era, the function of this kind of comedy was to emphasize a distinction between socially constructed love and romantically oriented love. Marriage and all the legal and moral structures that surrounded it are the social constructs of love–focused on social standing, convenience, and how one is seen. By contrast, there is romance—illogical, unruly, defiant, and focused on what a person feels. The real relationship between Charley and Kathryn is a thing of trust, companionship, and genuine romantic love, and yet what they have to hide is not love, but their marriage.

What we have here is a prototype of the romantic comedies that would come to dominate the movies in the aftermath of the transition to sound. Yet it stars Charley Chase and positions itself as a silent comedy in his wheelhouse. This may have been produced by Universal, with Chase "on loan" from Hal Roach, but the movie revisits several set pieces that Chase had developed in his short films at Roach.

In short, *Modern Love* is a trial run for a new kind of sound comedy, one that draws as much from Lubitsch as from Chaplin. Comedy did lead in this direction, and if this film hasn't spent so long out of public view it might be hailed as a key missing link between

The lobby card for the 1929 part-talkie feature *Modern Love* highlights Kathryn Crawford over her more established costar Charley Chase.

slapstick and screwball. All the while, it is clearly a Charley Chase vehicle. Many sequences feel familiar from his shorts, and his character is a generic office worker, just as he was in his short films.

Which is a way of saying, Charley Chase was naturally on the path of an organic evolution from silent slapstick to talkie romantic comedies. So, what would it have taken for him to continue on that path and finish the journey?

In my estimation, he'd have needed two things.

One. A full-fledged co-star.

To make this genre work, he needed at least a Thelma Todd (if you need to, flip ahead to next chapter to see her opposite Cary Grant, and evaluate how well she fit into the screwball tradition). Screwball changed the comedy landscape by elevating female performers to a place of equality if not priority. Kathryn Crawford is OK, but she doesn't have that star power that the genre demands. Thelma Todd worked with Chase and he had hoped to establish a lasting screen partnership with her, but there are perhaps more apt selections. I'd have loved to see him playing alongside Jeanette MacDonald, or Claudette Colbert.

Two. Screenwriters.

The romantic comedies of the 1930s were defined by writers more than directors, more than actors. Ben Hecht, Norman Krasna, maybe Robert Riskin—these are the true comedians behind screwball. Perhaps this is why these films didn't get the same adoring critical attention as slapstick. Film scholars fall over themselves to write about Chaplin and Keaton and Lloyd, but comparatively few invest the same effort in writing about screwball. Critics generally prefer directors and stars over writers, because it's too damned hard to figure out what writers do.

Chase had the stuff to be a romantic comedy star. Maybe not a first tier star, but a reliable presence. *Modern Love* points the way down a path that, for reasons discussed in the previous chapter, Chase was not allowed to follow. But the path was there, for others to exploit. And just a couple of years later, the ingredients of Hal Roach slapstick and Ernst Lubitsch bedroom farce would again be combined, in something that toyed with the ideas of Chase's comedies but turned them into something new. And out of that would come a new kind of comedy star, a man born Archibald Leach, who would do the things that Charley Chase never did.

# Meet Cary Grant

We come upon three men and a naked lady.

The lady is Thelma Todd, denuded as she often was in her brief screen career.

One of the men is Roland Young, a womanizing roué who has brought her home in this state. The other, Charlie Ruggles, is his mostly useless sidekick. The third man? Well, that'd be Thelma's husband—known to be a fiercely jealous man. He is also an Olympic javelin thrower (yes, that's right). Oh, and he has a quiver of javelins with him.

This, ladies and gentlemen, is the screen debut of Cary Grant. It is not an especially auspicious performance—Grant is quoted in numerous sources as disliking his contribution to this film. But it is for our purposes an extremely illuminating one. Here is a film that behaves like a modern dialogue-driven romantic comedy, but which is comprised of the DNA of silent comedy. Here is a missing link between one animal and the other—a glimpse into the evolution of talkie comedy. And it all hinges on Cary Grant.

The film in question is a Pre-Code comedy called *This Is the Night*, made in 1931 by director Frank Tuttle. In addition to the four stars we just met, there is a second female lead, played by Lili Damita. As a group, these five characters are caught up in a web of overlapping love triangles, mistaken identities, deceptions, and compromising positions. This is what they used to call "sophisticated farce," which is to say it involved lots of double entendres and a European setting. Ernst Lubitsch was making some of the very best of these bedroom farces, but Tuttle's *This Is the Night* is a pleasant enough entry in the canon.

The story of course begins with Thelma Todd getting her dress caught in a car door and ripped from her body—throughout the film, Todd keeps losing her clothing as a running joke.

It is the immediate fallout of this embarrassing incident that threatens to expose her relationship with Roland Young to her threatening caveman of a husband, Cary Grant. And so, in the heat of the moment, Charlie Ruggles comes up with a plan to save his friend. It is a ruse worthy of George Costanza: Ruggles makes out as if Young is already married, and all the things that Grant is picking up on that are making him think the rogue is carrying on with his wife, are really just symptoms of his being married to … um, married to … hang on…. Oh yeah, married to this girl, Lili Damita!

Damita is in fact an actress they hire to play the role of Young's wife, and she's contracted to come along on their trip to Venice to maintain the lie.

The contours of this story are probably easy enough for you to predict, regardless of whether you've caught this rarity before: the enforced intimacy between Young and Damita will kindle a genuine romance between them. What begins as a purely commercial transaction, and one rooted in dishonesty at that, blossoms into something pure and true. The rogue will settle down at last—here is a woman worth giving up everything else for.

It is easy to appreciate this as an example of the faux-Lubitsch "sophisticated" farce genre of the early talkie era—all the conventional elements are in place, from the European setting to the light operetta songs that blanket the soundtrack. But at the same time, this is familiar silent comedy stuff.

For example, the running gag of Thelma Todd losing her dress. The opening scene is a virtual photocopy of the opening scene of Laurel and Hardy's silent short *Double Whoopee*. For that matter, throughout her run of two-reel shorts at the Hal Roach Studio, Thelma Todd routinely got caught in states of undress. If she didn't take her clothes off, it wasn't a Thelma Todd film. Later in the film, Ruggles and Young interrupt their scheming to stop and get drunk at a Venetian café, in a scene that owes much to similar drunk-act scenes in Laurel and Hardy pictures like *Their Purple Moment*.

In fact, I should mention that *This Is the Night* is in fact a genuine remake of an actual silent comedy, *Good and Naughty* directed by Malcolm St. Clair in 1926 (St. Clair was the only director other than Buster Keaton credited on Keaton's run of silent shorts; he collaborated on Harold Lloyd's first talkie *Welcome Danger*, and finished his career directing Laurel and Hardy's late period features like *The Big Noise*). Sadly, it looks like *Good and Naughty* is lost to posterity—certainly it is unavailable for easy viewing now, so I'm not in a position to compare the two directly.

Without access to *Good and Naughty*, let's turn our attention instead to what real estate professionals might term a "comparable"—that is, a film of similar ambition and tone, from roughly the same period—for example, Bebe Daniels' *Miss Bluebeard* from 1925.

Daniels had been Harold Lloyd's longtime onscreen foil until she branched out on her own. In *Miss Bluebeard*, she plays a French actress (very much like Lili Damita's character in *This Is the Night*) who is pushed by contrived circumstance to pretend to be married to a rich playboy (again, like *This Is the Night*) while she also cultivates a friendship with his goofy sidekick (more parallels), and the vague sexual hostility of the fake marriage eventually gives way to genuine romantic attraction (you get the point).

In other words, the two films share a similar agenda, but the ultimate effect is very different, and it is the addition of the soundtrack that makes *This Is the Night* the more enjoyable and ambitious of the two. Now, it's a bit unfair of me to pick some random film out of the ether and say, *Ahem, this one isn't as good.* But, you see, I *didn't* pick *Miss Bluebeard* randomly out of the ether. In fact, Frank Tuttle directed both pictures—I selected this to see how the same director, working with substantially the same comic material and plot, responded to the addition of sound.

Take for example a joke structure shared by both films. In *Miss Bluebeard*, the playboy character is played by Robert Frazer, and he's fake-married to the French actress played by Bebe Daniels. The more Frazer's heart sings for Daniels, the more his friend Raymond Griffith (serving more or less as the Charlie Ruggles analogue in this film) tries to cover up Frazer's tawdry past to her. When one particularly noisy ex-girlfriend shows up, Griffith doesn't want Daniels to know anything about it. But she heard some commotion—*Oh, that?* says Griffith, *that was just a cat.*

It's a poor lie, but the situation is made worse by the sudden entrance of Frazer, who was alleged to have just disposed of this pesky cat but knows nothing whatsoever of this lie. To keep the ruse going, Griffith has to silently signal Frazer, while he's talking to Daniels, what the essence of the cover story was.

Now, a similar scene appears in *This Is the Night*. Cary Grant, suspicious of Lili Damita and not at all willing to accept the story that she is Young's wife, grills Young about the circumstances of their wedding. Young extemporizes, claiming for example they met in Cincinnati. Later Grant gets some alone-time with Damita, absolutely clueless about the lies Young's just spun about her immediate past. Grant starts chatting with her—and Young realizes that the jig is up if she contradicts what he's just said. So poor Young struggles to clue Damita in, while she struggles to interpret his unhelpful clues.

Something crucial shifted in the joke structure once sound was added. In *Miss Bluebeard*, the comedy is inherent almost exclusively in Raymond Griffith's contortions and silly mimicry as he tries to signal silently to Frazer. We are aware of Frazer's dilemma in trying to convincingly speak about this stuff while trying to make sense of Griffith's behavior, but the joke is all in Griffith's nutty attempts to mime being a cat. But once you add sound, the punchline in the joke switches hands. The joke structure has mutated, and now the joke is at least partially if not mostly in Damita's attempts to interpret the clues, not just in Young's attempts at charades. Damita's mistaken interpretation of Cincinnati as "*I was living in sin. I was naughty*" is, you have to admit, a lot funnier than watching Raymond Griffith act like a cat.

*Miss Bluebeard* is not a bad film, but it is hampered by the lack of a soundtrack. The film is constantly interrupted by title cards, and feels stagey and claustrophobic. It is not an especially visual concept—not compared to the outsized comic antics of Chaplin or Keaton. There's a nice bit of characters coming in and out of doors and just missing each other, which apparently Griffith improvised on the set. But it amounts to a small fraction of the overall running time of a film that otherwise seems desperate to say something, but lacks the ability. And for that matter, the scene that Griffith allegedly improvised is borrowed largely stroke-for-stroke from Charley Chase, who'd been doing this kind of farce for years by this point.

The specter of Charley Chase haunts both films—this was his métier, and it's an almost an insult he was left out of *This Is the Night*. The film is so close to being plagiarized from his playbook, he might as well have been an official part of it. The premise is not far off from Chase's 1922 short *Too Many Mammas*, in which a group of men and women are constantly swapping partners like a sexed up game of hot potato in an effort to collectively deceive one another about who's actually with whom.

But for all that, it is not clear exactly where in this thing you'd fit Charley Chase. And the more one thinks through alternative casting scenarios, the more something weird about this movie bubbles to the surface. Charley Chase could theoretically have played the Charlie Ruggles role, but Ruggles did it so perfectly there's no advantage to recasting him. One can imagine Chase in the Roland Young role—they have a similar effete fussiness—but now all of a sudden the world starts to appear upside down. *Why in the world is Roland Young in this role in the first place?* I'm not saying he isn't excellent. He is terrific throughout. But the character is supposed to be the man that Thelma Todd is choosing *over Cary Grant*. In any rational universe, Thelma and Cary would pair off in the first scene and be done with it, and Roland wouldn't even enter into it. Roland Young has been deliberately miscast—and much of the fun of the movie lies in the ironic gap that opens up between who this character is apparently meant to be according to the logic of the story and the actual prissy nerdlinger he is.

Now that we've broached the subject of deliberate miscasting for comic effect, it's finally time to take stock of Cary Grant. Whatever dismissive nonsense Grant may have spouted later, the fact is he oozes charm and steals every scene he's in. Like Lucille Ball in *A Girl, a Guy, and a Gob*, he is blatantly operating in a whole other league to his costars—this is the debut of a star. That being said, he is also completely wrong for this role.

His character is supposed to be a brute of a man, an athlete known for throwing objects at great distances, a controlling man with a fearsome temper. And what we get is Cary Grant—with a suave James Bond–like cool, a voice of

**Cary Grant's ironic delivery and detached attitude undermines the literal meaning of his dialog, contradicting or enhancing it.**

cultured erudition, and constantly winking at the audience. Every line is delivered with a sarcastic inflection. It's not that we can't picture him chucking spears—it's that we can't picture him chucking them seriously.

Grant's ironic delivery allows him to insert an additional layer of commentary into his dialogue. He says the words that the script gives him—and thereby conveys the strictly literal meaning of those words, plain and simple. But because he says them with this detached attitude, he also undermines that literal meaning, contradicting or enhancing it.

This is something about screen comedy that changed with the arrival of sound, and in order to see it clearly, let's take a look back at another Bebe Daniels silent comedy from 1928, *Feel My Pulse*, directed by the great Gregory La Cava. This film finds Daniels more in the ex-Harold Lloyd vein, in a plot that has echoes with Lloyd's *Why Worry* and features a lot of physical slapstick and stuntwork by Miss Daniels. The premise is that she is a rich hypochondriac who heads off to a sanitarium she owns in order to recuperate. Little does she know that while she's been living the germophobic life, her sanitarium has been taken over by bootleggers. When she arrives, the rum runners decide to pretend to be doctors and patients to fool her.

It is a romantic comedy, and true to the screwball form there is the classic triangle. Daniels is the runaway heiress, doing increasingly nutty things; There is the good boy, played by Richard Arlen; And then there is the king of the rum runners, played by William Powell. And it is Powell's performance that concerns us here.

William Powell and Cary Grant were similar kinds of performers in the 1930s—each one specialized in the charming rogue, but in different inflections. Grant had that transatlantic voice, an accent that screamed of culture, the impossibly handsome looks, and was often cast in roles where these marks of class and class were at odds with the social standing he was alleged to have. Grant as gangster, as soldier, as con man.

By contrast William Powell had a wild sort of look about him. He had a voice like single malt Scotch and a suave manner somehow equal parts immensely cultured and rough. In the glory days of 1930s romantic comedies, he was a king. William Powell was the 1930s equivalent of Fonzie. He was untouchably cool. In any of his 1930s films, Powell would have been the default romantic lead for a picture like this—the story would be about Bebe Daniels ending up in his arms. Sure he's a violent gangster, so what? He's a charming gangster—or at least, he could be. The trick however is the way Powell's sardonic charm undercuts whatever literal awfulness the script has him say. But in 1928, when *Feel My Pulse* was made, no one had yet heard Powell speak. Instead, his dialogue is rendered in title cards. The film shows Powell's character as a ruthless criminal, and the things he says and does are monstrous. Funny, but monstrous. Without Powell's inherent sarcasm to undercut those lines, they stay on that literal level—Powell is the bad guy.

The film has a lot of fun in its final reel, with Bebe Daniels confronting the entire gang and singlehandedly defeating them. She channels the best of Harold Lloyd as she brings total slapstick chaos to bear on their operation—and while Richard Arlen is the good guy she ends up with, he doesn't save her—she saves him, in a nice touch. *Feel My Pulse* can't effectively end any other way—to have her end up with Powell would have been bizarre. Powell is unambiguously the villain. Except, if you were to remake this film in the sound era with the exact same cast and without changing any of the dialogue, Powell's naturally sarcastic delivery would turn his "villain" into a charming rogue.

This was the most significant gift that sound gave comedy. Sound made it possible to layer two different sets of meanings onto the same scene. Once we get actors like William Powell and Cary Grant delivering their dialogue with wry, ironic distance, all of a sudden, it becomes possible for a movie to do two things at once. It can chug its way through a literal series of plot steps (this happens, then this happens) while also commenting on, contradicting, undercutting, and otherwise lampooning those very things. A person with Grant's kind of sarcasm can have his cake and eat it too.

When critics called these things "sophisticated comedies" they mostly just meant it involved lots of double entendres and a European setting. Snicker snicker, let's make some crude jokes about the size of Cary Grant's "javelin." Ha ha, this is *Beavis and Butthead* circa 1932. But the real double entendres come every time Cary Grant speaks—double and triple entendres, quadruple and beyond. And let's be clear—sound is key to this. You can have irony in silent film, sure, and you can miscast on purpose to play with the disconnect between the literal meaning of a character and the specifics of the actor's performance. But there's a ceiling on how far you can go with it—whereas the ability to deliver dialogue in such a way as to convey the words but also consciously slip out of synch with those words depends on actually hearing the actor's voice.

It's not that silent comedy was incapable of irony, merely that the limitations of silence made it tricky. The arrival of sound opened up new possibilities to explore ironic humor, and the ascendancy of performers like Cary Grant and William Powell made that into widely popular and increasingly common form. The strictures of screwball comedy, by distributing the comic responsibilities across a larger cast, provided opportunities to indulge in quirkier or more unpleasant characterizations because they no longer had to completely anchor an audience's sympathies. Put all these things together, and sound comedy had the tools to do things silent comedy didn't.

*This Is the Night* does very little with this power. It is at best an amiable way to spend a long hour. To really take advantage of what you could do with this technique would depend on having a much more nuanced screenplay than *This Is the Night*. But let's just say that a truly gifted writer—maybe a writer/director who specialized in how his words came alive on movie screens—set out to do the very things that an old-timey silent comedy would have done. Would it be possible to translate, say, the crudest, most primitive kind of violent, anti-social Keystone havoc into a genuinely sophisticated and entirely dialogue-based romance? Is that even possible? And if you did, would the result live for the ages as one of America's best comedies?

# The Worst People in the World

We have gathered here today to discuss a landmark of American screen comedy.

It is a film about a reporter, and he is a reprehensible example of the most caricatured excesses of his profession. He is selfish and callous, gleefully exploiting the sufferings of others because it makes good copy. He has his eyes on a girl, but she's already involved with another man—a decent citizen, who will become the butt of our protagonist's abuse. The reporter will do everything in his power to punish this rival, including framing him for various crimes. Although this character's behavior is unambiguously villainous, he is not the villain of the film—he's not quite its hero, either, but he's the central anchor of all that happens, and we in the audience are not expected to boo him but to relish in his monstrous actions. All this awfulness is presented for our entertainment.

But here's the riddle: what movie am I talking about? Is it Howard Hawks' *His Girl Friday*, starring Cary Grant? Or Mack Sennett's *Making a Living*, with Charlie Chaplin? Ah, there's the rub—and therein lies our tale.

Admittedly, if you fell for the Charlie Chaplin of *The Gold Rush*, sitting down to *Making a Living* must feel like a bait and switch. Not only is the whole Tramp persona not yet in place, but the very notion of making Chaplin into the heroic figure with whom we are expected to sympathize was actually going to be years in gestation. Instead, the first film Chaplin made for Sennett belongs to a wholly different tradition, one that Keystone had turned into a profitable formula: exaggerated parodies of Biograph-style melodramas, in which all the characters are turned into grotesques.

The entertainment value of such things was meant to lie in the transgressive thrill of watching people behaving badly. Keystone stars were expected to spend their screen time kicking each other in the pants, and trying to cheat, rob, or attack each other.

But let's take a moment to consider what this transgressive thrill was all about. Because it was genuinely transgressive. Movie audiences were unprecedented in the way they commingled races, classes, and other social divisions. Other forms of entertainment had higher ticket prices and assigned seating, to keep out the riff raff or at least control who was sitting next to whom. Movies were cheap, and the hoi polloi could find themselves side by side with illiterate immigrants. This is what got moralists of the age so hot and bothered about movie censorship—the mixed audiences presented a socially volatile situation and the stuff shown on the screen could provoke reactions in parts of that crowd.

So what did Keystone go and do? Make the most aggressively provocative stuff they could think of, that's what. They lampooned authority, ridiculed the most basic and universal social values, and reveled in sex and violence. They sold themselves as outsiders attacking the establishment—and outsiders they were. Chaplin himself was an immigrant who knew from poverty: in his recent memory were bouts of homelessness and serious want.

Chaplin's poverty was the most extreme example, but the rosters of silent comedies were stuffed with the poor, the outcasts, the migrants and immigrants. And this makes perfect sense—if you came from the middle class or privilege and had an interest in show business, you wouldn't go into movies in the 1910s. It was too unproven and risky. You'd opt for the established businesses like Broadway, where the prestige and money were better and more importantly where there was some guarantee of stability. Movies were a novelty and no one knew when the bubble might burst. Only the people with nothing to lose and everything to gain would take that kind of gamble—and so Hollywood filled up with the once-poor, the ex-desperate, the nouveau riche.

And they sold rebellion to the masses.

This is the context in which *Making a Living* has to be understood. The grotesque behavior of its characters and its unrelieved nastiness wasn't about promoting antisocial attitudes, but providing a safety valve by which those sentiments could be vented publicly and defused.

*His Girl Friday* is by no means a remake of *Making a Living* (it is a remake of a previous film called *The Front Page*, which was an adaptation of a play by the same name, but that's not what interests us here). Just putting it alongside *Making a Living* seems an incongruous juxtaposition. *Making a Living* is a silent film, that runs about 10 minutes or so. *His Girl Friday* is so packed with talk, so overstuffed with dialogue, that even at 90 minutes it feels like it takes four or five hours to watch. Not only does every character talk at an exhaustingly accelerated pace and change topics on a dime, but in any given scene there may be multiple such supercharged conversations overlapped on top of each other so the viewer gets whiplash just trying to follow it all.

On that level, the difference between the silent comedy and its talkie cousin would seem to be an uncrossable gulf. But as we noted above, the basic story being told in each film is fundamentally the same set of story beats … so there is something else here at work that needs our attention.

The antisocial comedy of *Making a Living* existed within the context of the film industry and audience of the 1910s, but *His Girl Friday* is a work of a corporate Hollywood, an established institution in its Golden Years. The rock and roll aesthetic no longer applies. But what do we find in this film?

It is a romantic comedy, for one, which means (as we've been discussing) that it makes equal room for Cary Grant's costar Rosalind Russell, and the thrust of the story is about

**Cary Grant, Rosalind Russell, and Ralph Bellamy do the institution of the press no favors in *His Girl Friday* (1940).**

bringing them (back) together. When we first meet her, she is happily engaged to a decent, upstanding man, and looking forward to the "normal" suburban life of an American house-wife. Her fiancé Ralph Bellamy may be a tad naïve and boring, but he's the kind of person I aspire to be: trusting, forgiving, loving. He recognizes the allure Rosalind's career had and is willing to adjust his plans to give her a chance to pursue one last story. He admires Cary Grant's charms, he accepts many of his tribulations with equanimity. Sure, he sells life insurance—but even there he does so because he says he wants to help people (although, he sheepishly admits that he's not helping them much while they're alive).

And what does he get for all this? Insulted to his face, manipulated, robbed, thrown in jail repeatedly for crimes he didn't commit, forced to tarnish his own reputation and seek bail from his colleagues back home, his mother is very nearly killed, and in the end he loses his fiancée to this tawdry world.

That's the happy ending? That she breaks up with him? Sends him back home, pen-niless and lovelorn with his bruised and injured mother? That's what we were rooting for?

Along the way, of course, there's the case of soon-to-be executed murderer Earl Williams. His fate is tossed around casually—he is just a pawn in this game, and whether he lives or dies has nothing to do with justice and everything to do with the cynical machi-nations of powerful people, including Cary Grant and Rosalind Russell. People will be shot, some will have their livelihoods threatened or destroyed, bribes will be paid, people will be conned, and an innocent woman will throw herself out a window. And yet none of these calamities and calumnies will strike our heroes in any way as tragic or unfortunate.

Rosalind Russell hears a siren in the distance, her ears prick up. "That sounds like a swell fire." This, our hero.

It isn't as if Howard Hawks was a ruthless cynic who thought this was how people ought to behave. Nor Cary Grant nor Rosalind Russell, nor the writers Charles Lederer or Ben Hecht. These people were not monsters.

If we step back far enough and try to take in the broadest view, we can see that the message of the film isn't necessarily so cruel: it tells us that people will be happier doing what they love, and they're more likely to love doing what they're good at; People who share the same interests and attitudes are probably a good romantic fit; The world is a dan-gerous place, and smart people who think fast have a better chance at surviving it.

It's hard to disagree with any of that.

But then when you get down to the details, on paper at least it sounds like this film is a cesspool, right? But that's not how it plays at all. These may be the worst people in the world, but they are immensely entertaining to watch, and *His Girl Friday* deserves its lasting reputation as a comedy classic. The key to its success is the ability in dialogue comedy to say and mean two different things at the same time.

*His Girl Friday* does several things towards this end, and all of them are dialogue-based. One is a sense of self-awareness: the movie knows this behavior is reprehensible, and Rosalind Russell's character is the key conduit by which that self-recrimination is conveyed.

Then there's self-referentiality. One of the most celebrated jokes in the film (kept in place over the objections of the studio) describes Ralph Bellamy's character as looking like, well, like Ralph Bellamy.

Things like this are a way of winking at the audience, at maintaining that ironic distance necessary to present this story and have it feel like a delicious satire instead of a tragedy.

Cary Grant especially, as discussed in the prior chapter, is an absolute boon to anyone who wants to make ironic comedy. He has the rare ability to be enormously charming and seductive no matter what he says, and so he can be given a role that in narrative terms functions as the villain, but which his performance treats as the hero. Cast Jimmy Cagney or Peter Lorre in this role and suddenly you've got a very different movie. As Alfred Hitchcock found out the hard way, it doesn't matter what you've written, Cary Grant can't play a villain: he'll come across as the hero no matter what.

*His Girl Friday* succeeds in a way that *Making a Living* cannot because its characters are capable of being emotionally engaging and attractive while at the same time being unpleasant and villainous.

It's not that Chaplin isn't capable of being charming—that would be a stupid position to take. And it isn't the case that Chaplin can't be charming while behaving badly—again, his body of work belies that. But Chaplin's films require a significant amount of effort to establish him as a bad-behaving good guy, and need to shift his behavior within the film into that "good" space to maintain the audience's sympathies. *His Girl Friday* briefly flirts with having Cary Grant do something noble and selfless in its finale, only to discard that idea and ridicule it.

And so this is where I've been driving throughout this discussion of the nexus between silent comedy and talkie comedy: it isn't the case that sound killed silent comedy. Sure, some of the great silent comedians who dominated screens in the 1920s saw their careers hitch up, but let's be careful about sweeping generalizations: Keaton's personal troubles (a rotten marriage and the alcoholism it triggered) were a greater hurdle for him than MGM's corporate policies (as we've seen, MGM was clearly amendable to making the kinds of movies Keaton should have been making, if he hadn't been drinking himself to death at the time). Chaplin continued to make great films well into the 1930s and '40s, and then blew up his audience goodwill with his own personal problems (a tendency to rob the cradle, coupled with an affinity for Marxism at a time when Red baiting was a popular sport). Roscoe Arbuckle was done in by the notorious scandal well before sound came along. Charley Chase made the change to sound with aplomb but found his career hindered by studio politics. And then there's Harold Lloyd, who wasn't held back by sound in any meaningful way, in fact willingly embraced it, and then showed an ability to adapt his comedy to the new aesthetics of screwball comedy.

The list goes on, but the point is, the conspicuous examples of silent comedy stars "undone" by sound are really better explained as individual cases of unique circumstances. Meanwhile the traditions of slapstick marched on just fine.

The advent of sound gave comedians and filmmakers a set of tools to do the things that silent comedy had already been doing, but do them more efficiently.

# Slut Fabulous

We began this conversation 50-odd chapters ago (and I agree, some of them were pretty odd). I started out with a question: *why did silent slapstick disappear?* It was a trick question, of course—slapstick didn't really disappear, at least not all at once.

For the benefit of those of you who opted to skip the preceding chapters, or who suffer from one of those *Memento*-style memory impairments, here's a quick summary:

- Some of the great practitioners of silent slapstick saw their careers falter for unique personal reasons;
- Some of the great practitioners of silent slapstick kept on truckin' well into the middle of the 20th century;
- The advent of sound film gave comedy filmmakers tools with which to emphasize irony; and social and aesthetic changes ushered in a new approach that prioritized female-centered ensemble comedies that explored cultural tensions between the classes, a genre identified as "screwball."

Which begs a different question: *why did screwball disappear?* The 1930s and early 1940s were chock-a-block with runaway heiresses and wacky dames in a constant battle of wits with disreputable journalists and various rogues. They brought up baby, learned the awful truth, and insisted nothing was sacred. Then what?

One answer is that screwball never did disappear. Just as slapstick never really died, neither did screwball.

Billy Wilder's *Some Like It Hot* is as definitive a take on the screwball form as anything we've discussed so far, and it came along in 1959, a chronological anomaly like Charlie Chaplin making *Modern Times* in 1936. Frank Tashlin's *Will Success Spoil Rock Hunter?* from 1957 is no mere throwback, but a thoroughly mid-century rethink of the genre. The year 1998 brought John Cleese and Charles Crichton's superb *A Fish Called Wanda*; the Coen Brothers updated (and upstaged) Frank Capra's legacy with 1992's *The Hudsucker Proxy*; Amy Schumer's 2015 *Trainwreck* used screwball's style in service of a sort of slapstick feminist pseudo-memoir.

Meanwhile, much as *The Jazz Singer* and the arrival of talkies posed a technological disruption that changed Hollywood economics, the competition between cinema and television forced filmmakers towards making splashy, Technicolor widescreen spectacles. In response, television became a natural home for screwball—what else was *I Love Lucy* than a 90-hour-long screwball epic played out in weekly installments on broadcast television over the course of six years?

There were also social and aesthetic issues at play. For one thing, the Depression-era obsession with pitting the Haves against the Have Nots in romantic combat lost a lot of its allure as the economy rebounded.

More significantly, the Second World War called most able-bodied men into service in one form or another, and women found themselves taking places in the working world that were previously unthinkable (or at least largely unthought). This set of conditions challenged wounded male egos and unresolved social misogyny. Screwball offered brassy, liberated women who outshone their male counterparts—and returning GIs came home ready to show those brassy, liberated women back to their place. The conditions of the Second World War made the very ethical foundation of screwball seem suspect. Insecure men trying to reassert their dominance in a postwar world were a lot less inclined to find the antics of screwball heroines appealing.

As far as comedy goes, the 1940s took a hard swerve back towards the male-dominated, solo comedian or comedy team-based, vaudeville-inflected slapstick. You can't tell me that slapstick died when sound arrived, when the biggest box office draw of the 1940s were Abbott and Costello.

Say what you will about Abbott and Costello, when they were on their game they were outstanding. Audiences loved them for a reason, their classic routines have stood the test of time, and they have left a lasting influence on American comedy that can be measured in the likes of Jerry Seinfeld and Larry David. They were also lazy wastrels given to unseemly petty in-fighting. My first insight into how dysfunctional they were came in off-handed and back-handed comments by the likes of Groucho Marx or Buster Keaton. Eventually I came to understand what Groucho and Buster were hinting at—here were a pair of movie stars who had the clout to force Hollywood to their will. They could have demanded and received a level of creative autonomy that Groucho and Buster could only dream of, but instead they could barely be bothered to show up to their own set on time and deliver their lines semi-competently. They put the minimum amount of effort into making their films, while indulging the most pointless and fractious grudges against one another. Watching their films is an exercise in squandered opportunities: it's like discovering that yes, Superman landed on Earth from Krypton, but that instead of becoming either a crusading journalist or a planet-saving superhero, he was content to become a pretty good bowler, but never even won a municipal tournament.

In 1942, two of the top 10 box office draws were Abbott and Costello pictures (and Bob Hope claimed another two). Meanwhile, *Palm Beach Story* and *To Be or Not to Be*—hailed earlier in this book as absolute pinnacles of the screwball art—did not even rate. It should not escape your notice that *Palm Beach Story* and *To Be or Not to Be* are films that directly challenge prevailing values, and demand their audiences be actively engaged in thinking about the sexual and political morals they lampoon, whereas Abbott and Costello made cheap jokes intended for no more permanence than the passing moment—the movie equivalent of Cheetos.

Whether by accident or design, the move away from screwball back to a slapstick ethos in the 1940s was a marked retreat from the 1930s' pre-feminist inclinations towards women's lib.

Consider *Theodora Goes Wild*, an underrated gem from 1936. Prior to this film, Irene Dunne was a dramatic actress who looked down her nose at comedy; after this film her career swerved hard into comedy. Dunne stars as Theodora Lynn, a mousy church-going spinster bookworm from the suffocating small town of Lynnfield. That name's no coincidence—her family founded the town and has dominated it since. As such, her behavior is closely watched and judged by her aunts, the town gossip, and an entire community of tongue-clucking busybodies.

And she has a secret.

Theodora, you see, is none other than "Caroline Adams," best-selling author of an incendiary novel called *The Sinner* (think the 1930s equivalent of *Fifty Shades of Gray*). The Lynnfield Literary Society has worked itself into a book-banning frenzy over *The Sinner*, which is a little awkward because Theodora sits on the Society herself. If these self-appointed guardians of morality knew she and Caroline Adams were one and the same, the fallout would ruin her life and potentially the lives and happiness of everyone she holds dear.

Into this powder keg of a situation breezes the artist behind *The Sinner*'s book jacket, Michael Grant (Melvyn Douglas at his smarmy best). He knows her secret, and what it's worth to her. He exploits that knowledge to blackmail her into spending time with him. Which would be pretty unpleasant behavior, if it weren't for the fact she actually does enjoy spending time with him.

For roughly the first hour of the movie, this is how it goes: Michael and Theodora do silly, childish things together, argue worldviews and philosophy, debate the merits of small town values versus big city thrills, and shuffle awkwardly to keep Theodora's secret identity under wraps. Oh, and they play house with an Asta-like dog standing in as an ersatz child.

It's too much for her to bear. Everything she enjoys, Theodora does in the shadow of fear; the people she loves are turned into antagonists that she has to deceive. This is no way to live, and it breaks her. In one gloriously cathartic outburst, she tells off the clucking hens of the town that she is no longer willing to hide her love for Michael, and she is unwilling to feel shame for it. Read what metaphors into it what you will—it's a form of coming out, a person declaring they are tired of being bullied into hiding who they love.

As satisfying as the scene is, it's not enough. Theodora "came out," but only by exposing *one* of her many secrets—and easily the least explosive of them. The opening titles made a promise to us: *Theodora is going to go wild*. One self-righteous speech does not equal "going wild." And the film has a good 40 minutes left to go.

Theodora discovers that Michael is not the free spirit he pretends. He is trapped in a loveless marriage with a shrewy witch but cannot divorce her without damaging the political career of his wealthy and well-connected father. He spent all this time convincing Theodora to escape the confining mentality of her small-town, but he is a prisoner of the same need to please others.

It is here, in the back half of the picture, that this otherwise mild-mannered amusement turns into a sharp-edged satire. It is the screwball equivalent of *Safety Last!* Just as Harold Lloyd spent the first two-thirds of his iconic comedy carefully establishing the plot logic that would then oblige him to scale a skyscraper with his bare hands, *Theodora Goes Wild* spends its first two thirds boxing its heroine into becoming "Caroline Adams" for real.

Theodora outs herself publicly as the author of *The Sinner*, starts dressing herself as the vampish man-eater everyone seemed to think she was, and proceeds to invent as many outrages as possible around herself. She becomes a walking sex-scandal, a sort of Jezebel-meets-Midas for whom everything she touches turns to scandal. If a few minutes have gone by without someone leveling a new charge of dishonor her way, she gets itchy.

And it is so joyous to watch. Irene Dunne can't suppress her giddy smile, like that of a toddler who has discovered how to use a bulldozer. The sheer thrill of destruction is intoxicating.

Like some avenging angel, she buzzsaws her way through both New York and Lynnfield, tainting everyone she meets with scandal until no one is left to presume moral authority over anyone else. She systematically deprives everyone of the ability to judge, and does so while forcing everyone to confront the worst, most exaggerated caricature of herself. When finished, she can discard the Caroline Adams persona and go back to being herself, secure in the knowledge that there's no one left to give her stick about anything she does.

The gossipy matrons of Lynnfield mistakenly think they can just stare at her "and she'll fall through the floor from the shame." They haven't realized that Theodora is now bulletproof, a slut-fabulous superhero. There's no stopping a woman who no longer cares what other people think of her.

**Irene Dunne puts on her battle armor in *Theodora Goes Wild* (1936).**

As powerful as *Theodora Goes Wild* is, I do not think it is especially *funny*. You'll be pretty deep into this movie before anything recognizable as a joke occurs. Although this might seem like a liability for a comedy, frankly I find *Theodora* far more enjoyable than *Bringing Up Baby*, which is wall-to-wall jokes but is utterly exhausting to sit through.[1]

Nevertheless, I have always held a soft spot in my heart for the many charms of

*Theodora Goes Wild*. It revels in a tension between the coastal elites and fly-over country that is still very much a fault line in American life, but does so by emphasizing how much more important are the things those communities share in common rather than their obvious surface differences. Theodora is a sort of proto-feminist, a rambunctious rule-breaker who came from a small town and independently established herself as a big city success in a man's world. I assumed these virtues might shine through, even if the rest of the film wasn't all that funny, when I forced my family to watch it with me.

And "forced" is the right word. To be clear—my family are veteran watchers of classic movies. My wife and both kids have all happily sat through any number of silent slapstick films in theaters and at home—if I'd insisted on watching *Safety Last!* they'd have been quite content.

Because here's the thing: Theodora's rampage was successful. She and all the other heroines of the screwball era helped rewrite American mores, to create a new kind of society in their wake. Charlie Chaplin's *A Woman of Paris* is hard to appreciate today because the social values that drive all of its drama have changed, to the point that the plot no longer makes a lot of sense. The same problem plagues *Theodora Goes Wild*. Far from "going wild," Theodora seems to go mild. In one scene she lays waste to a sitting governor's political career—and she does so by simply engineering a paparazzi snapshot of her in the governor's company. That's it. That's the extent of that "scandal," time to move on to her next conquest. The world of Theodora is so very quaint.

Meanwhile, although the world of *Safety Last!* is substantively less like ours in many respects, the very style of silent film helps make it seem *less* so. Silent film, like opera or comic books or musical theater or the Muppets, is a highly stylized aesthetic experience. There's not much point complaining in a Muppet movie that Kermit is just a puppet—you have to accept a certain amount of buy-in to the premise when you buy your ticket. In other words, you sit down to a silent comedy already predisposed to accept a fair degree of variance from your own world and experience. Some aspects will feel familiar and will connect to you emotionally, some won't and will be interesting to remark on, others may slip by unnoticed.

By contrast, we are far less likely to find the aesthetic style of a screwball comedy like *Theodora Goes Wild* from 1936 as especially foreign. It's in Black-and-White and paced more slowly than more modern films, but by and large Hollywood has spent the last century determined to adhere to a consistent, mostly realistic aesthetic model. And the more cues we get telling us that the film is supposed to feel "normal," the weirder its variations become. It's awfully hard to imagine what a 21st-century remake of *Theodora* would look like—how one could possibly adapt a story about weaponizing shame for a society that no longer feels it.

Let me share an anecdote: When I was producing my DVD compilation of the restored films of Harry Langdon, I had gone to my bank to take out a loan to help finance the project. I sat down with a banker and started to explain what my company did, and what this specific project entailed. She listened, and nodded her head politely. But she was puzzled. "*Silent* comedies? How does that work? How do people hear the jokes?"

Every once in a while I find myself getting dragged into some arcane argument with other slapstick nuts like myself (the sometimes controversial stances I take in this book should clue you in to why that happens to me a lot). And when the arguments get heated—

over such trivia as the proper frame rate for silent comedies, or whether that's really Mal St. Clair as "Deadshot Dan" in Buster Keaton's *The Goat*—I like to remember that as passionate and fanatical as we can get, there are a great many Americans who don't understand how a silent comedy could even exist. *How d'ya hear the jokes?*

*And they outnumber us.*

And it is at times like that when I curse the nostalgia merchants.

When I first pitched my Harry Langdon DVD project to Image Entertainment, back in the early part of the 2000s, their senior management weren't too impressed. The only way to do what I was proposing was to spend a lot of money (see my encounter with the banker above), and even my most conservative budget figures were horrifically underwater from their most liberal sales projections. They had a track record with silent films on disc—a deep history of data that told a single story: there are about 3,000 silent movie fans in the United States who would buy DVDs. It didn't matter if the silent film in question was some obscure title or the restored Mutual shorts by Charlie Chaplin, it didn't matter if they put in promotional efforts or not. The sales targets were as predictable as the tides. I wasn't prepared to agree to that logic, and was convinced that it was possible to connect to a new audience, a newbie audience.

Spoiler alert: I failed. In the end my sales figures on the Langdon set were indistinguishable from sales of slapstick compilations which I never even bothered to advertise or promote at all. And, yup, my numbers lined up with what my distributers had pessimistically projected.

I bring this story up as evidence that I've been giving this problem a lot of thought, and trying to put my money where my mouth is. In promoting the Langdon set, I gave a few interviews to newspapers and radio, and I presented live screenings in several cities—and in these appearances, I was always careful to define Langdon's legacy in terms of contemporary comedy. I invoked Monty Python and Pee Wee Herman, Steve Martin and Sacha Baron Cohen, Jerry Seinfeld and Larry David.

It was a calculated strategy—on one hand I was keen to sneak these references into publicity materials and blurbs to increase the likelihood that my disc would pop up in Google searches for these other comedians. But that sounds manipulative and dishonest, when my main motivation was sincere—Langdon was an anti-comedian, who performed a kind of 1920s performance-art comedy built around subverting familiar comic forms, and emphasizing discomfort and embarrassment. The best way to describe this kind of comedy is to reference his contemporaries who play in the same sandbox.

I also attended a number of film festivals and conventions, and found that my "sales pitch," so effective when talking to people who didn't know silent comedy and had never heard of Langdon, provoked an entirely different response from film geeks. I was surprised how many hardcore fans of slapstick comedy expressed such hostility and revulsion to contemporary comedy.

It is not a zero-sum game—liking one doesn't preclude liking the other. Now, to be fair, I think that pop culture in this country can seem very ageist at times. Outside of a handful of major cities, there is no longer a concept of revival screenings of older films. Black and White movies scarcely get shown on TV at all except by channels such as Turner Classic Movies, and silent films are often banished to late night timeslots. So, it wouldn't be hard to take from this a feeling that American pop culture believed that anything old is bad and anything new is good—and if you resisted that formula, it could be a reflexive act to just invert it: *anything old is good, anything new is bad.*

It's ludicrous when you put it like that, and obviously indefensible, but there are film fans who seem to adhere to that very rubric. Yet as I went from conversation to conversation at places like Cinefest and Cinecon and Slapsticon and so on, promoting the Langdon set, I encountered a shifting definition of what counted as "old" and "new." For one person, any pop culture later than 1958 was worthless and to be avoided. For another, 1966 was the line in the sand.

I got the feeling that the magic year was whenever the speaker came of age—crossing that threshold from carefree youth into the burdens of adulthood. The pop culture that succored you on one side of that divide would remain touched by nostalgia forever after—the pop culture that assaulted you in the later years would only make you feel old.

The nostalgia merchants are an exclusionary force, their hostility to contemporary entertainment only sends the signal that if you like modern music and TV, then this oldster stuff isn't for you. Nostalgia is the enemy of building new audiences.

Nostalgia was especially an enemy force in promoting the films of Harry Langdon, since his work had been mostly out of circulation for years and what critical reputation he had was mostly negative. Chances are, if you'd heard of him before, you had a bad impression—I absolutely needed to cultivate an audience of newbies and outsiders.

I don't deny that nostalgia is a powerful force, and the warm glow of happy memories can forgive many a flaw in some old movie. But my objection to nostalgia as a selling point for movies is that is a death sentence. If the *only* thing you have to say in some movie's favor is that it appeals to those who grew up with it, once that audience grays and dies, there's nobody left. If you didn't grow up with it, there has to be *some* appeal made to explain why, out of universe of competing forms of entertainment, you should choose to let *this* one in.

And the irony is, the silent comedy fans I've met in my life—well, the oldest of them are in their '60s and '70s. And 70 years ago was already *after* silent comedy had ended as a form. In other words, even the most nostalgic amongst us jumped on this bandwagon after it had left the station. If we could be drawn into a passé form, then why do we distrust the ability of others to follow?

I used to do a presentation at elementary schools, in which I would bring my 16mm projector and screen and show the kids how the moving images are actually sequences of tiny still pictures. Then, I'd thread up and present the very first public film show, duplicating the Lumière Brothers' premiere, starting with *Leaving the Factory.* Then I would show Charlie Chaplin's *The Immigrant,* and the third film in the set was a rotating slot—Laurel and Hardy's *Big Business,* Buster Keaton's *One Week,* it depended on my mood. From the teacher's standpoint, it was an hour's worth of science, history, and social studies disguised as an entertaining distraction. From my standpoint, it was proselytizing.

And it worked—more than once I've been stopped in public, years afterward, by some kid who recognized me. They come up and say, "Hey, you came to my school and showed that Charlie Chaplin film!"

Let me pause here to let that sink in. I've been stopped by little kids—less than 10 years old—*who remembered Charlie Chaplin's name.* These are kids who will not grow up to be bankers who don't know what silent comedies are. All it took was one afternoon, one film, just a single exposure—and that gateway drug was enough to bring Chaplin into their lives.

During my promotional tour to publicize the DVD box set collection of the silent films of Harry Langdon, I had engaged Chicago's Portage Theater to screen a package of Langdon's silent shorts to be accompanied by live music from a local jazz band. Being keen to bring new audiences to silent comedy, I really wanted people to come to the show with their families. I brought my niece Haven … but being distracted by my responsibilities hosting the show, I failed to give her any useful context or preparation for what she was about to see. Haven was four at the time—she had never before seen anything in Black and White, and certainly never seen anything silent.

The house lights dimmed, and the movies began. First up was *The Hansom Cabman*. Langdon wakes up with a wicked hangover, to discover he also now has a furious fiancée he's never met (sober).

Haven scrunched her face up, staring at the screen, trying to make sense of what she was seeing. It was *funny*, and she was laughing in all the right places, but she was obviously worried. Finally, her face brightened as she figured it out. She grabbed my sleeve, and excitedly whispered, "They're doing something tricky with their mouths. They *are* talking, but you have to be in the movie with them to hear it."

I've been studying and writing about movies in one form or another my entire conscious life, and I've never heard a better explanation of silent film. And she came to it all on her own, without help, in a matter of minutes.

It gets better! On the way home, she asked whether Harry Langdon was a child or a grownup. Give that girl the gold star! Take that, Walter Kerr!

All I did was take her, I never shoved this down her throat, never pushed her. All I did was provide access, the first introduction. There are many in the classic film community who wring their hands over some misplaced worry that today's generation isn't sufficiently interested in old movies. Pshaw. *Of course* most of them aren't. Neither are they all that enamored of opera, or baseball, or the Theater of the Absurd, or utopian literature, or *Jeopardy!*, or any other of the almost endless niche appeal cultural pursuits humanity has thought up over the years. But *some* of them are, and those that do find their way to the pleasure of old movies will be captivated for life. And all it takes is mere exposure. Nothing else, just exposure.

Someday, decades from now, those kids will have their own nostalgic memories for these films—but if that's all the movies can claim, then they'll have been mostly forgotten long before that day. A movie made close to a century ago that can captivate a youngster's attention all on its own terms is a movie that doesn't need nostalgia to thrive.

Slapstick and screwball never died. Every single movie described in this book still exists. Go watch 'em.

# Filmography

*A comprehensive filmography of all silent slapstick and screwball comedies is beyond the scope of this book. What follows is a filmography of key films discussed or referenced in the text, presented in chronological order of U.S. release. The run time of silent films is reported in physical length instead of minutes, because variances in frame rate will affect the playback times.*

*L'Arroseur arrose* (1895); Producer: Louis Lumière; Director: Louis Lumière; Screenplay: Louis Lumière; Cast: François Clerc, Benoît Duval; Running time: 45 seconds; Released June 10, 1895

*The Melomaniac* (1903); Producer: Georges Méliès; Director: Georges Méliès; Screenplay: Georges Méliès; Cast: Georges Méliès; Running time: 1/6 reel; Released Aug 15, 1903

*Those Awful Hats* (1909); Producer: D.W. Griffith; Director: D.W. Griffith; Screenplay: uncredited; Cast: Flora Finch (Woman with Largest Hat), Mack Sennett (Annoyed Patron); Running time: 1/4 reel; Released Jan 5, 1909

*The Curtain Pole* (1909); Producer: D.W. Griffith; Director: D.W. Griffith; Screenplay: uncredited; Cast: Mack Sennett (M. DuPont), Harry Solter (Mr. Edwards), Florence Lawrence (Mrs. Edwards); Running time: 3/4 reel; Released Feb 15, 1909

*The Lonely Villa* (1909); Producer: D.W. Griffith; Director: D.W. Griffith; Screenplay: Mack Sennett; Cast: Marion Leonard, Mary Pickford, Adele de Garde, Mack Sennett; Running time: 3/4 reel; Released Jun 10, 1909

*Bangville Police* (1913); Producer: Mack Sennett; Director: Henry Lehrman; Screenplay: uncredited; Cast: Fred Mace (Sheriff), Mabel Normand (Della), Nick Cogley (Her Father), Dot Farley (Her Mother); Running time: 1/2 reel; Released Apr 24, 1913

*Noise from the Deep* (1913); Producer: Mack Sennett; Director: Mack Sennett; Screenplay: uncredited; Cast: Mabel Normand, Roscoe Arbuckle, Charles Avery, Nick Cogley; Running time: 1 reel; Released Jul 17, 1913

*Mabel's Dramatic Career* (1913); Producer: Mack Sennett; Director: Mack Sennett; Screenplay: uncredited; Cast: Mabel Normand, Mack Sennett, Alice Davenport, Virginia Kirtley; Running time: 1 reel; Released Sep 8, 1913

*Making a Living* (1914); Producer: Mack Sennett; Director: Henry Lehrman; Screenplay: uncredited; Cast: Charlie Chaplin (Sharper), Henry Leherman (Reporter), Virginia Kirtley (Girl), Alice Davenport (Mother); Running time: 1 reel; Released Feb 2, 1914

*Kid Auto Races at Venice* (1914); Producer: Mack Sennett; Director: Henry Lehrman; Screenplay: Henry Lehrman; Cast: Charlie Chaplin (Tramp), Henry Leherman (Film Director), Frank D. Williams (Cameraman); Running time: 1 reel; Released Feb 7, 1914

*A Film Johnnie* (1914); Producer: Mack Sennett; Director: George Nichols; Screenplay: Craig Hutchinson; Cast: Charlie Chaplin (Film johnnie), Roscoe Arbuckle (Fatty), Edgar Kennedy (Director), Virginia Kirtley (Keystone girl); Running time: 1 reel; Released Mar 2, 1914

*The Knockout* (1914); Producer: Mack Sennett; Director: Mack Sennett; Screenplay: uncredited; Cast: Roscoe Arbuckle (Pug),

Minta Durfee (Girl), Edgar Kennedy (Cyclone Flynn), Charlie Chaplin (Referee), Al St. John (Leader of street toughs); Running time: 2 reels; Released Jun 11, 1914

*Mabel's Married Life* (1914); Producer: Mack Sennett; Director: Mack Sennett; Screenplay: Charlie Chaplin, Mabel Normand; Cast: Charlie Chaplin (Husband), Mabel Normand (Mabel), Mack Swain (Ladykiller), Eva Nelson (His Wife); Running time: 2 reels; Released Jun 20, 1914

*A Florida Enchantment* (1914); Producer: uncredited; Director: Sidney Drew; Screenplay: Eugene Mullen and Marguerite Bertsch; From the novel by Archibald Clavering Gunther; Cast: Sidney Drew (Dr. Cassadene), Edith Storey (Lillian Travers), Charles Kent (Maj. Horton), Lillian Burns (Malvina); Running time: 6 reels; Released Aug 10, 1914

*The Rounders* (1914); Producer: Mack Sennett; Director: Charlie Chaplin and Roscoe Arbuckle; Screenplay: Charlie Chaplin; Cast: Charlie Chaplin (Mr. Full), Roscoe Arbuckle (Mr. Fuller), Phyllis Allen (Mr. Full's wife), Minta Durfee (Mr. Fuller's wife); Running time: 2 reels; Released Sep 7, 1914

*Love and Surgery* (1914); Producer: Henry Lehrman; Director: Henry Lehrman; Screenplay: uncredited; Cast: Billie Ritchie, Gertrude Selby, Henry Lehrmann, Louise Orth; Running time: 2 reels; Released Oct 24, 1914

*Tillie's Punctured Romance* (1914); Producer: Mack Sennett; Director: Mack Sennett; Screenplay: Hampton Del Ruth, Craig Hutchinson, Mack Sennett; Based on the play "Tillie's Nightmare" by A. Baldwin Sloane and Edgar Smith; Cast: Marie Dressler (Tillie Banks), Mabel Normand (Mabel), Charlie Chaplin (City Slicker), Mack Swain (John Banks); Running time: 6 reels; Released Dec 21, 1914

*A Night Out* (1915); Producer: Jess Robbins; Director: Charlie Chaplin; Screenplay: Charlie Chaplin; Cast: Charlie Chaplin (Reveller), Charles Allen Dealey (Restaurant Manager), Frank Dolan (Waiter); Running time: 2 reels; Released Feb 15, 1915

*The Champion* (1915); Producer: Jess Robbins; Director: Charlie Chaplin; Screenplay: Charlie Chaplin; Cast: Charlie Chaplin (Aspiring pugilist), Fred Goodwins (Spike Dugan), Edna Purviance (Trainer's daughter), Bud Jamison (Champion); Running time: 2 reels; Released Mar 11, 1915

*Courthouse Crooks* (1915); Producer: Mack Sennett; Director: Ford Sterling; Screenplay: uncredited; Cast: Ford Sterling (District Attorney), Minta Durfee (Judge's Wife), Charles Arling (Judge Grey), Harold Lloyd (Jobless Youth); Running time: 2 reels; Released Jun 15, 1915

*Fatty's Plucky Pup* (1915); Producer: Mack Sennett; Director: Roscoe Arbuckle; Screenplay: uncredited; Cast: Roscoe Arbuckle, Phyllis Allen, Edgar Kennedy, Joe Bordeaux; Running time: 2 reels; Released Jun 28, 1915

*A Submarine Pirate* (1915); Producer: Mack Sennett; Director: Charles Avery; Screenplay: Mack Sennett; Cast: Syd Chaplin (Waiter), Wesley Ruggles (Inventor's accomplice), Glen Cavender (Inventor), Phyllis Allen (Pugnacious Guest); Running time: 4 reels; Released Nov 14, 1915

*Fatty and the Broadway Stars* (1915); Producer: Mack Sennett; Director: Roscoe Arbuckle; Screenplay: uncredited; Cast: Roscoe Arbuckle, Ivy Crosthwaite, Mack Sennett; Running time: 2 reels; Released Dec 15, 1915

*A Movie Star* (1916); Producer: Mack Sennett; Director: Fred Hibbard; Screenplay: uncredited; Cast: Mack Swain (Handsome Jack), Louella Maxam (Nell), Mai Wells (Jack's Screen Mother), Ray Grey (Jack's Screen Rival); Running time: 2 reels; Released Jan 23, 1916

*Cruel and Unusual* (1916); Producer: George Kleine; Director: Louis Myll; Screenplay: uncredited; Cast: Harry Watson (Musty Suffer), Geoge Bickel (Willie Work), Rosa Gore (Dippy Mary); Running time: 1 reel; Released Mar 1, 1916

*Police* (1916); Producer: Jess Robbins; Director: Charlie Chaplin; Screenplay: Charlie Chaplin; Cast: Charlie Chaplin (Ex-convict),

Edna Purviance (Daughter of the House), Wesley Ruggles (Crook), James T. Kelly (Drunk); Running time: 2 reels; Released Mar 27, 1916

*Burlesque on Carmen* (1916); Producer: Jess Robbins; Director: Charlie Chaplin, and Leo White (uncredited); Screenplay: Charlie Chaplin; Cast: Charlie Chaplin (Darn Hosiery), Edna Purviance (Carmen), Leo White (Corp. Morales); Running time: 4 reels; Released Apr 10, 1916

*The Floorwalker* (1916); Producer: uncredited; Director: Charlie Chaplin; Screenplay: Charlie Chaplin; Cast: Charlie Chaplin (Tramp), Eric Campbell (General manager), Edna Purviance (Secretary), Leo White (Shoplifter); Running time: 2 reels; Released May 15, 1916

*One A.M.* (1916); Producer: Henry P. Caulfield; Director: Charlie Chaplin; Screenplay: Charlie Chaplin, Vincent Bryan; Cast: Charlie Chaplin (Drunk), Albert Austin (Taxi driver); Running time: 2 reels; Released Aug 7, 1916

*Luke Joins the Navy* (1916); Producer: Hal Roach; Director: Hal Roach; Screenplay: uncredited; Cast: Harold Lloyd, Snub Pollard, Bebe Daniels; Running time: 1 reel; Released Sep 3, 1916

*Luke's Movie Muddle* (1916); Producer: Hal Roach; Director: Hal Roach; Screenplay: uncredited; Cast: Harold Lloyd, Snub Pollard, Bebe Daniels; Running time: 1 reel; Released Dec 3, 1916

*The Rink* (1916); Producer: Henry P. Caulfield; Director: Charlie Chaplin; Screenplay: Charlie Chaplin, Vincent Bryan; Cast: Charlie Chaplin (Waiter/Sir Cecil Seltzer), Edna Purviance (Girl), James T. Kely (Her father), Eric Campbell (Mr. Stout); Running time: 2 reels; Released Dec 4, 1916

*Easy Street* (1917); Producer: Charlie Chaplin; Director: Charlie Chaplin; Screenplay: Charlie Chaplin; Cast: Charlie Chaplin, Edna Purviance, Eric Campbell, Albert Austin; Running time: 2 reels; Released Jan 22, 1917

*The Cure* (1917); Producer: Henry P. Caulfield; Director: Charlie Chaplin; Screenplay: Charlie Chaplin; Cast: Charlie Chaplin

(Inebriate), Edna Purviance (Girl), Eric Campbell (Man with gout); Running time: 2 reels; Released Apr 16, 1917

*The Immigrant* (1917); Producer: John Jasper; Director: Charlie Chaplin; Screenplay: Charlie Chaplin, Vincent Bryan; Cast: Charlie Chaplin (Immigrant), Edna Purviance (Immigrant), Kitty Bradbury (Her mother), Eric Campbell (Head Waiter); Running time: 2 reels; Released Jun 17, 1917

*The Rough House* (1917); Producer: Joseph M. Schenck; Director: Roscoe Arbuckle; Screenplay: Roscoe Arbuckle; Cast: Roscoe Arbuckle, Buster Keaton, Al St. John, Alice Lake; Running time: 2 reels; Released Jun 25, 1917

*Lonesome Luke, Messenger* (1917); Producer: Hal Roach; Director: Hal Roach; Screenplay: uncredited; Cast: Harold Lloyd, Snub Pollard, Bebe Daniels; Running time: 1 reel; Released Aug 5, 1917

*Bliss* (1917); Producer: Hal Roach; Director: Ald Goulding; Screenplay: uncredited; H.M. Walker (titles); Cast: Harold Lloyd, Bebe Daniels, Snub Pollard; Running time: 1 reel; Released Oct 14, 1917

*The Hobo* (1917); Producer: Louis Berstein; Director: Arvid E. Gilstrom; Screenplay: uncredited; Cast: Billy West, Oiver Hardy, Leo White, Virginia Clark; Running time: 2 reels; Released Nov 1, 1917

*A Gasoline Wedding* (1918); Producer: Hal Roach; Director: Alf Goulding; Screenplay: uncredited; Cast: Harold Lloyd, Bebe Daniels, Snub Pollard; Running time: 1 reel; Released Mar 3, 1918

*A Dog's Life* (1918); Producer: Charlie Chaplin; Director: Charlie Chaplin; Screenplay: Charlie Chaplin; Cast: Charlie Chaplin (Tramp), Edna Purviance (Singer), Syd Chaplin (Lunch wagon owner); Running time: 3 reels; Released Apr 14, 1918

*Triple Trouble* (1918); Producer: ; Director: Charlie Chaplin, Leo White (uncredited); Screenplay: Charlie Chaplin, Leo White (uncredited); Cast: Charlie Chaplin (Janitor), Billy Armstrong (Pickpocket), Edna Purviance (Maid); Running time: 2 reels; Released Aug 11, 1918

*Shoulder Arms* (1918); Producer: Charlie Chaplin; Director: Charlie Chaplin; Screenplay: Charlie Chaplin; Cast: Charlie Chaplin (Recruit), Edna Purviance (French woman), Syd Chaplin (Kaiser Wilhelm); Running time: 3 reels; Released Oct 20, 1918

*Take a Chance* (1918); Producer: Hal Roach; Director: Alf Goulding; Screenplay: uncredited; H.M. Walker (titles); Cast: Harold Lloyd, Bebe Daniels, Snub Pollard; Running time: 1 reel; Released Nov 24, 1918

*The Marathon* (1919); Producer: Hal Roach; Director: Alf Goulding; Screenplay: uncredited; H.M. Walker (titles); Cast: Harold Lloyd, Bebe Daniels, Snub Pollard; Running time: 1 reel; Released May 25, 1919

*Bumping into Broadway* (1919); Producer: Hal Roach; Director: Hal Roach; Screenplay: uncredited; H.M. Walker (titles); Cast: Harold Lloyd, Bebe Daniels, Snub Pollard; Running time: 2 reels; Released Nov 2, 1919

*The Garage* (1920); Producer: Joseph M. Schenck; Director: Roscoe Arbuckle; Screenplay: Jean Havez; Cast: Roscoe Arbuckle, Buster Keaton, Molly Malone, Harry McCoy; Running time: 2 reels; Released Dec 15, 1919

*One Week* (1920); Producer: Joseph M. Schenck; Director: Eddie Cline; Screenplay: Buster Keaton, Eddie Cline; Cast: Buster Keaton (Husband), Sybil Seely (Wife), Joe Roberts (Rival); Running time: 2 reels; Released Sep 1, 1920

*Convict 13* (1920); Producer: Joseph M. Schenck; Director: Eddie Cline; Screenplay: Buster Keaton, Eddie Cline; Cast: Buster Keaton (Golfer), Sybil Seeley (Warden's Daughter), Joe Roberts (Inmate), Joe Keaton (Inmate); Running time: 2 reels; Released Oct 27, 1920

*The Kid* (1921); Producer: Charlie Chaplin; Director: Charlie Chaplin; Screenplay: Charlie Chaplin; Cast: Charlie Chaplin (Tramp), Edna Purviance (Woman), Jackie Coogan (Kid); Running time: 6 reels; Released Jan 21, 1921

*The Haunted House* (1921); Producer: Joseph M. Schenck; Director: Eddie Cline; Screenplay: Buster Keaton, Eddie Cline; Cast: Buster Keaton (Bank Clerk), Virginia Fox (Bank President's Daughter), Joe Roberts (Bank Teller); Running time: 2 reels; Released Feb 10, 1921

*The Goat* (1921); Producer: Joseph M. Schenck; Director: Mal St. Clair; Screenplay: Buster Keaton, Mal St. Clair; Cast: Buster Keaton (Boy), Virginia Fox (Girl), Joe Roberts (Father), Mal St. Clair (Deadshot Dan); Running time: 2 reels; Released May 18, 1921

*The Playhouse* (1922); Producer: Joseph M. Schenck; Director: Eddie Cline; Screenplay: Buster Keaton, Eddie Cline; Cast: Buster Keaton (Stage Hand), Virginia Fox (Twins), Joe Roberts (Stage Manager); Running time: 2 reels; Released Oct 6, 1921

*Cops* (1922); Producer: Joseph M. Schenck; Director: Eddie Cline; Screenplay: Buster Keaton, Eddie Cline; Cast: Buster Keaton (Boy), Virginia Fox (Mayor's Daughter), Joe Roberts (Detective); Running time: 2 reels; Released Mar 22, 1922

*The Electric House* (1922); Producer: Joseph M. Schenck; Director: Eddie Cline; Screenplay: Buster Keaton, Eddie Cline; Cast: Buster Keaton (Electrical Engineer), Virginia Fox (Girl), Joe Roberts (Homeowner); Running time: 2 reels; Released Oct 22, 1922

*Safety Last!* (1923); Producer: Hal Roach; Director: Fred Newmeyer and Sam Taylor; Screenplay: Hal Roach, Sam Taylor, and Tim Whelan; H.M. Walker (titles); Cast: Harold Lloyd (Boy), Mildred Davis (Girl), Bill Strothers (Pal), Noah Young (The Law); Running time: 7 reels; Released Jan 25, 1923

*The Love Nest* (1923); Producer: Joseph M. Schenck; Director: Buster Keaton, Eddie Cline (uncredited); Screenplay: Buster Keaton, Eddie Cline; Cast: Buster Keaton (Sailor), Joe Roberts (Captain); Running time: 2 reels; Released Mar 23, 1923

*A Woman of Paris* (1923); Producer: Charlie Chaplin; Director: Charlie Chaplin; Screenplay: Charlie Chaplin; Cast: Edna Purviance (Mari St. Clair), Adolphe Menjou (Pierre Revel), Carl Miller (Jean Millet); Running time: 8 reels; Released Sep 26, 1923

*Our Hospitality* (1923); Producer: Joseph M.

Schenck; Director: John G. Blystone, Buster Keaton; Screenplay: Clyde Bruckman, Joseph Mitchell, Jean Havez; Cast: Buster Keaton (Willie McKay), Natalie Talmadge (Virginia Canfield), Joe Roberts (Joe Canfield), Leonard Clapham (James Canfield), Craig Ward (Lee Canfield); Running time: 7 reels; Released Nov 19, 1923

*The Marriage Circle* (1924); Producer: Ernst Lubitsch; Director: Ernst Lubitsch; Screenplay: Paul Bern; Based on the play "Only a Dream" by Lothar Schmidt; Cast: Florence Vidor (Charlotte Braun), Monte Blue (Dr. Franz Braun), Marie Prevost (Mizzi Stock), Adolphe Menjou (Prof. Stock); Running time: 9 reels; Released Feb 16, 1924

*Girl Shy* (1924); Producer: Harold Lloyd; Director: Fred Newmeyer and Sam Taylor; Screenplay: Sam Taylor, Ted Wilde, Tim Whelan; Thomas Grey (titles); Cast: Harold Lloyd (Harold Meadows), Jobyna Ralston (Mary Buckingham), Richard Daniels (Jerry Meadows), Carlton Griffin (Ronald DeVore); Running time: 8 reels; Released Apr 20, 1924

*Sherlock Jr.* (1924); Producer: Joseph M. Schenck; Director: Buster Keaton; Screenplay: Clyde Bruckman, Joseph Mitchell, Jean Havez; Cast: Buster Keaton (Sherlock Jr.), Kathryn McGuire (Girl), Ward Crane (Rival), Joe Keaton (Girl's Father); Running time: 5 reels; Released Apr 21, 1924

*The Hansom Cabman* (1924); Producer: Mack Sennett; Director: Harry Edwards; Screenplay: uncredited; John A. Waldron (titles); Cast: Harry Langdon, Marceline Day, Madeline Hurlock, Andy Clyde; Running time: 2 reels; Released Oct 12, 1924

*Too Many Mammas* (1924); Producer: Hal Roach; Director: Leo McCarey; Screenplay: uncredited; Cast: Charley Chase, Martha Sleeper, Beth Darlington, Olive Borden; Running time: 1 reel; Released Oct 12, 1924

*Hot Water* (1924); Producer: Harold Lloyd; Director: Fred Newmeyer and Sam Taylor; Screenplay: Sam Talor, Thomas Grey, Tim Whelan, John Grey; Thomas Grey (titles); Cast: Harold Lloyd (Hubby), Jobyna Ralston (Wifey), Josephine Crowley (Her Mother), Charles Stevenson (Her Older Brother); Running time: 5 reels; Released Nov 2, 1924

*Miss Bluebeard* (1925); Producer: Adolph Zukor, Jesse L. Lasky; Director: Frank Tuttle; Screenplay: Townsend Martin; From the play "Little Miss Bluebeard" by Avery Hopwood; Cast: Bebe Daniels (Colette Girard), Robert Frazer (Larry Charters), Kenneth MacKenna (Bob Hawley), Raymond Griffith (Hon. Bertie Bird); Running time: 7 reels; Released Jan 26, 1925

*Charley's Aunt* (1925); Producer: Al Christie; Director: Scott Sidney; Screenplay: F. McGrew Willis; From the play by Brandon Thomas; Cast: Syd Chaplin (Sir Fancourt Babberley), Ethel Shannon (Ela Delahay), James E. Page (Spettigue), Lucien Littlefield (Brasset); Running time: 7 reels; Released Feb 8, 1925

*His Marriage Wow* (1925); Producer: Mack Sennett; Director: Harry Edwards; Screenplay: Arthur Ripley; Cast: Harry Langdon, Natalie Kingston, William McCall, Vernon Dent; Running time: 2 reels; Released Mar 1, 1925

*Seven Chances* (1925); Producer: Joseph M. Schenck; Director: Buster Keaton; Screenplay: Jean Havez, Clyde Bruckman, Joseph Mitchell; Based on the play by Roi Cooper Megrue; Cast: Buster Keaton (Jimmie Shannon), T. Roy Barnes (Billy), Snitz Edwards (Attorney), Ruth Dwyer (Mary Brown); Running time: 6 reels; Released Mar 11, 1925

*The Gold Rush* (1925); Producer: Charlie Chaplin; Director: Charlie Chaplin; Screenplay: Charlie Chaplin; Cast: Charlie Chaplin (Lone prospector), Mack Swain (Big Jim McKay), Tom Murray (Black Larsen), Georgia Hale (Georgia); Running time: 7 reels; Released Jun 26, 1925

*Isn't Life Terrible* (1925); Producer: Hal Roach; Director: Leo McCarey; Screenplay: uncredited; Cast: Charley Chase, Katherine Grant, Oliver Hardy, Dorothy Morrison; Running time: 2 reels; Released Jul 5, 1925

*The Freshman* (1925); Producer: Harold Lloyd; Director: Sam Taylor and Fred Newmeyer; Screenplay: Sam Talor, Ted

Wilde, John Grey, Tim Whelan; Cast: Harold Lloyd (Harold "Speedy" Lamb), Jobyna Ralston (Peggy), Brooks Benedict (College Cad), James Anderson (Chet Trask); Running time: 7 reels; Released Sep 20, 1925

*Uncle Tom's Gal* (1925); Producer: Abe and Julius Stern; Director: William Watson; Screenplay: William Watson; Cast: Edna Marion, Larry Richardson, Les Bates; Running time: 2 reels; Released Oct 7, 1925

*A Night in the Show* (1915); Producer: Jess Robbins; Director: Charlie Chaplin; Screenplay: Charlie Chaplin; Cast: Charlie Chaplin (Mr. Pest, and Mr. Rowdy), Edna Purviance (Lady in the Stalls), Bud Jamison (Singer); Running time: 2 reels; Released Nov 20, 1915

*Hands Up!* (1926); Producer: Jesse L. Lasky, Adolph Zukor; Director: Clarence G. Badger; Screenplay: Monte Brice, Lloyd Corrigan; Story by Reggie Morris; Cast: Raymond Griffith (Jack), Virginia Lee Corbin (Alice Woodstock), George A. Billings (Abraham Lincoln); Running time: 7 reels; Released Jan 14, 1926

*My Stars* (1926); Producer: ; Director: Roscoe Arbuckle; Screenplay: Roscoe Arbuckle; Cast: Johnny Arthur, Virginia Vance, Florence Lee, George Davis; Running time: 1 reel; Released Jan 17, 1926

*Saturday Afternoon* (1926); Producer: Mack Sennett; Director: Harry Edwards; Screenplay: Arthur Ripley, Frank Capra; Cast: Harry Langdon (Harry Higgins), Alice Ward (Mrs. Harry Higgins), Vernon Dent (Steve Smith), Ruth Hiatt (Pearl), Peggy Montgomery (Ruby); Running time: 3 reels; Released Jan 31, 1926

*Tramp, Tramp, Tramp* (1926); Producer: Harry Langdon; Director: Harry Edwards; Screenplay: Arthur Ripley, Frank Capra; Cast: Harry Langdon (Harry Logan), Joan Crawford (Betty Burton), Tom Murray (Nick Kargas); Running time: 6 reels; Released Mar 21, 1926

*For Heaven's Sake* (1926); Producer: Harold Lloyd; Director: Sam Taylor; Screenplay: John Grey, Ted Wilde, and Clyde Bruckman; Ralph Spence (titles); Cast: Harold

Lloyd (J. Harold Manners), Jobyna Ralston (Hope), Noah Young (Roughneck), James Mason (Gangster); Running time: 6 reels; Released Apr 6, 1926

*Mighty Like a Moose* (1926); Producer: Hal Roach; Director: Leo McCarey; Screenplay: Charley Chase (uncredited); Cast: Charley Chase (Mr. Moose), Vivien Oakland (Mrs. Moose), Ann Howe (Maid), Charles Clary (Dentist); Running time: 2 reels; Released Jul 18, 1926

*The Strong Man* (1926); Producer: Harry Langdon; Director: Frank Capra; Screenplay: Arthur Ripley; Adaptation by Hal Conklin; Cast: Harry Langdon (Paul Bergot), Priscilla Bonner (Mary Brown), Gertrude Astor (Lily), Arthur Thalasso (Zandow the Great); Running time: 6 reels; Released Sep 19, 1926

*The Better 'Ole* (1926); Producer: uncredited; Director: Charles Reisner; Screenplay: Charles Reisner; Based on the play by Bruce Bairnsfather; Cast: Sydney Chaplin (Pvt. "Old Bill" Busby), Doris Hill (Joan), Harold Goodwin (Bert Chester), Edgar Kennedy (Cpl. Austin); Running time: 9 reels; Released Oct 23, 1926

*The Kid Brother* (1927); Producer: Harold Lloyd; Director: Ted Wilde, Harold Lloyd (uncredited); Screenplay: John Grey, Lex Neal, and Howard Green; Cast: Harold Lloyd (Harold Hickory), Jobyna Ralston (Mary Powers), Walter James (Jim Hickory), Leo Willis (Leo Hickory); Running time: 8 reels; Released Jan 22, 1927

*The General* (1927); Producer: Joseph M. Schenck; Director: Buster Keaton; Screenplay: Buster Keaton, Clyde Bruckman; From the book "The Great Locomotive Chase" by William Pittinger; Cast: Buster Keaton (Johnnie Gray), Marion Mack (Annabelle Lee), Glen Cavender (Capt. Anderson), Jim Farley (Gen. Thatcher); Running time: 8 reels; Released Feb 5, 1927

*It* (1927); Producer: Clarence Badger and Elinor Glyn (uncredited); Director: Clarence G. Badger; Screenplay: Elinor Glyn; Cast: Clara Bow (Betty Lou), Antonio Moreno (Cyrus T. Waltham), William Austin

(Monty Montgomery), Priscilla Bonner (Molly); Running time: 7 reels; Released Feb 15, 1927

*Long Pants* (1927); Producer: Harry Langdon; Director: Frank Capra; Screenplay: Robert Eddy, Tay Garnett; Story by Arthur Ripley; Cast: Harry Langdon (Harry Shelby), Alma Bennett (Bebe Blair), Priscilla Bonner (Priscilla), Gladys Brockwell (Harry's Mother); Running time: 6 reels; Released Mar 26, 1927

*His First Flame* (1927); Producer: Mack Sennett; Director: Harry Edwards; Screenplay: Arthur Ripley, Frank Capra; Cast: Harry Langdon (Harry Howells), Natalie Kingston (Ethel Morgan), Ruth Hiatt (Mary Morgan), Vernon Dent (Amos McCarthy); Running time: 6 reels; Released May 3, 1927

*Three's a Crowd* (1927); Producer: Harry Langdon; Director: Harry Langdon; Screenplay: Robert Eddy, James Langdon; Story by Arthur Ripley; Cast: Harry Langdon, Gladys McConnell, Cornelius Keefe, Arthur Thalasso; Running time: 6 reels; Released Aug 28, 1927

*The Missing Link* (1927); Producer: Darryl F. Zanuck; Director: Charles F. Resiner; Screenplay: Darryl F. Zanuck; Cast: Syd Chaplin (Arthur Wells), Ruth Hiatt (Beatrice Braden), Tom McGuire (Col. Braden), Crauford Kent (Lord Dryden); Running time: 7 reels; Released Sep 1, 1927

*College* (1927); Producer: Joseph M. Schenck; Director: James W. Home; Screenplay: Carl Harbaugh, Bryan Foy; Cast: Buster Keaton (Ronald), Florence Turner (Mother), Ann Cornwall (Mary Haines), Harold Goodwin (Rival); Running time: 6 reels; Released Sep 10, 1927

*Sunrise: A Song of Two Humans* (1927); Producer: William Fox; Director: F. W. Murnau; Screenplay: Carl Mayer; Based on the book "Excursion to Tilsit" by Hermann Sudermann; Cast: George O'Brien (Man), Janet Gaynor (Wife), Margaret Livingston (Woman from the City); Running time: 95 m; Released Sep 23, 1927

*The Jazz Singer* (1927); Producer: Darryl F. Zanuck; Director: Alan Crosland; Screenplay: Alfred A. Cohn; Based on the play by Samson Raphaelson; Cast: Al Jolson (Jackie Rabinowitz), Warner Oland (Cantor Rabinowitz), Eugenie Besserer (Sara Rabinowitz), May McAvoy (Mary Dale); Running time: 89 m; Released Oct 6, 1927

*Hats Off* (presumed lost) (1927); Producer: Hal Roach; Director: Hal Yates; Screenplay: H.M. Walker; Cast: Stan Laurel, Oliver Hardy, James Finlayson, Anita Garvin; Running time: 2 reels; Released Nov 5, 1927

*Soldier Man* (1927); Producer: Mack Sennett; Director: Harry Edwards; Screenplay: Arthur Ripley, Frank Capra; Cast: Harry Langdon, Natalie Kingston, Vernon Dent, Frank Whitson; Running time: 3 reels; Released Nov 27, 1927

*The Circus* (1928); Producer: Charlie Chaplin; Director: Charlie Chaplin; Screenplay: Charlie Chaplin; Cast: Charlie Chaplin (Tramp), Allan Garcia (Circus Proprietor), Merna Kennedy (Merna); Running time: 7 reels; Released Jan 6, 1928

*The Chaser* (1928); Producer: Harry Langdon; Director: Harry Langdon; Screenplay: Robert Eddy, Clarence Hennecke, Harry McCoy; Story by Arthur Ripley; Cast: Harry Langdon, Gladys McConnell, Helen Hayward, Bud Jamison; Running time: 6 reels; Released Feb 12, 1928

*Feel My Pulse* (1928); Producer: ; Director: Gregory La Cava; Screenplay: Nicholas T. Barrows, Keene Thompson; Cast: Bebe Daniels (Barbara Manning), William Powell (Her Nemesis), Richard Arlen (Her Problem); Running time: 6 reels; Released Feb 26, 1928

*Ladies Night in a Turkish Bath* (1928); Producer: Edward Small, Charles R. Rogers; Director: Eddie Cline; Screenplay: Henry McCarthy, Gene Towne; Based on "Ladies' Night" by Charlton Andrews and Avery Hopwood; Cast: Dorothy Mackail (Helen Slocum), Jack Mulhall (Speed Dawson), James Finlayson (Pa Slocum), Guinn "Big Boy" Williams (Sweeney); Running time: 7 reels; Released Apr 1, 1928

*Speedy* (1928); Producer: Harold Lloyd; Director: Ted Wilde; Screenplay: John Grey, Lex Neal, Howard Rogers, Jay Howe; Albert DeMond (titles); Cast: Harold Lloyd (Sppedy), Ann Christy (Jane), Bert Woodruff (Pop Dillon), Brooks Benedict (Steve); Running time: 8 reels; Released Apr 7, 1928

*Steamboat Bill, Jr.* (1928); Producer: Joseph M. Schenck; Director: Charles F. Reisner; Screenplay: Carl Harbaugh; Cast: Buster Keaton (Willie Canfield), Ernest Torrence ("Steamboat Bill" Canfield), Tom Lewis (Tom Carter), Tom McGuire (John James King), Marion Byron (Mary King); Running time: 7 reels; Released May 20, 1928

*Should Married Men Go Home* (1928); Producer: Hal Roach; Director: Leo McCarey; Screenplay: Leo McCarey, James Parrott; Cast: Stan Laurel, Oliver Hardy, Edna Marion, Viola Richard; Running time: 2 reels; Released Sep 8, 1928

*The Cameraman* (1928); Producer: Buster Keaton; Director: Edward M. Sedgwick; Screenplay: Clyde Bruckman, Lew Lipton; Cast: Buster Keaton (Luke Shannon), Marceline Day (Sally), Harold Goodwin (Stagg); Running time: 8 reels; Released Sep 22, 1928

*Heart Trouble* (presumed lost) (1928); Producer: Harry Langdon; Director: Harry Langdon, Arthur Ripley (uncredited); Screenplay: Arthur Ripley, Harry Langdon; Gardner Bradford (titles); Cast: Harry Langdon (Harry Van Housen), Doris Dawson (Girl), Lionel Belmore (Adolph Van Housen), Madge Hunt (Mrs. Van Housen), Bud Jamison (Contractor); Running time: 6 reels; Released Oct 1, 1928

*Spite Marriage* (1929); Producer: Edward M. Sedgwick; Director: Edward M. Sedgwick; Screenplay: Lew Lipton, Ernest S. Pagano; Cast: Buster Keaton (Elmer Edgemont), Dorothy Sebastien (Trilby Drew), Edward Earle (Lionel Delmore), Leila Hyams (Ethyle Norcrosse); Running time: ; Released Apr 6, 1929

*Unaccustomed as We Are* (1929); Producer: Hal Roach; Director: Lewis R. Foster; Screenplay: Leo McCarey; Cast: Stan Laurel, Oliver Hardy, Mae Busch, Thelma Todd; Running time: 21 m; Released May 4, 1929

*Mother's Boy* (1929); Producer: Robert Kane; Director: Bradley Barker; Screenplay: Gene Markey; Cast: Morton Downey (Tommy O'Day), Beryl Mercer (Mrs. O'Day), John T. Doyle (Mr. O'Day), Helen Chandler (Rose Lyndon); Running time: 8 reels; Released May 5, 1929

*Double Whoopee* (1929); Producer: Hal Roach; Director: Lewis R. Foster; Screenplay: Leo McCarey; H.M. Walker (titles); Cast: Stan Laurel, Oliver Hardy, Jean Harlow, Ed Brandenburg; Running time: 2 reels; Released May 18, 1929

*Modern Love* (1929); Producer: Carl Laemmle, Jr.; Director: Arch Heath; Screenplay: Beatrice Van, Albert DeMond; Cast: Charley Chase (John Jones), Kathryn Crawford (Patricia Brown), Anita Garvin (Brunette), Betty Montgomery (Blonde); Running time: 60 m; Released Jul 21, 1929

*Hotter Than Hot* (1929); Producer: Hal Roach; Director: Lewis R. Foster; Screenplay: H.M. Walker; Cast: Harry Langdon, Thelma Todd, Edgar Kennedy; Running time: 20 m; Released Aug 17, 1929

*Welcome Danger* (1929); Producer: Harold Lloyd; Director: Clyde Bruckman (sound version), Ted Wilde, Mal St. Clair, and Clyde Bruckman (silent version); Screenplay: Felix Adler, Lex Neal, and Clyde Bruckman; Dialogue by Paul Gerald Smith; Cast: Harold Lloyd (Harold Bledsoe), Barbara Kent (Billie Lee), Noah Young (Patrick Clancy), Charles Middleton (John Thorne); Running time: 115 m; Released Oct 12, 1929

*The Head Guy* (1930); Producer: Hal Roach; Director: Hal Roach (uncredited) and Fred L. Guiol; Screenplay: H.M. Walker; Cast: Harry Langdon, Thelma Todd, Judith Barrett (credited as Nancy Dover), Eddie Dunn; Running time: 22 m; Released Jan 11, 1930

*The Love Parade* (1930); Producer: uncredited; Director: Ernst Lubitsch; Screenplay: Ernest Vajda, Guy Bolton; From the play "The Prince Consort" by Leon Xanrof and Jules Chancel; Cast: Maurice Chevalier (Count

Renard), Jeanette Macdonald (Queen Louise), Lupino Lane (Jacques), Lillian Roth (Lulu); Running time: 107 m; Released Jan 18, 1930

*Free and Easy* (1930); Producer: Edward M. Sedgwick; Director: Edward M. Sedgwick; Screenplay: Richard Schayer, Al Boasberg; Cast: Buster Keaton (Elmer Butts), Anita Pge (Elvira Plunkett), Robert Montgomery (Larry), Fred Niblo (Director); Running time: 92 m; Released Mar 22, 1930

*Doughboys* (1930); Producer: Buster Keaton; Director: Edward M. Sedgwick; Screenplay: Richard Schayer, Al Boasberg; Cast: Buster Keaton (Elmer Stuyvesant), Sally Eilers (Mary), Edward Brophy (Sgt. Brophy), Cliff Edwards (Nescopeck); Running time: 81 m; Released Aug 30, 1930

*City Lights* (1931); Producer: Charlie Chaplin; Director: Charlie Chaplin; Screenplay: Charlie Chaplin; Cast: Charlie Chaplin (Tramp), Virginia Cherrill (Blind girl), Harry Myers (Eccentric Millionaire); Running time: 87 m; Released Jan 30, 1931

*Parlor, Bedroom, and Bath* (1931); Producer: Buster Keaton; Director: Edward M. Sedgwick; Screenplay: Richard Schayer, Robert E. Hopkins; From the play by Charles W. Bell and Mark Swan; Cast: Buster Keaton (Reginald Irving), Charlotte Greenway (Polly Hathaway), Reginal Denny (Jeffrey Haywood), Sally Eilers (Virginia Embrey); Running time: 73 m; Released Feb 28, 1931

*The Smiling Lieutenant* (1931); Producer: Ernst Lubitsch; Director: Ernst Lubitsch; Screenplay: Ernest Vajda, Samson Raphaelson; Based on the operatta "A Waltz Dream" by Leopold Jackson and Felix Doermann, and the book by Hans Muller; Cast: Maurice Chevalier (Lt. Nikolaus von Preyn), Claudette Colbert (Franzi), Miriam Hopkins (Princess Anna), Charles Ruggles (Max); Running time: 95 m; Released May 22, 1931

*Sidewalks of New York* (1931); Producer: Lawrence Weingarten (uncredited); Director: Edward M. Sedgwick; Screenplay: George Landy, Paul Gerald Smith; Dialogue by Robert E. Hopkins, Eric Hatch;

Cast: Buster Keaton (Homer Van Tine Harmon), Anita Page (Margie), Cliff Edwards (Poggle); Running time: 75 m; Released Sep 26, 1931

*Strictly Dishonorable* (1931); Producer: Carl Laemmle, Jr.; Director: John M. Stahl; Screenplay: Gladys Lehman; From the play by Preston Sturges; Cast: Paul Lukas (Gus), Sidney Fox (Isabelle), Lewis Stone (Judge), George Meeker (Henry); Running time: 91 m; Released Dec 26, 1931

*Rich and Strange* (1931); Producer: John Maxwell; Director: Alfred Hitchcock; Screenplay: Alfred Hitchcock, Alma Reville, Val Valentine; Based on "Rich and Strange" by Dale Collins; Cast: Henry Kendall (Fred Hill), Joan Barry (Emily Hill), Percy Marmont (Commander Gordon), Betty Amann (The Princess); Running time: 83 m; Released Jan 1, 1932

*The Man I Killed* (A/K/A *Broken Lullaby*) (1932); Producer: Ernst Lubitsch; Director: Ernst Lubitsch; Screenplay: Samson Raphaelson, Ernest Vajda; Based on the play by Maurice Rostand; Cast: Lionel Barrymore (Dr. Holderin), Nancy Carroll (Elsa), Phillips Holmes (Paul Renard), Louise Carter (Frau Holderin); Running time: 94 m; Released Jan 19, 1932

*Helpmates* (1932); Producer: Hal Roach; Director: James Parrott; Screenplay: H.M. Walker; Cast: Stan Laurel, Oliver Hardy; Running time: 21 m; Released Jan 23, 1932

*A Passionate Plumber* (1932); Producer: Harry Rapf (uncredited); Director: Edward M. Sedgwick; Screenplay: Laurence E. Johnson; From "Her Cardboard Lover" by Jacques Deval; Cast: Buster Keaton (Elmer Tuttle), Jimmy Durante (McCracken), Irene Purcell (Patricia Alden), Polly Moran (Albine), Mona Maris (Nina); Running time: 73 m; Released Feb 6, 1932

*One Hour with You* (1932); Producer: Ernst Lubitsch; Director: Ernst Lubitsch; Screenplay: Samson Raphaelson; Based on the play "Only a Dream" by Lothar Schmidt; Cast: Maurice Chevalier (Dr. Andre Bertier), Jeanette MacDonald (Colette Bertier), Lili Damita (Mitzi Olivier), Roland Young (Prof.

Olivier); Running time: 80 m; Released Mar 25, 1932

*This Is the Night* (1932); Producer: Benjamin Glazer (uncredited); Director: Frank Tuttle; Screenplay: Benjamin Glazer, George Marion, Jr.; Cast: Lili Damita (Germaine), Charles Ruggles (Bunny West), Cary Grant (Stephen), Thelma Todd (Claire); Running time: 80 m; Released Apr 8, 1932

*Speak Easily* (1932); Producer: Lawrence Weingarten (uncredited); Director: Edward M. Sedwick; Screenplay: Ralph Spence, Laurence E. Johnson; From "Footlights" by Clarence Budington Kelland; Cast: Buster Keaton (Prof. Post), Thelma Todd (Eleanor Espere), Jimmy Durante (James), Ruth Selwyn (Pansy Peets), Hedda Hopper (Mrs. Peets); Running time: 82 m; Released Aug 13, 1932

*Movie Crazy* (1932); Producer: Harold Lloyd; Director: Clyde Bruckman, Harold Lloyd (uncredited); Screenplay: Agnes Christine Johnson, John Grey, Felix Adler; Dialogue by Vincent Lawrence; Cast: Harold Lloyd (Harold Hall), Constance Cummings (Mary Sears), Kenneth Thomson (Vance), Sidney Jarvis (Director); Running time: 96 m (later cut to 84 m); Released Sep 23, 1932

*Trouble in Paradise* (1932); Producer: Ernst Lubitsch; Director: Ernst Lubitsch; Screenplay: Samson Raphaelson; Based on the play "The Honest Finder" by Aladar Laszlo; Cast: Miriam Hopkins (Lily), Kay Francis (Madame Mariette Colet), Herbert Marshall (Gaston Monescu), C. Aubrey Smith (Adolph Giron); Running time: 83 m; Released Nov 8, 1932

*Hallelujah I'm a Bum* (1933); Producer: uncredited; Director: Lewis Milestone; Screenplay: Ben Hecht; Cast: Al Jolson (Bumper), Harry Langdon (Egghead), Madge Evans (June Marcher), Frank Morgan (Mayor John Hastings); Running time: 82 m; Released Feb 3, 1933

*What, No Beer?* (1933); Producer: Lawrence Weingarten (uncredited); Director: Edward M. Sedgwick; Screenplay: Carey Wilson; Story by Robert E. Hopkins, Additional Dialogue by Jack Cluett; Cast: Buster Keaton (Elmer J. Butts), Jimmy Durante (Jimmy Potts), Phyllis Barry (Hortense); Running time: 66 m; Released Feb 10, 1933

*Tied for Life* (1933); Producer: Arvid E. Gillstrom; Director: Arvid E. Gilstrom; Screenplay: Dean Ward, Vernon Dent; Cast: Harry Langdon, Vernon Dent, Nell O'Day, Mabel Forest; Running time: 20 m; Released Jul 2, 1933

*Dinner at Eight* (1933); Producer: David O. Selznick; Director: George Cukor; Screenplay: Francis Marion, Herman J. Mankiewicz; Cast: Marie Dressler (Carlotta Vance), Lionel Barrymore (Oliver Jordan), Billie Burke (Millicent Jordan), Jean Harlow (Kitty Packard); Running time: 113 m; Released Aug 29, 1933

*Rafter Romance* (1933); Producer: Merian C. Cooper; Director: William A. Seiter; Screenplay: Glenn Tryon, H.W. Hanemann, Sam Mintz; Based on the book by John Wells; Cast: Ginger Rogers (Mary Carroll), Norman Foster (Jack Bacon), Robert Benchley (H. Harrington Hubbell), Laura Hope Crews (Elisa Peabody Whittington Smythe); Running time: 72 m; Released Sep 1, 1933

*The Stage Hand* (1933); Producer: Arvid E. Gillstrom; Director: Harry Langdon; Screenplay: Harry Langdon, Eddie Davis; Cast: Harry Langdon, Marel Foster, Ira Hayward, Eddie Shubert; Running time: 20 m; Released Sep 8, 1933

*Bombshell* (1933); Producer: Irving Thalberg; Director: Victor Fleming (uncredited); Screenplay: John Lee Mahin, Jules Furthman; From the play by Caroline Francke and Mack Crane; Cast: Jean Harlow (Lola), Lee Tracy (Space), Frank Morgan (Pops), Franchot Tone (Gifford); Running time: 96 m (later cut to 84 m); Released Oct 13, 1933

*Duck Soup* (1933); Producer: Herman J. Mankiewicz; Director: Leo McCarey; Screenplay: Bert Kalmar, Harry Ruby, Arthur Sheekman, Nat Perrin; Cast: Groucho Marx (Rufus T. Firefly), Margaret Dumont (Mrs. Teasdale), Chico Marx (Chicolini), Harpo Marx (Pinky); Running time: 70 m; Released Nov 17, 1933

*Design for Living* (1933); Producer: Ernst Lubitsch; Director: Ernst Lubitsch; Screenplay: Ben Hecht; Based on the play by Noel Coward; Cast: Fredric March (Tom Chambers), Gary Cooper (George Curtis), Miriam Hopkins (Gilda Farrell), Edward Everett Horton (Max Plunkett); Running time: 90 m; Released Nov 22, 1933

*Dancing Lady* (1933); Producer: David O. Selznick; Director: Robert Z. Leonard; Screenplay: Allen Rivkin, P.J. Wolfson; Cast: Joan Crawford (Janie Barlow), Clark Gable (Patch Gallagher), Franchot Tone (Tod Newton), May Robson (Dolly Todhunter); Running time: 92 m; Released Nov 24, 1933

*The King of the Champs-Elysees* (1934); Producer: Seymour Nebenzahl; Director: Max Nosseck; Screenplay: Arnold Yipp; Dialogue by Yves Mirande; Cast: Buster Keaton (Buster Garnier/Jim Le Balafre), Paulette Dubots (Germaine), Colette Darfeuil (Simone), Madeline Guitty (Madame Garnier); Running time: 70 m; Released Jan 5, 1934

*Six of a Kind* (1934); Producer: uncredited; Director: Leo McCarey; Screenplay: Keene Thompson, Douglas MacLean, Walter DeLeon, Harry Rsukin; Cast: Charles Ruggles (J. Pinkham Whinney), Mary Boland (Flora Whinney), George Burns (George Edward), Gracie Allen (Gracie Devore); Running time: 62 m; Released Feb 9, 1934

*It Happened One Night* (1934); Producer: Harry Cohn, Frank Capra; Director: Frank Capra; Screenplay: Robert Riskin; Based on "Night Bus" by Samuel Hopkins Adams; Cast: Clark Gable (Peter Warne), Claudette Colbert (Ellen Andrews), Walter Connolly (Alexander Andrews), Jameson Thomas (King Westley); Running time: 105 m; Released Feb 22, 1934

*Four Parts* (1934); Producer: Hal Roach; Director: Charley Chase (Charles Parrott), Eddie Dunn; Screenplay: uncredited; Cast: Charley Chase, Betty Mack, Florence Roberts; Running time: 19 m; Released Mar 17, 1934

*Twentieth Century* (1934); Producer: Howard Hawks; Director: Howard Hawks; Screenplay: Ben Hecht, Charles MacArthur; Cast: Carole Lombard (Mildred Plotka), John Barrymore (Oscar Jaffe), Roscoe Karns (Owen O'Malley), Walter Connolly (Oliver Webb); Running time: 91 m; Released May 3, 1934

*The Thin Man* (1934); Producer: Hunt Stromberg; Director: W.S. Van Dyke; Screenplay: Albert Hackett, Frances Goodrich; From the novel by Dashiell Hammett; Cast: William Powell (Nick Charles), Myrna Loy (Nora Charles), Maureen O'Sullivan (Dorothy Wynant), Nat Pendleton (Guild); Running time: 91 m; Released May 25, 1934

*Hollywood Party* (1934); Producer: Irving Thalberg; Director: Roland Boleslawski, Edmund Goulding, Russell Mack, Roy Rowland, Sam Wood, Charles Resiner; Screenplay: Howard Dietz, Arthur Kober; Cast: Stan Laurel, Oliver Hardy, Jimmy Durante, Polly Moran; Running time: 68 m; Released Jun 1, 1934

*The Merry Widow* (1934); Producer: Irving Thalberg; Director: Ernst Lubitsch; Screenplay: Ernest Vajda, Samson Raphaelson; Based on the operetta by Franz Lehar, libretto and lyrics by Victor Leon and Leo Stein, additional music by Richard Rodgers, additional lyrics by Lorenz Hart anb Gus Kahn; Cast: Maurice Chevalier (Prince Danilo), Jeanette MacDonald (Sonia), Edward Everett Horton (Ambassador Popoff), Una Merkel (Queen Dolores); Running time: 99 m; Released Oct 11, 1934

*The Gay Divorcee* (1934); Producer: Pandro S. Berman; Director: Mark Sandrich; Screenplay: George Marion, Jr., Dorothy Yost, Edward Kaufman; Cast: Fred Astaire (Guy Holden), Ginger Rogers (Mimi), Alice Brady (Hortense), Edward Everett Horton (Egbert); Running time: 107 m; Released Oct 12, 1934

*Ruggles of Red Gap* (1935); Producer: Arthur Hornblow, Jr.; Director: Leo McCarey; Screenplay: Walter DeLeon, Harlan Thompson; Based on the novel "Ruggles of Red Gap" by Harry Leon Wilson; Cast: Charles

Laughton (Ruggles), Charlie Ruggles (Egbert Floud), Mary Boland (Effie Floud), Zasu Pitts (Mrs. Judson); Running time: 90 m; Released Feb 19, 1935

*Top Hat* (1935); Producer: Pandro S. Berman; Director: Mark Sandrich; Screenplay: Allan Scott, Dwight Taylor, Ben Holmes, Ralph Spence; Based on the play "Scandal in Budapest" by Sándor Faragó and the play "A Girl Who Dares" by Aladar Laszlo; Cast: Fred Astaire (Jerry Travers), Ginger Rogers (Dale Tremont), Edward Everett Horton (Horace Hardwick), Helen Broderick (Madge); Running time: 101 m; Released Sep 6, 1935

*Hands Across the Table* (1935); Producer: E. Lloyd Sheldon; Director: Mitchell Leisen; Screenplay: Norman Krasna; Cast: Carole Lombard (Regi Allen), Fred MacMurray (Ted Drew), Ralph Bellamy (Allen Macklyn), Astrid Allwyn (Vivian Snowden); Running time: 80 m; Released Oct 18, 1935

*The Timid Young Man* (1935); Producer: Mack Sennett; Director: Mack Sennett; Screenplay: uncredited; Cast: Buster Keaton (Milton), Lona Andre (Helen), Tiny Sandford (Mortimer), Kitty McHugh (Milton's Fiancee); Running time: 20 m; Released Oct 25, 1935

*Alice Adams* (1935); Producer: Pedro S. Berman; Director: George Stevens; Screenplay: Dorothy Yost, Mortimer Offner, Jane Murfin; Based on a novel by Booth Tarkington; Cast: Katharine Hepburn (Alice Adams), Fred MacMurray (Arthur Russell), Fred Stone (Virgil Adams), Evelyn Venable (Mildred Palmer); Running time: 99 m; Released Nov 13, 1935

*A Night at the Opera* (1935); Producer: Irving Thalberg; Director: Sam Wood; Screenplay: George S. Kaufman, Morrie Ryskind; Cast: Groucho Marx (Otis P. Driftwood), Harpo Marx (Tomasso), Chico Marx (Fiorello), Margaret Dumont (Mrs. Claypool); Running time: 93 m; Released Nov 15, 1935

*An Old Spanish Custom* (A/K/A *The Invader*) (1936); Producer: Sam Spiegel, Harold Richman; Director: Adrian Brunel; Screenplay: Walter Greenwood; Cast: Buster

Keaton (Leander Proudfoot), Lupita Tovar (Luipta Malez), Esme Percy (Jose); Running time: 61 m; Released Jan 2, 1936

*Modern Times* (1936); Producer: Charlie Chaplin; Director: Charlie Chaplin; Screenplay: Charlie Chaplin; Cast: Charlie Chaplin (Worker), Paulette Goddard (Gamine); Running time: 87 m; Released Feb 5, 1936

*The Milky Way* (1936); Producer: E. Loyd Sheldon; Director: Leo McCarey; Screenplay: Grover Jones, Frank Butler, Richard Connell; Based on the play by Lynn Root and Harry Clork; Cast: Harold Lloyd (Burleigh Sullivan), Adolphe Menjou (Gabby Sloan), Verree Teasdale (Ann Westley), Helen Mack (Mae Sullivan); Running time: 88 m; Released Feb 7, 1936

*Mr. Deeds Goes to Town* (1936); Producer: Frank Capra; Director: Frank Capra; Screenplay: Robert Riskin; Story by Clarence Budington Kelland; Cast: Gary Cooper (Longfellow Deeds), Jean Arthur (Babe Bennett), George Bancroft (MacWade), Lionel Stander (Cornelius Cobb); Running time: 115 m; Released Apr 12, 1936

*Neighborhood House* (1936); Producer: Hal Roach; Director: Charley Chase (Charles Parrott), Harold Law; Screenplay: uncredited; Cast: Charley Chase, Rosina Lawrence, Darla Hood, George Meeker; Running time: 58 m; Released May 9, 1936

*The Princess Comes Across* (1936); Producer: Arthur Hornblow, Jr.; Director: William K. Howard; Screenplay: Walter DeLeon, Francis Martin, Don Hartman, Frank Butler; Based on the novel "Death Cab" by Louis Lucien Rogger; Cast: Carole Lombard (Wanda Nash), Fred MacMurray (King Mantell), Douglass Dumbrille (Inspector Lorel), Alison Skipworth (Lady Gertrude Allwyn); Running time: 75 m; Released May 22, 1936

*Disorder in the Court* (1936); Producer: Jules White; Director: Preston Black; Screenplay: Felix Adler; Cast: Moe Howard, Larry Fine, Curly Howard, Bud Jamison; Running time: 17 m; Released May 30, 1936

*My Man Godfrey* (1936); Producer: Charles R. Rogers; Director: Gregory La Cava; Screenplay: Morrie Ryskind; Based on the novel by Eric Hatch; Cast: William Powell (Godfrey), Carole Lombard (Irene Bullock), Alice Brady (Angelica Bullock), Eugene Pallette (Alexander Bullock); Running time: 94 m; Released Sep 6, 1936

*Theodora Goes Wild* (1936); Producer: Everett Riskin; Director: Richard Boleslawski; Screenplay: Mary McCarthy, Sidney Buchman; Cast: Irene Dunne (Theodora Lynn), Melvyn Douglas (Michael Grant), Thurston Hall (Arthur Stevenson), Robert Greig (Uncle John); Running time: 94 m; Released Nov 12, 1936

*Mixed Magic* (1936); Producer: E.H. Allen; Director: Raymond Kane; Screenplay: Arthur Jarrett, Marcy Klauber; Cast: Buster Keaton (Elmer), Eddie Lambert (Professor Spumoni), Marlyn Stuart (Mary), Eddie Hall (Hector); Running time: 17 m; Released Nov 20, 1936

*Make Way for Tomorrow* (1937); Producer: Adolph Zukor; Director: Leo McCarey; Screenplay: Viña Delmar; Cast: Victor Moore (Pa Cooper), Beulah Bondi (Ma Cooper), Thomas Mitchell (George Cooper), Fay Bainter (Anita Cooper); Running time: 92 m; Released May 9, 1937

*Easy Living* (1937); Producer: Arthur Hornblow, Jr.; Director: Mitchell Leisen; Screenplay: Preston Sturges; Based on a story by Vera Caspary; Cast: Jean Arthur (Mary Smith), Edward Arnold (J.B. Ball), Ray Milland (John Ball, Jr.), Luis Alberni (Mr. Louis Louis); Running time: 88 m; Released Jul 16, 1937

*Artists and Models* (1937); Producer: Lewis E. Gensler; Director: Raoul Walsh; Screenplay: Walter DeLeon, Francis Martin, Keene Thompson; Story by Sig Herzig, Gene Thackery; Cast: Jack Benny (Mac Brewster), Ida Lupino (Paula Sewell), Richard Arlen (Alan Townsend), Gail Patrick (Cynthia Wentworth), Ben Blue (Jupiter Pluvius); Running time: 97 m; Released Aug 4, 1937

*The Awful Truth* (1937); Producer: ; Director: Leo McCarey; Screenplay: Viña Delmar; Based on a play by Arthur Richman; Cast: Irene Dunne (Lucy Warriner), Cary Grant (Jerry Warriner), Ralph Bellamy (Daniel Leeson), Cecil Cunningham (Aunt Patsy), Molly Lamont (Barbara Vance); Running time: 91 m; Released Oct 20, 1937

*Nothing Sacred* (1937); Producer: David O. Selznick; Director: William A. Wellman; Screenplay: Ben Hecht; Based on the short story "Letter to the Editor" by James H. Street; Cast: Carole Lombard (Hazel Flagg), Fredric March (Wally Cook), Walter Connolly (Oliver Stone), Sig Ruman (Dr. Emil Eggelhoffer); Running time: 77 m; Released Nov 25, 1937

*True Confession* (1937); Producer: ; Director: Wesley Ruggles; Screenplay: Claude Binyon; From the play by Louis Verneuil and Georges Berr; Cast: Carole Lombard (Helen Bartlett), Fred MacMurray (Kenneth Bartlett), John Barrymore (Charley Jasper), Una Merkel (Daisy McClure); Running time: 85 m; Released Dec 24, 1937

*Bringing Up Baby* (1938); Producer: Cliff Reid, Howard Hawks; Director: Howard Hawks; Screenplay: Dudley Nichols; Based on the short story by Hagar Wilde; Cast: Katharine Hepburn (Susan Vance), Cary Grant (Dr. David Huxley), Charles Ruggles (Major Applegate), Walter Catlett (Constable Slocum); Running time: 102 m; Released Feb 16, 1938

*Vivacious Lady* (1938); Producer: George Stevens; Director: George Stevens; Screenplay: P.J. Wolfson, Ernest Pagano; Story by I.A.R. Wylie; Cast: Ginger Rogers (Francey), Jimmy Stewart (Prof. Peter Morgan, Jr.), James Ellison (Keith Morgan), Charles Coburn (Peter Morgan, Sr.); Running time: 90 m; Released May 13, 1938

*Holiday* (1938); Producer: Everett Riskin; Director: George Cukor; Screenplay: Donald Ogden Stewart, Sidney Buchman; From the play by Philip Barry; Cast: Katharine Hepburn (Linda Seton), Cary Grant (Johnny Case), Doris Nolan (Julia Seton), Edward Everett Horton (Prof. Nick Potter); Running time: 95 m; Released Jun 15, 1938

*Professor Beware* (1938); Producer: Harold Lloyd; Director: Elliott Nugent; Screenplay: Delmer Daves; Adaptation by Jack Cunningham and Clyde Bruckman from a story by

Crampton Harris, Francis M and Marion B. Cockrell; Cast: Harold Lloyd (Prof. Lambert), Phyllis Welch (Jane Van Buren), Raymond Walburn (Judge Marshall), William Frawley (Snoop Donlan); Running time: 93 m; Released Jul 29, 1938

*Too Hot to Handle* (1938); Producer: Lawrence Weingarten; Director: Jack Conway; Screenplay: Laurence Stallings, John Lee Mahin, Buster Keaton (uncredited); Cast: Clark Gable (Chris Hunter), Myrna Loy (Alma Harding), Walter Pidgeon (William Dennis), Walter Connolly (Arthur MacArthur); Running time: 106 m; Released Sep 16, 1938

*Room Service* (1938); Producer: Pandro S. Berman; Director: William A. Seiter; Screenplay: Glenn Tryon, Philip Loeb; From the play by Allen Boretz and John Murray; Cast: Groucho Marx (Gordon Miller), Chico Marx (Binelli), Harpo Marx (Faker), Lucille Ball (Christine Marlowe); Running time: 78 m; Released Sep 30, 1938

*Next Time I Marry* (1938); Producer: Cliff Reid; Director: Garson Kanin; Screenplay: John Twist, Helen Meinardi; Story by Thames Williamson; Cast: Lucille Ball (Nancy Crocker Fleming), James Ellison (Anthony J. Anthony), Lee Bowman (Count Georgi), Mantan Moreland (Tilby); Running time: 65 m; Released Dec 9, 1938

*Midnight* (1939); Producer: Arthur Hornblow, Jr.; Director: Mitchell Leisen; Screenplay: Charles Brackett and Billy Wilder; Story by Edwin Justus Mayer, Franz Schulz; Cast: Claudette Colbert (Eve Peabody), Don Ameche (Tobor Czerny), John Barrymore (Georges Flammarion), Mary Astor (Helene Flammarion); Running time: 94 m; Released Mar 15, 1939

*Pest from the West* (1939); Producer: Jules White; Director: Del Lord; Screenplay: Clyde Bruckman; Cast: Buster Keaton (Sir), Lorna Grey (Conchita), Gino Corrado (Martino), Richard Fiske (Bullfighter); Running time: 19 m; Released Jun 16, 1939

*Bachelor Mother* (1939); Producer: Buddy G. DeSylva; Director: Garson Kanin; Screenplay: Norman Krasna; Story by Felix Jackson; Cast: Ginger Rogers (Polly Parrish), David Niven (David Merlin), Charles Coburn (J.B. Merlin), Frank Albertson (Freddie Miller); Running time: 82 m; Released Aug 4, 1939

*Fifth Avenue Girl* (1939); Producer: Gregory La Cava; Director: Gregory La Cava; Screenplay: Allan Scott; Cast: Ginger Rogers (Mary Grey), Walter Connolly (Timothy Borden), Tim Holt (Tim Borden), Veree Teasdale (Martha Borden); Running time: 83 m; Released Sep 22, 1939

*Ninotchka* (Ernst Lubitsch); Producer: Ernst Lubitsch; Director: Ernst Lubitsch; Screenplay: Charles Brackett, Billy Wilder, Walter Reisch; Based on a story by Melchior Lengyel; Cast: Greta Garbo (Ninotchka), Melvyn Douglas (Count d'Algout), Ina Claire (Grand Duchess Swana), Bela Lugosi (Commissar Razinin); Running time: 110 m; Released Oct 6, 1939

*Hollywood Cavalcade* (1939); Producer: Darryl F. Zanuck; Director: Irving Cummings; Screenplay: Ernest Pascal; Story by Hilary Lynn, Brown Holmes; Cast: Alice Faye (Molly Adair Hayden), Don Ameche (Mike Connors), Alan Curtis (Nicky Hayden), Buster Keaton (Himself); Running time: 97 m; Released Oct 13, 1939

*The Shop Around the Corner* (1940); Producer: Ernst Lubitsch; Director: Ernst Lubitsch; Screenplay: Samson Raphaelson; Based on the play "Parfumerie" by Nikolus Laszlo; Cast: Jimmy Stewart (Alfred Kralik), Margaret Sullavan (Klara Novak), Frank Morgan (Hugo Matuschek), Joseph Schildkraut (Ferencz Vadas); Running time: 97 m; Released Jan 12, 1940

*His Girl Friday* (1940); Producer: Howard Hawks (uncredited); Director: Howard Hawks; Screenplay: Charles Lederer; From the play "The Front Page" by Ben Hecht; Cast: Cary Grant (Walter Burns), Rosalind Russell (Hildy Johnson), Ralph Bellamy (Bruce Baldwin), Clarence Kolb (Mayor); Running time: 92 m; Released Jan 18, 1940

*He Married His Wife* (1940); Producer: uncredited; Director: Roy Del Ruth; Screenplay: Sam Hellman, Darrell Ware, Lynn Starling, John O'Hara; Story by Erna

Lazarus, Scott Darling; Cast: Joel McCrea (T.H. Randall), Nancy Kelly (Valerie), Roland Young (Bill Carter), Mary Boland (Ethel); Running time: 83 m; Released Jan 19, 1940

*Remember the Night* (1940); Producer: Mitchell Leisen; Director: Mitchell Leisen; Screenplay: Preston Sturges; Cast: Barbara Stanwyck (Lee Leander), Fred MacMurray (John Sargent), Beulah Bondi (Mrs. Sargent); Running time: 91 m; Released Jan 19, 1940

*Goodness a Ghost* (1940); Producer: Lou Brock; Director: Harry D'Arcy; Screenplay: Harry Langdon; Story by George Jeske, Arthur V. Jones; Cast: Harry Langdon; Running time: 16 m; Released Mar 8, 1940

*My Favorite Wife* (1940); Producer: Leo McCarey; Director: Garson Kanin; Screenplay: Leo McCarey, Garson Kanin, John McClain, Samuel and Bella Spewack; Cast: Irene Dunne (Ellen Arden), Cary Grant (Nick Arden), Randolph Scott (Stephen Burkett), Gail Patrick (Bianca Bates); Running time: 88 m; Released May 17, 1940

*Foreign Correspondent* (1940); Producer: Walter Wanger; Director: Alfred Hitchcock; Screenplay: Charles Benson, Joan Harrison; Cast: Joel McCrea (John Jones), Laraine Day (Carol Fisher), Herbert Marshall (Stephen Fisher), George Sanders (Scott ffolliott); Running time: 120 m; Released Aug 16, 1940

*The Great McGinty* (1940); Producer: Paul Jones; Director: Preston Sturges; Screenplay: Preston Sturges; Cast: Brian Donlevy (Dan McGinty), Muriel Angelus (Catherine McGinty), Akim Tamiroff (The Boss), William Demarest (Skeeters); Running time: 82 m; Released Aug 23, 1940

*The Great Dictator* (1940); Producer: Charlie Chaplin; Director: Charlie Chaplin; Screenplay: Charlie Chaplin; Cast: Charlie Chaplin (Adenoiud Hynkel/Jewish barber), Paulette Goddard (Hannah), Jack Oakie (Benzino Napaloni); Running time: 125 m; Released Oct 15, 1940

*Christmas in July* (1940); Producer: Paul Jones; Director: Preston Sturges; Screenplay: Preston Sturges; Cast: Dick Powell (Jimmy MacDonald), Ellen Drew (Betty Casey), Raymond Walburn (Dr. Maxford), William Demarest (Mr. Bildocker); Running time: 67 m; Released Oct 25, 1940

*The Philadelphia Story* (1940); Producer: Joseph L. Mankiewicz; Director: George Cukor; Screenplay: Donald Ogden Stewart; Based on the play "The Philadelphia Story" by Philip Barry; Cast: Katharine Hepburn (Tracy Lord), Cary Grant (C.K. Dexter Haven), Jimmy Stewart (Mike Connor), Ruth Hussey (Liz Imbrie); Running time: 112 m; Released Dec 26, 1940

*Mr. and Mrs. Smith* (1941); Producer: Harry E, Edington; Director: Alfred Hitchcock; Screenplay: Norman Krasna; Cast: Carole Lombard (Ann Smith), Robert Montgomery (David Smith), Gene Raymond (Jeff Custer), Jack Carson (Chuck Benson); Running time: 95 m; Released Jan 31, 1941

*A Girl, a Guy, and a Gob* (1941); Producer: Harold Lloyd; Director: Richard Wallace; Screenplay: Frank Ryan, Bert Granet, Sarah Y. Mason, Victor Heerman; Story by Grover Jones; Cast: Lucille Ball (Dot Duncan), George Murphy (Coffee Cup), Edmond O'Brien (Stephen Herrick), Franklin Pangborn (Pet Shop Owner); Running time: 90 m; Released Mar 14, 1941

*The Lady Eve* (1941); Producer: Paul Jones; Director: Preston Sturges; Screenplay: Preston Sturges; Based on a story by Monckton Hoffe; Cast: Barbara Stanwyck (Jean), Henry Fonda (Charles), Charles Coburn (Col. Harrington; Running time: 94 m; Released Mar 21, 1941

*That Uncertain Feeling* (1941); Producer: Ernst Lubitsch; Director: Ernst Lubitsch; Screenplay: Donald Ogden Stewart, Walter Reisch; From a play by Victorien Sardou and Emile DeNajac; Cast: Merle Oberon (Jill Baker), Melvyn Douglas (Larry Baker), Burgess Meredith (Alexander Sebastian), Alan Mowbray (Dr. Vengard); Running time: 84 m; Released Apr 20, 1941

*Meet John Doe* (1941); Producer: Frank Capra; Director: Frank Capra; Screenplay: Robert Riskin; Based on a story by

Richard Connell and Robert Presnell, Sr.; Cast: Gary Cooper (John Doe), Barbara Stanwyck (Ann Mitchell), Edward Arnold (D.B. Norton), Walter Brennan (The Colonel); Running time: 122 m; Released May 3, 1941

*Sullivan's Travels* (1941); Producer: Preston Sturges; Director: Preston Sturges; Screenplay: Preston Sturges; Cast: Joel McCrea (John Sullivan), Veronica Lake (Girl), Robert Warwick (Mr. LeBrand), Robert Greig (Butler); Running time: 90 m; Released Feb 6, 1942

*To Be or Not to Be* (1942); Producer: Ernst Lubitsch; Director: Ernst Lubitsch; Screenplay: Edwin Justus Mayer; Based on a story by Melchior Lengyel and Ernst Lubitsch; Cast: Jack Benny (Joseph Tura), Carole Lombard (Maria Tura), Robert Stack (Lt. Sobinski), Stanley Ridges (Prof. Siletsky); Running time: 99 m; Released Mar 6, 1942

*Lady in a Jam* (1942); Producer: Gregory La Cava; Director: Gregory La Cava; Screenplay: Eugene Thackrey, Francis M. Cockrell; Cast: Irene Dunne (Jane Palmer), Ralph Bellamy (Stanley), Patric Knowles (Dr. Enright), Eugene Pallette (Billingsley); Running time: 78 m; Released Jun 19, 1942

*Palm Beach Story* (1942); Producer: Buddy G. DeSylva; Director: Preston Sturges; Screenplay: Preston Sturges; Cast: Claudette Colbert (Gerry), Joel McCrea (Tom), Mary Astor (Princess Centimillia), Rudy Vallee (J.D. Hackensacker III); Running time: 88 m; Released Jan 1, 1943

*Slightly Dangerous* (1943); Producer: Pandro S. Berman; Director: Wesley Ruggles; Screenplay: Charles Lederer, George Oppenheimer; Story by Aileen Hamilton; Cast: Lana Turner (Peggy Evans), Robert Young (Bob Stuart), Walter Brennan (Cornelius Burden); Running time: 94 m; Released Apr 1, 1943

*The More the Merrier* (1943); Producer: George Stevens; Director: George Stevens; Screenplay: Robert Russell, Frank Ross, Richard Flournoy, Lewis R. Foster; Cast: Jean Arthur (Connie Milligan), Joel McCrea (Joe Carter), Charles Coburn (Ben-

jamin Dingle); Running time: 104 m; Released May 13, 1943

*Heaven Can Wait* (1943); Producer: Ernst Lubitsch; Director: Ernst Lubitsch; Screenplay: Samson Raphaelson; Based on the play "Birthday" by Laszlo Bus-Fekete; Cast: Gene Tierney (Martha Van Cleve), Don Ameche (Henry Van Cleve), Laird Cregar (His Excellency), Eugene Pallette (E.F. Strabel); Running time: 112 m; Released Aug 11, 1943

*The Miracle of Morgan's Creek* (1943); Producer: Preston Sturges (uncredited); Director: Preston Sturges; Screenplay: Preston Sturges; Cast: Eddie Bracken (Norval Jones), Betty Hutton (Trudy Kockenlocker), William Demarest (Constable Kockenlocker), Porter Hall (Justice of the Peace); Running time: 98 m; Released Jan 19, 1944

*Lifeboat* (1944); Producer: Kenneth Macgowan; Director: Alfred Hitchcock; Screenplay: John Steinbeck, Jo Swerling; Cast: Tallulah Bankhead (Connie Porter), William Bendix (Gus), Walter Slezak (Willi), Mary Anderson (Alice MacKenzie); Running time: 97 m; Released Jan 28, 1944

*Hail the Conquering Hero* (1944); Producer: Preston Sturges (uncredited); Director: Preston Sturges; Screenplay: Preston Sturges; Cast: Eddie Bracken (Woodrow Truesmith), Ella Raines (libby), William Demarest (Sgt. Heffelfinger), Georgia Caine (Mrs. Truesmith); Running time: 101 m; Released Aug 9, 1944

*Cluny Brown* (1946); Producer: Ernst Lubitsch; Director: Ernst Lubitsch; Screenplay: Samuel Hoffenstein, Elizabeth Reinhardt; Based on the novel by Margery Sharp; Cast: Charles Boyer (Adam Belinski), Jennifer Jones (Cluny Brown), Peter Lawford (Andrew Carmel), Helen Walker (Betty Cream); Running time: 100 m; Released Jun 1, 1946

*The Sin of Harold Diddlebock* (A/K/A *Mad Wednesday*) (1947); Producer: Preston Sturges; Director: Preston Sturges; Screenplay: Preston Sturges; Cast: Harold Lloyd (Harold Diddlebock), Frances Ramsden

(Miss Otis), Jimmy Conlin (Wormy), Raymond Walburn (E.J. Waggleberry), Edgar Kennedy (Bartender); Running time: 89 m; Released Apr 4, 1947

*A Southern Yankee* (1948); Producer: Paul Jones; Director: Edward M. Sedgwick; Screenplay: Melvin Frank, Norman Panama; Cast: Red Skelton (Aubrey Filmore), Brian Donlevy (Kurt Devlynn), Arlene Dahl (Sallyann Weatharby), George Couloris (The Grey Spider); Running time: 90 m; Released Aug 5, 1948

*That Lady in Ermine* (1948); Producer: Ernst Lubitsch; Director: Ernst Lubitsch and Otto Preminger (uncredited); Screenplay: Samson Raphaelson; Based on the operetta by Rudolf Schanzer and Ernst Welisch; Cast: Betty Grable (Francesca/Angelina), Douglas Fairbanks, Jr. (Col. Teglas/The Duke), Cesar Romero (Count Mario), Walter Abel (Major Horvath/Benvenuto); Running time: 89 m; Released Aug 24, 1948

*The Beautiful Blonde from Bashful Bend* (1949); Producer: Preston Sturges; Director: Preston Sturges; Screenplay: Preston Sturges, Earl Felton; Cast: Betty Grable (Winfred Jones), Cesar Romero (Blackie Jobero), Rudy Vallee (Charles Hingelman), Olga San Juan (Conchita); Running time: 77 m; Released May 27, 1949

*Watch the Birdie* (1950); Producer: Harry Ruskin; Director: Jack Donohue; Screenplay: Ivan Tors, Devery Freeman, Harry Ruskin; Cast: Red Skelton (Rusty), Arlene Dahl (Lucia), Ann Miller (Miss Lucky Vista), Leon Ames (Grantland Farns); Running time: 71 m; Released Dec 11, 1950

*Singin' in the Rain* (1952); Producer: Arthur Freed; Director: Gene Kelly, Stanley Donen; Screenplay: Betty Comden, Adolph Green; Cast: Gene Kelly (Don Lockwood), Debbie Reynolds (Kathy Selden), Jean Hagen (Lina Lamont), Donald O'Connor (Cosmo Brown); Running time: 103 m; Released Mar 27, 1952

*L'Incantevole Nemica* (1953); Producer: Jules Borkon, Dario Sabatello; Director: Claudio Gora; Screenplay: Edoardo Anton, Jean-Bernard-Luc, Claudio Gora Age; Story by Vittorio Metz and Marcello Marchesi; Cast: Silvana Pampanini (Silvia), Robert Lamoureux (Roberto), Carlo Campanini (Albertini), Ugo Tognazzi (Factory Director); Running time: 86 m; Released Jun 14, 1953

*Abbott and Costello Meet the Keystone Kops* (1955); Producer: Howard Christie; Director: Charles Lamont; Screenplay: John Grant; Story by Lee Loeb; Cast: Bud Abbott (Slim), Lou Costello (Tubby), Fred Clark (Joseph Gorman), Lynn Bari (Leota Van Cleef), Mack Sennett (Himself); Running time: 80 m; Released Feb 21, 1955

*The Silent Partner* (*Screen Diector's Playhouse*) (1955); Producer: Hal Roach; Director: George Marshall; Screenplay: Barbara Avedon; Cast: Buster Keaton (Kelsey Dutton), Zasu Pitts (Selma), Joe E. Brown (Arthur Vail), Evelyn Ankers (Miss Loving); Running time: 25 m; Released Dec 21, 1955

*The Golden Age of Comedy* (1957); Producer: Robert Youngson; Director: Robert Youngson; Screenplay: René Clair, Robert Youngson; Cast: Stan Laurel, Oliver Hardy, Carole Lombard, Ben Turpin; Running time: 79 m; Released Dec 26, 1957

*Some Like It Hot* (1959); Producer: Billy Wilder; Director: Billy Wilder; Screenplay: Billy Wilder, I.A.L. Diamond; Story by Robert Thoeren, Michael Logan; Cast: Marilyn Monroe (Sugar Kane Kowalczyk), Tony Curtis (Joe/Josephine), Jack Lemmon (Jerry/Daphne), Joe E. Brown (Osgood Fielding III); Running time: 121 m; Released Mar 29, 1959

*When Comedy Was King* (1960); Producer: Robert Youngson; Director: Robert Youngson; Screenplay: Robert Youngson; Cast: Charlie Chaplin, Buster Keaton, Roscoe Arbuckle, Harry Langdon; Running time: 81 m; Released Mar 29, 1960

*Harold Lloyd's World of Comedy* (1962); Producer: Harold Lloyd; Director: (various); Screenplay: (various); Cast: Harold Lloyd,

Jobyna Ralston, Josephine Crowell; Running time: 94 m; Released Jun 4, 1962

*The Funny Side of Life* (1966); Producer: Harold Lloyd; Director: (various); Screenplay: (various); Cast: Harold Lloyd, Jobyna Ralston, Noah Young, Ann Christy; Running time: 99 m; Released Nov 9, 1966

*War Italian Style* (1967); Producer: Fulvio Lucisano; Director: Luigi Scattini; Screenplay: Franco Castellano, Pipolo and Fulvio Lucisano; Cast: Buster Keaton (General Von Kassler), Franco Franchi (Frank), Ciccio Ingrassia (Joe); Running time: 84 m; Released Jan 18, 1967

# Notes

## Introduction: The History of the History of Silent Comedy

1. I need to attend to a matter of pedantry: technically *The Circus* came out in January 1928, not 1927. But c'mon—January 1928. That's awfully close to 1927. And the film was delayed due to Chaplin's breakdown. I don't think I'm on thin ice lumping it in with the other 1927 features.

## Slapstick While Black

1. By the by, the girl in question is played by Dorothy Morrison (also known as Dorothy Morrison Green). If this name pops out at you, good for you. For everyone else, just keep reading—in a few pages' time you'll encounter her older brother Ernie Morrison.

2. I would be remiss if I did not point out here that Moe and Shemp Howard got their start in show business with a blackface act. So … nothing's ever just one thing, is it?

## @RealCharlieChaplin

1. This is a potentially apocryphal anecdote. Take it with a grain of salt.

2. The big distribution outfits handled the entire United States, but there were also small-scale local distribution companies that handled individual territories. These were called "state's rights" distributors.

## Eureka

1. Shortly after directing this film, Jules White became the head of Columbia Pictures' comedy shorts division, and as such was one of the key creative forces behind the Three Stooges. Other slapstick comedians who made talkie comedy shorts with Jules White at Columbia include Buster Keaton, Harry Langdon, and Charley Chase.

## What, What No Beer?

1. For anyone counting, this is his fourth appearance as someone named "Elmer" and his second as someone named "Elmer Butts."

## The Sin of Harold Lloyd

1. Although Laurel and Hardy beat him to theaters with *Unaccustomed As We Are*, a short film and the first time any silent comedian was heard to speak.

2. If you'll forgive the digression, I discovered the 35mm nitrate of Lloyd's *Bliss* was missing its finale thanks to nitrate decomposition, and that I personally owned the missing footage in a smaller gauge (9.5mm to be exact). So I arranged to have this and a few other Lloyd rarities on 9.5mm transferred to digital video for inclusion on one of my DVD collections. After doing so, I donated the video masters and the 9.5mm originals to Lloyd's estate. I called them up to make arrangements, and they told me that somebody would be by my house "later that morning" to pick them up. This was absolutely baffling. I live in a Chicago suburb, I was calling Lloyd's estate in California. How in the world were they going to have someone by my house in a few hours? Were there secret Harold Lloyd Black Ops agents in sleeper cells throughout the country? Turned out, a relative of Lloyd's lived in an adjacent 'burb and was going to come by on her way to the grocery store.

## The $30,000 Question

1. God bless this particular format war—Pathex was the world's first home movie format. It was created by movie distributer Pathé, and during its exceptionally brief life served as a platform for the home-market release of a number of Pathé's silent films. Then it was killed off by 8mm within a few years of its debut. Many of the Pathé rarities that were sold in this format were unceremoniously abandoned in attics when the projectors turned into obsolete relics. And so, a significant number of movies that are now officially "lost" in their orig-

inal form actually survive in partial scraps on 9.5mm reels. A few chapters ago I mentioned an anecdote about donating some film to the Harold Lloyd Trust—that was 9.5mm film I'd bought at an estate sale.

## Jean, Clara, Bombshell and It

1. I used to think the prevalence of smarmy European counts in screwball comedies was the result of filmmakers consciously modeling their pictures after *It Happened One Night*, but that fails to explain the presence of smarmy European counts in films that show no other obvious influence from *It Happened One Night*, much less something like this that was made before it.

## Girls! Girls! Girls!

1. Don't recognize the name Anita Loos? Then drop this book (or carefully set it down—your choice) and go read *Gentlemen Prefer Blondes*.

## Slut Fabulous

1. You may notice I have not allocated a chapter to *Bringing Up Baby*, despite it being one of the most famous landmarks of the genre. Like *It Happened One Night*, it is a film of massive historical importance, but there are other lesser known gems that are more fun.

# Bibliography

Adamson, Joe. *Groucho, Harpo, Chico, and Sometimes Zeppo.* New York: Simon & Schuster, 1973.

Anthony, Brian, and Andy Edmonds. *Smile When the Raindrops Fall: The Story of Charley Chase.* Lanham, MD: Scarecrow Press, 1998.

Aping, Norbert. *The Final Film of Laurel and Hardy.* Jefferson, NC: McFarland, 2008.

Balducci, Anthony. *The Funny Parts: A History of Film Comedy Routines and Gags.* Jefferson, NC: McFarland, 2012.

Barnes, Peter. *To Be or Not to Be.* London: British Film Institute Publishing, 2002.

Benayoun, Robert. *The Look of Buster Keaton.* New York: St. Martin's Press, 1983.

Cahn, William. *Harold Lloyd's World of Comedy.* New York: Duell, Sloan and Pearce, 1964.

Cahn, William. *The Laugh Makers.* New York: Bramhall House, 1962.

Capra, Frank. *The Name Above the Title: An Autobiography.* New York: Macmillan, 1971.

Chaplin, Charles (Designed by David King, Introduction by Francis Wyndham). *My Life in Pictures.* New York: Grosset & Dunlap, 1975.

Crichton, Kyle. *The Marx Brothers.* London: William Heinemann, 1951.

Dardis, Tom. *Buster Keaton: The Man Who Wouldn't Lie Down.* New York: Penguin, 1979.

Dardis, Tom. *Harold Lloyd: The Man on the Clock.* New York: Penguin, 1983.

Epstein, Jerry. *Remembering Charlie: A Pictorial Biography.* New York: Doubleday, 1985.

Everson, William K. *Hollywood Bedlam: Classic Screwball Comedy.* New York: Citadel Press, 1994.

Eyman, Scott. *Ernst Lubitsch: Laughter in Paradise.* Baltimore: Johns Hopkins University Press, 1993.

Gehring, Wes D. *Carole Lombard: The Hoosier Tornado.* Indianapolis: Indiana Historical Society Press, 2003.

Gifford, Denis. *Chaplin.* New York: Doubleday, 1974.

Harter, Chuck, and Michael J. Hayde. *Little Elf: A Celebration of Harry Langdon.* Albany, GA: Bear Manor Media, 2012.

Harvey, James. *Romantic Comedy in Hollywood: From Lubitsch to Sturges.* New York: DaCapo Press, 1998.

Horton, Andrew (ed). *Buster Keaton's Sherlock Jr.* Cambridge: Cambridge University Press, 1997.

Jenkins, Henry. *What Made Pistachio Nuts? Early Sound Comedy and the Vaudeville Aesthetic.* New York: Columbia University Press, 1992.

Keaton, Buster and Charles Samuels. *My Wonderful World of Slapstick.* Garden City, NY: Doubleday, 1960.

Kerr, Walter. *The Silent Clowns.* New York: Alfred A. Knopf, 1980.

King, Rob. *The Fun Factory: The Keystone Film Company and the Emergence of Mass Culture.* Berkeley: University of California Press, 2009.

Knopf, Robert. *The Theater and Cinema of Buster Keaton.* Princeton: Princeton University Press, 1999.

Lahue, Kalton C., and Sam Gill. *Clown Princes and Court Jesters: Some Great Comics of the Silent Screen.* Cranbury, NJ: A.S. Barnes and Co., 1970.

Louvish, Simon. *Keystone: The Life and Clowns of Mack Sennett.* New York: Faber & Faber, 2003.

Louvish, Simon. *Stan and Ollie: The Roots of Comedy.* New York: St. Martin's Press, 2002.

Macleod, David. *The Sound of Buster Keaton.* London: Buster Books, 1995.

Maltin, Leonard. *The Great Movie Comedians.* New York: Crown, 1978.

Massa, Steve. *Lame Brains and Lunatics.* Albany, GA: Bear Manor Media, 2013.

Mast, Gerald. *The Comic Mind: Comedy and the Movies.* Chicago: University of Chicago Press, 1973.

McCaffrey, Donald W. (ed). *Focus on Chaplin.* Englewood Cliffs, NJ: Prentice-Hall, 1971.

McPherson, Edward. *Buster Keaton: Tempest in a Flat Hat.* New York: Newmarket Press, 2005.

Mitchell, Glenn. *A-Z of Silent Film Comedy.* London: Batsford, 1998.

Moss, Robert F. *Charlie Chaplin: An Illustrated History of the Movies.* New York: Jove Publications, 1975.

Neibaur, James L. *Chaplin at Essanay: A Film Artist in Transition 1915–1916.* Jefferson, NC: McFarland, 2008.

Okuda, Ted, and David Maska. *Charlie Chaplin at Keyston and Essanay: Dawn of the Tramp.* Lincoln, NE: iUniverse, 2005.

Oldham, Gabriella. *Keaton's Silent Shorts: Beyond the Laughter.* Carbondale: Southern Illinois University Press, 1996.

Parish, James Robert, and William T. Leonard. *The Funsters.* New Rochelle, NY: Arlington House, 1979.

Paul, William. *Ernst Lubitsch's American Comedy.* New York: Columbia University Press, 1983.

Payne, Robert. *Charlie Chaplin (The Great God Pan).* New York: Ace Star Books, 1952.

Poague, Leland A. *The Cinema of Ernst Lubitsch.* Cranbury, NJ: A.S. Barnes and Co., 1978.

Rapf, Joanna E., and Gary L. Green. *Buster Keaton: A Bio-Bibliography.* Westport, CT: Greenwood Press, 1995.

Rhueban, Joyce. *Harry Langdon: The Comedian and*

*Metteur-en-Scene.* East Brunswick, NJ: Associated University Presses, 1983.

Rickman, Gregg (ed). *The Film Comedy Reader.* New York: Limelight Editions, 2001.

Roberts, Richard M. *Smileage Guaranteed: Past Humor, Present Laughter: Musings of the Comedy Film Industry 1910–1945 Volume One: Hal Roach.* Phoenix: Practical Press, 2013.

Robinson, David. *Buster Keaton.* London: Sight and Sound, 1969.

Robinson, David. *Charlie Chaplin: Comic Genius.* New York: Harry N. Abrams, 1995.

Schelly, William. *Harry Langdon: His Life and Films.* Jefferson, NC: McFarland, 2008.

Schelly, William. *Harry Langdon: The Fourth Genius of Screen Comedy.* Metuchen, NJ: Scarecrow Press, 1982.

Schickel, Richard. *Harold Lloyd: The Shape of Laughter.* Boston: New York Graphic Society, 1974.

Sennett, Mack. *King of Comedy.* Garden City, NY: Doubleday, 1954.

Sherk, Warren E. *The Films of Mack Sennett.* Lanham, MD: Scarecrow Press, 1998.

Slide, Anthony. *Eccentrics of Comedy.* Lanham, MD: Scarecrow Press, 1998.

Smith, Imogen Sara. *Buster Keaton: The Persistence of Comedy.* Chicago: Gambit Publishing, 2008.

Sobel, Raoul, and David Francis. *Chaplin: Genesis of a Clown.* London: Quarter Books, 1977.

Sturges, Sandy (ed). *Preston Sturges by Preston Sturges.* New York: Simon & Schuster, 1990.

Sweeney, Kevin W. (ed). *Buster Keaton Interviews.* Jackson: University Press of Mississippi, 2007.

Vance, Jeffrey. *Chaplin: Genius of the Cinema.* New York: Harry N. Abrams, 2003.

Vance, Jeffrey, and Suzanne Lloyd. *Harold Lloyd: Master Comedian.* New York: Harry N. Abrams, 2002.

Walker, Bill, and Brian Anthony. *Nothing On a Stage Is Permanent: The Harry Langdon Scrapbook.* Walker and Anthony Publications, 2016.

Walker, Brent E. *Mack Sennett's Fun Factory.* Jefferson, NC: McFarland, 2010.

Ward, Richard Lewis. *A History of the Hal Roach Studios.* Carbondale: Southern Illinois University Press, 2005.

Weinberg, Herman G. *The Lubitsch Touch.* New York: E.P. Dutton, 1968.

Yallop, David. *The Day the Laughter Stopped.* New York: St. Martin's Press, 1976.

# Index